Women of Vision

VISIBLE EVIDENCE

Edited by Michael Renov, Faye Ginsburg, and Jane Gaines

Public confidence in the "real" is everywhere in decline. The Visible Evidence series offers a forum for the in-depth consideration of the representation of the real, with books that engage issues bearing upon questions of cultural and historical representation, and that forward the work of challenging prevailing notions of the "documentary tradition" and of nonfiction culture more generally.

VISIBLE EVIDENCE, VOLUME 9

Women of Vision

Histories in Feminist Film and Video

Alexandra Juhasz, Editor

 University of Minnesota Press

Minneapolis

London

For information about the video *Women of Vision,* contact:
  The Cinema Guild, Inc.
  1687 Broadway, Suite 506
  New York, NY 10019–5904
  (212) 246-5522
  http://www.cinemaguild.com

Copyright 2001 by the Regents of the University of Minnesota

Published by the University of Minnesota Press
111 Third Avenue South, Suite 290
Minneapolis, MN 55401-2520
http://www.upress.umn.edu

Library of Congress Cataloging-in-Publication Data

Women of vision : histories in feminist film and video / Alexandra Juhasz, editor.
        p.   cm. — (Visible evidence ; v. 9)
      ISBN 0-8166-3371-1 (alk. paper) — ISBN 0-8166-3372-X (pbk. : alk. paper)
      1. Women motion picture producers and directors—United States—Interviews.
    2. Feminist motion pictures.   I. Juhasz, Alexandra.   II. Series.
      PN1998.2 .W666 2001
      791.43'082—dc21

                                                                        00-011270

Printed in the United States of America on acid-free paper

The University of Minnesota is an equal-opportunity educator and employer.

12 11 10 09 08 07 06 05 04 03 02 01   10 9 8 7 6 5 4 3 2 1

For my children, the next generation,
Simone Irene Dunye and Gabriel James Robert Juhasz.
May their feminist histories flourish.

Contents

Preface

When one of my interviewees failed to show up to be videotaped, I didn't want to waste this precious hour of crew and studio time. My associate producer, Megan Cunningham, agreed to interview me. On camera, she asked me to reflect on the process of making my documentary Women of Vision: Eighteen Histories in Feminist Film and Video. *I had always planned to include my own voice in the documentary, given my feminist commitment to a self-reflexive methodology. So I spoke about what I had learned.*

I include this excerpt from my video interview (and another as the book's afterword) as a preface to the written aspect of this project to mirror the reflexive feminist process of the originary video documentary, to include some of my "live" recorded voice in the book so that I speak through the same technology as do the book's other interviewees, and to set out the book's central theme—the reclaiming of power through interactive remembering of feminist media history.

MEGAN CUNNINGHAM: *What have you learned while making this documentary?*
ALEX JUHASZ: I learned some things that surprised me even though I teach women's studies and spend a lot of time with younger feminists and women who don't call themselves feminists. Two things rarely happen:

First, we as women rarely get legitimate documents—documents on television, documents on video—that recount the lives of strong women who preceded us. What is so beautiful about the interviews that we have shot is to see articulate, self-controlled, self-confident (and sometimes not so confident), bright, committed women living their lives. They don't present themselves in all the demeaning, and painful, and violent ways in which women are typically portrayed. They are simply living full, rich lives of the head and the spirit. I found it surprising to realize this imagery's power.

And then second, I was surprised to see how we lack cross-generational conversation and how desperate we are for older women to hear the words of younger women and for younger women to hear those of older women. We as a movement—even though we are not a movement maybe—but we as women have neglected that, as does most of our culture. I'm in my thirties, and most of the women working on this project are even younger, and we all found it empowering to talk to women who are forty, fifty, sixty, who tell us a similar message: "I have lived a life, choosing it by my own rules, valuing what I know and believe, even though by doing so, I push up against the rules of the society. I want to show you my life so you know that it is possible to do the same."

When we do not know or cannot imagine that we have such opportunities, a new generation of young women inevitably comes along, and it is like they are inventing it again—that they could be an artist, or a scholar, or an active participant in the cultural and political life of our society.

Acknowledgments

One of the central themes of this book is the absolute necessity of infrastructural and material support for the possibility of feminist media work. Another is its reflexive methodology. I make the same thing that I study: feminist media and feminist media history. Self-consciousness about my own process becomes part of the study. For these reasons, I must honor the generous support of many individuals and institutions without which this feminist media project, as both documentary video and book, could never have been completed.

First, I would like to gratefully acknowledge the book's subjects, the twenty women who allowed me to interview them for the documentary and whose interviews appear transcribed here. This has been a long, interactive process based on their continual involvement. My work would not be possible without their contributions of time, memories, ideas, and images.

I also need to thank the nearly two hundred media feminists who attended the preproduction research meetings in Philadelphia, New York, Chicago, San Francisco, and Los Angeles. The issues and conflicts raised in these meetings formed my project. These meetings were in turn supported by individuals (and their institutions) who provided contact information, meeting spaces, food. Thanks to David Haas and Linda Blackabee at the Philadelphia Independent Film and Video Association, Terry Lawler at Women Make Movies, Jeanne Kracher at Women in the Director's Chair, Kate Horsfield at the Video Data Bank, Patricia Boero at the John D. and Catherine T. MacArthur Foundation, Gail Silva at the Film Arts Foundation, and Elayne Zalis at the Long Beach Museum of Art Video Annex. Monetary support for these meetings was provided by research grants from Swarthmore College and a Mellon postdoctoral fellowship at Bryn Mawr College.

This book is the companion to a documentary that was made with little funding over the course of four years. I did receive two outright grants that helped pay for research and editing of the documentary, these generously provided by the California Council for the Humanities and the Astraea National Lesbian Action Foundation. Ongoing research support from Pitzer College has financed a great deal of the project's production; especially valuable was its support for the transcription of the video interviews. Thanks to Robin Podolsky for her attentive and thoughtful assistance as she transcribed many hours of videotape. My documentary was also supported through trades and other in-kind support from several of the organizations and institutions that themselves play a central role in this history: Film/Video Arts, the Performance Art Department at New York University, the Video Department at the School of the Art Institute of Chicago, and the Video Annex of the Long Beach Museum of Art.

None of this work could have been accomplished without the loving (and usually unpaid) assistance of student interns. Swarthmore College students Katie Bowman, Heather Abel, and Valerie Casey helped organize the Chicago and San Francisco research meetings, and Kenrick Cato helped to log the videotapes of those meetings. Bryn Mawr students Truc Ha, Suh Kyung Yoon, and Lisa Lopez-Lopez organized meetings, recorded sound, and logged tapes. Pitzer College students Kathy Kiernan, Bonnie Gavel, and Matthew Cooke helped organize and shoot the Los Angeles interviews, while Zara Ayazi did archival research for the documentary. Aaron Rhodes designed the graphic elements for the documentary, and he assisted me with editing. Crosby Noricks did Web research to help with distribution of the completed documentary. Pomona College student Sylvain White helped with shooting stills and editing. My student assistants from Claremont Graduate University helped with research, postproduction, and distribution: Betsy Heilbrun, Jennifer Davies, and Jennifer Waits. Enid Baxter-Blader designed beautiful promotional materials for me, as well as all the video stills that illustrate the book.

My deep gratitude goes to several people who read the manuscript closely, and often more than once, offering me careful and considerable feedback: Julia Lesage, Suzanne Juhasz, Erin Cramer, my editor at the University of Minnesota Press, Jennifer Moore, and my copy editor there, Louisa Castner. B. Ruby Rich had several long, and lively, conversations with me about this history, as well as my historicizing of it. I appreciate the camaraderie and mentoring of all these women: another of the book's central themes proved true in its production. The gracious donation of a Web site for the project (www.pitzer.edu/~ajuhasz/wov) is another example of a feminist media community in action. Thanks to Kym Dolcimascolo and her staff at Planet Visions, Inc. (whom I met after a screening of the documentary at a film festival in Tampa, Florida) for their gift of its construction.

I lovingly credit family and friends (you know who you are) for providing me with that most rare support, one that I suggest in the book is a crucial condition to making feminist media: a sense of one's right and power as a woman to pursue engaged artistic and scholarly work. Finally, Cheryl Dunye helped me to build what all feminists desire—not just a room but a home of my own where our life's work is embedded, sustained, and entangled.

Introduction

▶

Twenty-One Histories in Feminist Media

> There was a blank where there should have been a
> recognition of continuities and a confrontation with past
> limitations. Following a well-established U.S. system of
> values, women's liberation set out to invent itself from scratch.
> :: Rachel DuPlessis and Ann Snitow, *The Feminist Memoir Project*

> But, as activists have known all along, neither the movement
> nor feminist individuals vanished.
> :: Nancy Whittier, *Feminist Generations: The Persistence of the
>   Radical Women's Movement*

I am certain that feminist media pioneers have not vanished. They are very
much alive and visible if you know where to look. They've been quite adaptive, and their lives and feminist media work continue to influence others.
By *feminist media* I mean the diverse work with or concerning film, video,
television, and digital production made by those who critique the many in-
equitable power relations that limit women. I situate this production within the field of *alternative* or *independent media,* by which I refer to work
made outside the sanction and profit motive of the industrial model. Since
the 1970s, feminist alternative media has been a most significant site of
personal, social, and political action for American women.[1] And yet I initiated this project, first as a feature documentary video[2] and here as a collection of the documentary's source interviews, because I too worry about
the remembering of the recent feminist past, and more specifically about
the forgetting of feminist media history.

   To enliven my feminist memory, in 1995–96 I videotaped interviews with twenty women involved in diverse feminist media practices (the twenty-first history in this introduction's title refers to my own). These women contribute to feminist history's reinvention by publicly recounting their distinct careers in the media. They want to remember and to be remembered, to fill the historical blanks and contribute to what Rachel DuPlessis and Ann Snitow see as an ongoing political necessity—the recognition of continuity with activism of the past. In so doing, they refuse the usual, debilitating system of loss and waste. "We live in a culture of oblivion that perpetrates a kind of self-induced denial in which the meaning of the recent past is continually lost or distorted," proclaims Carolee Schneemann in the book *Angry Women*. "The cultural history each generation creates is immediately turned into waste: 'That's *old* shit!'"[3]

Throughout this project I have attempted to make that old shit fertile by relocating the works of my colleagues and predecessors and claiming them as valuable historical artifacts. In the process, questions were raised about the making of both feminist history and documentary. In this introduction, I will discuss the strengths and limitations of how I make history in this project with a process-oriented, interview-based documentary method—a collaborative, supportive style of feminist work that has its own history and politics. I will also explain why I chose to situate this relaying of feminist media history squarely within the alternative media infrastructure: the institutions that support the funding, production, exhibition, education about, and criticism of media. DuPlessis and Snitow yearn for "a recognition of continuities." In this book, I respond by drawing connections among twenty-one women, as well as by linking them to many other media feminists and the material conditions that make feminist media and its history possible.

As a women's and media studies teacher of young women, I am certain of the necessity of this work because I find that those who need and want this history do not have enough access to it. I am consistently saddened to see how little feminist history is known by even those of my students committed to knowing it. Instead, I find a recurring cycle of feminist knowledge and action: feminists exist and are forgotten, make their work and see it disappear, are remembered and get lost, are rediscovered, erased, and re-represented yet again. In the 1970s, the feminist scholars who founded the academic discipline of women's studies had to search for real, but hidden, feminist legacies. At that time, Elaine Showalter wrote about the same feminist cycle of repeating historical research described earlier in this introduction by DuPlessis and Snitow: "Each generation of women writers has found itself, in a sense, without a history, forced to rediscover the past anew, forging again and again the consciousness of her sex."[4] With an eerie doubling, twenty years later, Ellen Willis, now historicizing 1967–75, the period when Showalter was decrying feminist loss, reminds us of the unstable foundation that underlines all feminist remembering. Willis bemoans how we remember (or don't) the formative period of radical feminism: "Radical feminism, along with civil rights, the most influential struggle of the 60s, transformed the cultural and political landscape: its imprint is everywhere in American life. Yet the radical feminist *movement* has largely disappeared from history."[5]

What are the consequences of this concurrent disappearance and re-remembering for (the) women's *movement*? And why the perpetual "re" for things feminist? When I *re*trieve and *re*lay too-seldom seen and too-quickly forgotten feminist films and videos from the recent past in my classroom, my students are nourished and inspired by work from another time and other generations. My project is founded on the certainty that across "generation," "wave," or merely time we need feminist memories to enable possibility and politics, even as such memory fades under the influence of individual and institutional amnesia. When first seeing this work, my students are also angry and perplexed—angry that this legacy seems erased, perplexed when considering whom or what to blame. Given such ambivalent response to *re*viewing this work, I believe that understanding the causes and consequences of forgetting feminist media history may be as equally important as remembering it.

With such motivations, *Women of Vision* records the voices of twenty-one articulate, passionate women whose work in media has ranged over five decades and across distinct careers (they are artists, educators, distributors, critics, scholars, archivists, activists, festival organizers). In their interviews, these women explain how they express their personal, political, and artistic commitments through a concurrent commitment to technologies that record and then re-present movement and ideas in time. That is to say, the diverse women interviewed in this book share little in common but "feminism" and "media." And even the feminism and media they share can be expressed with only the most general of terms. Yet all of the women interviewed here do political work within contemporary culture. All are motivated by the desire to speak to and alter the world; all believe that the media are a most powerful tool with which to effect the changes that matter most.

And here the interviewees' similarities end.[6] Their collective voices contain many oppositions and contradictions. This is a variety I sought out, and one I have struggled to preserve and even foreground in my presentation of these interviews. These women are well known, lesser known, and unknown. They are young, middle-aged, and old; straight, bisexual, and gay; white, Puerto Rican, black, Asian American, and biracial; leftist and centrist. For a variety of personal and political reasons, often related to feminism's ongoing troubles incorporating racial, sexual, or generational difference, some of the interviewees do not even call themselves "feminists," although none is averse to being labeled such by me. This hesitancy about, and even resistance to, the word *feminism* by women who are its vital constituents manifests one of the significant failures of the "movement," and one of the reasons feminism is so difficult to remember. A significant amount of feminist work gets done, never to be named or known as such.

For instance, several of the women in my study refuse the term *feminist* for their media work—even as they enact a gender-based critique of our society—because the history of the women's movement in America has been laced with racism and other insularities. Specifically, I refer to ongoing assumptions made by many women that race (or sexuality or class) is somehow a distinct, if important, condition that can be isolated from gender, and therefore, that the white (heterosexual, middle-class) experience *is* the female experience. Film and video producer Yvonne Welbon articulates this position in her interview: "It seems, from the little bit I know about early feminism, it wasn't very inclusive of black women. And then, what I know of black women's history is that we were always feminists. We were always doing stuff, from before early suffrage. Black women were doing a lot of things, and white women didn't want to include them. In theory, yes, I have to be a feminist, but I've never really used that word to describe myself."

Film- and videomaker Cheryl Dunye adds another dimension to this critique. It is not only feminism's whiteness that alienates her but also its age: feminists are her *professors,* feminism is institutionalized, whereas Dunye sees herself as young and marginal: "When I was exploring feminism, it was a bunch of *books* that made you a feminist. There was no movement that I, as a young black woman, could run into. It was about a lot of reading and feeling uncomfortable and standing around people I didn't like who said they were feminists." Similarly, activist videomaker Carol Leigh, whose work often focuses on prostitutes' rights, calls herself a "neofeminist" in her interview so as to differentiate herself from what she perceives to be the censorious, antisex position of institutionalized feminism. For Puerto Rican filmmaker Frances Negrón-Muntaner the label *feminist* can serve to diminish the range and complexity of her identity and work:

> I often identify as a queer filmmaker. . . . In other contexts, I am a diasporic filmmaker and feel most at home with other displaced peoples, since migration probably defines my adult life more than any other single process. . . . I relate to feminist work and I incorporate feminist concerns into my work. But

as an identity, it tends to exclude other concerns that have to do with migration (for instance, my diasporic sensibility), and being located at the intersections of power relations.

Such critiques of feminism's myopia, of the false limits and boundaries it often builds, have been foundational to the shape and method of this project: why I include the widest variety of committed work and women under the "feminist" mantle and why I draw the field as loosely as is necessary to include any woman who challenges the structures of dominance that hinder and contain her life, especially, but not exclusively, when these inequities are rooted in the gender/sex system. I have also drawn the field of feminist media history as an interactive domain where people who make media contribute only one component. This is not common, for artists tend to be regarded as the most valued, or at least interesting, link in the cultural production chain. But here, the amorphous inspiration of the gifted, isolated artist is understood to be the product of a larger web of ideas and institutions that are engaging in their own right. For instance, the work of distribution is given similar attention to the work of art that it circulates. In their interviews both Dunye and film archivist Pearl Bowser discuss the importance, and hard work, of building a responsive black film audience. They wonder: if you make feminist media but viewers don't know how or where to see it, what is its real value?

Importantly, the infrastructure that supports feminist media making is composed not just of institutions but also of women's usually thankless labor. Feminist media scholar Constance Penley illustrates this too common situation:

> A feminist film scholar and friend once saw me staggering down a hall with an armload of manuscripts, and she said, "I don't know how you can bear to put all that effort into other people's work instead of your own." I realized that I'd never thought of it that way. I thought of editing [Camera Obscura: A Journal of Feminist Film Theory] as my work, too. Most of the time, people just criticize us because we turned down their manuscript, or we spent too much time on psychoanalytic theory and still haven't recanted, or for being too dominant a voice in feminist film theory. But for me it's been a real labor issue. That was twenty years of work.

My inclusive method allows me to document a layered, loose, but interconnected vision of the many types of hard work that comprise feminist media history. I envision the field as a broad domain including diverse sets of practices, politics, and players. For instance, while all twenty-one of the interviewees discuss how they were profoundly influenced by the movements for social change of the 1970s, this means different things for different women. Some were immersed in the founding of the women's movement; others were inspired by the civil rights, socialist, or gay and lesbian rights movements. Younger women in the study only read of these movements or saw documentaries about them in school; they strive to remake a society that might again be predicated on social action. In addition, all twenty-one women discuss how they deal with the (in)accessibility of the various media technologies and institutions. While many women choose to work in video (first with the reel-to-reel portapak of the 1960s and 1970s, then the camcorder of the 1980s, and now the digital camera of the 1990s) because it is cheaper, easier to learn, and has less prestige than film, others commit themselves to ensuring that the elite medium of film, in its position of technological preeminence, opens its institutions to women. And others take on similar struggles, often for different reasons, within television or the digital terrain.

In the interviews, several more common themes and struggles define these women's careers. They talk about how difficult it is for women to acquire capital. They insist on, as I have already, the absolute necessity of an infrastructure. Many want to think through the complex relation between art and activism; others add their concerns about intellectual work like theory or teaching to expand this dyad into a complex triad. Many of these women use the media to interrogate the meanings and sensations of their bodies. They often focus on sexuality and sexual identity. Identity in and of itself is often a focus: identity in its formation, identity in its consolidation, and in its contestation and fragmentation. How does feminism relate to other political or personal investments? That is, how does a racial, Marxist, sexual, or other political identification affect one's feminism? The work of making history is also common: my interviewees research the past for undocumented stories or little-known art works; archive for later generations the images and words of valued contemporaries; write about and re-create the past for use in the present. Interpersonal relationships matter greatly: the compelling desire for or appreciation of role models; the complexity of attachment to mothers; the uncertainty about having or the attachment to children; the support of friends, colleagues, and lovers; the responsibilities of mentoring; the difficulty of intergenerational, interracial, and other boundary-crossing connections.

Contradictions arise: What do you do when you can't afford to make media? Are you still in the field? What is the difference between a history of those who understand media work as a career and those for whom it is a job? Do you even have a "career" if you are not recognized, or if your work can't be made? How do you acknowledge work that was never made due to lack of exposure, lack of self-confidence, lack of support? How do you create a life as an artist or media professional? What is the role of men in feminism? How do you continue to make feminist work over the span of a career, even as you change and feminism changes?

The voices in this book may not answer these questions, but they do reveal women's divergent attempts to make sense of such contradictions, critical to both feminism and the independent media at the past century's end and the new century's beginning. We learn that feminism is adaptive and alive, even as it is currently a political movement in crisis. We learn that the media is a most fertile if difficult arena for social change. We learn that feminist artists, academics, and activists influence each other and that such individuals, and the institutions that support them, change over time and in relation to each other. We are reminded that political action occurs, risks are taken, organizations are formed, relationships are built, artistic work is made—even as we are forced to acknowledge how precarious this all may be. We see that feminist media work proves to be (too) temporary for a variety of reasons. The ideas it is rooted in do not last, are too little under-stood, or are devalued; the work itself is underappreciated, unmentioned, unarchived, and so lost; original intentions get buried under new ways of understanding experience or politics; a steady drift toward capitalist insti-tutionalization and establishment careers makes the work seem preliminary. In fact, we find, dismayingly, that it is its very precariousness that may be feminist media's most salient common feature, one that begins to offer us insight into the contradictory relations between production and loss that underwrite its history.

This said, I want to add that these twenty-one histories do not make up *the history* of U.S. feminist media. There is certainly history to be found here, although it is neither comprehensive nor causal; rather, this history is multiple, personal, and sometimes mundane, as much the stuff of daily struggle as of fame, material success, or masterpiece. For reasons inherent to my process in developing this project (to be discussed shortly), in this book the reader will not find recorded a definitive beginning or end for feminist independent media, or an attempt to manufacture a neat, linear record, or to list important films, videos, artists, events, or organizations. In fact, I did not interview these twenty women because I believe that they are the most important players in the field. I learned from my research meetings that for media feminists *importance* is as relative as *feminism* is. So instead I map a field—its shape not entirely clear, its goals varying across time and for individuals, its method as diverse as any woman's ingenuity.

The project's very multiplicity, contradiction, and uncertainty locate me as a "third-wave" feminist, and this as a third-wave effort. This term is embraced by women my age and younger as we contribute our perspective on the past and current state of the women's movement. Actually, only after reading "third-wave" writing while researching this project did I willingly choose to self-identify as such. Before this, I had associated the term *third wave* with its typical usage in the mainstream media: defining an apolitical, nihilistic, angry swarm of bad daughters. On the contrary, third-wave theorists suggest—as I began to do above—that our generation is defined not just negatively through opposition to our foremothers, but also through the proactive embrace of a whole host of relationships and stances: for example, multiplicity, poststructuralism, postmodernism, postessentialism, postsubjectivity, pro-sexualism, transgression, performance, postcolonialism, and women-of-color feminism.

Third-wave feminists understand ourselves in relation to the feminisms that preceded us. Thus *Third Wave Agenda,* an anthology of personal/theoretical writings about what it means to be a feminist born during the period 1963–74, suggests that our agenda is defined by feminists who are educated in an already established tradition. Leslie Heywood and Jennifer Drake find that we third-wavers work from a recognition of "multiple, constantly shifting bases of oppression in relation to multiple, interpenetrating axes of identity, and the creation of coalition politics based on these understandings. . . . We know that what oppresses me may not oppress you, that what oppresses you may be something I participate in, and that what oppresses me may be something that you participate in."[7] They posit that acknowledging difference need not lead to isolation, just as I suggest that indicating memory loss need not foreclose remembering.

In this sense, third-wave feminists are as often "re" as we are "post." This particular use of "re" signals our proactive attempts to associate with our feminist past. We strive not only to move ahead but also to *re*member, *re*medy, and *re*combine. We insist that theories of gender, race, or sexuality wrought from identity—often first understood in isolation from each other—must be inter*re*lated. We understand that the dichotomies that have formed much of earlier feminist theory and politics do not explain all of our experiences. Third-wave videomaker Valerie Soe explains that she is driven to *re*present, in all its complexity, her experience of American race relations:

> My uncles all speak Spanish, and Chinese, and English, and Spanish was the first language a lot of them learned. My aunts heat up tamales in the rice cooker and my grandmother used to make really excellent flour tortillas. They listen to country music and wear those little bolo ties. Southwestern Chinese people. . . . So I want to talk about that a little bit, this culture that exists completely outside of the black/white dichotomy, which seems to be the only way that some people can think about race relations in this country.

Harder still, third-wavers believe that we can and must learn from identity positions outside those that we "know" merely through direct experience. Thus, women-of-color feminism, or lesbian feminism, or the writings of older or younger women must be politically and theoretically relevant to feminism more generally. In her contribution to *Generations,* a volume of writing by scholars from multiple generations speaking about the legacy of academic feminism, Mona Narain does such work:

> One of the challenges that a younger generation of third world feminists faces now is to devise a way of integrating the knowledge produced by third world feminists in prior years with the knowledge they have from mainstream white feminisms and charting their individual path. Furthermore, there remains the challenge of taking the production of feminist knowledge in new and different directions that are germane to the present historical moment while using the invaluable groundwork done by previous generations.[8]

Recent projects like *Generations* and *Third Wave Agenda* are invested in examining the links and continuities that bind distinct generations into a (sometimes) cohesive, communicative struggle, while also attempting to define the gaps and miscommunications that separate feminists. "We define feminism's third wave as a movement that contains elements of second wave critique of beauty culture, sexual abuse, and power structures while it also acknowledges and makes use of the pleasure, danger, and defining power of those structures," explain Heywood and Drake (3). Nancy Whittier also performs a productive example of such third-wave theorizing in *Feminist Generations,* her exploration of the lasting effects of second-wave feminism on following generations. By interviewing second- and third-wave women involved in the feminist community of Columbus, Ohio, Whittier finds that feminism does not disappear through some kind of lost/found model: "The 'post-feminist' myth proclaims both the death of the feminist challenge and its rejection by a younger generation of women. In contrast, I suggest that the women's movement has both survived and changed because of the lasting commitments of longtime feminists and the continual infusion of new participants who simultaneously challenge and carry on the feminist legacy."[9]

My goals for this book echo Whittier's position. I add to (and take from) a feminist legacy that was never really lost but may need to be reclaimed. I embrace feminism as I seek to broaden its scope. I intend to infuse my focus on radical female representation into a society that may be saturated with images of women, images that are produced and seen only through a conservative, politicized form that guarantees profits. I want to document the hard work of media women who came before me, create new possibilities for those who follow, and encourage intergenerational dialogue between these women. I am certain that the following narratives paint the lives of women who matter to history. Through this book, I imagine the possibility that later generations of media feminists might not have to do this work again: putting a stop, for a while at least, to this particular feminist "re"-cycle.

▶
_____

The Personal Is the Infrastructural: Making Feminist Media History

The remembering of feminist media history seems particularly important because to date so little of it has been done and because feminist alternative media is itself so precarious. Such remembering is difficult because of the overwhelming influence of major media institutions on how we think about the media and the possibilities they offer us. Cultural production in the United States, an increasingly larger sector of the national economy, produces a product that is simultaneously mass, popular, homogenized, profit-driven, corporate, and "universal." In contrast, feminist media work suffers from a lack of diffusion and an abundance of idiosyncrasy; one of its fundamental preconditions is a significant degree of inaccessibility. This is because the foundation for feminist media may include a commitment to things countercultural, nonindustrial, small-format, underfunded, highly intellectual, overtly political, transgressive, personal, sexual, racial, radical, or female. Thus, as Patricia Zimmermann suggests, "a truly feminist historiography" of alternative media practice investigates the noncommercial infrastructure that makes independent media possible. She writes that to understand alternative feminist media we must research and think differently: we "must analyze the institutions that created spaces where cinema could be imagined outside and as infiltrating the commodity exchange system of Hollywood and American nationalism . . . toward a larger terrain beyond films and toward an analysis of the institutions that give public life to most independent work and produce noncommercial media culture."[10] Such analysis is feminist because it values support systems over the individual, alienated, great (male) artist, or even his great works of art.

Feminist media has never received sufficient critical attention or a very large audience. This can be explained in many ways. It is still a relatively new field. Its work is tarnished in the eyes of the traditional academy and art establishment because it is often overtly political. When produced in video, its product is readily reproducible (not easily bought, collected, or sold), while being overly connected to either lowbrow, mass cultural forms like television or highbrow, artisan traditions of the avant-garde. Feminist media is quickly lost to view (or is never made at all) because it is more expensive than other forms of art, activism, or communication (even as it is less expensive than commercial film or television), is overshadowed by the for-profit model of the society's largest and most successful industry (entertainment), and continues to accrue less cultural capital for its makers and critics than other academic and artistic pursuits would.

As a result, traditional film histories deal very little with women in the media (not to mention feminists), and feminists themselves have written surprisingly little history about feminist media.[11] The recent feminist preoccupation with legacy sweeping academic fields like English literature and nonacademic feminist writing has seemed to have had little impact on feminist media studies.[12] With the 1998 publications of B. Ruby Rich's *Chick Flicks: Theories and Memories of the Feminist Film Movement* and Michelle Citron's *Home Movies and Other Necessary Fictions,* the recent publication of a collection of personal reflections on feminist film theory in the journal *Camera Obscura,* and the addition of Janet Walker and Diane Waldman's historiographic collection of essays, *Feminism and Documentary,* we see the beginning of an autobiographical and theoretical investigation by women who shaped this field.[13] These recent projects address how and where feminist media has developed since the 1970s. They begin to initiate a conversation about how feminist media knowledge and memory are and are not transmitted across time, place, and difference. They try to understand the effects of lineage in view of the multiple generations of media feminists who have created a field.

Perhaps not surprisingly, these studies and many more in English and women's studies, commonly use an autobiographical mode of memoir. In the first person, feminists raise the same contradiction with which I begin this study: how to explain second-wave feminism's successes while also making sense of its decline. In her autobiographical history of academic feminist literary theory, *Around 1981,* Jane Gallop says that she seeks to explain why "in the American academy feminism gets more and more respect while in the larger society women cannot call themselves feminists" (10). Similarly, Gloria Hull ends an essay on her personal development as a black feminist critic by musing, "I remind myself that the 1990s are not the 1970s. Women's Studies—though still vulnerable—and feminist scholarship have been institutionally recognized. There is now a generation for whom feminism is largely intellectual. There is no longer the same precise need for the consciousness we carried of being infiltrators and subversives."[14] As these many, now midcareer feminists seek to understand their guerrilla legacy, they also seek to preserve what it meant (and might mean) to be a subversive infiltrator. "Better get it on record before it disappears," quips Ann Jones to Gayle Greene, coeditor of an anthology of personal essays about the making of feminist literary theory, *Changing Subjects*.[15]

These critical-historical writings address the glaring lapses in the public memory of feminism while also manifesting a mode of history making that has itself been of central concern to feminist historians. This and other interview- or memoir-based feminist histories are structured through a contradiction: how to contribute to the struggles of feminism by validating the words that real women use to describe their experiences without creating yet another authoritative (even if personal or experiential) narrative that erases or contains. Susan Stanford Friedman elucidates this feminist historiographic contradiction: "The insistence on making history, on narrative as a potentially transformative mode of knowing, expresses the desire to transfer power to those who have not had it, while the problematizing of history making reflects the dangers of empowerment as a re-establishment of power over others."[16]

Black women historians have also addressed the problems and advantages of using personal narratives to re-create their undocumented histories. Deborah McDowell labels this tension as one between "black feminist criticism" and "poststructuralist theory." She explains how black feminist theory strives to "assert the significance of black women's experience" just as poststructuralism dismantles the authority of experience; how the former calls for "non-hostile interpretations" of black women's production, while the latter calls the very act of interpretation into question; and how reclaiming the work of unknown black women writers contradicts a theory that challenges both the concept of "the author" and a canon.[17] To resolve such conflicts, Friedman suggests a strategy that incorporates both "the need to make history by writing history as a political act; and the need to problematize that activity so as to avoid the creation of grand narratives" (42).

Following the lead of such feminist historiographers, I attempt to value the experiences of real women and also preserve the ambiguity of personal reflection. I want to do contradictory things simultaneously: I hope that I can mobilize a structure that can respect each interviewee's voice *while* demonstrating the contradictions both in an interview and between interviews *while* pointing to the larger forces that support these women's histories *while* never losing sight of the power and specificity of my own voice. To do so, I make history by juxtaposing twenty-one distinct interpretations of feminist media. These voices speak to, against, at, near, around, and in contradiction to each other. There are many authors here. They speak about multiple experiences of feminist media history, experiences that are sometimes in tandem and sometimes in contradiction.

This allows for singular and several truths. When two women indicate that the same person, film, or event is formative in their lives, a singular node of historical significance emerges. Some examples: the same, few, pivotal organizations that teach or exhibit alternative media emerge again and again across the interviews. Carol Leigh learned to make video through public access in Tucson, Arizona, and Yvonne Welbon was first introduced to the idea of video while she was in Taiwan running a magazine where she employed a man who had left public access in Austin, Texas. Women's work affects others, even as they may never have direct knowledge of this relationship. In her interview experimental filmmaker Barbara Hammer says that she shows viewers that film can manufacture a kinetic disturbance to reality: "I want people to change places between the screen and their seat while they're watching. I want them to see the camera move fluidly so that they understand the world can be seen upside down and that's as valid as right side up. Gravity happens to be a circumstance that we're forced to comply with. We can make the world antigravitational with a camera." Meanwhile, AIDS activist videomaker Juanita Mohammed discusses her response to first seeing a Barbara Hammer film using the very terms conjured up by Hammer: "I realized you don't have to make a film where people talk all the time: there can be movement. The camera can be upside down. I had wanted to make stuff weird. That film [*Superdyke,* 1975] gave me the freedom to mess with the camera: upside down, sideways, things out of order. That gave me a big sense of power."

Yet to me, if one woman identifies how another woman helped her with some aspect of her work, I see this assistance as no more or less significant than another woman's regret about how a *lack* of support marked her career. When history is constructed through the conflicting truths of women's experience, a confluent node has no more value than a conflictive node identified by the tension created by opposing answers to a question. At the five preproduction research meetings for this project (held in Philadelphia, New York, Chicago, San Francisco, and Los Angeles), lively dialogue and debate ensued when large numbers of feminist media women met for the first time in decades. For instance, at these meetings debates about origins become a more productive way to look at history than my choosing and listing the starting points for feminist media history. Cauleen Smith, a filmmaker finishing her MFA at UCLA when she participated in the San Francisco meeting, pointed to the fields of music and literature as starting points for *her* history of feminist film and video: inexpensive, accessible media in which African American artists could thrive and set the artistic agenda. Meanwhile, in a memorable debate that occurred at the New York City research meeting Annie Sprinkle, feminist pornographer and performance artist, suggested that the prehistory of feminist film went back as far as the 1880s when women sat and modeled naked for the pre-cinema cameras of Daguerre and his contemporaries. She sees in these images self-employed, sexual subjects in control of their own bodies. In her interview Pearl Bowser says that she cannot search solely for stories of African American women as she archives and historicizes early black film production, because too few women participated in the field. As she seeks for origins in black film history, only some of them are female or feminist. Smith, Sprinkle, and Bowser suggest that origins are debatable, flexible, and contextual. Defining an origin is an act shaped by the needs and perceptions of the person who searches.

I make room for several opinions because larger conclusions about feminist media history are created out of this multiplicity. My history making results from narrating both the specificity of each woman's history (how real-world events, forces, and people shape and are shaped by the personal, psychological, and political structures of her life) and the more general themes that are raised *across* histories. In so doing, I did identify four major generalizations as central to this history that I will discuss here only in brief: first, the relation between feminist media history and infrastructure; second, how technology affects feminist possibility; third, how theories of politics and art influence feminist practice; and fourth, the relationship between the women's movement and feminist productivity.

▶──

Alternative Institutions and the Facilitation of Feminist Media

Alice Echols describes radical feminism of the '70s as conversant with a more general radicalism of the '60s that sought to move beyond reforming society to transforming it.[18] While all of the women involved in feminist media are by no means "radical feminists,"[19] the creation of counter-institutions, an explicit tactic of radicalism, helped to create the thriving feminist, alternative media that initiates this history and makes feminist careers in the media possible. "Alternative institutions provide the space for something different, something oppositional, something aimed at trying to transform, revolutionize, the existing order," write the editors of the film journal *Jump Cut* in an overview of alternative film periodicals.[20] They explain that forums for writing about alternative film are a significant component in facilitating their production and use. However, in her interview Kate Horsfield, the executive director of the Video Data Bank, an organization that distributes art video, worries that an earlier, "'70s" preoccupation with infrastructure has adapted, over the course of twenty years, into a '90s focus on individual success, inspiring many once "alternative" media makers to move into the "mainstream." It is true that more and more feminist makers now attempt to work within standard forms, have institutional sanction, or constrain their content. This is because, in part, the alternative structures that might have supported their more radical work have become harder and harder to find. In this vicious cycle, less work gets made and institutions that rely on this work are forced to close down.

But this 1990s move into individual professionalization will prove to be shortsighted and dangerous. Each of the book's interviewees (whatever her "generation") attests to how an established, organized, available infrastructure is the most significant factor responsible for enabling her feminist media practice. This infrastructure is composed of a significant variety of institutions and services, including those related to production, distribution, and education. I will discuss briefly a few of the most important institutions and services.

Film clubs. Leftist and/or avant-gardist organizations where people screen and discuss alternative media.[21] These institutions are still lively venues in other countries, but most have died out in the United States.

Film libraries, collections, and archives. Museums, colleges, and media centers build collections that provide opportunities for media makers to sell their work, and forums where viewers can see it.[22]

Associations for media makers, media scholars, and media centers. These support organizing that furthers collective needs and often serve as fiscal sponsors or overseers for individual producer's grants.[23]

Conferences and professional meetings. These are often but not exclusively hosted by professional associations and allow people to meet face to face and share their latest work.[24] The '70s and '80s saw a large number of feminist film conferences that brought together scholars, makers, and critics for productive dialogue.[25]

Artist collectives. These allow access to equipment, facilities, and other artists. In the '70s and '80s, a number of such collectives were formed, often espousing a radical political agenda as one of their founding principles.[26]

Nonprofit media centers. These provide education, production, and other services for media artists at low cost.[27] They usually run film/video screening series for the public and teach classes in media making, often to beginners.

Venues to show independent work, including for-profit art houses, museum, community, and gallery spaces, educational settings, and media centers. The *film festival* is a major setting for alternative exhibition. In the seventies, there were scores of women's film festivals across the country beginning as early as 1971, when the Whitney Museum sponsored a series of films by women. The year 1972 saw the First International Festival of

Women's Film and the First Annual U.S. Women's Video Festival, both in New York. At present, there are yearly U.S. women's film festivals in New York City, Chicago, and Seattle. The current dearth of such events seems especially confusing given that there are now gay and lesbian film festivals in almost every major U.S. city, as well as many smaller cities and towns.[28]

Film writing in journals, magazines, and books. Critical writing allows audiences to learn about current and past work. It also educates about the changing interpretations, themes, and approaches to both making and thinking about media so as to allow for collective dialogue and the progress of ideas. As John Hess and Chuck Kleinhans explain in a summary article of U.S. film periodicals, "The film magazine forms an essential institution for the critical analysis of cinema and the existence of a film culture that allows and encourages its development."[29] Feminist film publications first emerged in the 1970s: *Women and Film* was founded in 1972, *Jump Cut* in 1974, and *Camera Obscura* in 1977. And 1973 proved to be a watershed year for feminist book publishing about film with the release of Molly Haskell's *From Reverence to Rape,* Marjorie Rosen's *Popcorn Venus,* and Joan Mellen's *Women and Their Sexuality in the New Film.*[30] Many would argue that the publication of Claire Johnston's "Women's Cinema as Counter Cinema" in 1973 and then the 1975 publication of Laura Mulvey's "Visual Pleasure and Narrative Cinema" were the originary moments for the immensely productive subfield of feminist film theory.[31] However, the same professionalization that haunts '90s independent media making also haunts feminist media criticism, which focuses mainly on Hollywood film and broadcast television. Very little is written about independent media, feminist or otherwise.

Distributors. These crucial businesses ensure that media made outside the entertainment industry gets to its audience, to the venues that support such work, and to collectors, educators, and others who buy it. In the '70s, there were a significant number of feminist distribution companies, including New Day Films, Iris Films, Women/Artists/Filmmakers, Women Make Movies (WMM), the Women's Film Co-Op, Video Data Bank, Third World Newsreel, and Serious Business. Today WMM is this country's only dedicated feminist distributor, and the majority of the businesses listed above have folded.

Media education. This is a broad-based endeavor that occurs in colleges, universities, and high schools as well as at nonprofit community organizations and public access stations. In the '70s, a great deal of energy went into creating organizations that taught media production and media literacy at low cost to low-income and working-class people. Only some remain viable.

Hollywood and commercial television. No counterinstitution exists outside or without the influence of the dominant model. All of the manifestations of alternative infrastructure listed thus far, at least in part, define themselves both in opposition to and in dialogue with the profit-driven, globally powerful industries of traditional narrative filmmaking and broadcast television.

Funding. Given that film and even video are arguably the most expensive media for art or communication, a significant factor in this history has been women's ability to acquire capital. Because women have had little access to money and the power associated with wealth, women's roles have been minimal in Hollywood film, somewhat larger in television, and larger still in video, documentary, and experimental media. However, while some women work in nonindustrial forms simply because they are less expensive, most feminist media is also rooted in an explicit critique of the inherent sexism in the forms and functions of mainstream media and industrialized capitalism.

Further, given that its motivation is many things before economic (political, aesthetic, personal, social), feminist media history is mostly composed of work made despite a lack of available funding or with little possibility for profit. Julia Reichert reviews the founding principles of New Day Films, the film distribution collective that she cofounded, in such terms:

> It's based on principles from the women's movement: the idea of collective action, not individual genius; and artists, or cultural workers, as I prefer to think of myself, taking control of their work. That means controlling the whole process, including getting the film to the audience. Your life could be about having an idea, making it work, distributing the result, and having that inform your next work. It's not just a business cycle, but a learning cycle.

Kate Horsfield similarly explains the motivations behind the many artists' interviews that she shot on video in collaboration with her late partner, Lyn Blumenthal:

> We didn't do it for anything other than to participate in the ideas of our generation. We wanted to build an organization and we did. We wanted to create a legacy of ideas and we did. I'm proud of it, and I hope people will have the patience to wade through some of the difficult decisions we made in terms of that work. It's hard, not easy, not about entertainment. It's about really listening to somebody talk about what's important to them and hoping that another person finds value in that.

As is true for all of these women, Julia Lesage insists that her largely unfunded media work of the 1970s—which included the founding of a women's Super 8 collective; a women's studies program run by teachers, undergraduates, and staff at the University of Illinois, Chicago; the founding of the journal *Jump Cut* and the first Chicago Women's Film Festival—was inspired by a political movement that created the confidence that "we could learn anything and teach it to others."[32]

The waning of these movements, and the political hope they created, has allowed the logic of capitalism to fill the gaps. Here is another explanation for the mainstreaming occurring within feminist media. The making (and spending) of money and influence becomes a motivation in and of itself in a culture that can recognize value or power only in these terms. Valerie Soe, herself a student of Horsfield and Blumenthal, is depressed by this shift:

> I think that my life has been ruled less by hope than by despair. . . . A lot of that comes from coming of age during the Reagan administration. Growing up as a child in the '60s and '70s, I remember this as an incredibly optimistic period. People thought that they could be whatever they wanted—you know, a potter, a sculptor—nobody wanted to be a banker in the '70s. Then in the '80s, *everybody* wanted to be a banker.

For the few who don't want to be bankers, the availability of grants—directly to the artist or to the organizations that support media makers—has a significant effect on feminist production. Before the inception of the National Endowment for the Arts (NEA, founded in 1965), the Corporation for Public Broadcasting (CPB, founded in 1967), film cooperatives that allowed artists access to equipment at nonprofit prices, or film funding cooperatives that explicitly funded feminist or progressive work,[33] most women who produced film were either independently wealthy or were supported by wealthy husbands, fathers, or family.[34] For instance, in her interview, media educator Margaret Caples insists that many black or poor women never imagine that they can be artists, let alone actually get to work as artists, because their first commitment is to making a living for themselves and their families.

Thus, a massive expansion of arts and humanities funding in the late 1960s and early 1970s opened up possibilities for many female producers. In their early days, the National Endowment for the Humanities (NEH), NEA, and CPB supported liberal (and sometimes progressive) political art work, some of which was by women (this was before the ongoing attacks by right-wing politicians initiated today's self-defensive retreat by such cultural institutions). Recently, as these more established agencies have become increasingly traditional in their programming, the Independent Television Service (ITVS) was championed by media activists hoping to (re-)create some government support to fill the glaring lapses in broadcast programming. ITVS has a congressional mandate to fund television for and by people and communities underrepresented on broadcast (and public) television: for instance, women, people of color, the young and the aged, the disabled, and gays and lesbians. Of course, since the '70s, cable access has allowed many such Americans to make and locally air their television for free.

Just as funding possibilities enable work, in their interviews several women attest to the direct impact of the defunding of the arts. For instance, both Wendy Quinn (from the Women in the Director's Chair Film Festival) and Caples (from the Community Film Workshop) note a steady decline, respectively, in entries for the festival and programs they can offer, as art funding continues to dwindle in the United States. In their interviews, Horsfield and Schneemann discuss how the complete defunding of film and video preservation denies contemporary artists access to valuable resources created in the past. And even when successful in attaining funding, contemporary artists acknowledge how a general atmosphere of intolerance (often expressed through the defunding of institutions and organizations) affects their sense of artistic possibility. Many of this study's younger artists share a spirit of cynicism and despair. In her book on guerrilla video of the '70s Deirdre Boyle worries about the attitude of the youngest generation:

> Faith in the future, which seemed so natural to youth in the late 60s, is conspicuously lacking today if my graduate students are any indication. They are smart, talented, and deeply sensitive, but instead of boundless belief in themselves and in their ability to affect the world, many are plagued by depression, hopelessness, and doubt. The infrastructure created in the 60s to support budding talent and public channels for art and information is rapidly being dismantled.[35]

Lack of funding, and the myriad other supports necessary to imagine oneself a media maker and then to actually make work, has meant that a significant number of women have entered this field only to leave it, or have never even entered at all. We will never know the histories of absent women and can only point toward the space of *unmade* work and *non-careers*, as a truly invisible but key manifestation of (the lack of) funding and infrastructure.

▶

Technology and the Possibility of Feminist Media

A number of advances in media technology have directly affected feminist media production. As technologies for making media become more affordable and easier to operate, more women are able to use them. These technological changes have a history. In the '50s and '60s, people outside the film industry became able to make independent film because of the invention of the home movie camera (8mm and Super 8), the marketing of cheap 16mm technology to nonprofessionals (which included lighter cameras and film stock that did not need professional lighting equipment), and the marketing of lightweight synch-sound recording technologies (the Nagra, for instance). Women especially became active in media with the invention and marketing of handheld consumer video recording devices (the portapak in the '70s, the camcorder in the '80s, the digital camcorder in the '90s), the invention and marketing of consumer-grade videotape and editing equipment in the '80s (first ¾" video, then smaller-format video including VHS, Hi-8, and digital), and the invention and marketing of digital editing soft- and hardware in the '90s. These changes in video technology made media production more accessible because the materials were lighter, easier to learn and handle, cheaper, and accessible to individuals outside of industry settings. Such technological developments, often accompanying ideological shifts, prove to be the underpinnings of many progressive film or video movements—from the New American Cinema in the '60s made possible by consumer 8mm and 16mm cameras, to video collectives in the '70s working with portapaks,[36] to activist video in the '80s using inexpensive consumer camcorders,[37] to Web-based collectives of the '90s. In all of these instances, consumer-grade, consumer-priced technology allowed large numbers of women, people of color, and others to enter these otherwise costly and overly professionalized media fields.

New technologies allow changes in film culture beyond expanded access. As previously disenfranchised communities make artistic work, both media subject matter and style are renewed. In his writing on committed documentary, Thomas Waugh demonstrates this productive relation:

> The new lightweight cameras encouraged filmmakers to go beyond their traditional observational modes towards modes of participation and even collaboration, intervention, and social catalysis. New stocks permitted new environments to be added to the documentary arsenal, for example leading feminists to add the iconography of kitchen-table rap groups to that of classical street-corner demonstrations, enabling them to translate into filmic practice the political practice of intervening in the personal sphere.[38]

Most important, these new producers bring already viable political communities and networks to media technologies. For instance, Chela Sandoval, a member of the Santa Cruz Women's Media Collective in the 1970s, points out, "Women's media collectives, like the one in Santa Cruz, were a vital arm of the women's liberation movement and could be found in almost every major urban area. They would show their programs and hold discussion groups in community centers, women's bookstores, universities, and on public access channels."[39]

Ideas about Art, Culture, and Politics and the Possibility of Feminist Media

> *In the existence of feminist scholarship . . . we've presented*
> *fundamental challenges to the structures and institutions of*
> *society—marriage, the family, gender roles, the academic*
> *disciplines—and to the structure of knowledge itself. There*
> *was no equivalent to this in the first wave of feminism.*
> :: Gayle Greene, "Looking at History" in *Changing Subjects*

Gayle Greene proposes that the permanent contribution of second-wave feminism is (academic) feminist theory; if the women and their actions of the '70s are forgotten, the ways that they taught us to *think* are lasting because feminist theory changed "the structure of knowledge itself." If Greene is right, this is a change so deep that it would go unrecognized, become natural. However, initially these ideas felt like a revolution. In the '70s, women were inspired and changed by ideological forces like the liberation of women's voices through consciousness-raising, a New Left commitment to alternative media, and a countercultural do-it-yourself sensibility. In that political and intellectual climate, they began making their own personal and political films in unprecedented numbers.[40] An abundance of feminist media production continues to this day, its roots in these ideas no longer necessary to mention, or perhaps no longer known. While I cannot do justice here to the nuanced history of ideas that underlies this unprecedented women's media practice, I will discuss how feminist theory, theories of the media arising from other political movements, and academic feminist scholarship—all in dialogue with the women's movement—have contributed to feminist media possibility.

In the 1970s, a "feminist analysis" of one's life and society was an integral aspect of consciousness-raising, and more centrally of feminism itself. Lisa Maria Hogeland explains that the 1970s women's movement "was based on gender consciousness, on women's sense of themselves *as women*—as members of a group socially, politically, and economically positioned differently from *men*."[41] She suggests that a woman became a feminist when the recognition of this basic idea altered her experience of her self and her everyday reality. Founded on a politics of altered *perception,* it is not surprising that feminism emphasizes the political importance of understanding the relation between representation and gender construction as well as the related work of altering such representations.

In fact, a great deal of early feminist theory was explicitly about the power and function of images. Large numbers of women were affected by the publication of Betty Friedan's *The Feminine Mystique* (1963) with its critique of patriarchal media images of women, and by the later founding of the National Organization of Women (NOW), which supported Friedan's analysis.[42] Most of the collections of women's liberation writings published in books and journals during the '70s included analysis of media stereotyping.[43] Consciousness-raising groups often looked at our society's omnipresent stereotypical images of women so as to understand better the subjugation of women and how women are conditioned to participate in their own subjugation. In her book *Women's Reflections: The Feminist Film Movement,* Jan Rosenberg proposes that a critique of patriarchal representation of women was at the core of both mainstream and radical feminist theory and organizing.[44]

At the same time, feminist media practice was influenced by the more general radical political debate and spirit of the era. The ideological energy of the 1970s—rooted in the liberation rhetorics of socialism, civil rights, anti-imperialism and anticolonialism, antiwar activism, gay liberation, the counterculture, and feminism—energized women who lived through these times. These movements for a more humane and just society, one no longer based on arbitrary systems of power inequity, often took up this simple but radical position: cultural work is political work. For instance, as Tommy Lott attempts to devise his "No-Theory of Black Cinema," he realizes that "as a primarily oppositional practice engaged in resistance and affirmation, black cinema need not be presently defined apart from its political function."[45] For blacks, women, and other politicized groups, the "political function" of media work was theorized to occur on (at least) two fronts: through the mainstream, in critiquing dominant images and organizing to get more minorities into the media; and through forming alternative institutions and representations.

Media feminism was not only influenced by such ideas and struggles occurring in the "real world"; it also was shaped by the work of feminist scholars across traditional academic disciplines who developed interpretations of what it means to be female (or male) in a patriarchy. In the '70s, activist intellectuals insisted that their work (teaching, writing, creating and altering ideas) comes from and contributes to political change. "Like many feminists of my generation, my starting point in this arena was not my becoming an academic. My goals at that time were very much influenced by the Civil Rights Movements of the 60s, which moved me to the study of Afro-American history and literature as one means through which I believed a change in consciousness might occur in this country," reminisces Barbara Christian about her choice to become a feminist scholar.[46] In the same fashion, the editors of *Jump Cut,* a journal of scholarly film criticism founded in the 1970s, refer to their original goals with a language that completely integrates politics and culture: "We eagerly threw ourselves into building the cultural dimensions of political struggle and the political dimensions of cultural struggle, and we have both drawn our strength from and hopefully contributed to the revived feminist movement, the gay and lesbian movements, the civil rights movement, and antiwar and anti-imperialist movements."[47]

The feminist media community of the '70s flourished due to a relatively direct line of communication between media scholars, feminist activists, and media makers, perhaps even more so than was true in other fields. Much feminist media practice is immersed in, and inspired by, feminist theory; in fact, it could be argued that it is its most logical outcome. In the '70s and '80s, grassroots feminist distribution companies were not hesitant to carry and promote intellectual films to sites outside the academy. And feminist film theory was initially inspired by the ideas and actions of the women's movement. Laura Mulvey chronicles this development in a 1989 edition of *Camera Obscura* that historicizes feminist film theory through the memoirs of some of its founding practitioners: "Feminist use of the new theory and its application to popular culture grew directly out of the Women's Movement's concern with images, their contribution to fixing the connotations of gender and circulating images of women as signifying a patriarchal mythology of sexuality."[48]

Although the field of feminist media scholarship initially developed in response to the women's movement's interest in images, the field shifted focus within only a few years. Influenced by developments in film studies, the newly-translated-to-English theories of psychoanalysis, structuralism, semiotics, and the legacy of the New Left's interest in Marxism, feminist scholars began to ask questions about patriarchy with a different vocabulary; they were less interested in the power of images *of* women than they were in the very notion of woman "as image."[49] The 1975 publication of Mulvey's "Visual Pleasure and Narrative Cinema" introduced some key ideas about how Hollywood film promotes patriarchal "looking relations"— especially the gender-based pleasures of voyeurism, fetishism, and sadism. In her memoir of this period, Rich recounts how psychoanalytic feminist media criticism initiated the field's decided shift from supporting and critiquing the politicized film practice of the women's movement toward examining "the controlling power of the male gaze, the fetishization of the female body, and the collusion of narrative cinema with gender subjugation."[50]

As the questions around images changed, feminist scholarship about "voice" also shifted. Whereas scholars initially considered how disenfranchised people might "claim a voice" in the media, they began to consider how voice itself is constructed, mobilized, and legislated by dominant systems. While an impulse to "claim a voice" continues to encourage activist media practices by people of color, women, gays and lesbians, and AIDS activists, most academic feminists focus their criticism on mainstream or "deconstructionist" media where a feminist analysis of voice, voyeurism, or the construction of images can be their central concern. As Mulvey notes, "Feminist film theory lost touch with feminist filmmaking, that which had hitherto acted as its utopian other. In the meantime, the female spectator has tended to become the empirical consumer of television, advertising, shopping malls and so on."[51]

This rift between theorizing mainstream culture and making alternative culture may begin to heal as a generation of feminist media makers is educated in and through feminist film theory. As film and women's studies continued to be institutionalized in the '80s and '90s, college students have often learned feminist film analysis as part of their media studies and could even expect to find a feminist filmmaker or critic on the faculty. This younger generation is now becoming film studies and filmmaking professors themselves. They make work *and* write theory since they are conversant in the multiple traditions of feminist media work. Cheryl Dunye exemplifies this trend: "Of course, a lot of people have seen my work. There are black lesbians who have seen my work and a mass of white lesbians and gay men who have seen my work. That's about 30 percent of the audience. And then there's the academy. My work has been consumed by the academy. It comes from me being a thinker, an intellectual, dipping from the same cultural well. . . . In one sense, I've never left school."

Finally, in the 1980s and 1990s, the escalation of identity politics and multiculturalism as both theory and praxis, as well as the introduction of AIDS activism and the burgeoning fields of cultural and queer studies, have also had a great impact on feminist media practice. Continuing to be influenced by many of the core ideas of the movements for social change of the 1970s—particularly the notion that cultural work is political work, and often the theory that the personal is the political—these are contemporary arenas where art, thought, and action are highly integrated. Yet these present-day movements occur in a very different world from the United States in the '70s, and they respond to the mistakes and failures of earlier activists. Eve Oishi attests to the odd, but productive, array of forces that inspire contemporary careers in feminist film scholarship—in tandem, forces as diverse as theories and practices of race, popular culture, sexuality, fantasy, and violence:

> When I was looking back and trying to trace the path through which I became a feminist film scholar, or a feminist, it was interesting that I found all of these

roundabout histories that weren't traditionally feminist. They had to do more with trying to understand what my racial identity was, what my relationship to my Japanese American father was, what my relationship to American culture was. . . . And my relationship to popular culture, my relation to violence, and power, and my relation to technology. . . . Because for me, my love of film had to do with illicitness, voyeurism. It had to do with fantasy and fantasy that was often violent and that was often forbidden.

▶
───

The "Women's Community" or "Women's Movement" and Feminist Media

In her book on the feminist film movement, Jan Rosenberg documents how this "unique aesthetic/political movement [is] rooted politically in contemporary feminism." Writing in 1979, contemporaneously with the movement she studies, Rosenberg explains how the exuberant and productive communality of the women's movement inspired the birth of feminist film and its unprecedented body of production: "Understanding how the feminist film movement grew out of the women's movement provides a necessary preface to understanding the feminist film movement itself."[52] However, as I write this volume on the history and contemporary state of feminist media, it is less clear how the current *waning* of the movement affects feminist media production. Whereas the '70s saw an active and visible infrastructure of feminist organizations, political groups, consciousness-raising groups, collectives, schools, and the like, the '80s and '90s appear at first look more barren. Megan Cunningham, this study's youngest participant, knows only an isolated feminist media practice:

> It was already a downward spiral. . . . There wasn't that coalition that the women of the '60s and '70s described. Nor was there that spirit of leftist politics being almost mainstream. . . . It made sense to me that you would make your own little video in your room and show it to your friends because this was your own little personal crusade. It had nothing to do with launching a career or a larger political movement. It wasn't about joining forces; it was about surviving.

Certainly, some feminist production/distribution mechanisms and interactive spaces actually became more firmly established in the '90s, including video distribution (home video, cable, and the educational market), the Internet, the queer community, the academy, and goal-driven coalition politics. And without question, producers continue to make a great deal of feminist media work. But we must consider where and how this work actually gets made given our current climate: is it only "about surviving"? Perhaps the most viable public places left standing for feminism—where women do "join forces," if temporarily—are women's and now queer studies programs, which are housed in the university setting. Cunningham (as did I) came into her media feminism in such an environment. However, given that only some women go to college, most end up graduating and moving on, and only a few major in the often-perceived-to-be-threatening settings of "minority studies programs," we must celebrate the successes of such programs while also questioning how to maintain feminist community in other environments.

Evaluating how to create or maintain feminist possibility is especially difficult because there is no uniformity to feminism's understanding of its current condition. As I screen and discuss my documentary that accompanies this book with multigenerational groups of women, they debate whether or not feminism and feminist media are alive and well. No one seems to know for sure. They wonder: because young girls are not taught it in school, does it disappear—even as girls' lives have changed dramatically as a direct result of feminism? Because we are disallowed to say the "f-word," do the ideas that it encompasses evaporate? And what of the many, many of us who *do* say we are "feminists," who *do* participate in feminist organizing and feminist culture? Why is our steady production so hard to see? And just because it is invisible (to many), is that a reason to proclaim its failure? The older women at my screenings tend to mourn the loss of a clearly identifiable community and its steady organizing. Meanwhile, some of the younger women insist that this continues, but that such activism is unrecognizable to those who use a '70s model to locate it.

Many point to the terrain of the Internet as both a real site and a metaphor for the contemporary state of feminist activity: dispersed, privatized, boundaryless, mediated through technology. Given that the Internet is both unmapped and not yet universally accessible, the metaphor and practice of an Internet-based feminism describe less the magnitude of feminist production (it's hard to know how many are there and how much they may be accomplishing) than its very *visibility* (or lack thereof). If many women are finding lively sites of communal interaction in cyberspace, many, many more are denied this pleasure. And one of the definitive features of the Internet is that others on the system need never know of the microcommunities that fall outside of their surfing matrix. As feminism occurs on the Internet, it is visible only to those who use it. Contemporary feminism must consider the consequences of the invisibility, and perhaps actual lack, of real-world feminist community and organized activism in the face of the individual, privatized empowerment and political action of isolated, or at best, wired women.

The younger women with whom I speak about this project also indicate that their feminism occurs within goal-driven coalition politics. It is certainly true for me that when I trace the places where feminism was and is most alive for me (outside of my teaching in women's studies), I find it in my AIDS, queer, and antiracism media production, teaching, and activism. It is not only younger feminists who refuse to see feminist history as one in decline. In her response to a collection of memoirs about the '70s women's movement, most written by white women who proclaim feminism's sad demise, Barbara Smith postulates another interpretation: that the dismantling of (some of the) infrastructure does not necessarily speak to an end as much as to a better beginning:

> The 70s saw the growth of feminists of color organizing (often led by lesbians) all over the country. This organizing reached its peak in the early 1980s. This was also the period when those issues that had divided many of the movement's constituencies—such as racism, anti-Semitism, ableism, ageism, and classism— were put on the table. The most progressive sectors of the movement responded to the challenge to transform their analysis and practice in order to build a stronger movement that encompasses a variety of feminisms.[53]

Smith suggests that the groups and struggles that are informed by a feminism that is in dialogue with other political vocabularies do maintain their viable if less-than-visible work: "In 1997 there is still a feminist movement in the United States. Its most vital elements are grassroots activists who are committed to linking diverse communities and struggles. This is the part of the movement that never got major media attention, nor does it get to speak out in mainstream contexts about feminist issues" (481).

In this sense, the inaccessibility and lack of exposure that define feminist media are similar to the current state of progressive feminism, which also occurs in the most marginal of places: noncapitalist, anticommercial, multiracial, pan-sexual, radical, strategically organizing. Mainstreaming merely in the name of increased visibility has consequences. Here, I think that feminism has a great deal to learn from the (brief) history of queer activism. While gays and lesbians have certainly entered mainstream consciousness, this is necessarily at the expense of a more radical critique of mutually influencing, structural systems of dominance. The queer movement has a sexy product to sell, that is, if you reduce its demands to a matter of mere sexual openness, exploration, and tolerance rather than to a systematic critique of heteronormativity. It seems impossible to imagine how "feminism" could ever be so reduced and then advertised on the glossy pages of the many catalogues that now sell rainbow-or-red-ribbon tchotchkes to queers. On the other hand, feminists' current position may reflect the society's inability to hear feminist demands because the "movement" has not changed with the political tides, has not manufactured a media-savvy, sound-bite version of who we are and what we want. Instead, we have allowed the mainstream media to do this for us and thus to reduce feminists to that simplistic, dour image that most resembles their fears.

Projects like this one attempt to respond. But as long as feminism remains so unattractive in a society increasingly motivated by slick surfaces, my reach will be small, especially given that I make few concessions in my style or content to make my words more marketable. So perhaps this is where feminist legacy and generation can be mobilized in a productive way. Where my specific feminist history may disallow me from making this project marketable in the fresh new ways that speak to a more general twenty-first-century America, maybe new generations will build from this feminist history, eventually respeaking it in a way that can be more widely understood.

▶

The History of *Women of Vision*

> *To paraphrase Marx, a committed filmmaker is not content only to interpret the world but is also engaged in changing it.*
> :: Thomas Waugh, *"Show Us Life": Toward a History and Aesthetics of the Committed Documentary*

This book is my most current work as committed videomaker and scholar eager to both participate in and change my world. It is feminist practice about feminist practice. These interviews become part of the larger feminist legacy that they attempt to document, participate in, contribute to, and understand. The community I "study" is the community I feed, the community I know and care about, my own community. At best, I want the process of my media work to model the goals of the communities it engages, so I seek to trouble the kind of distance typically used by scholars and filmmakers to know their subjects by forefronting and valuing these relationships. In this way, my practice is similar to that of other feminist documentarians. For instance, Janet Walker and Diane Waldman write in their introduction to *Feminism and Documentary*: "Whereas American direct cinema and cinema verité traditions downplay the role of the filmmaker in the production process, feminist filmmakers have thought long and hard about the politics of people filming people."[54] In the following short history of my project, I will detail some of the consequences of working with a methodology that is supportive of and engaged with the real people that it studies. I will detail some of my own thinking about putting first the "politics of people filming people."

Of course, my feminist practice has a feminist politics as well. My methods for researching, interviewing, and producing and writing documentaries emerge from feminist models that I inherited and restructured for my own ends. As is true for my generation, I began my feminist education in the 1980s and was quickly immersed in institutionalized debates about "correct" and "incorrect" feminist method, debates sometimes decades old. I have had the luxury of learning from others—their established ideas and the mistakes they regretted; I have the burden of constructing my voice and career by evaluating a variety of methodologies, theoretical orientations, and subjects of study, all of which are always already understood as political, and sometimes personal, choices.

My mother, a feminist scholar, initiated my feminist education through her example. Then as an undergraduate in the mid-'80s I was inspired by the propositions and energy of feminist film scholarship and decided to go to graduate school to pursue media study's conjoining of the theoretical, the political, and the artistic. At the graduate level, I structured for myself an education within feminist traditions that supported the production of committed art and ideas. I studied cinema studies and ethnographic film at New York University and ideological/conceptual art production at the Whitney Museum's independent studio program. At the same time, I also absorbed myself in the AIDS activist video movement, making a number of educational documentaries about women's issues and AIDS.[55]

All aspects of this education valorize a reorientation of cultural production to incorporate a self-awareness about the position of the producer in relation to the subject and methodology of study. Feminist scholars have argued that the disengaged, expert scholar or artist—typically a white male authority figure who studies and uses others—relies on an implicitly politicized use of the powers of observation. Further, feminist theory suggests that the idea that a scholar must (or even can) divorce herself from the "real world," her community, or her political inclinations is the self-deceived privilege of those powerful enough to erase their own positionality. A number of the "fundamental tenets" of her "Black feminist critical approach," as enumerated by Gloria Hull, articulate this orientation toward scholarly production (I have here selected only some of Hull's tenets):

(i) The proper scholarly stance is engaged rather than objective.
(ii) The personal (both the subject's and the critic's) is political.
(iii) Research/criticism is not an academic/intellectual game, but a pursuit with social meaning rooted in the "real world."[56]

Like Hull, many of the scholars whom I most respect sought careers in the academy precisely because they believe that they could well accomplish their goals in this very real, if rarefied, world. "My academic writing has always been and will always be politically motivated," writes Bonnie Zimmerman. "I want to advance lesbian consciousness and visibility wherever I am placed, and where I am placed right now is the academy. That is why I write, and why I write lesbian criticism."[57]

This (black/lesbian) feminist academic tradition is not the only one in which I was trained. At the same time that feminist theory was radically restructuring (much of) academic practice, feminist theory also caused upheavals in the art world. In the '70s, feminism both politicized and gave more personal content to conceptual art, which was already moving the commodifiable art object into the more amorphous terrain of performance, video, installation, and the "real world" so as "to narrow the distance between art and audience and art and life."[58] In his article about the feminist art of Suzanne Lacy, Jeff Kelley lists the distinctive qualities of feminist art to "includ[e], to quote Lucy Lippard, 'collaboration, dialogue, a constant questioning of aesthetic and social assumptions, and a new respect for audience.'"[59] I worked hard to learn about such feminist art tactics from the '70s. When I was in graduate school during the high-theory '80s, this aspect of feminist (art) history was largely hidden under the table, understood as an embarrassing relic of an antiquated ('70s), antitheoretical, feminist "essentialism." It has only been in the '90s and beyond that feminists like myself have been interested in revisiting this period and revalorizing its process-oriented work by and about the artist's community.

I also studied other movements of media activists who attempted to participate in social change. Especially compelling for me was the legacy of what Deirdre Boyle calls the "grass roots" sector of the guerrilla media community. Founded in the '70s but still very much alive in New York City where I studied during the '80s, these groups espoused liberatory possibilities for the media. They used the camera to reestablish or at least reexamine subject-object relations in media practice: "Their aim was making changes in the community; making tapes was just a byproduct of this process."[60] Similarly, Chon Noriega describes how early films of the Chicano cinema movement "served the needs of an audience whose main concern was the organization of 'community' and not the craft of an autonomous, objective, or artistic statement."[61]

One of the real consequences for my project, due to this primary commitment to community building, is that the documentary ended up taking me four years to complete. With limited funding,[62] and a full-time job, I slowly chipped away at the documentary, and then the book, as I could afford to. The interviews were shot in 1995–96, the documentary was completed in 1998, and the book of transcribed interviews in 2001. Clearly, one consequence of my process is that the interviews are already dated at the book's initial publication. My subjects and I have kept the interviews true to their original content except to update women's work histories and other necessary factual information.

Work on my project was also slower than for the many documentaries because of another feminist strategy that structures my work: collaboration and collectivity. Given that I was telling the story of very alive, very active, very smart women, I felt that it was inexcusable to *not* hear their interpretations of this history rather than to individually, and in more traditional scholarly isolation, produce my own interpretation. Thus for the first year of the project, I organized and ran (with the help of many students and community film organizations) five research meetings across the country (in Philadelphia, New York, Chicago, San Francisco, and Los Angeles) where nearly two hundred women involved in this field came together and discussed their interpretations of its history. I learned a great deal from these meetings (especially about the significant differences between media communities, city by city, this itself worthy of a documentary). But most valuable was the lesson that there was no way to respect my own collaborative process and then produce a linear version of this history (even as video is itself a decidedly linear medium). Each one of these media-savvy women voiced as central to her feminist media history a different set of role models, political convictions, and stylistic strategies. I needed to produce a documentary that would reflect the diversity within this field rather than a simple trajectory of causality. Thus I selected for on-camera interviews twenty of the women whom I met during my research. These women could help me represent the immense diversity within the field. They would depict twenty different sites on the map of its terrain.

Importantly, the demands of shooting interviews on video (especially with minimal funding) define a great deal of the "choices" I actually made. I could only interview women who were in the cities in which I shot on the one or two days that I had financial access to a crew and equipment. In several, regrettable cases, I did not interview my "first choice." For instance, I had hoped to interview experimental filmmaker Yvonne Rainer and feminist critic B. Ruby Rich, both of whom were associated with the project but neither of whom was available when I was shooting. And I conducted several interviews with colleagues or friends with whom I already had a personal relationship. For it is a great deal to ask of anyone to dedicate an hour of her time (which becomes innumerable hours of rough-cut watching, transcript editing, data providing), not to mention her intimate life stories, to a project that is not hers and to a person whom she does not know. There is community and there is *community*. My friends and immediate colleagues were the easiest subjects for me to handle, given that I did not have the fiscal resources necessary to best undertake such a large study. Money usually provides the cushion that softens the demands of large-scale production and postproduction. In this case, friendship or collegiality provided some of what funds usually purchase. Even so, the documentary's slow but steady creation is (against my best hopes) yet another reflection of its subject: a field defined by production with limited fiscal—but a great deal of community—support.[63]

It took me about two years to shoot the twenty interviews and then another two years to edit them into the final documentary video. Editing—often thought of as women's work because it bears a relation to the thankless piecing together of sewing—is my favorite part of the video production process; it is the behind-the-scenes territory where real power lies. Here, interviewees' words meet up with my aesthetic and conceptual framework, which then adapts and grows to meet their words. In the documentary, I decided to edit the interviews so as to group them around large conceptual frameworks that would map the changing foci of the women's movement across the decades. The decision came from ideas illuminated in the research meetings and interviews. I realized that each woman articulated a relation to the politics of the '70s as she described her political identity. In fact, this was probably the only marker that was universal across the interviews.

I also broke up the whole into three PBS-style, half-hour-long segments that could be shown separately or all together. This form—besides being pedagogically useful—structured into the text the possibility of a television airing.[64] The first grouping, "Creating an Infrastructure," brings together six women who helped to build organizations during the fertile '70s and in the face of a barren cultural scene not open to women artists. The second section, "Mothers, Lovers, and Mentors," focuses on six women whose careers were energized (mostly in the '80s) by inspirational interactions with other women that were largely facilitated by the infrastructure put into place by the women's movement. In "Reassembly Required," six women speak about their constructive, sometimes critical, relation to the institutionalized feminism of the '90s. The video documentary is edited to mark elaborate shifts from the making of feminist institutions to the institutionalization of feminism. The tape moves with a loose chronology. It begins in the '60s when women were blocked by the male art world and patriarchal academy. It looks at the '70s with its communal networking, consciousness-raising, and critique of capitalism, racial inequities, and the nuclear family; and then it turns to the '80s when some women experienced dissension and disheartenment as feminism was enhanced by a new emphasis on sexual orientation and ethnicity. And finally, the tape looks at the '90s when new identities (for example, AIDS, queer, biracial) and new technologies (digital) began to shape how and where feminists make work and allegiances.

Editing of a slightly different sort occurs in this book. Unlike for the documentary video, I've created here a chronological order organized by the interviewees' date of birth, from oldest woman to youngest. I changed the structure because I feel the reader of this written text can have more power creating connections and, perhaps, historical relations than is possible when viewing the documentary. While both are linear forms, a video rolls forth (yes, stoppable and rewindable, but rarely viewed in this way) while a book is opened and closed at the reader's complete discretion. Furthermore, the lack of competing (and compelling) images allows the book's reader to consider the interviewee's words with closer attention. Date of birth is a relatively objective structure that allows the reader to form links and associations between the words of the diverse interviews without my preliminary grouping.

Like any imposed structure, this system of presenting history, both personal and political, clarifies some things while it complicates or obscures others. "There's a danger in being born with a decade," writes Nancy Miller. "One tends to conflate (solipsistically) things that might not have anything to do with each other."[65] Miller's point is well demonstrated by looking at changes that occur depending on which of the two organizing schemata I use. For instance, in the documentary video, I place Barbara Hammer in the second section (where she is the seventh interview) because she began her career as a filmmaker when she was already immersed in the organized lesbian feminist scene of the '70s. One of the few out lesbian filmmakers of this period, she became a filmmaker in *relation* to other organized women. In the book, her interview is placed third because she is the third-oldest interviewee.

This allows the book's reader to see the varied paths taken by women of a similar age to get to their careers, the varied forces that inspire or obstruct them. Interestingly, Carolee Schneemann, the same age as Hammer, had already been making art work for nearly a decade when Hammer began making film. Slightly younger than Hammer and Schneemann, Margaret Caples was employed in the '60s as a social worker and came to film through her commitment to civil rights. In her book on feminist generations, Nancy Whittier is quick to point out the difference between age and "political generations"—that is, when a woman becomes politicized or "the time that [she] enters a movement and experiences it as an activist" (226).

In this case, in the '60s three women of similar age were at different places in their feminist development. As Whittier writes, "More than an age group, members of a political generation are bound together by shared transformative experiences that create enduring political commitments and worldviews" (16). The structure of this book allows the reader to deduce for herself where age and political generation merge or part. The reader can see, for example, that for three women of a similar age it was their different political alliances and personal experiences that organized their sense of "generation." The civil rights movement brought Caples to film education; lesbian feminism brought Hammer to experimental filmmaking; the women's movement brought Schneemann, already working in film, to a community of female colleagues.

There were other considerations as I worked to produce this book from transcripts of interviews initially shot for a documentary video. Given that the heart of my documentary methodology resides in the relationships I establish in the making and distribution of video, would the questions and the kinds of answers they inspire have been different if my first project were a book? Yes. It is central to my methodology as a video documentarian to strive for supportive, collaborative relationships with my subjects because they present themselves to me as living, breathing people. Filming real subjects is different from writing about real people. As Ilisa Barbash and Lucien Taylor spell out in their handbook *Cross-Cultural Filmmaking*, "If you are writing a book or an article, you can go home and write it all up afterwards. With film, you have to shoot events and activities as they occur. . . . That's what is so special about film: it's linked absolutely, existentially to its object, a photochemical permeation of the world."[66] As a feminist producer, I am very aware of interpersonal and ethical considerations of video production because of this existential specificity. My actions affect real people to whom I already have political and personal allegiances. I record and own a person's videotaped image, to edit and reassemble with other images at will. I have a distinct obligation to and responsibility for that image—both in how I film people and what I do with the footage—different from those raised by the act of representation in its most general sense.

Feminists have argued that the phallic camera, much like a gun, has most typically been used to shoot and therefore control and own "others." Barbash and Taylor, like many other committed documentarians, propose a collaborative method as one response to (if never a "cure" for) the immense power imbalance structured into the filmic apparatus and interaction: "The incentive to collaborate stems from the recognition that it is only reasonable that people should have some input into how they are represented. Moreover, if a film is about someone's subjective or emotional life, it will probably only be enriched by their active participation" (86). Similarly, in her book on activist art production Nina Felshin illustrates how a collaborative method has a political effect:

> Participation is thus often an act of self-expression or self-representation by the entire community. Individuals are empowered through such creative expression, as they acquire voice, visibility, and an awareness that they are part of a greater whole. The personal thus becomes political, and change, even if initially only of community or public consciousness, becomes possible.[67]

As a feminist bent on using documentary as a tool for change, I do not use the act of interviewing as an opportunity to challenge, confuse, or undermine my subjects. Quite the opposite. I do everything in my power to make them feel supported, comfortable, and respected. For this project, my interviewees knew the questions in advance, all but one had previously met me, and all understood and supported the project's goals. After the interviews, I sent each person subsequent versions of her written transcript and video portrait. I invited each interviewee to edit, change, or approve each draft. I learned this method from others who had made committed documentary with vulnerable communities. For instance, my professor, eminent documentarian George Stoney, always screens drafts of his films to the communities depicted in them so that his subjects can respond to his representation, and so he can reedit the work in response to their critique.[68] Such a methodology stands as a direct critique of the traditional combative, distant, and judgmental style of most documentary production. Feminist documentarian Barbara Halpern Martineau elucidates how a collaborative method separates feminist documentary from the larger field: "The relationship of commitment between filmmaker and film subject, and between these two and the audience, provides a little-discussed dimension to the issue of how women are 'represented' in the [feminist] documentaries."[69]

I have used a collaborative method of video making to create history, and that raises certain conceptual questions. Needless to say, this method may not unearth the same kinds of "data" that an academic historian or theoretician seeks. One difficulty with using this method to understand history is that it is most often affirmative and descriptive rather than analytical or reflective. While the information my interviewees offer is neither ahistorical nor atheoretical, it is certainly less removed or abstract than information that is typically culled for writing social history. One way to understand the strengths of such a practice, particularly as a strategy for women's intellectual reflection, is to look at this as a (re)mobilizing of the '70s feminist practice of consciousness-raising. Julia Lesage argues that much early feminist documentary was organized by a deep structure analogous to the intellectual work of analyzing women's experience that was done collectively—and locally—by the consciousness-raising group. As a feminist documentarian, I participate in this tradition that, to quote Lesage, "sets the filmmaker in a mutual, non-hierarchical relation with her subject (such filming is not seen as the male artist's act of 'seizing' the subject and then presenting one's 'creation') and indicates what she hopes her relation to her audience will be."[70]

However, theories and practices of consciousness-raising have been widely debated in the feminist community. Some think that this particular feminist methodology creates solipsism, self-congratulation, and narcissism; others believe that it allows women to begin to interrogate the difference within supposedly homogeneous communities, and that it provides the necessary comfort for subjects to speak the stories that no outsider is allowed to hear. In her book on the consciousness-raising novel, Lisa Maria Hogeland gives the two, competing understandings of consciousness-raising (CR) the names "hard, theory-building CR" and "soft, self-esteem-building CR."[71] I believe that the two forms of CR can be productively interrelated. In her memoir of her history in academic feminism, Hull recounts a personal movement from self-esteem to theory, from soft to hard CR. She remembers how personal empowerment was the first step toward her politicized, professorial career: "We had to chant 'Black is beautiful' and 'Sisterhood is powerful' before we could declare that they were also legitimate scholarly subjects. Gestures of self esteem seem to be fundamental prerequisites to any kind of revolutionary change."[72] For her book on the women's movement and feminist theory, Katie King reads CR pamphlets and finds a similar transition—from personal to political change—articulated as the goal of CR: "Pam Allen, in her 1970 essay 'Free Space' talks about four processes in CR: opening up, sharing, analyzing, and abstracting. CR is not to exchange or relive experience, nor is it cathartic; rather, its purpose is to teach women to clarify and to clear ground for action."[73] It is this movement in CR—to clear ground for action—that I hope to replicate in my documentary process.

I strive to understand what I have gained and lost by using a collaborative methodology. While I create a supportive environment and public platform to allow my interviewees to ruminate on their past, their work, and their future, I may not have pushed them sufficiently to interpret their work or lives in new or self-critical ways, nor may I have been as critical as I might have been if analyzing art and artists from a distance and in the abstract. In conversations with me about this project, B. Ruby Rich labeled it "activist" in its structure, and "old-fashioned" in that it is based on a more '70s type of commitment to egalitarianism, identification, and communalism. However, I do not believe that my reliance on consciousness-raising or other "dated" structures necessarily entails a retreat or even a form of nostalgia. Rather, as I strive to present knowledge that will be empowering, and that can perhaps even "clear ground for action," I find that the more common poststructuralist method taken up by feminist scholars seems at once too cynical and too text-based for my real-world–based practice. In a similar way, Ellen Willis seeks to make sense of other contemporary returns to earlier feminist forms and methods: "Language keeps falling back on the tropes of an earlier era for the simple reason that in this [current] period there exists no legitimate public language in which to describe utopian vision or systematic opposition."[74]

I believe that we can learn from and adapt earlier feminist methods initially used at a time of greater engagement. While I want to invest these earlier techniques with current conditions, new passions, and contemporary critiques, I am still old-fashioned enough to believe that there is work to be accomplished outside (while still making use of) the text, and that there is much we can and need to learn from those who have struggled before us. Therefore, at the minimum I hope that my relaying of these twenty-one histories can function in much the same way that Kate Horsfield and Lyn Blumenthal intended for their hundreds of videotaped oral histories with artists from the '70s and '80s. As Horsfield says in her interview:

> The point was very much a feminist concept. We started out only shooting women. We wanted to give all of our colleagues in graduate school an opportunity to understand one thing: no matter what books say about how to become an artist, there isn't any one way. It's totally self-defined. It's a hard road with many accidents and curved spaces. We wanted to give everyone the concept that you can do whatever you want to do, that many women were doing it and making amazing accomplishments.

After exposure to the laborious, personal paths that these twenty-one women take to get to the difficult place of having a media career, I hope the reader will appreciate the media work each woman has made with a greater respect and will value the even harder work of making that career. Ideally, she will then begin to consider how she can contribute to furthering this tradition.

The Trouble with Generation

Is the idea of generation the most useful way to understand our history, our relation to each other, the way that our progress as women and as media makers is enabled or hindered? Does generation convey only the most obvious, comfortable, and perhaps even sexist or heterosexist metaphor—one of family, progeny, mothering, daughtering? Or does it acknowledge a formative structure (perhaps culturally constructed, perhaps even patriarchically useful) that most of us nevertheless use to organize our sense of ourselves in the world, in relation to others, in relation to time, to ideas, to our contributions? As Judith Roof says in her contribution to Devoney Looser and E. Ann Kaplan's *Generations*: "The irruptions of feminist consciousness seem to require a history, a set of precedents, a feeling of context. But insofar as the familial paradigm also imports other habits of mind—debt, legacy, rivalry, property—it may be time to think the developments of criticism differently."[75]

Despite Roof's and others' cautions, most studies of feminist history are structured, using a generational model. In a discussion that the feminist journal *differences* set up between "distinguished scholars" and "young Turks" in women's studies, distinguished scholar Joan Scott initiates her reflections by criticizing the very organizing paradigm of the special edition: "Generational differences [do not] characterize the proponents of the various positions (radical, cultural, liberal, socialist . . . feminism) that have been contested in the last several decades. . . . Instead of a contested field, feminism conceived as generational becomes a unified category and its history is recounted in terms of linear successions."[76] She argues that the concept of generation is potentially limiting in that it can be understood as stagnant, fixed, singular: a woman is born into one generation and there she must stay; a woman is influenced by her generation to the exclusion of other kinds of relationships or forces. Thus Chon Noriega and Ana López introduce their collection of essays on Latino media arts with fears about how their generational structure may blind them to other models of influence: "When individual filmmakers are identified with a generation (precursor, first, second, third) within the history of Chicano, Puerto Rican, Cuban American, or Latino gay and lesbian cinema, the specific ethnic genealogies being established effectively ignore 'other' film/video/art histories that these artists have participated in."[77] Generation also suggests a biological model based on genetic inheritance and resemblance. This makes third-wave scholar Devoney Looser fear overidentification from those who want to claim the position of feminist foremother: "Passing on carries with it the idea of linear movement, as well as a suppression of the inevitability of difference. . . . [A] transmission from second to third wave can never be fully achieved regardless of how much Steinem and others might like to see themselves in us—see their issues echoed in our own."[78]

However, even as I understand such dangers, I find that I am still motivated by the possibility of *feminist association*: generations learning from and working with each other. My study was biased in this direction from the beginning. For the very tenor of my interviews revolved around questions that I posed to my subjects—if initially with little self-consciousness—about influences, role models, and debt. While I acknowledge how my own history inspired this overarching generational concern (more to follow), what I learned while doing this project also became a powerful force maintaining my commitment to this particular conceptual structure. Through the interviews, I discovered the immense importance of the '70s for feminists. I learned that a definition of feminist self and other depends on when a woman hit up against the driving force of this era: was she already an adult and an artist? Was she in college? Did she learn about it from her mother? During the research meetings, I would consistently hear women in these multigenerational groups fiercely debate the significance of the '70s for my project. The women in the room who were formed by the women's movement of that time insisted on presenting its flurry of events, festivals, collectives, and magazines as *the subject* of feminist media history. Basically, for them a history of feminist media was nothing more than a detailed recounting of the events and issues of this period. However, other women who had not been there (for a variety of reasons) strongly resisted this impulse. For instance, many of the older women of color involved in the research meetings were participating in civil rights activism during this time, often aware of and learning from feminism, but not actively participating in a women's movement perceived to be fundamentally racist.

And I have other reasons to define this project in generational terms. I've lived a personal, political, and scholarly life both as feminist mentor and mentee. I am myself a biological (or at least cultural) product of just such a legacy. My work here is, in part, a testament to my mother's ability to pass on her feminism to me with grace and power (as she did with my two feminist sisters). For I am a second-generation feminist scholar, daughter of Suzanne Juhasz, one of those early feminists who helped found women's studies. Growing up, I remember her CR group in Lewisburg, Pennsylvania, her feminist poetry readings in San Jose and Boulder, and the ongoing tension and harassment she has always faced as a feminist scholar. I also was lucky enough to study with a number of inspiring feminist teachers: professors Cathy Portuges and Laura Wexler in college, Laura Mulvey and Faye Ginsburg in graduate school, and artists Yvonne Rainer and Martha Rosler at the Whitney Independent Studio Program in New York. Further, this project has benefited immensely from the support of more established women in the arts from across the country who have believed in it and could match that belief with institutional sanction and personal power:

Terry Lawler, then at Women Make Movies; Elayne Zalis, then at the Long Beach Museum of Art Video Annex; Jeanne Kracher, then at the Women in the Director's Chair Film Festival; Kate Horsfield at the Video Data Bank; Vanalyne Green at the School of the Art Institute of Chicago; Gail Silva at the Film Arts Foundation; and Linda Blackabee, then at the Philadelphia Independent Film and Video Association. Finally, scholarly supporters like B. Ruby Rich and Julia Lesage worked closely with me to think through the fundamental ideas that were necessary to best frame and make sense of this history.

With my own history as only the most obvious example, I find that while it may be useful on a theoretical level to challenge the concept of a reproductive lineage that moves knowledge or power neatly from one individual to another, from one "mother" to her "daughter," when it comes to any woman's lived experience this is a different matter. A messy but necessary connection *is* commonly understood between whom and what a woman is exposed to and what she feels she can become. Many of the women in this study search for what Schneemann calls "historical precedence": who was here, making feminist film or video, before me? She declares, "It's what I call 'missing precedence,' because if I don't have a realm of precedence, then I'm anomalous and my experience is constantly marginalized as being exceptional in that there is no tradition, there's no history, there's no language. But there *is* history, tradition, and language." Evidencing the same spirit that motivates this project, women in this study dedicate themselves to sharing with others what they learn about the quite alive history, tradition, and language of feminist media.

Many are also mentors—especially in their work as teachers (a majority of them make a living through teaching)—although or perhaps because they had lacked this themselves. For instance, Juanita Mohammed explains that her childhood as a working-class, urban, black girl allowed her little access to feminist filmmakers or a feminist education. She learned of the possibility of personal, artistic power from seeing Mae West acting in movies and realizing that Barbra Streisand directed films. Only later did she seek a film school education. After these experiences, she strives to immerse her daughter in feminist and countercultural possibility. Mothering, mentoring—both can be about granting another woman what you wanted but didn't have. "Recognizing how much the presence of a single, congenial female colleague in my field mattered . . . I have felt a moral imperative to act as a mentor to new female faculty and graduate students," writes Shirley Nelson Garner in her essay "Mentoring Lessons."[79] She also goes on to specify how being a mentor and a mother are different roles: mentors assume their position in professional settings; this relationship is often mutually chosen and developed rather than given; and it can just as easily be ended. "Our love is not nearly as unconditional as a mother's is supposed to be nor is our tenure with our students long enough to entitle us to call ourselves parents," echoes Barbara Christian.[80] And Garner also cautions in her lessons: "While many women have welcomed my support, the painful lesson I have to learn is that many do not. As a mentor I have had to stand back, let go, and even protect myself from disappointment or anger as I relate to another generation of female scholars" (9).

Like Garner, I have also learned through mentoring as well as through struggles with mentoring: deciding when and when not to mentor others; figuring out other systems of support when feminists mentored me poorly or not at all. However, for the most part the joy and power of my feminism have revolved around the relationships I have created with others—and the work we have accomplished together—through our interactive (and often contentious) learning, activism, or art making. Many of the other women in the study were also lucky enough to experience the intense passion, conflict, and excitement of feminist interaction. Videomaker Susan Mogul studied at the Feminist Art Program in Los Angeles in the 1970s:

> We were a tight group and very supportive of one another. There was a sense of excitement and exploration. We were finding something new. For the first time, a teacher, other than my chemistry teacher who liked me even though I wasn't good at chemistry, said "I can identify with you." Judy Chicago said, "I can understand you." When she was telling me that, she was sitting on one toilet in the basement of Cal Arts in the ladies' room and I was on another. Tears were streaming down my face. Now, that's not an exact quote, but there was something very powerful about an instructor ten years my senior saying that she identified with me.

Mogul describes a powerful feminist interaction where she is both acknowledged in her own right and is connected to another woman, one who is older than she is.

Getting to experience "something very powerful" is, finally, what this and other feminist media projects are all about. But understanding, and thus gaining power, is complicated, especially in a feminist context. In her analysis of the phenomenon of "postfeminism," Diane Elam recommends that feminism interrogate its internal struggles and acknowledge its handling of power: "Feminism needs to take account of the fact that it does not simply stand outside of institutional power structures at the same time that it tries to imagine new ways of standing together. The problem with actually doing this seems to revolve around a lack of specifically feminist models of power and tradition."[81]

Making use of Elam's terms for this discussion of feminist media history,

I find that the generational model is certainly an imbalanced institutional power structure, just as it is an old way of standing together. Yet my interviewees have convinced me that there *is* something specifically feminist about this mechanism for the sharing of power and tradition. When I ask interviewees what they are owed or what they owe, this is rarely returned with a straightforward (male) claim to entitlement or legacy. Rather, most of these women have an ambivalent relation to their own place in history and the succession of property and power this typically permits. As is true for many women in a patriarchy (even feminists), they are hesitant to make demands on others, are modest where they could be boastful, and claim the gaining of their own agency as reward enough.

For most of my interviewees, their hardest work was building for themselves that sense of personal entitlement that enables them to think of themselves as artists, and that allows them to imagine that they are not just permitted to but are capable of using a technological medium. Many men in a patriarchy assume these positions as givens. Women struggle to possess a sense of their own importance and the value of their work. Carol Leigh dreams, "I wish I had tried even harder. I wish I had never slept. I wish—and women don't do this enough—I had thought big." Feminist educators, mentors, and practicing artists in the media often do nothing more valuable than to represent to other women their unique version of female entitlement to agency. Pearl Bowser sees the power in her work as a film educator as her ability to enable possibility: "Working with young people in the '60s and '70s to expose them to those secret areas of filmmaking allowed them to imagine themselves as filmmakers because you talked about it with a facility or ease that allowed people to feel like, 'Yeah, that is something I can do.' Although you did not have a camera to hand to them, there was always a temptation and the idea that it was possible."

The radical possibility of a woman having artistic and political agency is powerful in and of itself. Horsfield insists:

> Every generation decides to take the risks they want. I'm not owed anything. The pleasure of it all has been a selfish pleasure. I have gotten a lot from what I've done. I've been able to live a life of almost perfect freedom. I've been able to make my own choices, to live how I wanted. . . . I've been very privileged, and I'm not unhappy with the way that things have turned out. It's up to everyone else to figure out whether I did something valuable to them.

Her "selfish pleasure" defines what I see as a distinctly *feminist legacy*—open and available to those who follow but never mandated, a legacy only for those who choose to seek. For instance, Yvonne Welbon couldn't find films, or even names, of other black lesbians at her graduate film program at the School of the Art Institute of Chicago, so she created and curated the film festivals that would allow her to find the work and peers she needed. Only then did she learn about, and eventually meet, fellow African American lesbian videomaker Cheryl Dunye. Now Welbon is committed to making images of diverse African American women more easily available to other black women and, particularly, to black girls.

Yet feminists in this study articulate critiques of power as often as they describe strategies for women to gain more of it. They describe a range of qualities or degrees of power: from what it feels like to work in the places and ways typical to men (filmmaking) to the particular strengths of working through marginal, and more liberated, media practices (video or digital). While experimental filmmaker Michelle Citron and media educator Margaret Caples wonder why so few female students take film production classes, why they resist this avenue to (male) power that is now more available to them, videomaker Vanalyne Green asks why women are abandoning video, one of the few places that has readily afforded women the power to enter into media: "I don't understand why more women don't stand up and fight for this more economical form—video—that has had really interesting moments in the community, instead of looking at art as social power. Why do women defect to film? Why not legitimate this thing that is so much more politically interesting?" Horsfield describes the particular kind of political power gained through video. It is little like film's traditional "social power" of fame or money: "I was on a panel with someone in Chicago a few months ago who said, 'I got five thousand hits on my Web site.' And I said, 'How does that translate into meaning for you?' We [the Video Data Bank] have smaller numbers, but we had a tremendous intimacy and exchange of ideas with the audience. We didn't do it for anything other than to participate in the ideas of our generation."

Intimacy over influence, participation over numbers—these, along with responsibility, are specifically feminist modes of power. In their interviews, both Wendy Quinn and digital artist Victoria Vesna caution that while gaining power is crucial, this must always also be accompanied by an increased awareness of how to use that power. Quinn is happy to demonstrate that she learned at least this one lesson from her traditional film school education:

> It is a hierarchical structure where the director is "God." That's why people want to be directors. It's the only place where you can be the "King" or "Queen," and no one disputes it. *You* are the one, and these people are there to serve you. That's sexy. That kind of autocratic power is wild. That made me uncomfortable, actually. There's a responsibility with that. When you are

the King or Queen, you have a responsibility to your subjects, to take care of them. . . . Power, yes, but with responsibility.

A feminist critique of hierarchical power relations organizes many of these interviewees' media-making practices, just as it structures this study. Documentary filmmaker Julia Reichert explains the distribution company she cofounded in the '70s:

> At New Day, decision making was democratic. There was no president or anything like that. We made decisions together. That comes out of the original women's movement insight that patriarchy is one of the roots of all evil. It is not just that men are in control, but also that hierarchies are a big problem—hierarchies based on money, education, being better looking, letting "experts" do it. Especially as women, we were against that. We had to hold the camera, take sound, run the projector, learn to do it ourselves. That nonhierarchical way of doing it yourself fired us up.

To best understand what is particular to the movement of power through feminist generation, the hierarchical, legislated, and linear structure of legacy must be rethought within an associative, responsible, interactive model: women collaborating or arguing with, educating or learning from, first themselves and then others. A history of feminist media must consider that in this work, the interpersonal as well as the personal are political. This shared (and sharing of) knowledge and power embolden women to struggle for change. Although we have inherited ready-made language to describe the movement of knowledge and power between people and across time, my interviewees actually use a range of words when they narrate their life's work, and they inflect this terminology with the specificity of feminist power. From these twenty-one histories arise sometimes contradictory metaphors to describe the actual experiences women have had within their own feminist media generation and across generations: mothering, smothering, mentoring; loss, absence, severing; matrix, web, conduit; sister, lover, friend. Even as we have trouble with generation, the desire to associate with those before and after us so as to contribute to change for many of us—rather than isolating oneself in hopes of individual power—is what motivates, and differentiates, feminist work in media, and its short but inspirational history.

[1] *Pearl Bowser*

Pearl Bowser works to ensure that African Americans, and others, can learn from the contributions that people of color have made within film. As a scholar, teacher, documentarian, and curator of early black cinema, Bowser attests to the critical relationship between knowledge of the past and the possibility for change in the present. By first locating, then analyzing, and finally passing on the work of African Americans who preceded her in film, Bowser helps us to better understand our own position. Her story is a powerful opening to this study. As a film historian who has worked for nearly thirty years and by whatever means available, Bowser models much of what this project aspires to. For instance, her search for predecessors often demands a reframing of the questions we use to understand ourselves, as well as our subject of study. To unearth the African American presence in film history, Bowser must research outside the traditional terrain of classic film study: she must ask questions other than those about the aesthetics and content of film.

Most studies of film history look to the work and output of directors. Yet very few African American women directed film (or were credited for the directorial work that they did do) before the '60s movements for social change (civil rights, women's, gay and lesbian rights, and the black arts movement). It was during this period of social and political upheaval that real possibilities for black women's expression in commercial cinema began to emerge. Eloice Gist, Lita Lawrence, and Zora Neale Hurston each directed films in the early part of the twentieth century;[1] to date, the list of African American women who have directed feature films is relatively small.[2] But Bowser has learned that black women play a more central part in film history as writers, editors, script supervisors, designers, actors, builders and managers of theaters,[3] and of course viewers. This was especially true for the subindustry of "race films," Bowser's primary area of research: black-produced, black-consumed pictures that flourished from the teens until the 1940s. Yet given the small presence of black women directors in even this subindustry, Bowser must adapt her questions to best understand these women's significance: not simply, did they have jobs, but how did they get them? What did they give up to have them? How did a black woman get to a career in film? And how does the difference between thinking of work in film as a job rather than as a career affect one's work?

A focus on gender alone is not the most productive way to frame her research; class and racial oppression are equally relevant. In their influential manifesto "A Black Feminist Statement" (1981), the Combahee River Collective defines work like Bowser's—which does not make distinctions that separate gender from race, class, or other systems of oppression—as black feminism: "We are actively committed to struggling against racial, sexual, heterosexual, and class oppression and see as our particular task the development of integrated analysis and practice based on the fact that the major systems of oppression are interlocking. The synthesis of these oppressions creates the conditions of our lives."[4] Bowser's research reveals the conditions of the lives of black people in the past, nourishing contemporary African Americans with their hidden legacy of entrepreneurship, creativity, and expression.

As one of a small group of African American women who have been working in film since the 1960s, Bowser's own career evidences much that is similar to what her research unearths. To work in film, she has been forced to be adaptive. She is the founder of African Diaspora Images, a collection of film, photographs, posters, oral histories, and memorabilia that document the history of independent African American filmmaking. She has collaborated as editor or contributor to a number of projects including a special issue, "The History of Black Film" with Jane Gaines for Black Film Review *and the catalog* Oscar Micheaux and His Circle *(with Charles Musser and Jane Gaines); and she is coauthor of* Writing Himself into History: Oscar Micheaux, His Silent Films and His Audiences *(with Louise Spence). She codirected the documentary* Midnight Ramble: Oscar Micheaux and the Story of Race Movies *(1994) and is currently working on a dramatic film on the pioneers of black film. Since 1971, she has organized seminars and workshops on African American and African film at colleges, museums, libraries, and in community settings. She has mentored and inspired countless African American scholars and filmmakers who have gone on to have their own careers within the media. And from 1978–87, she created and toured film packages from the African diaspora as director of the Theater Project at Third World Newsreel, this country's largest distributor of independent film and video by people of color.*

Bowser's central commitment to distribution and exhibition is shared by most political film organizations. Ada Gay Griffin, former executive director of Third World Newsreel, writes: "The moving-image medium, now one hundred years old, is currently the primary apparatus for the communication of information, ideas, and history in this country. The issue of consumption of media is becoming inconsequential next to that of ownership of production, and now distribution."⁵ Coming into film by way of the civil rights movement, Bowser remains committed to the politicized work of getting this lost history out to the black community.

As she does this work, she performs another equally important function: she lives her life as a committed, productive, political woman whose work matters to both herself and her community. A film scholar, filmmaker, and film educator, Bowser prefers to understand her work as activism. In this respect, she joins other feminist media scholars who practice the work of committed intellectualism: making sure that ideas and knowledge flow from higher education into the community and back again.

▶

I Stumbled into Film

Please describe your career in film.
I didn't have a professional background in film. Nothing in my academic studies prepared me for a career in film. I accidentally stumbled into it, so to speak, through friends who asked me to work on their projects. Documentary filmmaker Ricky Leacock suggested that I come work in his office.⁶ The two years I spent there doing his billing, ordering the equipment, sitting in on the editing sessions and production meetings opened up a whole new world to me. I was exposed not only to film projects from concept to fine cut, but also to a group of artists and craftsmen whose work would have a lasting impact on both the technology and aesthetics of documentary film. Shirley Clark, Willard Van Dyke, and Don Allen Pennebaker, prominent independent artists in media, were part of the group known simply as Filmmakers. Other artists such as the Maysles brothers and still photographer Morgan Smith would visit from time to time.

My film education began in the 1960s at Filmmakers where I was exposed to documentary films and had my first hands-on editing experience. At one point Ricky gave me a negative to cut. I had never cut a negative. The experience gave me the confidence to approach the technology of film without fear.

Years later at Third World Newsreel, I became involved in production and exhibitions. I began to think about my own film project when I was collecting and gathering materials in the field while showing old black films. I met and interviewed people who had not only been part of the audience in the '20s and '30s for race films, but who had worked in front of the camera as actors, performers, and extras. Many of the actors and performers who came forward with their stories gave me scrapbooks and mementos documenting an all-but-forgotten chapter in American film history. So I had to learn to do my own copy work and use a still camera—make slides and that sort of thing—in order to share the work that I was accumulating by illustrating my talks.

▶ ───

The Excitement in Seeing Race Movies

It became my passion to share the story that I was uncovering of race movies and the involvement of African Americans in cinema as early as 1909 and from so many different perspectives: actors and actresses, people who worked behind the camera, people in front of the camera, people who were distributing, and so on.

The films, and the stories of the making of these films, embraced so many different aspects of black culture: the obvious images of pride absent from mainstream cinema; the way the characters dressed and the roles they played; the physical surroundings and sense of place captured in familiar settings. I could identify with the stories. The characters on screen looked like my neighbors or my own family whose skin color varies from dark chocolate to creamy vanilla. More important, there was a level of awareness shared with the audience in a character's back story—the little details and seemingly insignificant twists and turns in the plot that triggered information about the African American experience I had always known but had never seen portrayed on the screen.

The first race movie I saw sitting in the screening room of the American Film Institute in Washington, D.C., in 1970, was *Scar of Shame* (1927). This forty-three-year-old silent melodrama, critical of intragroup social behavior, struck a familiar chord—it still seemed relevant. For once I could suspend the usual stereotyped images and react to the unhappy story of a black woman, Louise, who just would never be good enough for the man who married her. I watched the actress, Lucia Lynn Moses, move across the screen, her face and gestures not measured and rehearsed but natural. She was playing herself, her joy or sorrow coming from someplace inside her. Lucia was a dancer at the Cotton Club and Connie's Inn. She had traveled abroad in the musical *Black Bottom* and performed before the king and queen of England. Years later, interviewed in her home in the Williamsburg section of Brooklyn, Lucia dismissed the title of actress, saying, "We are all actors; we act every day of our lives."

Part of the research and the recorded interviews that I was doing took place in Harlem, where I was born. In some ways the lives of the people I met during this project (Lucia, her sister Ethel Moses, Alfred "Slick" Chester, Lorenzo Tucker, Clarence Jones, and others) were interconnected with my own. I discovered during my research that I was born in the same apartment house in a section known as Sugar Hill where a number of the performers still lived in the late 1970s, and at least one apartment in the building had been used as a set for productions made in the '30s. I felt a kind of intimacy with the subject of race movies because parts of my own life were connected with some of the information that I was uncovering.

As you show work from your archive, what do you think is the power of being able to see for the first time work that is so often invisible?
The excitement for me personally revisiting some of the films I may have seen as a child growing up in Harlem was the way in which blacks were represented on the screen and the knowledge that some of the films were made by blacks. For instance, Oscar Micheaux, one of the early pioneers of race films, attempted to tell stories relevant to black life. Seeing black people in very natural ways on the screen was, for lack of a better word, thrilling. I was a product of the Hollywood movie. Movies were a kind of babysitter as I was growing up. My mother would give my older brother money—I was the youngest of six children and the only girl—and we would go to the movies for three or four hours at a time, watching cartoons, Westerns, serials, and features, all on the same program, while a matron in a white uniform kept order in the children's section. My mother worked as a domestic and frequently had to work on Saturdays. This way she knew where we were. I felt embarrassed seeing blacks with bulging eyes, hair standing on end, or practically turning white when frightened.

I remember as an adult seeing early race movies like *Swing* (1938) and *Body and Soul* (1925), two Oscar Micheaux films, where the characters looked like my neighbors and people that I knew.[7] And they were acting out stories that I could identify with because there was some aspect of my own life there. When I say "my own life," I am sure that many other people who were seeing these films were having this experience as well. Audiences expressed their kinship with what was happening by talking back to the screen, laughing, and applauding. These films were more than stories about music, singing, and dancing, or comedy. They were about stories of people's lives; moments of triumph and defeat; mother-daughter relationships; the church; and romance, which was totally absent from the Hollywood films that I grew up with. It has been said that the first black kiss appeared in a 1929 Hollywood film, *Hallelujah* (King Vidor). A peck on the cheek demonstrated the extent of black intimacy that the censors would allow. But it was wonderful seeing glamorous, beautiful black people on the screen in films made by and for African American audiences. The characters in race films celebrated the achievement and progress of the race.

▶

Women in Race Films

Can you talk more specifically about women's involvement in race pictures and how that history is part of the larger history I am investigating?
I came to film in the '60s and began working in film in the '70s. There were few black women working as independent filmmakers. Thus, this earlier period of film is fascinating for me because there were many black women who were involved on various levels. If you think of the earliest period, back as early as 1916 (and probably earlier), women were basically writing scenarios and producing their own films. On occasion they were identified as editors. Although their names rarely appear in the credits, they are documented in the black press, magazines, personal diaries, and letters from that period. We know there were husband-and-wife teams like Jennie Louise Toussaint Welcome (James Van der Zee's sister) and her husband who were independent producer-directors of at least two films celebrating black participation in the war effort at home and on the battlefield.

I met and interviewed Haryette Miller Barton, one of the few black women who had worked in film behind the camera in the '40s. She worked with William Alexander, whose newsreels and feature films bridge the gap between the end of race movies and the beginning of independent black cinema in the '60s. Barton worked in various capacities. She was a production manager, casting agent, screenwriter, and she was also a director of some of the soundies the company produced. But because women were not admitted into the union, she was not able to function officially in that role. (Alexander always worked with union crews.) She functioned in that capacity on the set, but her name does not appear in the credits.

When Barton worked as a casting director for Alexander, she was aware of the prevailing attitudes toward skin color and leading roles for women. On one project the question arose about casting Ruby Dee. This was during the early part of Dee's career. They said she was "too dark" for the part. This was a black producer making this assessment. Ultimately, Barton won out, convincing the producer to hire Dee because she was the most talented actress around.

Barton's film career was very brief. She was with Alexander Productions for a little more than two years. Her story is interesting because it indicates the kinds of choices that women had to make in this period. She had a son to raise as a single parent. Both the hours and instability of a job in film would not allow her to give her son the type of life that she thought he should have. So she moved out of film, which is a decision that she regrets because there was a degree of excitement in that career. Of course, she hadn't thought of it as a career. It was a job. She hadn't thought of it as something that would ultimately become historically important.

There is another woman who was a feature filmmaker in Kansas. She has been promoted as the first black woman feature film producer, director, and writer. The film that she made, *Shadowed by the Devil*, was reviewed in *Half Century Magazine* in 1920. The magazine was founded by two women in 1916. But the review of the film manages to omit her name. So the only way to identify her name would be to backtrack in the newspapers of that period, perhaps finding an ad for the film somewhere.

There is another woman filmmaker, Eloice Gist, who emerges later in the '30s, whose work is just beginning to surface. This research is being done by Gloria Scott Gibson, who is also involved in the restoration of one of Gist's films. She is reassembling the film frame by frame, using modern technology. Gist and her husband made what could be described as morality plays that were based on the Bible. These enactments joined elements of reality and fiction, commenting on social behavior and the abuse of women. As far as we know, this was the direction of the films made by Gist. They were religious in content, using biblical stories and events acted out in the community, stories related to interfamily relationships, male-female relationships, greed, the seven deadly sins.

Women were also involved in the exhibition and distribution of films—because they owned theaters. It was an entrepreneurial opportunity open to women, especially during the establishment of all-black towns. And in the far West, in particular, there were women who built and ran those theaters: Mrs. Loula T. Williams in Tulsa, Oklahoma, appears in *Half Century Magazine* with a photograph of her theater in an advertisement. And Mrs. Zelia N. Breax financed and built the Alderidge Theatre in Oklahoma City. Women were involved in a variety of areas of the filmmaking process. This history is not only about what black audiences were exposed to, but it is also about the job choices that they had or the opportunities that emerged as the result of one entrepreneur becoming a kind of mentor, training others.

There's been a lot of debate, as I've been doing this research, about what is "feminist" and what is "feminist film/video"? I'm wondering if you characterize the work you just discussed as feminist. And the women you have talked about in early film history: would you characterize them as feminist?

It is difficult to look at the history of black filmmaking from the basis of gender. That aspect does emerge in a variety of different ways, but you can't go to the subject with the idea in mind that you are going to discover something specific about women. It happens because the broader history is about both men and women. But men do indeed—and I'm thinking about black film history—dominate the arena. There is a kind of dovetailing of the role of women in black cinema with women in the social history of that period. When I did learn of a woman working in race films, it was of particular interest to me as a woman. I was interested in other women's stories. But I couldn't focus primarily on gender, because there weren't enough women involved in a professional way in filmmaking. When their names did surface, it was very intriguing to discover their presence, as well as how they got there and what roles they played and how long they were involved.

▶━━

Political Activism through Film

Let's talk about another kind of history. Your work in the '60s in film is part of the history I'm trying to retrieve. Can you talk about yourself as a historical subject for awhile?

Working as a woman in the '60s in film, I was aware of the fact that there were few of us involved. I was not actually making films in the '60s; I was exhibiting film, which took me in and out of the community. I became a kind of educator. The research that I was doing, the films that I was collecting, and the oral histories were something that I shared with students on campuses across the country. My initial thrust outside of the community was to share that information with students at black colleges.

So I became a sort of lecturer/educator and workshop leader; I even developed a course in black and Third World cinema at Rutgers. I talked to students who were very interested in cinema and in black history who then graduated and moved on to other universities for advanced degrees and to teach. I have been at it so long that former students, as professors, now invite me to speak to their classes at different colleges around the country. I think of the relationship between myself, students, and other teachers as the political activism part of my career. Thinking of my own personal life, this was how I was involved in the civil rights movement . . . through film. I took material anywhere I could get an audience—whether it was a community center, a library, or a classroom.

One story. I did some work in a halfway house in New York with black teenagers. I set up a film discussion group one day a week. I would take my films and show them just to provide some sort of social activity for the young people. It became a platform, to talk not just about black history, but about life choices. What emerged in these workshops was an interest from some of the girls in my job. At the time I didn't think of what I was doing as a career. I was not a filmmaker or a distributor. I did not think of myself as an educator. I was an activist and I was sharing material in whatever forum was open to me. This young woman asked how she could get to do what it was that I do, and that question stayed with me for a long time. I didn't have a quick answer. I simply wanted to share the history — a part of our culture that was not immediately visible. But I realized that when you do something in a public space, in a community where you're involved in attempting to share the history, you become something — not a role model, because I do not think of myself as a role model — but you become a key or kernel from which people can be challenged, from which they can build other things, or from which they can see possibilities.

I always thought of film before I got involved, before I was hired by Ricky, as something very distant, and it was not something that I could pursue because it was outside the realm of my experience. As a young person growing up, I had not encountered people who were more than just part of the audience. Discussions about black film history during the civil rights movement encouraged audiences to imagine themselves as filmmakers — chroniclers of the history taking place all around them. The realization that others, less equipped than the present generation, had done it, reawakened the notion to record events. Still cameras and tape recorders were everywhere, and the Bolex 16mm equipment wasn't far behind. While television dominated the scene, a film package could be rented from small independent organizations like Third World Newsreel at a reasonable rate.

I have the feeling that many people who were part of that turbulent era and who were making films were driven by the need to document their struggle and to tell their own stories. The camera was simply a tool, perhaps even a weapon, in the struggle.

► ───────────────────────────────────────

Translating the History to Contemporary Audiences

Can you talk about the contemporary film world? What happened after the '60s that allows us to see the relative explosion of African American film that we now see?

Hollywood entertained the black spectator with a rash of urban, action-driven, crime, and sex films in ostentatious settings (and with great sound tracks!). Black independent filmmaking opted for a more community-based cinema. Charles Burnett's classic urban story *Killer of Sheep* and Julie Dash's *Daughters of the Dust*[8] are almost bookend examples of a community-based cinema, bringing together historical and cultural details validating black family and community. These are the kinds of stories that were told and retold sitting around the kitchen table or in small social gatherings. They are part of a shared reality rarely seen in mainstream or commercial films. To encounter these narratives in film is exciting, and this accounts for the sustainability of these films.

In the film *Tongues Untied* (1989) filmmaker Marlon Riggs presented a personal narrative exposing the unspoken taboo surrounding homosexuality within the African American community.[9] In relating his own story to the sexual politics within the community, he opened up a dialogue that historically had been closeted and bolted. The impact of the film, laced with a range of human emotions and a shared history, reverberated throughout the black community and sent echoes through the halls of Congress. Marlon's well-crafted, intense filmmaking is more than a piece of polemic; his brilliant use of culturally specific art forms (poetry and dance included) is provocative and engaging. The film continues to be an important document that reaches out, not only to the black community at large, but beyond.

Can you think of contemporary African American women directors who accomplish that kind of work?
Cathy Collins comes to mind immediately in the kinds of stories she dramatized in *Losing Ground* (1982). I also think of Ayoka Chenzira and *Hairpiece: A Film for Nappy Headed People* (1982), which deals with this aspect of identity within the culture with humor to diffuse a very sensitive issue and force us to look at how we see ourselves, using hair as a metaphor. I think of women filmmakers like Maya Angelou in her *Sister, Sister, Sister* (1980) and *Georgia, Georgia* (1972); they were impactful films because they were very different from the Hollywood films that we were exposed to. Zeinabu irene Davis comes to mind, thinking of young women going through puberty and romantic relationships in *A Powerful Thang* (1991). In films like these, it is not only the images but the stories being told from a certain perspective that stay in your consciousness. Alile Sharon Larkin's *A Different Image* (1982) compares commercial images on billboards and images in cinema and how young black women perceive themselves not only in relation to society but in interpersonal relationships.[10]

▶
Getting It Out There

What is characteristic of most of this filmmaking (as is true for the earlier filmmaking) is that it does not get to as large an audience as it needs to. Distribution becomes once again that imponderable; that mountain that yet again needs to be overcome. One tries to control this by self-distribution, by creating small companies that work within limits but do not give us the potential for reaching the maximum audience. That remains a challenge for filmmakers and people that work on the periphery of film, like myself and others, who attempt to create distribution models in different ways, by touring packages of films, by programming films at different types of venues, and creating an audience.

There are some films that are beginning to be picked up by commercial distributors. *Daughters of the Dust* is handled by a commercial distributor [Kino International]. But again, it is not enough for a film to sit in a catalogue; it still has to find its audience. There is a dynamic that is missing from a film that gets picked up and put in a catalogue and then nothing else is done. Something else needs to happen in between to make sure that an audience gets to see and use the work. That is a challenge to those of us working in film. The other aspect of filmmaking, getting a work to an audience, is as important as the product itself. Because that is who we want to talk to, because that is who we want to share the work with. It is not about making money—it is about finding that audience and having the audience experience the story that is told by the artist.

Where do you see yourself in the history of feminist film and video?
I see myself as someone who has persisted in an area that was not always welcome outside my community. I have maintained a foothold in the field by working in film in whatever capacity I could. Whether it was as a programmer, as a consultant, as a producer, as a distributor, as a historian. I did all those things that were connected in some way, but they did not always provide job opportunities for me as a woman. But I persisted. I was motivated by wanting to share the history—not particularly as a woman per se, although that was important.

I see myself as an activist using film to enlighten and inspire, as I was enlightened. I work to encourage other blacks to become involved in making film, telling stories, and documenting aspects of our culture. At this stage of my life I am excited about more and more people, and more and more women, becoming involved in cinema because there are still so many more stories to be told, and histories to be learned. There is so much of our social and political lives that needs to find expression through this very powerful medium. We have used it in the past. It was a part of the early beginnings of cinema in the 1900s to use film to document aspects of our culture, and that is a continuum.

The power of this tool, film, is so important. It is something that I cannot *not* talk about at every opportunity in order to stress the importance of controlling it. Controlling it means that we have to produce our own films, tell our own stories on film, and get them to the maximum audience, not only to demonstrate the possibilities but to educate. I think of controlling cinema in these ways as activism, and it is that aspect of cinema that I find the most engaging.

◆————————————————————————————

PEARL BOWSER

Founder

1969 to present	African Diaspora Images (programming, distribution, and audience development)

Festival Director

1971–85	Harlem Cultural Council
1978–87	Third World Newsreel
1989, 1990	Celebration of Black Cinema V

Guest Curator

1980	Black American Film Festival, Paris
1985, 1987, 1989	Pan African Film Festival, Burkina Faso
1986	"Third World Women and Women of Color," Dorothy Arzner International Film Festival, Boston
1990, 1991	"From Harlem to Hollywood," American Museum of the Moving Image
1995	Festival International de Arte Negra, Brazil

Films and Publications

1993	"The History of African American Film," *Black Film Review* (with Jane Gaines)
1994	*Midnight Ramble: Oscar Micheaux and the Story of Race Movies*
2000	*Writing Himself into History: Oscar Micheaux, His Silent Films and His Audience* (with Louise Spence), Rutgers University Press
Forthcoming	*Oscar Micheaux and His Circle* (with Jane Gaines and Charles Musser), Indiana University Press

[2]   Carolee Schneemann

Carolee Schneemann has been making transgressive art for more than thirty years. She uses her own body as her primary medium in her vast oeuvre of performance, photography, painting, film, and video. Ancient and contemporary Goddess-based feminist theory coupled with her intuition and dreams provide the moorings from which she hangs on ropes, pulls strands of text from her vagina, makes love, kisses her cat, and then records these outrageous acts as feminist art. In a brief written biographical statement, Schneemann describes her work as "characterized by research into archaic visual traditions, pleasures wrested from suppressive taboos, the body of the artist in dynamic relationship with the social body. [My] work . . . has transformed the very definition of art especially with regard to discourses concerning the body, sexuality, and gender."[1]

Whatever the decade in which it was originally produced—from the '60s to the '90s—Schneemann's art continues to break taboos because it is created from her insistence on being an autonomous person who is fully sexual, entirely an artist, and defiantly a woman. Even currently, depictions of a self-defined, transformative, female sexuality, especially those made by and about the woman so empowered, are virtually unheard of—and are beyond outrageous. If her work is still difficult for audiences, imagine when it was first viewed in the '60s and '70s, when there was no artistic or social context in which to place such work. B. Ruby Rich discusses the cultural scene in the early '70s when she first saw Schneemann's film Fuses *(1964–67):*

> Is there any way to convey the sense of risk and courage that accompanied those early screenings, back when scarcely any films by women had been seen, received, or apprehended as such? . . . The only models for open female sexuality in the early seventies were the boyfuck orgies of hippie culture, the Living

Theater gangbang model, [and] the porn movies to which all cool girls had to accompany their boyfriends.[2]

At that time, and for that matter currently, Schneemann makes this raucous work, and takes up this unseemly position, at great cost. For most of her career practically unfunded, Schneemann has only recently had her first major retrospective at an American museum: "Carolee Schneemann: Up to and Including Her Limits," at the New Museum of American Art (1996). Sadly, her enormously prolific, highly regarded, and almost fully unfunded career represents the most common pattern for women in the arts.

The making of feminist art and a feminist life has always been treacherous because there are so few models, so little support, and so many sacrifices. Schneemann and her American contemporaries, women who managed to make art in the early '60s and before, were what Schneemann calls "women on the edge." They were trying to make their mark as female artists in their own right, even as they were situated on the margins of the male avant-garde; they were trying to live outside the crushing confines of bourgeois-nuclear-family-white-picket-fence-suburban-monogamy even as they remained entrenched in a patriarchy. In her book on women, power, and politics in the New York avant-garde cinema, Points of Resistance, *Lauren Rabinovitz describes the contradictions experienced by the generation of women filmmakers who preceded Scheemann in the pre- and proto-feminist '50s and '60s. Filmmakers like her subjects Maya Deren, Shirley Clarke, and Joyce Weiland "were the exceptional women who balked enough at conventions that they achieved a measure of success in artistic areas usually considered 'masculine.' . . . But they did so without entirely understanding how the cultural institutions, including the family, constructed and organized women's social subordination."[3]*

It would take the political activism of the 1970s to establish for these and other women an organized women's movement that espoused a systematic critique of sexism and patriarchy. Only then, according to Schneemann, was there the possibility for community among women, institutional support for women, and the beginnings of a shared vocabulary that could explain some of the contradictions that constrained women artists. In her interview, Schneemann discusses living through the unsettling change from this protofeminist art world of the '60s to the fully mobilized scene of the organized women's movement only ten years later. This shift from marginalization to communal exuberance, so fundamental to Schneemann's career, is hard for me to comprehend. I can only know this as her memory, and this gap in perception marks a real obstacle between us: separating our ex-

periences as feminist artists and potentially unsettling the history that con-
nects us and of which I attempt to write.

And yet what motivates my feminist history project is the desire to
understand differences while also pursuing the certain links between
women. I set out to interview Schneemann because I had had two, highly
memorable introductions to her. First, I had seen her most infamous film,
Fuses, *when I taught a course on feminist film at Bryn Mawr College in*
1995. The film had been made thirty years previously, and yet the class was
held in the grips of its entirely relevant representation of female sexuality,
female heterosexuality, female desire, female orgasm, female creativity.
What was particularly overwhelming for my students and myself was how
this film seemed to foretell our "current" fascination with the sexualized
experiences of the female body. The feminist work that we had been more
commonly exposed to (largely from the '80s) was different: dry, intellectu-
alized, abstracted representations and interpretations of both feminist sex
and bodies. Schneemann's film was so fresh, so new, so bold that it seemed
hard to believe it was so "old."

As I watched and taught Fuses *and other protofeminist films as re-*
search for this project, I began to recognize that women like Schneemann
did not foretell, *they* told, *and that telling had been nearly erased and for-*
gotten. Why don't we get to hear—often enough, or loud enough, or hon-
estly enough—the lives and words and stories of the women we dream of
becoming? It's not as if Schneemann hadn't been getting her work out there.
She has made twenty or more experimental, political, usually erotic films
and videos (these are alongside her work in installation, performance, paint-
ing, and writing). Plumb Line *(1968–71) marks the filmic dissolution of a*
relationship through freeze-frames and mirror printing. Kitch's Last Meal
(1973–78) is Schneemann's diary of her daily life shared with her lover and
also her cat, Kitch. In the '80s, Schneemann collaborated with video artist
Victoria Vesna (interviewed here as well) on another piece about bestiality,
Vesper's Stampede to My Holy Mouth. *Many of Schneemann's films are*
artistic documents of her performance and kinetic, interactive sculptures
such as Interior Scroll *(1975), which displays Schneemann's "body as a*
source of knowledge" as she reads her semiotic text extracted from within,
and Known/Unknown-Plague Column *(1996), a video/installation that*
explores cancer treatment as a metaphor.

Schneemann also writes and is written about.[4] My second exposure to
her, before I had the opportunity to interview her on video, was through her
inclusion in the book Angry Women, *a gift to me from a feminist boyfriend*
committed to subcultural excess.[5] Images of her body splattered with mud

and writhing among a sea of similarly slimy bodies, or kissing cats, or pulling snakes (or so it seemed) from her vagina were etched into my memory. And then there she was in the flesh! My very first interview for my documentary, a major feminist influence—to be shot with a broken camera provided by a much-needed grant from Film/Video Arts—and she was wearing horns. The bumpy, irregular video image of Schneemann now seen in my documentary permanently marks my own project's place in the longer legacy of feminist art: underfunded, non–profit-reliant, but nevertheless realized.

When I met her, Schneemann spoke at length about one of her ongoing projects, work that had eerie similarities to my own. She explained that she had spent a great deal of her career searching, mostly unsuccessfully, for female teachers and role models, "historical precedence"—those women who could help her locate a "female genital and pronoun"—before having to invent a life, language, and genital on her own: "I was negotiating a universe that denied me authority as an authenticating voice and denied me the integrity of my own physicality. This declivity—no pronoun, no genital—became the tripod on which my own vision would be balanced." Only from this more stable feminist place could she later go on to mentor other female artists (like Vesna). Yet besides her relationship with Maya Deren,[6] Schneemann sees her early career as one largely aided and abetted by the male artists who made up her world. In this respect, Schneemann, a proud and vocal lover of men, touches on another important question for this study: what is the role of men in feminist film history, men who were women's lovers, teachers, fathers, artistic and political influences, and sometimes women's providers or muses?[7] Although Schneemann's work has been exhibited as part of the traditions of dada, neodada, Beat culture, performance art, video art, the Theater of Cruelty, happenings, and Fluxus, her career has not matched the fiscal and other artworld successes of the mostly male artists with whom her work is typically shown.

Thus, beyond her search for historical precedence, another of her legacies is that of struggle, underrecognition, anger, and frustration initiated by the very sexism that her career attempts to dismantle. But perhaps some of the questions that Schneemann and I raise about the loss of feminist legacy have also begun to be answered here and in the following interview: records of living artists are shot with broken cameras; films rot in garages; women's artistic accomplishments are lost in histories that reframe them within the traditions of men; women become too discouraged due to lack of money and support and drop out, their stories forgotten. Most women are not as resilient as Carolee Schneemann.

An Obsession with Space, Images, Time, and Language

Please narrate your own personal history as one demonstrative history within the larger history of feminist film and video. I'm particularly interested in what allowed you to make your work, what was or wasn't there for you, how you could have and still can have a career.

I'm glad you said the word *career* because I've never considered that I had a career. I don't know what a career is. I imagine it's something one chooses to do and advance in certain ways, going through certain disciplines.

I was born a painter. There was never any choice for me. It's never been a "career," something that is so considered or planned. My work has rarely been supported except in the most minuscule of ways. So I dog it out by scrounging around on the edges of my culture. There are things I have to see, problems I have to consider. I'll work with whatever I can get my hands on: if it means typing on an old typewriter or doing black-and-white Xerox obsessively for months. What helped me was my attachment to and obsession with making images. From the time I was four years old, I couldn't survive if I wasn't examining what line could encapsulate on a page. My earliest drawings as a child were sequential, filmic. Any one idea would take about nineteen pages on a little tablet because I had this obsession with space containing time.

I'd also like to discuss my obsession with language because women have really forgotten that in the past twenty years we have repositioned ourselves as central to language. But when I was in the university, all the books said: "Man and *his* image," "The artist and *his* model." And the university's messages would be: "Each student will clean out *his* locker or have a penalty," "No student will park *his* car in front of the art building." That wasn't me! So I figured I would not clean out my locker, and I would park my car, if I had one, in front of the art building. I was fighting all the time. The men always said, "But it means you, too!" I said, "I don't want to be 'too'! Why am I the caboose? Why am I only included by your grace?"

Double Knowledge

Tell me more about art school. How did you get there?

I came from a working-class, rural, German, Lutheran, Mennonite, Amish, and Nazi town in Pennsylvania. It was one of the important farming villages for the German American Bund. So I had no idea what it was to be an artist.

Once I had a glimpse, it was intoxicating. And then they couldn't stop me—which they would subsequently try to do along the way.

But I was lucky. I kept finding people who, unexpectedly, would see that there was something special. For instance, at some point I discovered—probably when I was about eleven—a strange set of works by someone I thought might be female, Cez-Annie. That person became my secret mascot because Annie was a girl's name. I would subsequently grow up and find out that this great misogynist had been influencing my work—Cezanne! But Cez-Annie gave me the secret clue that *maybe* there was an important woman painter, and that is why the figures were so strange looking. I didn't ask anyone—I was afraid what they would tell me.

What I call "double knowledge" had started: the double knowledge of being a criminal instigator in your own culture, burrowing within to find out what had been denied and hidden. I wondered, "Had there ever been other women artists? If so, where were they? And why was I both encouraged and discouraged?" My father thought that girls didn't go to college. His compromise was to send me to a two-year, typing, finishing school, and I wouldn't go. I knew I couldn't do that.

And then, unexpectedly, a lanky man appeared in the infirmary of my high school from Bard College and offered me a full scholarship—tuition, room, board, everything! I had applied to Bard and Black Mountain and other strange places. My father refused to fill out a financial statement. Now, he's not a criminal in all of this. He's a very inspiring person. But he was in his own set of cultural conventions. He couldn't imagine what type of life I was drifting away to. And with the best will in the world he wanted to shape my life—not in an overtly aggressive way; he also gave me the courage to jump off the edge. My mother's position was to uphold the morality of the patriarchy because she knew of no other possibility.

So when did I find art? Well, certainly at Bard. One of the first paintings I did there was an open leg self-portrait with my knees up, holding a paintbrush: painting with exposed vulva. It was the first painting of mine that was stolen. I sure would like to see it again. It was very red. It was very angry. I was only seventeen years old. I'm sure it also was very mannered with too much encaustic on it. But I knew that I had to put inexplicable impression in view.

A lot of splendid things happened at Bard, but the contradictions were already in place. What I learned at Bard and what would obsess me by the time I had a fellowship at the University of Illinois in painting—always in painting—was that there was no feminine pronoun and no feminine genital. I was negotiating a universe that denied me authority as an authenticating voice and denied me the integrity of my own physicality. This declivity—no pronoun, no genital—became the tripod on which my own vision would be balanced.

▶ ───

Missing Precedence

You said you were looking for women artists as a young child. Do you have a memory of when you began that kind of historical research?
Yes, absolutely, it's so vivid. I was able to go to Putney School in Vermont for one year in 1959. There was a book bus that would come around. Each month we could look inside the back of this station wagon and pick books! I chose two. One had a beautiful, painterly, flowered cover, and it had a strange name, a woman's name, which had double letters like my name—Virginia Woolf—with two o's. The book was called *The Waves*. I took that book to the barn and I recognized then—I was fourteen—that this was how I had to work, that it was possible. I entered this surge of simultaneities. It was musical. It was structured. It was associative. It was metaphoric. It was colored and emotionally generative. And so *The Waves* became a talisman for me.

Also in 1959, I found Simone de Beauvoir. I felt all alone while my sense of gender politics was revealed by *The Second Sex*. Later I found out that there were thousands of other women *all* alone with de Beauvoir: de Beauvoir just lays it right open. It's crystal clear. Now I understand everything! From de Beauvoir, I can go to [Antonin] Artaud for other suppressed meanings of the body and its larger extensivity. At the same time, my lover, the composer James Tenney, and I were reading Freud and Wilhelm Reich. Reich, with de Beauvoir and Artaud, gives me permission to begin to introduce the body into a literal space.

But there weren't any other women. I want to make that absolutely crystal clear. The young women were in a kind of fog. I began to work with the Judson Dance Theater in 1961.[8] This was even before there is a Judson Dance Theater, but there's this coming together of young dancers, almost all women: Yvonne Rainer, Deborah Hay, Trisha Brown, Elaine Summers, Lucinda Childs, Ruth Emerson, Judith Dunn. . . . We knew that no one was going to take over the meaning of the body and new forms of motion except us. It was protofeminist. We were getting a lot of power from each other. We were very conscious of the meanings that women were going to discover and construct together, or in dissension together, because we soon began to have intense formal falling-outs.

Let's talk about the '60s and the women's movement.

Well, there was no women's movement in the '60s, of course. In the '60s we began to be consumed with women being able to work together as artists, but we had no sense yet of it as a movement. We were all like wild cats. At the same time, women at Judson and at Charlotte Moorman's avant-garde festival were beginning to put things together in cultural ways that hadn't existed to our knowledge before.

Meanwhile, the political configuration becomes consuming and really intense. Feminism is building from civil rights, from the Weather People, from the tremendous upheavals for justice against the destruction of Vietnam. There are only two positions in the '60s, and that begins to tear everything apart. Politics become ferocious. The country is polarized by the Vietnam War. It's enough to have a certain hairstyle to have rocks thrown at you, even on Sixth Avenue. People are running off to communes, to Canada evading the draft, to Europe, relationships split, people kill themselves.

I go through a breakdown and leave. Everything cracks apart about 1968 or 1969. With that dispersal comes a sense of energy, of being absolutely sure one could make a better culture—a deeper sense of communality, a deeper sense of sensitivity to the issues of community. These issues are taken out of the centralized places and into the country: farming, self-sufficiency, in smaller cities and villages. I'm in London, in a kind of exile for four years. When I come back in 1976, feminist theory is in place. It's clarified itself. There's A.I.R. Gallery in New York City and Women's Space in L.A.: women-run, women-directed galleries. Soon, anthropology, archaeology, science, religion, law, medicine—intellectual territories—are penetrated with feminist analysis and feminist insight.

My early dream to tear it all apart and put it back together again is being taken up by a vast movement; it's thrilling. It's also full of dissension and contradiction and pain. I work on the *Heresies* magazine issue on the Goddess in which we also discovered that if there were knives and labryses, half of us would have killed the other half. Feminism is not always the idealized communication that we expect! There are painful dissensions and disillusionments. Also in the '70s, when I show *Plumb Line* at a film festival that's mostly for woman-identified women, the lesbian women in the audience see the man's image and they give it about five seconds. Then they began howling, "We don't need him!" It was the only time I had to leave a showing of mine—not because of the police or the men going crazy—but because of women going nuts. I had to crawl out of the showing on my hands and knees. I crawled down the aisle, trembling, and out into the hall, into the elevator, and left. By the '90s, I find myself having to defend heterosexuality as an ecstatic, sacred possibility.

Why is finding female role models and colleagues so important to you? Why, even now, in 1995, do we need both female contemporaries and memories of those women who came before us?

It's what I call "missing precedence," because if I don't have a realm of precedence, then I'm anomalous and my experience is constantly marginalized as being exceptional in that there is no tradition, there's no history, there's no language. But there *is* history, tradition, and language.

It's also part of being able to exist with increased paradox and complexity. Because we live within a culture that's constantly retreating from the variousness of human experiences and trying to recodify and police the variousness of what people actually can know and experience. It's absolutely essential that we don't lose the struggle of this history. The horrible thing is—especially for people of my generation—that it fucking never ends! You have to do it again and again. We already did that work. But, yes, again and again. And with as much risk, and certainly in 1995, without any kind of political focus or organization. It's a terrifying abyss.

▶

Speed My Frame

When did film enter this for you?

Painting was too slow. At some point I was mounting paintings on wheels and spinning them. I needed the implicit energy of abstract expressionism to become more materialized, more dimensional. So in graduate school I was cutting through and slashing my paintings in great misery. It was an existential grief worked out on a beloved corpse.

All my work is about trying to find other ways to paint. Film became another way to paint in time—to speed my frames simultaneously. I was also dealing with the paradoxical fixity of photographs that carry image or energy or referent from a past moment. The photograph was the way in which I could be most subversive. That's where I could begin to tear up the image of a woman's body from *Playboy*. That's where I could situate a patriarchal scientist—Sir Henry Francis Taylor, shot by Julia Margaret Cameron, Virginia Woolf's great-aunt—embedded in my own universe in a set of associative painted objects. So film has to do with real time, and it's an incredible melancholy that I'm grasping. I want to encapsulate time, and it's always fleeing. And even when I can fix it, it's part of this momentive worry.

My beloved companion during these years was James Tenney, the composer and conductor, and we were sharing information. In graduate school he was reading [Erwin] Schrödinger and material about entropy,

I was reading Proust, and we were reading everything to each other. So we were building an interconnective way to work with the implications of philosophy, space, time, technologies, and the poetry of language and image. Stan Brakhage is his early friend from high school, and he's one of the first friends of Tenney that I met.[9] They both went to South Central High School in Denver, and Brakhage was ahead of Tenney a couple of years. Brakhage introduced film and film process to us. I introduced the issues of painting and real time to Brakhage, who was making surrealistic drama-narrative films when we met. Tenney brought in all the information on sound and space. The three of us divided up the art of the future and how it had to be transformed and penetrated!

So I came to film through Brakhage, and through him I met Maya Deren. That was a horrible lesson. I saw a beautiful, fierce woman praised for important work who was also trying to raise money to pay lab bills and having all these guys live off her! She was not just an inspirational artist— she was simultaneously a mother figure. The young men would go to her and expect her to inspire them, confirm their work, show them what she was doing and thinking, and cook! I decided that whatever this is about, I was not going to cook. I ended up cooking, of course, but heterosexuals usually have to cook—that's part of the deal for your pleasure.

Some lesbians have to cook, too.
[Laughter.] I think so! Someone has to cook! There's a Kate Millett story from the farm.[10] Kate has established her ideal feminist arts farm community. We're good friends, and I go over there for a harvest festival in the fall. Some years it's completely stressful to organize a meal for seventy women, or even twenty women. But other years, it's completely harmonious and smooth. Those are the years when Kate finds the woman whom they call "Mother" who agrees just to be the cook with associates who will agree just to clean up. So Mother takes the role. There's no conflict. There's no sharing. That's what she does: she feeds us.

▶ _____

Fuses

Fuses, my first film, develops after my first performative works. My sense of time is now pushing the frames of painting through the exigencies and energies of my body into a lived circumstance that is going to tear apart the projected superimpositions of male mythologies that have been deforming everything I know. And the crazy thing about *Fuses* is that the men lend me their cameras. The underlying film structure is already montaged because all the cameras for *Fuses* are borrowed (from Stan Brakhage, Stan VanderBeek, Robert Breer, Ken Jacobs, and Elaine Summers).[11] First, Brakhage gives me a lesson in how to hold the Bolex. Now the 1964 Bolex has a thirty-second windup motor with a parallax viewfinder! So what you're seeing through the camera lens is only kind of what you're seeing. You have to make all these subtle adjustments.

The way they taught me to operate the camera was the way men teach you, so that you know you are doomed, almost as if you were going to menstruate on it. Oh, they were so reluctant to lend me their cameras. And then it took a special courage because every time they explained it to me, I went into my blanking-out mode, like it was second grade and I was learning multiplication. I had to take those borrowed Bolexes and put them so close to my body and do a mystical thing with them that would somehow transcend everything I had been taught. The first 100 feet that I ever shot, with Brakhage's borrowed Bolex, was impeccable. It's an early sequence in *Fuses,* of the green leaves in the window, bright light behind, cat in front, perfect focus and exposure. Once I got that 100 feet back, I knew that I didn't have to worry anymore. I was going to be able to do what I felt like with it.

▶ ──

The Missing $400

When did you take control over the technology by owning it yourself?
After thirty years I still don't have anything. I work with Super 8. I have a little box, a Bell & Howell. At some point, I believe it was in 1976, I lectured about how I didn't have any equipment. And a man in the audience says, "I was really impressed by your films. Meet me at my hotel. I'd like to give you a camera that I don't use anymore." I was suspicious of the man in the hotel, but I'd do anything. I had a vision of a Beaulieu. I knew that this is going to be the camera I really deserved. I go to the man's hotel. He's very nice. He comes down to the lobby, and he's carrying something that looks like a cigar box. No Beaulieu could be in there unless it was in pieces. And he hands me this pitiful little thing, it's a Super 8 camera. It's got a hole here and a hole there. And that's about it—you push a button. I say, "Thank you very much" and go away with it. And that's how *Kitch's Last Meal,* my three-year, twenty-hour diary film is made—it begins with this little box. And I still reach for it, that Bell & Howell, it's alive and responsive.

I am trying to get a computer. I still work with a typewriter. My friends are always saying, "You *have* to get a fax. You *have* to do this. You *have* to do that." But I do it out of bare bones because the culture does not support my work. I don't even have a gallery now. So it's a case of "the Missing $400."

It's all a struggle with time or acquiescence; most of my important painting constructions are in a shed with mice living in them. If you want to dissolve epoxy resin, mice urine works like a charm. But everything is on video now.

Just be careful because video itself has a shelf life. In preparation for this documentary, I've been watching early '70s video. I was at the Long Beach Museum of Art Video Annex, and a lot of the videotapes in their archive have deteriorated. You can't watch them now. As my generation is getting excited about reclaiming this history, the history itself is dissolving. So, then, I have to ask: Were these made as permanent documents in the first place, since they were shot on video?

We hoped that they would at least have the permanence of a human life. We didn't have information about how the material itself would disintegrate. And we had the illusion that all these early technologies would be communal and that we would have constant access to shared cameras and editing decks. Of course, it's been a huge disillusionment for all of us that we don't all have access.

In order to preserve any one artist's body of material, you would need a little staff that would—every year—retransfer all these videotapes. And the films get mold. Every time I open a can of work from the '60s or '70s, there are potential unpleasant surprises. Now the NEA has just cut all the funds for preservation, completely cut.

▶—————————————————————

Mortal Coils

Could you talk about your more recent work?

The most recent work is an installation on death called *Mortal Coils*. In 1993 and 1994, first thirteen and then fifteen close friends died. They died of various things, unknown causes. It wasn't just AIDS or heart attack. I wanted to commemorate the friends and to stay with their images. It was very confusing work. I finally had a dream instruction. And in the dream I ask my dear friends for guidance. I didn't want to advance my position in the art world by absorbing their loss, but I had to stay with them. It was a lot of asking them what to do and waking every morning and going first to their photographs. I'd have them out on the table, and I was Xeroxing, going into them further, enlarging, examining details. Then I had a dream that showed me ¾" manila rope suspended from the ceiling with a coil on the bottom and the rope was moving in the dream, very, very slowly like a snake. And the dream said, "6 rpm." I called my friend Jim, we rigged up a length of ¾" manila rope, and a 6 rpm motor. And it was just beautiful when the rope turned! That was the first key to the energy of this piece.

And that's the installation that I just did two months ago in Vienna in a museum space with 30-foot-high ceilings. It was one of the rare times when I could build what I had envisioned: images 25 feet high, both dissolving and moving through mirrored systems so that they're projected, they're in dissolution, and they're moving. The walls are covered with huge blown-up in memoriam statements—which is how our culture is superstitious, printed in the *New York Times,* under the obits, where the living talk to their dead.

How was it funded?
The Kunstraum in Vienna brought me there. I've only sold two works in my life in the United States, only two. I've only had one commission, and that was for the San Francisco Museum of Modern Art. And that is it. I've never shown in a Whitney Biennial or Documenta or . . .

Would you like to?
Oh, yes. Yes. The work needs it; it's not even me. I now have this huge trust of all this material, and maybe it doesn't mean anything. That's why my position seems very schizophrenic. I'm always surprised if anyone's interested in the work at all; the discrepancies have been so huge.

▶ ━━━

You Owe Me the Vulva

I would like you to talk about the legacy of your work. I want to know what we owe you.
You owe me the vulva. You owe me the concept of vulvic space. You owe me bestiality. You owe me the love of the presence of the cat as a powerful companion and energy. You owe me heterosexual pleasure and the depiction of that pleasure. And you owe me thirty years of lost work that's never been seen. That's what you all owe me. I guess what I'm also owed is a living, an income. I'm owed the chance to produce the work that I've envisioned that I've never been able to do. I'm owed the chance to preserve the works that already exist. And I'm glad you've asked. Nobody has ever asked me. And you can see, I'm fuming underneath.

Well, it's a history of anger and frustration. It's also a history of loss.
Tremendous loss. Personal loss. Partnership loss: the underlying secret conflict in my lovers between the pleasure and excitement and equity of being

with an artist and their final decision always to become a father and have a traditional marriage. That's a big layer of loss. Of course, we lose everything sooner or later, but one would prefer later.

And anger . . .
Well, anger always has to go with humor and pleasure. Anger has to be honed; with your biggest iron mallet you take the anger and you go at it long enough so that you can tune it. It has to become funny and outrageous and made back into something aesthetic. It's not good enough on its own. But it's good.

Would you want young women to be artists? To be filmmakers?
Oh yes. As many as possible. We should flood the place. To some extent, proportionally, there's now a flourishing of women working to the point where it's also a morass. The mixture of qualities is totally confusing to everyone.

Would you warn them of anything? Or tell them about things to cherish?
I would admonish them to really consider structure and form, to realize that the history of perception and making is volatile and vital. And that they need as much rigorous information as they can get. It's not enough to have a good idea, or a problem to display and relate. We've got too much "stuff" going on. Almost no one has heard of the works in film that I think about all the time.

Can you tell me what those films are?
Oh, I can try, but I'm very forgetful. Luther Price's *Warm Broth*—that's an astonishing, sinister, creepy, unforgettable, feminist, gay male film. Dark and luminous, very simple. The Canadian Jack Chambers, who was a painter in the '70s, began to photograph time durations in his house and the roads near his house and then a visual history of building a city circled into a slaughterhouse, *Hart of London*. Very extraordinary and completely neglected. There's as much by men as by women.

Why are you wearing horns?
I'm wearing horns because I want to show everybody that the phallic principle originally belongs to the feminine. When Mapplethorpe and the boys wear horns, they're usurping the original symbology of the bull that was an attribute of the Goddess. The horns always belonged to the Goddess, and all of us can now have horns equally.

Selected Films and Videos

1964	*Meat Joy,* 16mm, 12 min., documentation of performance
1964–67	*Fuses,* 16mm, 22 min.
1967	*Body Collage,* 16mm, 6 min.
1968–71	*Plumb Line,* 16mm, 18 min.
1973–78	*Kitch's Last Meal,* Super 8, from 20 min. to 4 hr.
1975	*Interior Scroll,* ¾" video, 40 min.
1974–77	*Up to and Including Her Limits,* ¾" videotape, 1 hr.
1980–91	*Infinity Kisses,* documentation of performance
1982	*Vesper's Stampede to My Holy Mouth,* with Victoria Vesna, video
1990–91	*Scroll Painting with Exploded TV,* installation with video complement
1992–97	*Instructions per Second,* with Mirek Rogula
1993	*Imaging Her Erotics: Carolee Schneemann,* with Maria Beatty, video, 10 min.
1995	*Interior Scroll—The Cave (1993–95),* video, with Maria Beatty, 12 min.
1996	*Known/Unknown–Plague Column,* installation documentation
1999	*Vespers Pool,* installation documentation

Distribution and Contact Information

Films available from Filmmakers Coop, 175 Lexington Ave., New York, NY 10016; (212) 889-3820

Videos available from Video Pool, #300–100 Arthur Street, Winnipeg, Manitoba R3B 1H3, CANADA; (204) 949-9134; vpdist@videopool.mb.ca

Or from the artist, Carolee Schneemann, http://209.100.59.3/artists/index.html

[3] Barbara Hammer

Barbara Hammer is the Grande Dame, the mother—no, the Fairy
Godmother—of lesbian, experimental cinema. Since the late '6os, she
has made seventy-four short and six feature-length experimental films,
continually attempting to create a filmic language most expressive of les-
bian experience and desire. Hammer's film language, life, and sexuality
are adventures into uncharted territory. Although born the same year as
Schneemann, her early professional life was influenced not by a frustrated
search for compatriots but, rather, by an immersion in the lifestyle, politics,
and energy of the women's movement, particularly that of lesbian femi-
nism. Although both Schneemann and Hammer sought for foremothers
and found few besides Maya Deren, Schneemann first did so in the late
'5os and '6os and from a world populated mostly by temperamental if
talented men. Meanwhile, Hammer, a housewife until the late '6os, only
then to be inspired by the women's movement, began to create her vast
body of feminist film work as she participated in the radical experiment
of building a world composed almost entirely of women.

As a direct consequence of the politics of consciousness-raising and
other feminist strategies, women were propelled into speaking and showing
with film (and other media) what had been previously forbidden, hidden,
ignored. Hammer tells Judith Redding and Victoria Brownworth in their
book of biographical sketches of independent women filmmakers, Film
Fatales: *"My films talk about all the things we [women, lesbians] were told*
never to talk about: orgasms, personal desire, the body, sex. I wanted des-
perately to break that taboo of not talking, to smash through that silence
I had been raised to believe was the way women had to be—the way we all
had to be."[1] *As Hammer smashed through silence and into representation,*
her short films mirrored a contemporary, feminist understanding of women's
experience—later deemed "essentialist" or labeled "cultural feminism"—

that championed women's exploration of the specificity of their female power, particularly that which was acquired from the natural rhythms and functions of their bodies. The iconography in Hammer's early oeuvre is based in playful and sometimes serious depictions of menstruation, women's rituals, Amazonian tactics, circular or vaginal patterns, and the forms of women's organs and orgasms (e.g., Multiple Orgasm, 1976; Eggs, 1976; Superdyke, 1975; Menses, 1974; Dyketactics, 1974; and many others). For one active cohort of the feminist community, lesbianism was the ultimate form of such feminist expression. Hammer's lesbian feminist films of this era give us access to a more idealistic time when some women (as did the counterculture more generally) believed that they could form better communities and better selves by abandoning the patriarchal, punitive mainstream culture to create more humane, more female traditions.

I knew more about Hammer than I did about Schneemann, first because I had seen her work (both new and in retrospective) in early '90s lesbian and gay film festivals: the independent and avant-garde film community's first and only growth industry since AIDS activist video in the mid-1980s. And second, because she had been more widely written about in academic journals and books. When I was a graduate student at NYU in cinema studies in the mid-1980s, her work had been used primarily as an exemplar of what feminist film should not be: an exploration of an essential female body or sexuality, rather than images focused on how such a body and sexuality come to be known through the representational systems of culture. By the late '70s, feminist film theory had made a quick but decisive theoretical shift from a celebration of the representation of women's "truth" by female filmmakers to an interrogation of how the cinema was complicit in "creating a patriarchal way of seeing."[2] This was only one example of a widespread academic interest in the cultural construction of meaning that was most commonly articulated through a critique of "essentialism." The antiessentialist position countered beliefs that had inspired much of '70s radical or cultural feminism: that there are biological or other essential traits that make women different from men, and that it is around these shared traits and interests that women must unify. In counterdistinction to a body- or biology-based feminism—while at the same time embracing current theories of semiotics, psychoanalysis, antiessentialism, and poststructuralism—feminist film theory, according to one major study, turned its focus to feminist films that "dealt explicitly with issues of representation, language, voyeurism, desire and the image."[3]

As was true for many feminist filmmakers, Hammer's work was not perceived to fit these strict criteria, and the effects on her career were significant. Hammer insists that she experienced these intellectual debates *both materially (in loss of prestige, income, support) and personally as she was often attacked or ignored for certain of her artistic positions.*

I am less interested in here replaying these debates as I am in signaling how critical to feminism such controversies around "theory" have been. B. Ruby Rich reflects on how such debates about theoretical or political positions mattered greatly at the time: "The 70s were an intensely politicized era: intellectual positions were still identified as part of political activity and, as such, fair game for dispute. They were viewed as principled stands that should be taken at their word(s)."[4] The debate about "essentialism" versus "social constructionism" was one front where feminists waged often bitter debates over competing interpretations of the meanings of women's sexuality. These debates were never merely rhetorical struggles. Rather, feminists debate theory to better understand women's power and oppression, what structures maintain and create these conditions, what strategies might best address these conditions, and who can be one's allies in such struggles. The processes of understanding and countering oppression are well served by debates about "correct" and "incorrect" theories. As women talk, position, and counterposition, they strive to hone their critique of patriarchy.

However, as is true for Hammer, these intellectual debates created lived effects for many women artists. For many of the other women I interviewed, the absence of feminist scholarship about their work led to the direct consequence of unarchived, unrented, now-deteriorated films and videos, the winning of fewer grants and shows (based on written recognition, to a large extent), and a sense of being betrayed by the very community that should have been the most appreciative and responsive. Although many tensions between feminist makers and scholars became evident while conducting this study, two seemed most common, at least from the filmmakers' point of view: first, this perception of a direct relationship between the (scholarly) writing about an artist's work and her success; and second, the inaccessibility of the (scholarly) writing that is available about feminist media. Even so, feminist film scholarship and criticism do work to support feminist filmmaking, Hammer's massive oeuvre included. When professors write about films, a market for those films is established; when professors teach films to students, an audience for those films is born; and when professors teach filmmakers their craft, formal traditions and ideologies are passed on.

Importantly, Hammer perceives cycles of academic and artistic thought not as fixed but, rather, as rapid and responsive: what is out for one scholarly (micro) generation (about every ten years) swings right back in for the next. In the '90s, both Schneemann's and Hammer's body-centered films from the '70s have found a much-deserved renaissance. Yet Hammer's '70s *films were only the beginning of a still-active career. Her films have changed as have feminism's views of sexuality and sexual politics. For instance, in the '80s Hammer worked with new stylistic approaches, ever experimenting with the representation of lesbian experience: she took women out of the frame entirely in a cycle of landscape work (*Bent Time, *1983, and* Pond and Waterfall, *1982), and she explored computer-altered representations of lesbian images (*No No Nooky TV, *1987, and* Bedtime Stories, *1986). Hammer's current work investigates the construction of lesbian experience through culture, history, and language. In* The Female Closet *(1998),* Nitrate Kisses *(1992), and* Tender Fictions *(1995), she situates the private experiences of individual lesbians into a public and political framework. In perhaps her most infamous and controversial work,* Nitrate Kisses, *Hammer explores three deviant sexualities—S/M lesbianism, mixed-race gay male lovemaking, and the passions and sexual practices of older lesbians—by linking these erotic, private images into a more complex cinematic matrix of public history (particularly that of Nazi crimes against gays and lesbians), theory (particularly that of queers and feminists), and public space (burned, charred, or rotting buildings). When Hammer shows us these "private" sex acts, she argues that sex can never be seen in isolation from the world we live in— and escape from. In her autobiographical film* Tender Fictions, *Hammer situates her own lesbianism within a complex montage of personal, cultural, political, theoretical, familial, and formal traditions. This work is a decidedly important contribution to the construction of lesbian history.*

Like Schneemann, Hammer is an experimental filmmaker. For she cannot represent lesbianism's difference from and critique of mainstream, heterosexual society using the very language—Hollywood film or mainstream television—that has served to silence lesbians. Her film practice is always multiple: interrogating the relationship between the form of film and that which it represents. For most audiences this also means that her films are challenging. They do not conform to Hollywood's pleasures of closure and continuity. But given that traditional filmic style has led to a standard of voyeuristic, demeaning, heterosexist depictions of women's sexuality, Hammer must expand the form of film to expand consciousness of the diversity of sexual experience. Her films allow us to learn to see new subjects through new forms.

▶ ───

Something to Express

I have been making films since 1967, when somebody gave me a Super 8 camera. I was studying to be a painter because I was a bored housewife and I felt I had something to express. I made a number of Super 8 films. Those films have rarely been shown except in the early lesbian feminist women's coffeehouses. The women reacted strongly against some of them because they came out of my heterosexual past.

My own work in 16mm film coincided with my coming out as a lesbian. It was fortuitous because making love with a woman changed my life. I touched a body similar to my own, and it awakened a sense of delight in my body that I hadn't known in my heterosexuality. I was stimulated by the new sensations and experiences of same-sex love to make the film *Dyketactics* (1974). Every image in the film has a sense of touch about it, either a hand touching the skin or water, or animals crawling across the body; there are all kinds of skin aesthetics in the film. I wanted to let other women know that they too could celebrate life through touch and through sexuality with a woman.

Dyketactics was the first explicit sexual film about lesbian sexuality made by a lesbian. Bisexual filmmaker Connie Beeson had made a film, *Holding* (1971), before that about lesbian sexuality, and it was very explicit.

I feel a great urge to make film. There is always this compelling rush and energy to make work because there are things inside that need to be expressed. People often say to me with a mixed message of admiration and envy, "You are so prolific." I never know quite how to read that. I just do what I need to do. In the '70s, the films just rushed out. I was in school, but I didn't make them for classes, I just made them for myself. A high point along the way might be a simple film like *Superdyke,* a performance film where a group of us take over the institutions of San Francisco, like City Hall and the Erotic Art Museum, where we put paintings of our vaginas up over the phallic symbols on display. We had Superdyke T-shirts made, and we bull-dyked our way through the streets and the crowds. We danced at the women's coffeehouse and presented Sally Gehrheart with a Superdyke T-shirt. It was easy and fun. It was all shot in a day.

Then there were serious films like *Double Strength* in 1978. That film came out of the closure of an important relationship with Terry Sengraff, the performance artist. She and I performed on trapezes and suspended apparati, and often in the nude. I went through what, at the time, I thought were the stages of a lesbian relationship. But after screening some of these earlier films, I realized that I was explaining my aesthetic to an audience and I needed to put those ideas into a film. *Sync Touch,* made in 1980–81, is a film about lesbian aesthetic. My lesbian aesthetic is a screen that comes alive to the body, to the sense of touch. It's a connection between eyes and touching.

Recognition Changed My Life

Who gave you permission?

My mother gave me a lot of attention; she saw me as special. She thought I was a performer and gave me acting lessons, dramatic lessons. She saw a precocious, cute little girl with pigtails and bangs and freckles who liked to talk to strangers and who wasn't afraid of putting her personality into the world. My mother was born into a poor immigrant family. She grew up without a running toilet in the house. I was born in Hollywood at a time when Shirley Temple was making more money than any other woman in the United States. My maternal grandmother, Anna Buchack Kusz, was a cook for Lillian Gish and D. W. Griffith. I was told that I was introduced to Gish and Griffith when I was five. My mother took me for an audition at the Hollywood studios, but I wasn't accepted. I didn't have professional lessons. We didn't have the money for that, so I just took neighborhood classes. It was her encouragement, I think, and belief in me that has given me the strength and self-confidence to become a self-defined independent filmmaker.

It took me three years to identify as an artist. That wasn't easy. We don't have rules to be an artist. From the age of twenty-seven to thirty, I went through the process of self-identifying as an artist. Those were also the last three years of my marriage. I studied painting, aesthetics, and art history. I wrote poetry. My painting instructor, William Morehouse, recognized my artist's energy in a way that confirmed my evolving identity.

Recognition changed my life. *Schizy,* my first film, went into a film festival in 1968 and received an honorable mention award. *Schizy* was projected onto a screen larger than any canvas I was painting. The audience couldn't leave the theater because it was dark and, voilà, I had a captured audience, which is what I wanted. I wanted an audience and I wanted a large image.

After that experience at the Sonoma State Super 8 Film Festival, I never questioned that I should continue to make film. When I went to study film a few years later at San Francisco State, I saw Maya Deren's films for the first time. Before I saw her work, I had only seen men's cinema. I knew that there was a women's cinema, but I hadn't seen it, the screen was blank. I knew when I saw Deren's work that there was a role for me, a place to fill: there were images to make for that blank screen. The fact that there had not been a developed woman's cinema reinforced the sense that I was on the right path.

AJ: *Were you, at that stage, aware of any other women filmmakers?*
No. I wrote a poem to [Vsevolod] Pudovkin's wife, or to the woman who plays the mother in Pudovkin's [1926] film.[5] A few years ago Ron Levaco, my teacher of Russian film, gave that [poem] back to me and I saw how angry I was. We were angry feminists, a few of us, who sat in the first row, questioning the professor: "Where were the women's films?" No, I wasn't aware of any other women's cinema at that time besides Maya Deren.

▶

The '80s: Women out of the Frame

I felt that the '80s were a very repressive period in the United States. I couldn't get a show in the art establishment. I was only showing my films to women's groups, to feminist groups. It was very difficult; I hadn't received a grant at that time. For ten years, the works were all funded out of my pocket. I wasn't being recognized as an artist, but merely as a "lesbian filmmaker." I decided that if I took women out of the frame, the films couldn't be objected to, especially by the Museum of Modern Art and the Collective for Living Cinema.

I began to work with landscape imagery, with underwater cinematography. In *Pools* (made with Barbara Klutinis), *Pearl Diver,* and *Pond and Waterfall,* three films for which I used an underwater camera, I represent the world on the two levels a woman has to negotiate: the patriarchal and the personal. It is like coming up to the horizon of a swimming pool and being able to go underwater and above at the same time and have both in focus. A woman must function on two levels in order to survive in late–twentieth-century patriarchy.

There was always great intention and thought behind a work that may look like a simple exploration of a pond going into a river and down a waterfall out into the ocean. There is often danger involved in my films. I like to take risks because I feel that is part of lesbian filmmaking. Being a lesbian was risk-taking, at least when I came out. For *Pond and Waterfall* I stood under a waterfall with the camera, swam out into the ocean with a 50-pound Bolex and underwater housing, and when a wave broke over me and the camera got stuck on the bottom, I didn't know if I would save myself or the camera. The camera got saved first.

Finally, I was invited to show work in museums and avant-garde film houses, and I began to get grants. I got a Jerome Foundation grant here in New York in 1984. Actually B. Ruby Rich was on the panel, and I submitted *Pond and Waterfall.* I had actually moved to New York so that I could apply for a Jerome grant. California was number forty-eight out of the fifty states in terms of money given to filmmakers, and New York was either first or second. It was a very calculated idea, but if you feel that you have something to express, you must make the moves that you see necessary for your professional life. I never saw myself or my work as unimportant. I want to make a contribution to world culture.

I taught your article in Queer Looks *about the debates about essentialism in your career.[6] Can you talk about the effects on your work due to the institutionalization of feminist film theory?*
I studied film theory in graduate school. I read *Screen* magazine. I read Christian Metz in Xerox copies before he was published.[7] I knew about signs and signifiers. But when I first heard that my work was being called "essentialist," I didn't know what that meant. As the *Camera Obscura* women returned from their studies in Paris and brought back one criteria for "good feminist film," my work became déclassé. Seemingly, it identified a biological woman on screen as if all femininity occurred in biology rather than in culture. This nature/culture issue is older than feminist film theory. Feminist critics swung very far to the right in terms of antiessentialism in the '70s. In the late '80s, when postmodern deconstruction became de rigeur and people were studying questions of authorship and appropriation, theory entered into my work in a big way. It was exciting: these were great ideas and interesting material to work with. Now, there's a return to the body. Theory, like art, swings. It goes too far one way, causes a reaction, and swings back the other way. After abstract expressionism, you have pop art, and after that, theoretical work, and then in this year's Whitney Biennial, abstraction and narrative.

▶

Nitrate Kisses

Certainly the dismissal of my work hurt my career. It was one of the reasons I didn't get shows and grants. My work still isn't being written about except in isolated journals. It was disturbing because I never felt like I was saying we are our genetic makeup. I know that, as a lesbian, I always construct myself. What you wear, what gestures you make, how you drink your beer are all signifiers in the lesbian community. I thought that the representation of those codes would come across as constructions within the films. They didn't, until I purposefully made them do that in *Nitrate Kisses*.

So I think that to a lot of people my work has been challenging. Chuck Kleinhans wrote an article about my work for a catalogue for the Mary Riepman Ross Theater at the University of Nebraska in Lincoln, where

I had a retrospective. He said that my films didn't quite fit into the experimental camp because of the lesbian feminist content or the feminist camp because of the experimental challenge. I straddle the two camps. If I have a lesbian feminist audience perhaps unfamiliar with experimental films, I introduce them to the meanings and uses of disjunctive sound/image relationships. To experimental film-going audiences, I talk about the politics of identity, the need for representation of marginal communities, and why that is avant-garde, or why it is experimental to represent women's bodily functions on the screen. So that has been the life, traversing those two venues.

Can you talk a little more about the effect of a history of objections on your work.
It's really changed now.

I'm interested in how institutions change.
The idea of how the work has been received is very interesting and provocative. I have made films for thirty years, often films that include explicit lesbian sexuality. I have run into censorship issues numerous times. But there is an evolution. In the late '80s I began to receive the recognition I deserved. I received government, NEA funds, for *Nitrate Kisses.* I also reidentified with the burgeoning queer movement. It was time to reintroduce lesbian sexuality to the screen in my cinema and to also include that which I did not know firsthand, such as gay male sexuality, and some of the S/M practices.

Nitrate Kisses is about the histories of diverse sexualities on the screen. It is concerned with how history is made, who is left out, who is in the margins. I asked myself who, among queers, are most left out of history. I thought about mixed-race couples denied screen representation by the Hayes Code for twenty-five years. I asked two friends of mine who are actors and experimental filmmakers, Jack Waters and Peter Cramer, if they would simulate lovemaking for me on camera. When I was shooting, I thought it was a documentary. Jack and Peter later reminded me that it was dramatic and that they were following my directions. Then, I met two women who looked terrific. They had shaved heads and tattoos. I saw them in a coffee shop and asked them, "Would you be in my film making love?" Julie Tolentino, who runs the Clit Club (a lesbian bar/dance floor in New York's meat market area), and Alistair Fate, her sculptor lover, said, "Yes." I shot them inside Alistair's sculpture of a burnt-out house, which for me represented a burnt-out history, a history we don't have.

I was in Judith's Room, a New York women's bookstore, when two women came in wearing motorcycle leathers, J. C. and Selena Barone. It was a hot day—clearly, they were exhibitionists because everyone else was in shorts. I asked the leatherwomen if they would make love on camera for me. They said, "Yes." They arrived with whips, chains, and masks at my Westbeth apartment (federally supported artist housing). They roared up on motorcycles. I set up lights, and this was the first lesbian sex scene that I shot since *Dyketactics* in 1974. They were a little stiffer than the other couples. Maybe that goes with the codified sexuality that S/M can have, with its rules and limits and materials.

I was well into editing, still thinking about who else had been left out, when I realized—old women! I use *old* as a neutral and descriptive adjective. I would love to talk more about ageism in the lesbian community. When people say, "Oh, you don't look fifty-six, Barbara," I say, "This is what fifty-six looks like." The most radical of politicos will forget that it's no compliment to tell somebody she doesn't look her age. I went to an Old Dyke's Award Ceremony for outstanding old lesbians in the community. I asked women there who would make love for me on camera. They all said, "Frances Lorraine." I saw Frances walking down the aisles in her tight white Levis and her silk blouse opened to her bra, and I thought, "Mmm, perfect." She said, "Yes, I will." I asked if she knew someone who would do it with her, and she said that she would find someone because her lover worked for the city government and wasn't willing to come out on camera. Frances asked a friend of hers, Sally Binford, a bisexual woman who had been in earlier films on sexuality. They both arrived at my home in San Francisco. I had bought props of latex gloves, sexy underwear, but they already had them. They needed no coaching. I felt so familiar with filming them. I circled the bed, stroked them with the camera, encouraged them when I got something through the viewfinder that I liked.

In the NEA-funded film *Nitrate Kisses* sexuality was intercut with missing parts of history. I consider it my greatest work to date. It was ambitious. It took a large commitment. I was nervous during the making of it because of the NEA struggles surrounding people who were using explicit sexual imagery in their work.

I sneak-premiered the film in Washington, D.C. The first question to come up from the audience was hostile. It was, "Do you think you'll ever get another NEA grant, ha, ha?" I said, "Of course, I will. I have a lot more work to do." This man went to my files at the NEA and alerted them to my film. He read my grant proposal and said that I had made a different film from the one I proposed. It was supposed to have focused on gay men at the turn of the century. I was interested in looking at *Lot in Sodom*, directed by James Watson and Melville Webber (1930), the first gay film in

America, in terms of the AIDS crisis. I had expanded the project to include lesbian as well as gay male history.

After a year of deliberation, the NEA called and asked me to take their name out of the credits of the film. The film is out on home video, and it doesn't have the NEA logo on it, but I am reissuing a master tape and putting it back in! I have talked to the press. I've never hidden what happened. I have spent too much energy, first worrying during the making of the film, and then considering what to do afterward. No artist should have to go through that. We should be given the utmost freedom and encouragement to use our poetry and art to address society about repression—race, age, sexual representation, issues that need to be talked about, that are hidden under the rugs—not to perpetuate the status quo.

▶

Funding Film

ERIN CRAMER (associate producer): *You said that you were not grant-funded until the '80s. Can you talk about how you funded your films? What it cost you? Did you have access to equipment?*

One of the reasons I went to film school was to have access to equipment. I got a master's degree in film in two and a half years, and in that time I made thirteen short films. Not all of those films were for class assignments. They were films I personally had to make. I got the camera and sound transfers for free. All I had to pay for was the film stock. People would work for free, and we became friends and colleagues. In the '80s, I started teaching production out of my studio in Oakland, California. I would earn enough from six to eight students in my studio, using my equipment, taking them through the filmmaking process, that I could support myself. In 1982, my income was $8,000. Today, it would probably be equivalent, but I now teach at colleges and universities as a visiting artist.

One of the other ways that I have been able to fund my films is by not putting a lot of value in capitalism and the accumulation of material goods. I have always driven a secondhand car. Until recently, I never owned my own home. I am extremely thrifty, but I will spend money on my films and travel. When I was a painter, I'd pay $100 for a roll of canvas. As a filmmaker, when I had money it would go into the film. Now that I get grants, I set that money aside and only spend it on the film. *Nitrate Kisses* cost $21,000 exactly. A distribution company forwarded an advance of $2,000 to make an internegative print for them to make copies from. Most of the films eventually pay for themselves, and in the very long run they make money.

Influences

What women influenced you?

Maya Deren. She was the first strong female presence on screen, in directing, and in challenging cinematic form. As I learn more about her as an ambitious, political woman who set up venues for her films in the United States, I respect her more. I also question her sexual preference. She worked with women in her films who were lesbians. I'm not sure she didn't have lesbian experiences.

I began to look for women in experimental film. I wrote to Jonas Mekas at the Film Anthology saying, "Out of thirty people whom you have decided represent Essential Cinema, only two, Shirley Clarke and Maya Deren, are women."[8] He didn't answer my letter, which went on to say that I would help him to find more. I found Storme de Hirsch. She did a number of very challenging films on Super 8. They were psychedelic and concerned with other realms of reality. There's Sarah Arlidge, whose work is not well known. I interviewed her in Pasadena and had it printed in *Cinema News*.[9] She made six or seven films with glass slides that she painted and burned and etched with smoke. She dealt with questions of representation and gender. She made a film called *What Is a Man?*

Lately, I've been influenced by more intellectual feminist filmmakers such as Trinh T. Minh-ha and Yvonne Rainer.[10] Their work inspires me both in terms of style and the use of thought and reflection in the frame. Hollywood cinema, being based on action, is devoid of such thought. I like Su Friedrich's work.[11] *Sink or Swim* (1990) is as near to a perfect film as I've ever seen. I thought about it while working on *Tender Fictions*. I want to use segues and transitions in the way that she so beautifully uses an image and sound narrative montage.

Wishes

What do you wish for?

I hope that before I die I can start a Barbara Hammer Fund for lesbian filmmakers who use experimental form in their work and do not replicate the status quo. I would love to have a larger budget. I would love to share the load. I have to do everything myself. I shoot my own titles. I do my own optical printing. I edit and take my own sound, do my own transfers. There are no labor costs, and I don't pay myself out of the grant.

And I wish for health. As you age and you see more and more friends with AIDS, breast cancer, chronic fatigue syndrome, arthritis, I wish for health because that will give me the energy to continue. I'd love to make a larger-budget film. I've taken some directing classes and worked with actors, and I know that I have talent in directing that I have yet to be able to use. I'd like to work with a group of people. Usually, I work as a solitary artist.

Do you want to make a crossover film?
No. I'd like it to be cross-dressed, cross-gendered, not crossed-over. I want the audience to grow to meet me; I don't want to reduce the complexities of the film to meet them. You should do the work as best you can, do what the work tells you it should be, and then see what it becomes. Don't start with [the idea] that it should be crossover, or you've set yourself up for failure because you have a proscription in mind.

Do you want to talk about ageism?
There's a transition taking place in my life since the age of fifty. Now I'm a role model. Before, I was just working. Suddenly, I'm looked at with the admiration and respect I've wanted. I don't want to hold back from trying risky things because I'm afraid to fail. Idolization doesn't help. There has to be a way that the people whom we respect and admire can be colleagues, not isolated.

Intergenerational experiences are important to me. I want to be a part of your piercing ceremony, your coming out. I want you to come to my parties, interracially and intergenerationally. When I go to a movie and I'm the only white hair in the audience, it feels lonely. Where is my generation? Where are the dykes I danced with? Are they all professionals who have changed their lives and won't be seen in public now?

When you get older, you feel like the same person you were at thirty, only more articulate with better-formed ideas. You still feel like that playful flirt who is sensitive, who can be hurt by criticisms or brash movements or hurtful comments. You don't walk around knowing what you look like. It's always a bit of a shock when someone relates to you in a way that points out that you have a lot of wrinkles and liver spots and that you are an aging female, when someone doesn't recognize the "you" that is still you inside. It's a curious process, but I'm intrigued to go through it. It's fantastic that we have change. Even death and dying as a process will be a one-time, fresh experience, and one to acknowledge when it comes.

One of the failures of the women's movement is the lack of intergenerational interaction.

EC: *It is confined to teacher/student relations.*

When I teach my students this work—and that's why I want to make this film because they know so little of it—it's a surprise for my students to learn that women lived powerful, complex, artistic, free lives. I can't believe they lack that. Women leave the class and say, "Those are wonderful films . . . but who are those women?!" After interviewing Carolee, we all said, "It is so amazing to meet that woman. She is so wonderful! She's so intelligent. I want to be her." My mom was in CR, I see it in my mother. But I don't see it in most other areas of my life.

CHERYL DUNYE (cameraperson, New York interviews): *It's still considered marginal. It's still not ever going to be incorporated into the dominant culture. But it is so important to have your experience, your difference, become part of the dominant culture. It's this cyclical thing: to know that twenty years ago lesbians were going through similar things.*

EC: *It's been situated as a cycle of conflict and renunciation: this is in reaction to that. So you swing to the other side. When you get to the reaction to the reaction, you're not aware of what came before. And people got burned out from trying to make change, and so they receded for the successive generations. They weren't putting themselves forward to share their experiences; they were shell-shocked.*

They went off into the "Me Generation," too, doing our own work, which wasn't necessarily feminist. A group of us older ladies got together who were involved in Berkeley in the '70s. We had two meetings: how could we be active again? The group fell apart. I thought we should have a meeting at the Women's Building and all be on a panel and talk about the old days, just share the history, young women would want that.

AJ, EC, CD: *Exactly!*

▶ _____

A Multiple Place

What is your place in feminist film history?
I've been working to make a multiple place for the films and for the teaching. I also want to bring people together and encourage them to talk, whether that means in a class or a conference. I've been instrumental in encouraging African American, Latina, South African, and Taiwanese lesbians to make strong work and know there is space for their expression. Politically, as a board member of AIVF [Association of Independent Video and Filmmakers] I work to get media artists to make strong statements to the press and to legislators.

I hope that my own work will be seen as a progression of sophistica-
tion and development as it traces one lesbian's life in the second half of the
twentieth century. This is a space now filled where, before, there was a none,
a lack, a void. Now, I have sisters and brothers around me—there's a lot of
queer cinema. I want to keep working with my eyes open, learning from
others, going to see new work, trying to do the best I can to develop further
my "visual language."

I hope there's a new language of experiential cinema, where people feel
in their bodies what they're watching in a film that's not primarily based in
action or intellect. I want people to change places between the screen and
their seat while they're watching. I want them to see the camera move fluidly so that they understand the world can be seen upside down and that's as
valid as right side up. Gravity happens to be a circumstance that we're forced
to comply with. We can make the world antigravitational with a camera.
The world can be seen in many ways, all valid. I want people to walk out
of the cinema and see the world freshly, as a child. I want them to see the
most humble piece of garbage with fresh eyes, without a prescription for
how to see. So that grain of sand Blake talked about can become a world
in itself. And that's my next film.

What do we owe you?

I need to grow into owning what I'm owed: respect, a place in history, a
chance to tell my history, support to publish my autobiography, and to go
into those journals. I need to come out in print and be available in other
ways since the films have such limited distribution. The world owes those
of us who make independent cinema a place in the history of film. We need
to break down as national cinema viewers into an international cinema
audience. We'll come alive in our seats as we look at new worlds and cultures that we learn to understand. Whole, complex relationships will open
for us—instead of that piece of sand or garbage, worlds that we could not
understand because we've been such a nationalist country.

So, I'll take a MacArthur. A home in the country, a garden for my old
age and my horse Silver. And rollerblades.

◆————————————————————————————

BARBARA HAMMER

Selected Films and Videos

1968   *Schizy,* Super 8, silent, 4 min.
1972   *I Was/I Am,* black and white, 16 mm, 7.5 min.
1973   *A Gay Day,* 16mm, 3 min.

1974	*Dyketactics,* 16mm, 4 min.
1974	*Menses,* 16mm, 3 min.
1975	*Superdyke,* 16mm, 20 min.
1976	*Women I Love,* 16mm, 27 min.
1976	*Multiple Orgasm,* 16mm, silent, 6 min.
1978	*Double Strength,* 16mm, 16 min.
1981	*Our Trip,* 16mm, 4 min.
1982	*Pond and Waterfall,* 16mm, silent, 15 min.
1983	*Bent Time,* 16mm, 22 min., sound composition by Pauline Oliveros
1985	*Optic Nerve,* 16mm, 16 min., sound composition by Helen Thorington
1986	*Snow Job: The Media Hysteria of AIDS,* shot on Hi-8, mastered to Beta and ¾" video, 8 min.
1987	*No No Nooky TV,* 16mm, 12 min.
1989	*Still Point,* 16mm, 9 min.
1990	*Sanctus,* 16mm, 19 min., sound by Neil B. Rolnick
1991	*Vital Signs,* 16mm, 9 min.
1992	*Nitrate Kisses,* 16mm, black and white, 67 min.
1994	*Out in South Africa,* shot on Hi-8, mastered to Beta and ¾" video, 55 min.
1995	*Tender Fictions,* 16mm, 58 min.
1998	*The Female Closet,* shot on Hi-8, mastered to Beta and ¾" video, 60 min.
2000	*Devotion,* a film about Ogawa Productions, mini-DV mastered to Beta and ¾" video, 84 min.
2000	*History Lessons,* 66 min.

Distribution and Contact Information

Canyon Cinema, 2325 3rd Street, Suite 338, San Francisco, CA 94107; (415) 626-2255

Facets Multimedia, 1517 West Fullerton Ave., Chicago, IL 60614; (312) 281-9075

Frameline, 346 Ninth Street, San Francisco, CA 94103; (415) 703-8650

Women Make Movies, 462 Broadway, #500, New York, NY 10013; (212) 925-0606

Barbara Hammer, bjhammer@aol.com

[**4**] *Kate Horsfield* _____

Kate Horsfield, an artist and arts administrator, is perhaps most important to this history in her role as cofounder and current director of the Video Data Bank, a major archive and distributor of art video. The Video Data Bank houses four large collections: "On Art and Artists," more than 250 interviews with contemporary artists shot by Horsfield and her partner, the late Lyn Blumenthal; "Independent Video and Alternative Media," which includes recent experimental and documentary video by emerging videomakers; "Early Video Art," which houses work from the '70s; and "Americas With/ Out Borders," a collection of works made by Latino videomakers from north and south of the border. Horsfield has also produced compilations of alternative video that are distributed to schools, art centers, museums, and galleries: "What Does She Want" (with Blumenthal), a collection of feminist video; "Video against AIDS"; and "Surveying the First Decade: Video Art and Alternative Media in the United States: 1968–1980."

As graduate art students at the School of the Art Institute of Chicago (SAIC) in the early seventies, she and Blumenthal were shaken out of the quietude of the mid-1960s by the social, political, and technological upheavals of the decade's end. As is true for most of their generation—individuals who came to their sense of purpose through the many movements for social change—Horsfield and Blumenthal understood that social change was rooted to institutional change. They also believed that formal or aesthetic change would facilitate institutional growth. Horsfield's career and organization were enabled by the specific technological developments that allowed consumers and artists access to portable video recording technologies in the form of the portapak, first put on the market in the late '60s. A new medium—a new message. In her study of guerrilla video Deirdre Boyle articulates this early vision of the medium: "Fueled by adolescent rebellion and utopian dreams, video promised an alternative to the slickly civilized, commercially corrupt, and aesthetically bankrupt world of Television."[1]

Horsfield's interview also confirms how the history of video is inextricable from radical politics, the art world, and significantly, feminism.[2] "The arrival of video also coincided with the beginnings of feminism," writes JoAnn Hanley in the catalogue for her landmark video exhibition, "The First Generation: Women and Video, 1970-75." "By turning the camera back on themselves and their daily lives, and by presenting the world from their perspective, women artists used video, as Martha Gever has stated, 'to propose a redefinition of reality by asserting the validity of women's existence and experience.'"[3] Here was a medium easy to use and easy to learn. A medium that allowed for a more interactive, collaborative process because of the possibility of immediate playback. A medium yet to be territorialized by male artists. A medium that spoke back to mainstream, status quo, patriarchal culture in the very language—television—that it used to create sexist visions that functioned to contain women.

Not surprisingly, then, at this time large numbers of women artists came into a career through the medium of video. "Access to video (as to performance, photography and installation art also emerging in the 1970s) allowed women and others—until then marginalized by the mainstream— to have an equal voice," explains Mary Jane Jacobs in Hanley's catalogue.[4] Like feminist film scholarship that was soon to follow, video was a space of cultural production largely inspired by feminist thought and peopled by women. Horsfield and Blumenthal were no exception. With their portapak, they shot hundreds of hours of interviews with female (and male) artists with the same investment that motivates my project: if you can hear and see (or read) a woman talk about her life and work, it does not appear so strange, so inaccessible, and so hard to do yourself. "You can look at someone's work, and you may not like it very much," Horsfield reflects. "But once you've heard them explain how they made that work—particularly women, they work so hard to get there, even to a midlevel place—when you hear them talk about what they sacrificed, the amount of commitment they've put into it, and how hard it's been, there's no way to be critical of that work in a nonpersonal way."

By founding the Video Data Bank, Horsfield and Blumenthal archived their interviews, and other's art tapes, to ensure that they would not be lost. As distributors, they made certain that their work, and that of others, would go into the world and continue to be seen. Today, the tapes in the Video Data Bank need to be preserved, and this becomes the latest challenge. The defunding of the arts has been particularly unkind to preservation. Horsfield warns that losing histories like the one she has archived means *that only Hollywood and television will remain as an indication of the ideas of any given generation. A chilling prospect, for feminists have created radical representations and opportunities: gains have been made, an infrastructure was built, and women's lives and possibilities changed accordingly. Yet if we can't see records of such changes and what enabled them, we become disenabled to easily continue this work. Currently, the defunding and dismantling of the very institutions created by Horsfield's generation signal how very closely we did touch on the structures that matter and how important it is to stop us from working in those places.*

My generation did not need to create an infrastructure, because one was in place when we sought to establish our careers. We took for granted these institutions that allowed us the luxury to make work about ourselves and our interests, to imagine that we could be artists, and that this wasn't such a big deal. It was a gift, really, one that in its very obviousness became invisible and expected. We only saw this support system when the organizations began to close down. Horsfield also knows of a time when the world around her was a blank space, a void, at least as far as a feminist, cultural presence is concerned. "In the '70s, we were interested in creating an infrastructure and alternative organizations because when we looked out into the world, we saw nothing. There was no place to exhibit, to bring in poets, to have performances, to make video." Let us hope we do not need to return to that place before women are motivated to remake the feminist organizations that support us.

▶
─────────────────────────────────────

The '70s

I want to start by talking about the '70s. Now that we have perspective on that time, we can look at it as a space, as an arena. It was a tremendous moment for accomplishment and ambition, for people to create things. It was close to the driving force of the '60s with its politics, its radicalism that had the agenda "We can change the world, and we can do it now." Following right upon this was the feminist movement. Before this was a blank space. In Chicago, for example, I can remember in the '50s when there were only a few art galleries. There were no opportunities for anybody.

The '70s was a period of tremendous creativity and ambition for people my age; and this ambition took a different direction in the '90s. In the '70s, we were interested in creating an infrastructure and alternative organizations because when we looked out into the world, we saw nothing. There was no place to exhibit, to bring in poets, to have performances, to make video. The infrastructure was unbelievably valuable. There were many involved with this effort, and from it, other things have grown. It was like putting down stones so that the next generation would have a place to stand and from which they could move quickly. Younger producers of video and film, who are now in their early thirties, are not interested in creating organizations or infrastructure. They're interested in speaking out and creating their own work. In the '70s, a lot of people felt that no one could speak unless we had an infrastructure. That came straight out of the '60s. We wanted alternative organizations to carry alternative voices. That was successful, not just for the Video Data Bank, but for lots of other small organizations. All of them are under reevaluation at this point.

In that spirit, several things were created in Chicago in the early 1970s. Before we started the Video Data Bank, there was N.A.M.E. Gallery and Artemesia. Artemesia was particularly important to us. It was a local gallery that showed women's art exclusively, mostly painting and sculpture. My career and the Video Data Bank owe a little debt to Artemesia. In 1974, they invited Marcia Tucker, who was then a curator at the Whitney, to present a slide lecture in Chicago about the work of women artists. Lots of women went. It was a seminal, validating lecture in which she said, "Look at this fabulous work. It's all done by women."

▶ _____

The Interviews

A few months before this, my partner, Lyn Blumenthal, and I bought a portapak. We weren't sure of what to do with it. It weighed about two tons, and you had to carry it on your shoulder. We started by going to Lincoln Park in the middle of winter and turning the camera on, but we weren't getting anywhere. In March of 1974, Marcia Tucker came and Lyn said, "Why don't we just go and tape her? It might be stimulating." We shot fifty minutes of Marcia Tucker, sort of like we're doing right now. She said, "Before you show it to anyone, I want to see it myself." We were ecstatic! We thought, "Oh, cool!" We were also freaked out.

At the time I was thirty and Lyn was twenty-six. We had no idea what we were doing. We got there and Marcia looked at the tape. She said, "Well, this is kind of interesting. You know, Joan Mitchell is in town for her retrospective at the Whitney.[5] Why don't you do an interview with her?" We thought that this was a sign saying to go from the first step to the second. But we didn't realize that we'd kind of been set up. Joan Mitchell has a reputation as a terrorist. She was a hard-core abstract expressionist. She drank, she ran off with men in the middle of the night, she had a good time, she smoked, she painted. She was a tough old girl, and she was our first real interview with an artist.

That's how we started. In a practical sense, one thing led to the next. Lyn and I were about to go to graduate school, but we didn't start school until several months after we started our video project. She was in sculpture and video, and I was in painting and video. We were at the Art Institute of Chicago. We were dropout girls. Lyn, at the time, was married to a man and she was selling real estate. I was living with another woman and illustrating children's books. The feminist movement started to swirl around us. Both of us felt as though we weren't getting anywhere with our lives. She was driving a taxi and selling real estate, and I was drawing about four or five hundred children's tennis shoes a week. When we met, there was an electromagnetic reaction. It was like jet fuel. Once we met, we started talking about ideas, ways of working together, how to get out of the backwater or cul-de-sac that we felt we were in.

Nineteen-seventy-four was the year in which we started working together; it was also the year in which Panasonic came out with portable video equipment that was stuff that guys had. Girls weren't allowed to touch any kind of technological apparatus. Still true today, but it was really true back then. So, very quickly we saw our mission was to focus on the creativity of women. We were frustrated as graduate students because this was the first wave of high theory. There was such a distance between the motivations that artists had and the way that art was described in *Artforum*. There was also the omission of women's work.

We wanted to go to women and ask, "How do you feel about this? Why do you work in these ways? Why are you a sculptor or a painter? What got you from point A to point B?" These tapes were very intimate and very long, about two to three hours. We did not believe in editing. We wanted everyone to hear every word that Nancy Grossman, Arlene Raven, or Agnes Martin said. It seemed to be a cheap shot to edit. That approach didn't function so well with our audiences. Although the information was fabulous, people wouldn't sit still for that long. It was too intense for them.

We divided into roles on the night we did Joan Mitchell. I ended up doing the interview and Lyn ended up doing camera. Lyn was a very radical cameraperson. Her framing was like this [makes a box around her face with her hands]. If the subject moved, then you'd be looking at an ear for about ten minutes because she'd be in the background somewhere, smoking. We can look at television now and see close framing, but in the '70s everything was a perfect studio shot. Lyn just went straight in. The effect went beyond intimacy into a fearful relationship between the image on the monitor and the audience. There were a couple of our interviewees who terrified people.

Audiences couldn't watch them. Lyn would say, "I don't care what people think about it. This is my aesthetic, and this is the way we're gonna do it." We did 250 like that.

What's the link between feminism and video?
It was sort of accidental in the beginning because feminism was linked to the '60s, and so were video and performance, which also began during the same period. Video made it possible for people to create their own media. Equipment was available and cheap. It was a technological revolution that provided a means of expression for the range of ideas linked to the social agenda of the '60s.

The important thing about women and video was that, before this, the primary representation of women came from mainstream media; these were images created by the patriarchal structure. Video was important to women because they understood that to make social change they had to take control of production and their own representation. We had to make a functional, alternative representation that could help others understand the distinction between patriarchal representation and that created from and by feminism. Look at Martha Rosler's work.[6] It's incredible in its ability to describe how representation will affect a population of women. Video was the perfect medium. It was cheap and accessible—tapes could be bicycled from one feminist collective to the next—and it was easy.

▶
_____

The Video Data Bank

Was that the beginning of the Video Data Bank?
The Video Data Bank started in 1972 as an adjunct to the Video Department. The school started its video department very early, only a few years after people started thinking about video. The "Video Data Bank" was an in-house collection of about 150 student tapes and interviews with visiting artists and speakers such as Baba Ram Dass, Buckminster Fuller, and Joseph Beuys. No one believed in tapes at that time. Students were recording over some of these tapes. We had a tape of Anaïs Nin, another of Robert Smithson. The policy was so loose in that department that interviews were lost as students processed images over them.

In truth, the Video Data Bank was a wooden box adjacent to the video department. Inside was a red rug, pillows, a monitor, a playback deck, and a lock on the door. Students would go into the Video Data Bank for a couple of hours and lock the door. The school finally thought, "We can't have this going on." So between the tapes being recorded over and the private—

probably illicit—activity going on in the Data Bank, they decided to move it into the school library and make it a legitimate resource. This was simultaneous with Lyn's and my graduation in 1976. We parlayed the school's need to take care of the collection, and the fact that our interviews had become wildly popular, into a one-year job "cataloging" the collection.

We showed tapes every Thursday for the painting department. The point was very much a feminist concept. We started out only shooting women. We wanted to give all of our colleagues in graduate school an opportunity to understand one thing: no matter what books say about how to become an artist, there isn't any one way. It's totally self-defined. It's a hard road with many accidents and curved spaces. We wanted to give everyone the concept that you can do whatever you want to do, that many women were doing it and making amazing accomplishments.

That spirit was the real beginning of the Video Data Bank. There had been no ambition to make it bigger than a shelf of tapes until Lyn and I came along. We wormed our way into being employed at the school. No one understood why we were hired except the dean. He offered each of us $1,000 for one year to recatalog the collection. That was nineteen years ago. No one actually knew what we were doing. Every year, we'd go back to the dean and fabricate a reason why we had to stay one more year.

Something I've never said before is that Lyn and I had a domestic relationship, emotionally and sexually and professionally. In the '70s it was pretty unusual to have two women, who were lesbians, in the same job. We each had half a job. We worked at the Data Bank three days a week and had the rest of the time off for private work. We were both still co-directors, still making interviews, still working three days a week, and still making other work. It lasted like that until 1988, when Lyn died.

▶————————————————————————————

Influences

Whose work has been influential to you?
We didn't realize this, but the effect of doing the interviews was making us grow. We were learning everything. We were shooting in impossible situations. The most impossible was Agnes Martin, who lived in New Mexico. We interviewed her for the first time in the fall of 1974 before we started graduate school. Even now, nineteen years later, nobody has had the impact on me that she had. She was a self-defined woman. Her values were spectacular. She always lived alone. Once she started to become well-known in the art world in New York, she got out. She traveled in a pickup truck for two years. No one knew where she was. She landed in New Mexico and

built an adobe house for herself there, brick by brick. She made the bricks. So, we were influenced by the work we were creating. The tapes changed us. The work helped me to have a sense of values that were important to me. That was a tremendous gift.

There are three people who have been tremendous influences: Agnes Martin, Elizabeth Murray, who's just a few years older than me, and Louise Fishman. Louise Fishman was a painter who came out as a lesbian in the art world in the '70s and did a fabulous series of paintings called *Angry Women*. She was an out lesbian in 1973 or 1974 when it wasn't popular to be a lesbian. She paid for it, but she stuck with it, remained a committed painter, and now in her fifties, it's paying off for her.

▶ ————————————————————————————————————

Preserving the Legacy

When we started out, it was a different world. The risks were different than they are now. You could say that the feminist movement was a driving force, but it was a very controversial movement. There was still an antipathy to feminism, a lot of pressure on women to be very, very conventional. Having said that, I want to give a little compliment to this institution. They hired two lesbians for one job, they created space for us to do what we do because they thought it might be important to them, and they let us do it. Because of that, it was possible to put this collection together. That's not something that could happen in today's climate, even in our institution. Things have shifted culturally. We've moved full circle so that we face an uncertain future. Some things really stuck and have an influence, and other things have dropped away.

The period of time in which we began was a time of expansion. There were more and more dollars for small organizations. In 1971, Nelson Rockefeller took the New York State Council for the Arts budget from $4 million to $50 million in one year. They didn't know how to spend all that money, so they started funding film and video. Now, we're in a different period, a period of decline. You can't be sure that all your effort will net the dollars you need to keep going.

We're in a period that looks like contraction. Let's hope it's temporary. But this raises questions about the alternative history that we have created. The Video Data Bank is a record of the art world of the '70s, '80s, and early '90s. It's a record of the changing politics of the art world as it went from modernism, with Lee Krasner talking about "nature is here and I am here," and the whole foundation for abstract expressionism, through the changing politics, into postmodern representation and identity politics. So when you look at our collection, you can spot and mark the changes in art theory and practice.

We've gone into a period where we are not sure what, if any, of this alternative history will be saved. Video is not stable. We have two to three hundred open-reel ½" tapes that need to be preserved. And more recently, two thousand ¾" tapes.[7] A lot of us are now fifty-plus years old. We're very interested in how to preserve these histories. It's the preservation of ideas that are important, images and ideas that make a counterdistinction against commercial ideas. If we lose a record of this particular era and counterculture, with such an ambitious social agenda, what are we really passing on? We're passing on Hollywood, and that's it.

What has been the impact of your work?
We didn't do it because we wanted impact. We were doing it because it was Lyn's and my work together. It was what we created, and there was a place for both of us in it. The influence is tiny. If two or three people got something that helped them to see quickly that there was a wide variety of ideas that they could experiment with to get closer to themselves, then it was a success. It was never a success in terms of dollars or television. Only a few of the interviews have been broadcast. Most of them have only been shown in closed-circuit situations.

I was on a panel with someone in Chicago a few months ago who said, "I got five thousand hits on my Web site." And I said, "How does that translate into meaning for you?" We have smaller numbers, but we had a tremendous intimacy and exchange of ideas with the audience. We didn't do it for anything other than to participate in the ideas of our generation. We wanted to build an organization and we did. We wanted to create a legacy of ideas and we did. I'm proud of it, and I hope people will have the patience to wade through some of the difficult decisions we made in terms of that work. It's hard, not easy, not about entertainment. It's about really listening to somebody talk about what's important to them and hoping that another person finds value in that.

Video

Is video still the perfect medium?
I'm not so sure. Video really was connected to the '60s and '70s. Its agenda came from *Radical Software,* Guerrilla TV, and Spaghetti City Video.[8] It was a package deal that had to do with civil rights, community-based media, and inclusion of marginalized voices. The agenda was set up by Beryl Korot

and Ira Schneider and the people who wrote for *Radical Software* and were part of the Raindance Collective. So you look at video and ask where it is now. I'm not sure where it's at, because to some extent it has completed its mission and it's time to move on.

The problem with video is we don't have enough writing about it. We've never been able to plug into art journals, film journals, TV reviews, or mainstream publications. People get frustrated. They do work, but it feels like no one looks at it. There's no critical apparatus for video even though academics are the main users.

My feeling changes about this. I'm not saying that there's no work to be done in video. While we were happy with small audiences from our community, now a lot of people are frustrated because they want more. They want bigger audiences. They want backing from ITVS or Britain's Channel 4. They want to be seen on PBS's documentary series *POV*. Now people are frustrated with the small scale of video. There are still new things happening and there are still successes. But there's not the same connection to the original agenda that there was even ten years ago.

▶

A Biological Blip on the Screen

Can you talk about the values you learned from making your work?
I see myself as part of a generation. We were born after the war. There was something crazy about a lot of people my age. Maybe we were a biological blip on the screen. I was at the Democratic Convention in Chicago in 1968. I was in the park when we were trying to roll police cars over, breaking windows, the whole thing. I see a correlation between that and what we tried to translate into a sense of an alternative organization with a social, political, *and* aesthetic mission. I was extending the sense of values I got in my early twenties from the civil rights and antiwar movements and from the first phases of feminism. Those are incredible values that were about expanding democracy. My generation, and the group immediately younger, was intent on changing the world to become more socially conscious. We wanted to end racism, poverty, and the subjugation of women. We failed in a lot of ways. But I've been fortunate to spend my life so far trying to work on these issues.

How do you see 1996?
My head is filled with the '60s and '70s, when I was in my twenties and thirties. I believe that ideas start in small spaces. For example, many have debated the value of AIDS tapes. A lot of people say that none of them did

anything. It didn't work, didn't have the influence it should have had. But that's impossible to say. You would have to be a major theoretician to say how people are influenced by small ideas. Big ideas come out of tiny ones.

It took all the arts organizations to make a tiny effect. People will say it didn't do what we thought it would do, it didn't change society. But it's all still unfolding. Now we're seeing some independent video and filmmakers go on to bigger audiences. That's an accomplishment that wasn't a possibility for people in the '70s. All of this is relational and keeps moving forward. For instance, your project will create conceptual links, showing how some things led to other things. You're creating a lineage by clarifying what happened before. You're also building an agenda, a whole range of creative ideas for the future.

What do we owe you?
I'm not sure I can see it that way. Every generation decides to take the risks they want. I'm not owed anything. The pleasure of it all has been a selfish pleasure. I have gotten a lot from what I've done. I've been able to live a life of almost perfect freedom. I've been able to make my own choices, to live how I wanted. I had an employer who was supportive of me through a lot of difficult things. I don't feel I could take an attitude that anyone owes me anything. I've been very privileged, and I'm not unhappy with the way that things have turned out. It's up to everyone else to figure out whether I did something valuable to them.

Executive Director
Video Data Bank, 1976 to the present

Collections
On Art and Artists
Independent Video and Alternative Media
Early Video Art
Americas With/Out Borders

Productions

1984	Video Drive-In: Chicago, Lisbon, Barcelona, New York City
1987	*Ana Mendieta: Fuego de Tierra* (with Nereyda Garcia-Ferraz and Branda Miller)

Compilations

1986	*What Does She Want,* 6 hours
1989	*Video against AIDS,* 6 hours
1996	*Surveying the First Decade: Video Art and Alternative Media in the United States: 1968–1980,* 17 hours

Boards
Independent Television Service
Lyn Blumenthal Fund, president

Contact Information
Video Data Bank, 112 South Michigan Ave., #312, Chicago, IL 60603; (312) 345-3550

[5]   *Margaret Caples*

Margaret Caples is currently executive director of the Community Film Workshop (CFW) in Chicago—one of seven Workshops founded across the country in the late sixties to provide minorities job training in film and television. She is a social worker and arts administrator who comes to film from a lifelong commitment to social change: especially for African Americans and women. Her early career in film was enabled by the civil rights movement's investment in a politics of images. In his article about Black Journal, *a local PBS-sponsored magazine program by and about the black community in New York that aired from 1968–71, St. Clair Bourne describes the close relationship between civil rights and media access:*

> A specific complaint was the lack of presence in the electronic media and the negative distortion that took place when we were represented. Therefore, programs, funds, and positions were made available to provide media access for Black images so that Black issues could be addressed. . . . These changes . . . were the result of pressure by the revolutionary potential of the black protest movement, pressure from the people in the streets who disrupted the normal flow of business and demanded in one form or another—some with bricks, other with pencils—a share in social processes as they perceived them.[1]

While Caples readily claims such goals of the civil rights movement as formative, as is true for many women of color, she is less ready to acknowledge that she is now or has been influenced by "feminism," a movement that especially in its early stages catered primarily to the needs of middle-class white women. In her history of black women and feminism, Ain't I a Woman, *bell hooks revisits the early women's movement from a black feminist perspective: "Few, if any, white women liberationists are willing to acknowledge that the women's movement was consciously and deliberately structured to exclude black and other non-white women and to serve primarily the interests of middle and upper class college-educated white* women seeking social equality with middle and upper class white men."[2] Audre Lorde explains how feminism was and is commonly underlined by racism: "As white women ignore their built-in privilege of whiteness and define woman in terms of their own experience alone, women of Color become 'other,' the outsider whose experience and tradition is too 'alien' to comprehend."[3] Thus, like many black women activists, Caples may not choose for herself the term feminism and the history of othering it encompasses. Even so, she acknowledges a lifetime commitment to social change for women (and others), as well as a place within the history of politicized media work told here.

Caples identifies her part in this history as allowing underrepresented people to have a voice within the media field: women, people of color, poor people, gays and lesbians, the physically challenged. As is true for many of her generation, Caples devotes her career to ensuring that there is an infrastructure in place that will allow the broadest base of people to make use of the power of the media for themselves. As administrator at CFW and board member for countless media arts organizations (like the National Black Programming Consortium, the National Alliance for Media Arts and Culture, the Chicago Area Film and Video Network, and the Chicago Access Corporation), Caples makes certain that the needs of underrepresented people are on the media agenda. "I think the impact of my participation in the media arts field has been that we've broadened the voice," she explains.

Caples is not committed to film because it is "art" but for two, more practical reasons: it is a lucrative field of employment and a powerful tool of self-expression. In this respect, her relationship to feminism and film is closely linked to stories of the many women who have struggled to find employment in the film industry. Caples's work connects her to the early pioneers in the feature film industry (Lois Weber and Alice Guy-Blache, who were successful directors in the silent period;[4] Dorothy Arzner and Ida Lupino, the only two women directors during the heyday of the studio system;[5] and Eloice Gist, Lita Lawrence, Eslanda Goode Robeson, and Alice B. Russell, black women who worked in race films),[6] as well as to contemporary women who struggle to make it in today's still nearly all-male (and nearly all-white) film and television unions. While women have historically worked as editors, costume designers, and writers, there are still only a small percentage of women in camera, sound, or directing jobs or unions. And people of color, too, are significantly underrepresented in the more technical, lucrative, or public aspects of the film industry. Organizations like CFW are committed to changing this through access and education. To this end, a significant amount of CFW's mission has been directed toward getting their students into Chicago's film and television unions.

*I also interviewed Caples because her career in film speaks to a sig-
nificant subcategory of feminist media history: that of media education
and media literacy. In the '70s, countless media collectives and nonprofit
organizations like CFW were organized to get hands-on education to
communities that had never had access to these expensive and intimidat-
ing technologies. Miles Mogulescu, who spent the '70s working at one
such institution, University Community Video in Minneapolis, voiced the
attitude of the era: "Most people probably get most of their information
from television, so why not open it to ordinary people to express their
views to the world? Anyone can learn with a few hours' training. And just
like everyone knows how to read and write, everyone ought to know how
to use television."[7]*

*While many of the organizations founded in the '70s have since closed
down—due primarily to the steady defunding of the arts, especially those
connected to a politicized position—the cause of media literacy has found
support through other avenues. For instance, Caples now does a significant
amount of her work through the public schools. She developed CFW's arts
in education program, which teaches media literacy to students at Chicago
public high schools. Don Adams and Arlene Goldbard delineate the expan-
sive goals of the contemporary media literacy movement: "Complete media
literacy means mastery of the electronic media . . . knowledge of the social,
economic, and political characteristics of the media . . . and knowledge of
the debates over the media's effects, psychological, physiological, and social."[8] They suggest that significant change in public policy, education policy, and technical facilities are all necessary for media literacy to truly succeed. As expensive and difficult as such changes might be, they counter with
the grim consequences of denying literacy: "To enter our social discourse as
a full participant one must also break the thrall of the magic box and enter
its secrets. If we fail to adopt media literacy as an essential goal of public
culture policy, we doom ourselves to enter history as its objects, not its
makers."[9]*

*Schneemann's and Hammer's work is rooted in an art-school training
and an art-world milieu (even as they turn most of the values of these institutions on their heads) that is primarily motivated by an investigation of
the connections among language, sexuality, politics, identity, and images.
Caples represents a career committed to a more straightforward economic
and political critique of film as an industry: all citizens should be provided
equal access to film as cultural capital; all citizens should be provided the
ability to read and/or make media. It would be an oversimplification to
posit these schools of thought and practice as entirely distinct. Yet it is
equally important to establish that there are multiple criticisms of American*

culture that have inspired women to come to careers in the media. And what makes film and video so exciting is precisely the murky space in which they most precariously and uniquely lie—both art and industry, technology and ideology, work and indulgence, recorder of reality and creator of fantasy.

▶

Advocate

Please discuss your work in film.
I came to Chicago to get a master's degree in social work and met a photographer named Jim Taylor. In 1971, he became the director of the new Community Film Workshop of Chicago (CFW). At the time I was working as a school social worker for the Chicago public school system. So I enrolled in the first class because I wanted to use video with student groups. I worked in the public schools, so I had to work with students in groups because I had so many schools to cover. That's how I got involved with CFW. Then, I worked on the board of directors. And in 1973, I married Jim, so that tied me even closer to the work that was going on. In 1982, I became actively involved because I went down to help Jim and ended up staying and becoming the assistant director. And now I'm the executive director.

The way I see my role in the field is as an advocate. I don't have a major work, or a major body of work. But even so, I have contributed to helping women to have a voice. I work on a lot of boards. One such board is the Chicago Area Film and Video Network: I've worked on that board for twelve or fifteen years, just to make sure that film and videomakers in Chicago have a voice, and to create a sense of community here. I've worked on the Chicago Access Corporation's board for six years. I've worked on the NAMAC [National Alliance for Media and Culture] board for six years. I've done this work so that I could have input, so that I could make sure that the voices of women and people of color are heard, and so that I could help expand the participation of those groups in the dialogue around cable, the media arts, culture, and the whole broader agenda of media.

▶

The Community Film Workshop

Can you explain to me what the CFW does?
Well, originally it was organized so that we could get minorities into the film industry. So it started out as a job training program through the Office of

Economic Opportunity. The first workshop was started in New York, and then they developed seven workshops throughout the country. The CFW in Chicago was the last. It trained in 16mm film. At that time, a lot of the television stations were still shooting and editing on film. A lot of our students went into the local market and into smaller television stations. Many went on to work on union shoots, and some joined the unions.

But we've always had to fight people on the issue that we prepare people for the industry, that it was an employment program rather than art. It's very difficult for people to understand—no, it's not difficult, they care not to—that black people just don't have money lying around on the kitchen table so that they can produce film. People have to work, people have to eat. Why do you go to school? So you can work. It has been one of the stumbling blocks: film is so expensive to produce, most people don't want to invest in training someone. You can't guarantee that the trainee will get a job. We did get money through the Mayor's Office of Employment and Training, but other organizations weren't as supportive of the employment aspects of filmmaking.

Most people who sit on panels went to art school, and they define art in the way that they talk about it there. But we define it differently. We train people to tell a story with a beginning, middle, and end, to cut on action. Maybe our pieces do look a little slick. To me that is "art." We don't have jump cuts; we don't have people panning and zooming the camera. We have particular restrictions in terms of how we train. That is so people can have a clean piece through which they can learn. Once they do their second or third projects after the workshop, then they can pan and zoom.

How do you recruit people to attend your workshops?
We put ads in the newspaper and on cable access. We have a lot of people who call for information. We start with a screening program where people have to attend four film history classes so that we can get some preliminary things out of the way. When people actually come into the program, we do hands-on training. The first week involves working with—and getting over your fear of—equipment. The students complete two films: one with voice-over and the other with synch-sound. There's no use of children, animals, or old people, because they're too unpredictable. These restrictions are implemented so that people can have a good piece to show in order to get an internship, to show as their visual résumé. These are two good films you can put together on a reel. You want people to see that you can tell a story, you can cut on action, you can expose film properly.

The program is very successful. We've had students who take our program and use that reel to get into graduate school, to skip courses at film institutions, for leverage to get money to do a small project. For instance, I'm pleased with the work of Katherine Nero. She got her master's in film from Northwestern University, and she went through our program first. She has produced two thirty-minute pieces: *The Choice* (1990) and *Wedding Bell Blues* (1995). Most of her work is about relationships between men and women.

Katherine stands out because she works as a substitute teacher so that she can get money to do her films. Most of the people who come through the workshop don't go the grant route. It's just too much rejection. A lot of times, people of color don't fit the mold of what we "should be," or what kind of work we "should be" doing. What we want to do may not always be acceptable to people who are looking for a particular kind of work. Our people just don't want to go through that rejection for $5,000.

And it gets more and more competitive for less money. You spend more time writing grants than working on your film.
Independent filmmakers today are competing with Hollywood. A lot of independent features come out of Hollywood, but they have budgets of half a million dollars to make a twenty-minute film. So you're really up against a lot of slick productions. But Hollywood still doesn't tell good stories; that means we have to deal with content. Do it as slick as you can, but more importantly, have a good story. If you keep your eye on what you see as the importance of why you're doing a piece, why you came to filmmaking, what changes you want to see occur, then you can compete with anybody.

And of course, there's been an ongoing defunding of the arts in the past ten years. What have been the effects of that on your organization?
A lot of the organizations are redefining themselves, looking at their mission, and deciding what they can do better. We're "being lean," "downsizing," all that corporate terminology. But we have to stay focused on what is key— why we got started, what was the original mission, who are the people that we serve. Right now, we still serve the same people because nothing has changed; women and people of color are still basically the people we want to serve because they are not adequately represented in this field.

▶

Black Women Come from an Activist Background

How has the women's movement affected your work? And are there other movements for social change that have been important to you as you work in this field?

I never knew I was affected by the women's movement. Black women just come out of an activist background most of the time. You just have to do what you have to do to get the job done. That's how you get into it. That's why I'm still in this field. I've tried to leave it several times.

How do you feel about being considered a part of "feminist" film and video history?
If I am among a group of strong women, then I feel good. That's what I think a feminist is—a strong woman. You have to be that in any field, but especially in media. It's not soft. The things that you come up against are very hard. It's a male-dominated field, even in the independent area. When I think about it, most of the administrators of media arts centers are women. Does that say anything? And we advocate so that we can have resources, and possibly most of the people who use our centers are men.

Is that as true today as it was in the '70s?
Yes.

I teach, and it's also true that when push comes to shove, many more boys take classes in film and video, and then, even if it's fifty-fifty in the classroom, the men have a privileged relationship to the equipment.
That's right.

You think, it's 1996, and we've come so far, and then I'll teach a class . . .
This year with our Build Illinois Grant we gave out twelve grants, and we only had one woman.

How do you explain it?
The way we train girls. We have to really look at that. Boys are reared one way and girls another. We have to start very early. Because we carry for our whole lives all those images that our mother, and aunts, and cousins, and other women around us provide. We need to train our girls to think differently about media, to think about becoming the director, the person who controls the image.

Power in Images

Can you speak about your initial mission at the CFW—to get more people of color into the industry? Why do you think it is important to have people of color working in the film and television industry?
I really think that times are just as bad as they were in the 1970s. If you look at any movie set, there still are not many of people of color—or women—

on a shoot. And that's because there's power in those images, and there's power in who controls those images. People develop their attitudes about a particular group from what they see on TV. Most people go to a movie or watch television, and even though they know some person made that story up, they *believe* it.

Times haven't changed much. We have token black filmmakers out in Hollywood, with token budgets, and with token press releases. Even with the new black programs on television, the images of blacks are still stereotypes, most are comedies, most are someone else's version of who we are. I don't see too much difference in the clowning that goes on in most of the sitcoms now and how things were previously on TV. A lot of them are cartoon characters. They aren't even as good as *Amos and Andy.* At least Andy had a job, he had a family structure.

That's why it's important to have an independent voice. We have a Build Illinois Filmmakers Grant that allows filmmakers to do longer projects. There's no money—it's just access to cameras, and Nagra sound recording equipment, and lights, and postproduction. It's important for them to have that option to make films: to create another voice, to create another vision, to create new images. For instance, we still don't see images of working-class people on TV. We don't see real family stories coming out of the many communities here in Chicago. It's difficult when you don't put money behind that kind of effort. We tend to want to build a new football stadium and not look at the kinds of images that our children are ingesting daily, and what that does to their self-image, and to the image of Chicago, the image of our communities.

Why media? What is the particular power of film or video for people in various struggles?
It's the image. People don't remember the dialogue. They remember the images. It's powerful, and you can just say so much. You can speak to people's spirit. You can touch people in their hearts. You can just get so much done. It's the image. It's the image, the image. That's what it is.

▶

Broadening the Voice

What has been the impact of your work, both at the CFW and as you sit on these various boards?
I think the impact of my participation in the media arts field has been that we've broadened the voice. People talk multicultural, they talk about inclusion. It's a great word to have in your mission statement, or in your program

guide, but it's a difficult thing to put into action. But NAMAC has worked very hard to be inclusive: for women, people of color, gays and lesbians, the handicapped. The organization has tried to include more people in the dialogue. My contribution has been to help expand that discussion around media, to include not just people of color, but more voices, period.

When I asked you the question about media you answered, "Image, image, image." But the other word you use a lot is "voice."
I do because I'm so very conscious that our voice has been stolen. Other people always run into our communities with their cameras to make a statement about us. And I really believe in "first voice." Women filmmakers have to be really careful not to make the same mistake: rushing in to give your impression of what another group is about. Instead, you really need to listen to the first voice of the people of that community. That's why independent media is so important. Because handicapped people can have their own voice, they don't need someone to come in and tell their story for them. And it's the same with ethnic groups. And we are still being raped. That's what it is—it's rape—by groups who come into our community to speak for and about us.

Twenty-Fifth Anniversary

MEGAN CUNNINGHAM (associate producer): *You've been doing this work for so many years. Where did your patience come from?*
I married a man who has a lot of patience, and he would be happy to hear you say that. I've earned my patience. As you get older, you don't let a lot of things bother you. It comes with age. This is the twenty-fifth anniversary of the Community Film Workshop. If we had given up the first year when they called one day and said, "You will not be receiving further funding," or at any of the times when we didn't know where the rent money was coming from, we wouldn't have made it. That's an attitude that filmmakers have to take: it won't be easy. But if you persevere, you get wiser and you become stronger. You learn what's important, something you don't know when you're young, just starting out. At the end, you become a better filmmaker because you bring all these experiences with you. That also happens with an organization. We bring twenty-five years of experience to helping new filmmakers.

This field started with just a bunch of people who said, "What do we do?" We helped each other. Four or five people collaborated and then they had an organization. Now young people have these organizations in place with the background to really help them. Don't waste your time reinventing the wheel. I tell young people that. Sometimes they want to start an organization. That's hard. Let somebody else do that, and you go off and make your film.

MARGARET CAPLES

Executive Director
Community Film Workshop, 1980 to the present

Panels

1989–91	Illinois Arts Council, Media Arts Panel
1991	Chicago Filmmakers, Funding for the Independent Filmmaker
1991–92	ETA Creative Arts Foundation, African-American Women in the Arts Conference
1994–97	Michigan Council for the Arts and Cultural Affairs
1995	Chicago Office of Fine Arts, City Arts Panel

Affiliations
National Black Programming Consortium
Chicago Area Film and Video Network
National Alliance for Media Arts and Culture
Chicago Access Corporation
School for the Performing Arts at Bowen High School
National Coalition for Multicultural Media Arts

Contact Information
The Community Film Workshop, 1130 S. Wabash, Suite #302, Chicago, IL 60605; (312) 427-1245; CFWChicago@earthlink.net

[6] *Julia Reichert*

Julia Reichert is best known for her leftist, historical documentary films created with her partner, James Klein, and dedicated to preserving and passing on women's and working-class history. Throughout the '70s, she and Klein made several award-winning, widely distributed "talking heads," oral history documentaries, all the while claiming they were "cultural workers" not "filmmakers." Films like Seeing Red *(1983), a feature documentary on the lives of American Communists,* Union Maids *(1976), an Academy Award–nominated film that looks at the early labor movement through the stories of three working-class women, and* Growing Up Female *(1970), a documentary on the socialization of the American female, demonstrate their simple but elegant approach to a kind of political organizing that uses film as its method. Reichert and Klein's camera gives authority and stature to voices of individuals whose lives brushed with, or even shook up, history and yet whose stories are typically left ignored, devalued, or unrecorded.*

Like all of the women discussed thus far, Reichert was initiated into her filmmaking career through the radicalism of the late '60s and early '70s. In the '70s, Reichert and Klein melded art, research, and activism. They were interested less in aesthetic innovation or personal expression than in encouraging viewers' insights into, and their own participation within, the historical, economic, and political forces that organize and limit Americans' class mobility. Reichert maintains this commitment to building a more equitable and humane society, even as her work alters in both form and content with the changing American political landscape. As the leftist movement eroded in the '80s, Reichert took a job as a film professor at Wright State University in Ohio and produced a feature-length narrative film, Emma and Elvis *(1992). She is currently working on two documentaries, one concerning prehistoric images of the female and the other, a feature-length*

*cinema verité film about children living with cancer; she also produced
with her current partner, Steve Bognar, a feature narrative about two at-
risk youths hitchhiking across America,* The Dream Catcher *(Ed Akira
Radtke, 1999). In recent years she made the decision to put effort into
mentoring emerging minority and women fiction filmmakers from Ohio,
such as Ed Akira Radtke, Aralee Strange (*This Train, *currently in postproduction), Laura Paglin (*Nightowls of Coventry, *in preproduction), and
Michelle Davis (*Mecca's Lot, *in scriptwriting stage).*

*Reichert believes that her service to the independent filmmaking com-
munity is equally important to her productivity as a documentarian. In the
'70s, she cofounded the still-thriving feminist distribution company New
Day Films as well as the now-defunct Film Fund. These organizations
demonstrate Reichert's commitment to a socialist feminism that values
cooperative, nonhierarchical institutions that seek to redress the systematic
inequities of gender, class, and racial oppression. New Day's mission is to
distribute politically progressive films. In their first catalogue the founders
wrote, "This is what New Day means to us: personal commitment, responsibility, and the desire to create a society responsive to human needs."
Still committed to Marxist socialism, as well as feminism and antiracism,
Reichert sorely misses the commitment to building services and organizations that was shared by activists in the '70s. Reichert seeks to continue
these goals as she organizes film exhibitions and contests throughout Ohio,
teaches working-class students, and serves on numerous arts councils, film
commissions, and media organizations.*

*Although Reichert acknowledges that leftist politics continue in Ameri-
ca, she says that she misses two aspects of her formative years in the American left: its collective, productive spirit and its economic critique of capitalism. She counters this with our current reliance on identity politics as both
critique and stance. The idea that the particularities of each individual's life
story are* political—*one's race, ethnicity, religious upbringing, hometown,
sexual orientation, age—was enabled by feminism's credo, the personal is
the political. However, in that all humans experience their identities uniquely, and in isolation, the identity politics of the '80s and '90s have often inspired a political landscape broken up into factions based on personal experience rather than on shared ideas or goals. Reichert's interview narrates
one socialist feminist's career in film from the '60s through the '90s. She
has spent these years making and teaching film in the service of social, not
personal, change. She allows us to see how individuals both contribute to
and are shaped by forces bigger than (if still related to) their own personal
experience.*

Growing Up Female

How did you become involved with film?
My involvement came directly out of the women's movement. In the late
'60s, I was actively participating in feminist activism—I joined the protest
of the Miss America Pageant—and in consciousness-raising [CR] groups.
I was also very interested in photography. At twelve or thirteen, I started
taking photographs, and I continued seriously all through college. I also
did radio. In 1968, I had a women's radio show called "The Single Girl,"
which shows the consciousness of the times. Later, I had a show called
"Sisters, Brothers, Lovers, Listen." Eventually, as the women's movement
developed, there was a need for voices to speak out about all these experiences, to break out of college CR groups. Photography and radio didn't seem
like the best way to speak out, because they were too specific and local.

For my senior project in college, I decided to make a film. It turned out
to be *Growing Up Female.* I had a few months, training. My teacher, David
Brooks, handed everybody in class a little windup 8mm camera. He told us
nothing about f-stops or anything like that, so it's fortunate that I already
knew about photography. He said, "Go out and shoot what you see." I had
three months like that. Then David was killed. He was twenty-four years
old. That was a big turning point in my life. I remember thinking at his
funeral service, as I sat there with flowers in my hand, that I was going to
carry on his work. All these things—my interest in photography, inspiration from David Brooks, who was an experimental filmmaker, and the
movement with its heady ideas—added up to a sense that there was a film
to be made and I was in a position to make it.

On New Year's Eve in 1970, the idea for this first film, *Growing Up
Female,* came to mind. In late 1969 NOW had just begun in Ohio. I thought
about making a film about the women's movement, perhaps interviewing
Gloria Steinem. I thought about filming our CR group. Then it occurred to
me that what was needed was a film about average women, about women's
conditions and actual lives, a film that could be shown at high schools and
college campuses that were not as radical as Antioch, where I was going to
school. I wanted to film people of several ages, from little girls to women
who were what I thought of as middle-aged. The interviewees were four,
twelve, sixteen, twenty-one, and thirty-five (thirty-five was the end of the
line in my mind at the time).

I made that film in the spring of 1970. It was shot in three weeks. While
Jim and I were editing, all the campuses closed down because of the invasion
of Cambodia. We got permission from the radical committee, which we

supported, to do our work. Kent State happened. We had refugees from Kent at Antioch. The film fit into a larger picture of a movement that included the antiwar movement, the black power movement, the women's movement, and so on.

Please talk about the distribution and reception of Growing Up Female.
It's an hour-long, black-and-white film, shot on a 2½-1 ratio.[1] We edited on an old upright Moviola that broke every day, so we learned how to fix a film editing machine while also learning to edit film. We had no idea how to use Nagra synch-sound equipment, so we got a handbook and learned from the manual. A year later, the film came out. At that time, film was not the main thing we were doing. My partner, Jim Klein, and I didn't think about showings in museums or a theatrical release. We saw that film as a tool to help the women's movement grow.

My whole thrust was to get it to colleges, high schools, YMCAs, churches. I went on the road with it. I had one print. I went to Cleveland where I had friends in the women's movement, and they arranged showings in people's living rooms. I earned enough bus money to get to Pittsburgh, where I earned enough bus money to get to New York. I went to Washington, to Boston, with this one print, calling people on the phone to arrange showings. There weren't even women's centers yet, just networks of people. Everywhere I went, I wrote down names and addresses.

My first speaking gig was in Norman, Oklahoma, in 1971. I showed the film to a big group of men and women on campus. The film was actually quite upsetting to mixed audiences. Looked at now, it appears mild and moderate, but at the time it was seen as very radical. It offended men and made women angry. I was physically threatened by a couple of men from the audience. These were big men who came up with their fists clenched and threatened to beat me off the stage for what I was saying. It was a very scary moment. Luckily, the audience realized this was outside normal behavior.

But that, of course, was the whole point. We wanted to leave women at the end of the film in a state where they were feeling that we are an oppressed group, second-class citizens, and yes, this is embedded in society. A number of women actually got that from the film. In several places a woman would stand up at the end of the film and say, "I think the women need to discuss this film alone." This was before women's centers, before any of that. It was difficult for women to say what they felt. But someone would say, "I propose that the men all leave." All hell would break loose. The men would start screaming and people were threatening each other physically. There was a burgeoning consciousness of needing separate space. Now, that's not just because of the film, but it was a catalyst for some things that were about to happen.

▶

New Day Films

By fall of 1971 we started New Day Films. This happened in the course of taking *Growing Up Female* to New York and trying to get a distribution contract. We met distributors and heard their offers. We felt as though we would be giving up our work. We would be handing it to others, all men, who did not share our goals. Their reaction when we told them about the audiences for which we intended the film—high schools, YMCAs, prisons—was, "They don't have money. Why them?" We decided to get it out ourselves. Good people gave us advice. We learned how to run a printing press and printed a poster with ordering information on the back. Out of our dorm in Yellow Springs, Ohio, we mailed eight thousand copies of the poster. Our friends came over to help fold them. By then, we had five copies of the film. Orders poured in. Pretty soon, we had thirty, then thirty-five copies, and they were going in and out; we were running to the post office every day. We did it ourselves, the billing, the phone calls.

We noticed that, at first, the film went to Brandeis and Radcliffe and NOW, the sophisticated East Coast. Then, within a couple of years, it went to state schools, then a couple of the bigger high schools, then it started renting in the South. As the women's movement spread over the next few years, we could see its growth in where the film was being used. It went to Alabama, to Catholic schools. It was really a first-step film. Every woman's group wanted something for outreach, to help them start talking to people about women's oppression. This little film was the tool.

We realized that distribution was important to the larger community of people making oppositional media. New Day was born as a co-op in 1972. We began to meet other people who were making what we thought of as women's liberation media. We met with Liane Brandon and Amalie Rothschild. Rothschild had made *It Happens to Us* (1971), a film about abortion, and Brandon, *Anything You Want to Be* (1971). We said, "Since this distribution thing works, let's do it as a group. Instead of mailing one poster, we'll mail three." New Day Films grew and is still a viable option. It's based on principles from the women's movement: the idea of collective action, not individual genius; and artists, or cultural workers, as I prefer to think of myself, taking control of their work. That means controlling the whole process, including getting the film to the audience. Your life could be about having an idea, making it work, distributing the result, and having that inform your next work. It's not just a business cycle, but a learning cycle. You learn to know your audience.

At New Day, decision making was democratic. There was no president or anything like that. We made decisions together. That comes out of the original women's movement insight that patriarchy is one of the roots of all evil. It is not just that men are in control, but also that hierarchies are a big problem: hierarchies based on money, education, being better looking, letting "experts" do it. Especially as women, we were against that. We had to hold the camera, take sound, run the projector, learn to do it ourselves. That nonhierarchical way of doing it yourself fired us up. At this time, I also made slide tapes, in addition to films, because they were cheaper. Film, let's face it, is an elite medium. That always bothered me.

[Holds up catalogue.] This might be our first catalogue. David Brooks used a sun with three rays as his signature. We adopted the sun as our symbol. In the catalogue pictures, one sees all of us, collectively. We wrote, "This is what New Day means to us: personal commitment, responsibility, and the desire to create a society responsive to human needs." And this is a distribution company! This paragraph tells the story of how we started out as a women's group and then later included films about men and broader social issues as well. We felt that feminism wasn't just about women's issues. It seemed wrong to just distribute films by and about women, so we broadened our goals. For feminism to achieve its goals, families would need to change, the lives of children and men would need to change.

▶────────────────────────────────────

Union Maids

Union Maids was shot in three days in Chicago in 1974. We shot it on video: one inch, open reel. We interviewed three women who had been labor organizers in the '30s and had been part of forming the CIO, a big step forward from the elite craft unions. They organized rank-and-file workers, a lot of them foreign born. It was a huge mass movement. We sat these women down, didn't research our subject, just sat at these women's feet and said, "Tell us your story," and they did. Over time we edited it. We were filmmakers in a community of organizers. We were doing so much movement work in Dayton that we'd get back to the film for a little while every few months.

Union Maids is a little black-and-white film, fifty minutes long. We saw it as a tool for the movement. That's how we saw filmmaking. We did not see ourselves as artists or even primarily filmmakers. I saw myself as an activist who has skills to make film. I'm still a little uncomfortable with calling myself an artist. It denotes elitism, a certain kind of individuality, as though you make art for art's sake, for yourself, not to make a difference.

We looked for activity, people in motion. With *Growing Up Female,* we had known that women would be on the move. Then we got interested in the labor movement and thought that working-class people and unions would be on the move. *Union Maids* was a great tool for bringing together the insights of the women's movement and those of labor. It often brought those groups together in union halls and at high schools and conferences. It still inspires people. It's not so much the filmmaking as it is those great stories that the women told. If I had died right after making that film, I would've added something to the movement for social change in this country. I feel very proud of it.

When we chose to make *Union Maids,* we had made two films already. We were part of a radical movement of people making media for social change. So we were faced with the question of how to make filmmaking less elitist, how to change things so that people without a lot of money could make films. Most of the people making independent work—including Newsreel and most independent makers—were from very wealthy back-grounds. That's how they were able to do it, and that's something that's not often brought up. I'm from a working-class background. So the issue of how to make film for less money was a big item on my agenda. We heard about video, and we knew Skip Blumberg and others doing community-based video projects. So we said, "We're going to try a big experiment. We're going to shoot on video, rough-edit on video, transfer what we know we want to film, and fine cut on film. We'll save a lot of money!" Actually, we didn't save that much: the transfer was so expensive. But that process did let the women talk for three hours straight without us interrupting because we weren't watching the dollars roll by. In that way, video was liberating.

Oddly enough, when that film came out, we got a huge amount of praise. It got strong reviews in New York and San Francisco—Vincent Canby thought it was great. Stylistically, it was rough-looking black-and-white. It was not slick. The critics thought that the visual style worked well with the story and where it came from, which was the left-wing movement. So our experiment didn't save money, but it worked as an artistic statement in ways that we had never even considered. As I said, things worked out. *Union Maids* was used by the movement a lot. It also played in twelve cities theatrically and got great reviews. It also got us an Academy Award nomination in 1977.

After that, we started saying that we were "filmmakers." It was hard to admit that maybe we did have some kind of special skill or talent. But there were ways in which we were becoming hooked on the beauty and power of film beyond its utility as a tool for social change. You can see it in the editing. I edited a sequence where people are coming into Chicago. It's just trains running down the track, not there for any social change reason, it's just a cool sequence. It's exciting. Kinetic. Visual. So without really saying it to ourselves, we began to get into the beauty of the medium. You can see it in the use of music and archival footage, along with the editing.

▶

Oppositional Media

One thing that was high on our agenda was the making of oppositional media. We were not working in the system, although that was the route some women took. They wanted to work for PBS or their local TV station and change things that way. I felt that they were fitting into what existed, not changing it. They still had to put on the nylons and make themselves up and deal with the bullshit bosses. How much were they changing things by just being a woman there, running the camera and so forth? Okay, they were changing things some. But, for me, the important thing was the creation of alternative institutions that would prefigure what society could be. We wanted to create institutions that would last—a women's center, a food co-op, a worker's health co-op—alternative institutions that do not depend on the powers that be in the patriarchal system that now exists.

For example, there was an organization called the Film Fund that existed for about ten years, that started right after we completed *Union Maids*. We were involved in the Film Fund with others like Barbara Koppel, who made *Harlan County, USA* (1977). We joined forces with some rich leftists like George Pillsbury and David Crocker and Obie Benz. We got the insight that radical films definitely can help to create social change and to support and broaden social movements, but making them costs money. The idea was that wealthy folks could funnel money to filmmakers through an organization with good politics that could help choose how to spend it. It would not be about who you know, as it would be if I personally went to my wealthy contacts and asked for help. This was a democratic way to distribute rich people's money. It actually did fund a number of movies by all kinds of oppressed people. I'm glad I put time into it. There, too, I, along with Barbara, brought in a sense of class politics. I always worked believing that we're doing what we're doing to change our society. It was not just personal expression.

SIMON POOLIO (cameraperson, Chicago shoot): *How has living a rural life affected your work?*

I made a decision after college to live in a small city, Dayton, Ohio. I wanted to organize in a regular community. There were already lots of radicals in the "good places" like Berkeley and Cambridge and Ann Arbor. If we were going to have a test screening, we would invite our next-door neighbor, who was a postal worker, and his wife, who were both Catholics. We would invite people from around the block with whom we played softball. That's who we wanted to reach. We felt as though, if we lived in a big city in a community of artists, filmmakers, and other sophisticated people, we would lose touch. To this day, when I edit, I see my mother sitting there with me. My mom is a nurse and an Irish woman with a great heart and a great ability to understand people. If there's something in the film that she wouldn't understand, then I say, "We've got to think of another way to say it."

Later, I moved into the Ohio countryside. All the neighbors were farmers; we went through a severe drought. I learned a lot from those four years of really rural life. Now my partner, Steven Bognar, and I live in town near Dayton. There is a big filmmaking community here to which we are very devoted.

Seeing Red

By 1977, important changes had taken place in the world. One was that the women's movement as a whole had moved through some phases in its development. We started from the realization that women are oppressed and we should be pissed off about this, and moved to the belief that we should do something about it collectively. You then saw attention paid to specific issues—abortion, healthcare, childcare—and a whole group of films that addressed those issues. Those followed the films of the first phase, the "angry films," such as our film and those of Newsreel like *The Woman's Film* (1971). Then came the "issue films." Then what I call the "grandmother films," films that looked to the past for mentors and models. *Union Maids* is one of those.

There then came a sophisticated interest in radical history: women's history, black history, working-class history. This was linked to a belief that our movement could be a mass movement that could actually take over. We became very interested in looking at earlier movements that actually wanted to contest for power. So, of course, we were interested in understanding the Communist Party. The three women who had been interviewed in *Union*

Maids were all Communists, and we didn't know it. We found it out the night of the premier screening, when we were all sitting around and talking. How we found out was this: it was the night of the world premier of *Union Maids,* in a theater in Dayton. All three women had come from Chicago to be there onstage. It was a fantastic night. Later, we were all sitting around our kitchen eating and drinking and talking, and they started referring to "the party this and the party that." We asked what that was about, and they said, "Oh yeah, we all knew each other back then, and we were all in the Communist Party." They started telling us about being party members, telling great stories long into the night. They cried and laughed; it was clearly a huge part of their lives. So Jimmy and I said to each other, "Let's make a film about the Communist Party." Then sarcastically, "Oh, right, that would be a really smart move." We tried to shake it, but it was one of those ideas that would not go away.

So *Union Maids* led us to *Seeing Red,* and we spent six years of our lives running around the country talking to Communists. We felt as though we were doing original research. There were no books on the subject that were useful to us until much later. Existing stories were either procommunist or anticommunist. There was nothing that tried to synthesize an understanding of this as a social movement that had shaped people's lives. We tried to take a point of view that was neither pro nor anti but, rather, understood people's motivations.

It took a long time to make that film. We had a kid. The collective in which we'd been living for six years stopped being a collective. A lot of us became more isolated. The whole sense of being in a collective movement really started to break down. The election of Reagan was very demoralizing. We didn't know where we were in relation to the country. We had thought we were swimming in a river, and then we were stranded on the shore watching that river flow right on by us. It was a depressing time, and in that context *Seeing Red* came out.

Seeing Red is a feature-length color film made for theatrical distribution. I think of it as very much a feminist film because it's about personal life stories and has strong women characters. It focuses on the oppression of women within the party. That film and *Union Maids* are the best expressions in my work of what I call a socialist feminist politics or ideology. We really tried to look at working-class oppression along with female oppression. We tried to locate the potential for liberation in combating capitalism as well as patriarchy. *Socialist feminism* comes closest to identifying my politics, and those two films exemplify that perspective for me. They are inherent critiques of capitalism and calls for action on the part of regular folks, along with warnings about possible dangers in that action.

Emma and Elvis

Then my relationship with Jim broke up. That was horrible; it took several years. I made a feature fiction film on 35mm on my own. I cowrote the script for *Emma and Elvis* and made it in Ohio on a low budget. It was not financially successful, but it was a pretty good film. The main character is a forty-year-old woman, and there's not a lot of interest out there in the stories of forty-year-old women.

I'm glad I made it. I learned a lot and had fun. *Emma and Elvis* was an attempt at a political fiction film about the ways in which movements for social change become different over time in that the focus of activity changes. It tells the story of a woman who has lost touch with the world around her. She doesn't think that there are any radical developments until she stumbles onto the new generation. That's sort of what happened to me in real life. She comes into contact with gay liberation movements, punks, people with values that are different from hers but who are also antiestablishment. They don't have the theory, but they hate consumer culture and are anticapitalist and antiracist. They want to see the system changed. So the film is about two generations finding some common ground. Like *Union Maids* and *Seeing Red, Emma and Elvis* is a story about activists. But it's a dark story. It's about someone who lost her way and then reconnects. All my films have a positive ending. That's just my outlook on life.

Distribution Supported Us

How did you fund the last two big projects, and how do you support yourself?
I paid my way through college. I had a job as a waitress just to get *Growing Up Female* out of the lab. My mother gave us her life savings—which amounted to about $1,100—to finish *Growing Up Female*. We paid her back, several years later, by taking her to Europe for a month.

Seeing Red was our first big-budget film. Making it probably cost about $400,000. We got an NEH [National Endowment for the Humanities] grant in the waning days of the Carter administration. They were funding great stuff back then. Then we did what is now the usual fund-raising routine. We got other grants. For a year, I went around and threw parties at which I showed clips and gave a pitch. When we finished the film, we were not much in debt. *Emma* was a $700,000 project. We set up a limited partnership with investors. Those were the kind of people who I had earlier felt were on the other side of the barricades. Who else has $5,000 to $10,000 to throw into an independent film? It was an interesting couple of years. I'm working on a film now and looking for grant money like everybody else.

Distribution supported us. In addition to being good political work, it turned out to be profitable. Jim and I supported ourselves on our work for eighteen years. But funding sources have been eroded since the Reagan administration. Mass-market video took a lot of profit away from independent films. So I started teaching in 1986 and really loved it, especially because we teach nonprivileged, mostly working-class kids. Now teaching is how we support ourselves. Teaching was a new challenge; and it turned out to be a damn lucky break as well as a great source of health insurance.

Do you want to talk about the films you didn't make?
Jim and I wanted to make a film on women in prison, and I wanted to make another about women's work lives and daycare, the ways in which women are torn in several directions. Those never got made. There were several films about women that never got made, partly because I was in partnership with a man. He was great—a good partner and a good filmmaker—but there were certain subjects in which he couldn't participate. Actually, his resistance to the idea of doing a film on daycare and the stresses on women's lives was part of what led to our breakup. He didn't want me to do it. We talked about it, off and on, for a whole year.

Come to think of it, all the films I never made were a little more weird and radical, stylistically, and all were about women.

▶

No Mentors

Can you talk about the work of other people that is important to you?
I'm a member of a generation without mentors. No one showed me the ropes as I do regularly for young women now. Especially not in Ohio. Other than David Brooks, who died very quickly after I met him, I didn't have a mentor. I did feel part of the larger world of Newsreel, which was an influence. However, it's probably a good thing that we weren't invited into Newsreel. Newsreel was a radical, national film collective. They made quick, rough, down-and-dirty, black-and-white films, specifically for organizing. We followed that model. But Newsreel found us to be a little too soft politically, too interested in women's stories, and in the aesthetics of film—beautiful editing, beautiful sounds. We wanted to make something a

little more polished. But we had tons of friends in Newsreel, and it was definitely an influence. I would say that in my formative years I was influenced by Edward K. Murrow's *Harvest of Shame* and by the Robert Flaherty Film Seminar. I look at all kinds of work now. I teach film and have a seventeen-year-old daughter who's very culturally hip. The person I live with, my partner, is thirty-three, so he's in a whole other generation.

What is your place in the history of feminist film?
Because I was part of that early generation without role models, there weren't that many of us, and we had great influence. I think I've been a role model in a couple of ways. One was in promoting an understanding of the need to do your own distribution and to get out and meet your audience face to face. The other influence I've had, as a working-class person, has to do with insights about class analysis and the related oppression of race. That's always been very high on my agenda. I always tried to make that part of what we did in film. There were very few of us who were working class. Today, I see that influence less. I don't quite know where it went. But if I stood for something, it was the empowerment of working-class women and women as a whole, and the empowerment of filmmakers to distribute their own work.

It's now 1996. The '70s are remembered with nostalgia. Where are the movements for social change now? What was the impact of what you did in the '60s, '70s, '80s?
Movements are here today, still critiquing sexism, racism, discrimination based on sexual preference. They are still based in an antiestablishment, even anticapitalist, perspective, although not consciously. There's not much emphasis on Marxist theory. I'm still basically a humanist Marxist. It's too bad that's gone away. People are still doing oppositional acts and revolutionary acts, but there's less emphasis on creating organizations that will last. That's a sign of the times. People are more atomized and less inclined to trust each other. I believe that there's power in collective action, in lots of people doing similar kinds of things. So it's too bad that the world is a less trusting place.

I've learned a lot from younger activists. They've taken the notion of doing away with patriarchy and gone a long way with it. I was at a demo on the West Coast after the L.A. rebellion. Everyone got together, about fifty young people, and said, "Well, what are we going to do?" Everyone was to put in his or her two cents. I was appalled. I said, "Isn't there any leadership? You guys have to have a plan!" But they evolved the plan in an hour or less of discussion. This was a big group, everyone had their say, and it all worked. I was amazed. We had a great demonstration—it was wonderful. I feel positive about that energy and ingenuity, but there is a lack of class and economic analysis. We should be talking more about capitalism and putting less of an emphasis on identity.

JULIA REICHERT

Films

1970	*Growing Up Female,* 16mm, 50 min. (with James Klein)
1974	*Methadone: An American Way of Dealing,* 16mm, 60 min. (with James Klein)
1975	*Men's Lives,* 16mm, 45 min. (with James Klein)
1983	*Seeing Red,* 16 mm, 100 min. (with James Klein)
1991	*Emma and Elvis,* 35 mm, 105 min.
1999	*The Dream Catcher,* 35mm, 99 min., produced with Steve Bognar (directed by Ed Akira Radtke)

Service to the Field of Media Arts

1972	New Day Films, founding member
1978–82, 1986–89, 1996–97	The Film Fund, founding member
1986–87, 1996–97	Ohio Arts Council
1987 to present	Ohio Valley Regional Media Arts Coalition
1997	Cincinnati Film Commission

Distribution and Contact Information

New Day Films, 22-D Hollywood Ave., Hohokus, NJ 07423; (201) 652-6590; www.newday.com

[7] *Michelle Citron*

Michelle Citron, experimental filmmaker and film production professor at Northwestern University, has been teaching and producing films and videos since the mid-'70s. Her early works like Self-Defense *(1973),* Integration *(1974), and* Parthogenesis *(1975) are experimental films that speak from a feminist position to the male traditions of avant-garde film in which Citron was educated in the sixties. With* Daughter Rite *(1978) and* What You Take for Granted *(1983), Citron perfected her unique integration of film experimentation and feminist content through a complex mix of autobiography, documentary, fiction, and experimental style. In response to the increasing difficulties of actually making* film *due to the steady defunding of granting organizations in the 1980s and 1990s, and also due in part to the effects of ageism, Citron has recently chosen to work in other media: "Film, as it's construed now in this culture—meaning the Hollywood, indie culture—is young, exciting. It's a generational thing. The older you are, the harder it is to raise money. Because of the political climate, there's no more public funding. I've been doing performance for the past four years. That's really satisfying, but it leaves me with nothing tangible to hold." In response to the ephemeral nature of performance, Citron recently completed an experimental written memoir about memoirs,* Home Movies and Other Necessary Fictions *(1999). She also continues writing and performing about her ongoing interests in families, mothers, daughters, autobiography, incest, and feminism. However, she is quick to reflect that personal barriers connected to her working-class upbringing may, in fact, compel her even more than issues raised by her gender.*

Her large body of work notwithstanding, Citron is perhaps best known for one film, Daughter Rite, *an experimental documentary about women's relationships to their mothers. Citron believes that this film, one of the most written about and widely screened works from its era, has been so important because it effectively bridges the gap between experimental style and feminist content. The tension between these two concerns has been on-going and highly productive within the feminist film community. There has been a great deal of academic debate pitting self-consciously "theoretical" films (like the '70s films of Chantal Akerman, Laura Mulvey, Sally Potter, Yvonne Rainer, and Jackie Raynal)[1] against more "realist" political films (for example, the documentaries of Julia Reichert), which were inspired by consciousness-raising and feminist organizing.[2] The antirealist position questions whether a radical critique of patriarchy, or other dominant systems, can be expressed using the very structures, forms, or language that is used so effectively to espouse the sexist ideologies under attack. "So what actually happens then," writes Eileen McGarry in an early contribution to these debates, "is that those relationships already coded within the dominant ideology enter into the film unquestioned by the aesthetic of realism."[3] If your goal is to change a reality that is itself formed in and through systems of discourse like film, can this be possible if you do not also image reality differently, or at least make the audience self-aware of the imaging of reality that is always taking place? No, E. Ann Kaplan suggests: "Realism as a style is unable to change consciousness because it does not depart from the forms that embody the old consciousness."[4] Claire Johnston explains why: "The 'truth' of our oppression cannot be 'captured' on celluloid with the 'innocence' of the camera: it has to be constructed/manufactured."[5] On the other hand, if you are trying to reach average women, to express to them radical changes and possibilities, will they be interested in or capable of also unraveling a new* form *as they attempt to digest new content? "Sometimes, it is important, in analyzing a feminist documentary, to recognize other priorities than those involved in challenging dominant coding," writes Barbara Halpern Martineau.[6] She goes on to identify some of these priorities: education, granting authority to unconventional figures, advocacy, stimulating change.*

Importantly, Citron points to a crucial and often obscured truism underlying these debates. Yes, "critical theory" can often be used as a tool to silence, confuse, or overpower, sometimes serving as a kind of "If you can't speak this language, then you are not invited here" system. However, she reminds us that "theory" is nothing more than a systematic attempt to explain to one's self, and then to others, one's experience and world. "Theory opens up everything. It takes the world and shifts it on its axis a sixteenth of an inch. You see the world with fresh eyes." Her move toward theory and theoretical films, and then her more recent move toward what she now understands to be the more universally understood discourse of narrative, remains primarily motivated by her need for self-knowledge. "Briefly, my own work is fueled by a desire to understand my life in relation to larger cultural forces, as well as a yearning for a presence in the world."[7]

Although Citron established her career making avant-garde forms accessible to average viewers, in her late-'80s scholarly article "Women's Film Production: Going Mainstream," she foretells a great deal about the contemporary state of feminist film.[8] *Currently, a surprising number of once avant-garde film and videomakers believe, as does Citron, that it is through more* mainstream *forms, such as narrative features, that feminist ideas can reach wider audiences and therefore effect real change. Citron writes that independent feminist avant-garde production and distribution, although certainly forums for disseminating radical ideas and forms, are necessarily limited through mechanisms as varied as lack of distribution, media (il)literacy, and feminist backlash. In an analysis of changes in the feminist film movement from the '70s to the '80s, B. Ruby Rich suggests that technology also contributed to feminists' move toward the mainstream, which began to occur "when the feature-film format decisively became the only choice for directors in need of prestige, investment, and industry recognition. The parallel development of video in this same period further eroded the formerly lucrative educational market for 16mm and diminished the status of women working in shorter forms (documentary, personal film)."*[9]

Although it remains certain that the most radical of feminist principles will be watered down and potentially even quashed within the more conventional systems of Hollywood feature or broadcast television production, it is also true that these systems are adaptive and that their audiences also adapt. Thus, Citron now dedicates a certain amount of her professional energy to writing feature narrative screenplays, still admittedly experimental, but produced for the broader film industry, not the avant-garde. In Home Movies and Other Necessary Fictions *she explains her move toward narrative even as she continues to attempt to represent personal, psychological, familial traumas within a politicized framework: "Narrative can integrate experiences for which memory has not always functioned adequately. Narrative renders the incomprehensible understandable. Narrative offers the much needed illusions of coherency and cause and effect where there were none. Narrative puts the author at ease."*[10]

Citron's, and the field's, move from margin to center evidences a broader cultural shift in that many of the core values and critiques of the '70s women's movement have influenced and altered the larger culture, have themselves become "mainstream." Meanwhile, it seems that marginal culture becomes more and more absent because it has become either so demonized as to be erased or so commodified as to be absorbed. This said, perhaps the central question that defines contemporary feminist film projects (like Citron's and my own documentary, Women of Vision*) is just how mainstream one is willing, or able, to go.*

▶───

Give Me a Voice

How did you become involved with film?
I was in graduate school completing a doctorate in cognitive psychology, studying how the brain processes multiple channels of information. I used images as stimuli in my experiments. My adviser said, "You know, there's a film department here. Why don't you take a course and learn how to take photographs?" I found a Super 8 film production class, and for five hours, once a week, I watched experimental films. I'd never seen anything like them in my life. I'd grown up working-class and all I knew about film was Hollywood. After that semester I decided to become a filmmaker. I finished up my dissertation in 1974, started making films, and found a job teaching film. In 1974, there were hardly any women teaching film production in U.S. universities. The school that ultimately hired me had three lawsuits filed against it for not hiring women. All they cared about was that I had my Ph.D., had made films, and knew enough about film to teach.

When you took that first film class, what made you realize you had to be a filmmaker?
I've always felt verbally insufficient and that I was a terrible, terrible writer. That came from my childhood, my class, which has followed me. I felt that those images from the avant-garde—[Stan] Brakhage, [Scott] Bartlett, [Kenneth] Anger, [Maya] Deren—were eloquent, accessible.[11] It was shocking to me that these nonnarrative films had so much feeling without stories. I could speak through this medium; I thought it would give me a voice.

What was important to you about the avant-garde films you made, and can you focus on one film in particular?
I was very influenced by structuralist film, and in 1974, I made a film called *Self-Defense,* which was made entirely of optically printed, manipulated images. It's a short film, about five minutes long. In the first half, a woman performs Tai Chi, and in the second half you see first one woman, then multiple women, doing karate. The beginning images are abstract and very hard to read, and slowly as the film unfolds they become clear. The images of women doing karate are layered; they are symbols of what, at the time, I called socialization.

So I made this film, an experiment with form that had, I felt, a strong feminist content. The people in my film class, who were almost all men, loved the film and wanted to talk exclusively about the techniques I had used to get the visual effects. But when I showed the film to women's groups, the women were bored. They were also confused, having no access to that experimental film language. I felt split by the experience. So I split my creative self. I made two films. One was a documentary and the other was a structuralist film. I just split my creative sense. It wasn't until *Daughter Rite* that I could take those two parts of me—the part that cared about the form, the material, and the language of film, and my feminist part—and meld them back together.

Was there a relationship between the women's movement and your experimenting with a new feminist film language?
Definitely. I started college in 1966. In 1968, I became active in the women's movement at the University of Massachusetts in Amherst. Then in my senior year, I was one of two undergraduates hired to teach a discussion group for the introductory psychology class; I taught a section on feminism. So I was very involved in feminism, but in psychology, not in film. In the film class, the only woman whose work we saw was Maya Deren. The emphasis of the course was "expanded cinema," how consciousness was expanding through drugs and spirituality and how we needed new forms to express this experience. It was very '60s. This idea of new forms clicked with my understanding of feminism. I made avant-garde films for years with an intense need. I believed that you couldn't talk about women's experiences with old Hollywood forms.

▶━━━

Daughter Rite

Please talk about the reception, the life of Daughter Rite.
My father gave me my family's home movies when my parents got divorced. I spent three years obsessed with those movies and was determined to create something out of them. The film evolved through a long process and many dead ends. When it was completed, I sent it to the festivals where my work had been shown before. It was rejected. The judges would write comments like, "Send this woman back to film school. She doesn't know how to edit, she doesn't know how to write."

Mark Weiss saw the film at the Alternative Cinema conference at Bard College in 1979. Frances Reid and Elizabeth Stevens from Iris Films, a women's film distribution company, also saw the film there. The New Day people were there, too. They were my heroines and I had sent them the film, but they were confused by it. When it was screened at the Alternative Cinema conference, it found its audience: women and men who were aware of the theoretical earthquakes, such as psychoanalysis and semiotics, that were shifting film theory. That conference changed the life of the film, and suddenly it was invited everywhere. Probably the most important place was the Edinburgh Film Festival. In 1974, Edinburgh ran, in addition to the festival, a conference on women in film. Important work from British feminists was presented at that conference. Then they organized a conference in 1979, and *Daughter Rite* was invited.

I had been reading theoretical work from Europe. At the same time my political work was based in grassroots organizing, and I had had the experience of watching my avant-garde films be inaccessible to women. Somehow, in *Daughter Rite* all these threads came together. I wanted to make a film that would critique the notion of a transparent documentary and, at the same time, critique avant-garde film practices that I thought were inaccessible. At Edinburgh, there was tension between women who came out of grassroots organizing and believed that documentary film was the only kind of politically correct film to make, and, on the other side, the more theoretically based women who believed that the only politically correct film was one grounded in an avant-garde practice. When *Daughter Rite* was shown at the Edinburgh Festival, it became the lightning rod for these discussions. It was the right film at the right time in the right place. It was magic.

I really believe that so much of filmmaking is luck. Of course, you need a tremendous amount of discipline, and I actually do believe in talent, whatever that means, but you also need luck. After Edinburgh, *Daughter Rite* was picked up by film festivals all over the world. Even now, twenty years later, it's accessible and emotionally moving to women. Last year I was in Taipei showing *Daughter Rite* at a women's film festival. At the end, a woman shyly stood up with a translator. She asked me if I thought that the betrayal by a mother through silence was worse than betrayal through criticism. She was talking about the moment in the film where the daughter, Stephanie, describes being raped and its aftermath: when she tells her mother and is met with silence. Then the young woman in the audience talked about her own life: how she was raped and how, when she told her mother, her mother screamed at her for bringing shame down on the family. It was an electrifying moment. And it started an intense conversation between the women in the audience that had nothing to do with me. I faded into the background. It's amazing that the film still has that kind of emotional power.

That's not luck.

It's not luck. But I could've made the film at a historical moment when no one would have seen it or cared. That's the luck part.

▶ ———————————————————————————————————

Theory, the Avant-Garde, and Politics

One of the hardest things that I deal with is trying to make this documentary for a general audience for whom the intricacies and stakes of academic theoretical debates are very inaccessible. You started talking about some of those positions being bridged by your film. You're a woman who makes film and you also work in the academy. Could you explain the tension between academic work and filmmaking practice?

I think that my attraction to theory is linked to my relentless upward mobility, my intense need to escape my family. I was determined to make "art." "Art," with its upper-class and middle-class resonance was important to me psychologically because it was a way to put distance between my family and myself. I could make something that nobody in my family could understand.

On the one hand, I sometimes feel intimidated by theory and understand why my students find it difficult. On the other hand, I understand the importance of theory. You see the world with fresh eyes. Theory opens up everything. It takes the world and shifts it on its axis a sixteenth of an inch.

I grew up very confused and with a lot of pain. I think that's true of most people. How do you make sense of that? Theory is one way. I tried to take all the ideas that helped me understand my life and the chaos I was drowning in and transform it into something accessible to people. I'm critical of pure theoretical positions, just as I'm critical of positions that don't recognize theory at all, that look at the world naively. I don't like naïveté. When I teach directing, I tell my students that you have to direct from your head and your heart, from your intellect and your body.

This is a history of feminism and film, and theory . . .

. . . is essential to that! Theory is essential to all avant-garde film. When I first saw avant-garde film in the early '70s, I was reading Gene Youngblood's *Expanded Cinema.*[12] Whatever you think of that book, he was trying to approach film historically *and* theoretically. It's not the high theory of psychoanalysis and Marxism, but theory is just a tool to help you understand the world: how things work, why you get seduced by the image, why you lose your sense of self while you're watching a movie, why you cry when you watch Bambi's mother die.

In your career, as you've written about it, you made a move away from the avant-garde.
Right. Now I'm trying to do narrative.

Can you talk about that?
There are things I've wanted to speak my whole life. I have strong self-censors that make it difficult to talk about things like class and power dynamics within the family. Avant-garde film gave me a way to avow and disavow at the same time—to speak but not too clearly. Now I'm more attracted to narrative because it allows me to say things more directly than I could with an avant-garde language. My narratives aren't conventional. The work I'm doing now has anywhere from two to five intertwined narratives. It's not mainstream, but it's storytelling.

The choices that a woman artist makes—what she says and what forms she uses, what she understands intellectually, what she's feeling emotionally, what's going on politically—are fueled by both the micro and macro. As a feminist, I believed that I was making films for women. Well, guess what? I was also making them for myself. I was using politics as a way to obscure my own need to speak. Yet talking about something personal doesn't deny the political dimensions.

▶

Influences

What work has influenced you?
The two women who have influenced me the most are Adrienne Rich and Maya Deren. One's a filmmaker, Maya Deren, the Great Mother of avant-garde film. *Meshes of the Afternoon* (1943) is an extraordinary film, even now. I just showed it. It went over the heads of most of the men in my class. Yet the women understood it as an expression of a woman's fragmented identity. The theoretical work that has been most important to me is feminist writing, but not necessarily feminist film writing, although that, too, has been important. But more important has been the work of Adrienne Rich as a poet and theorist, her ability to bind metaphor, art, and politics. *Of Woman Born* contains intensely personal descriptions of being a mother and raising children together with an analysis of the institution of motherhood as a political construct.[13]

Are there other artistic, theoretical, or political traditions that influence your feminism?
I came out of the antiwar movement. And Marxism really influenced my feminism. I have a more complex relationship to psychoanalysis. Because

I was trained in psychology, I have an acute awareness of how it's used in a therapeutic situation involving two living people. I also have to ask: how does one take theoretical constructs from that practice and use them in completely different contexts? Yet it can be useful. So Marxism and psychoanalysis have influenced my feminism. Isn't that what everybody says?

No.

Isn't that interesting? Semiotics. I was intensely influenced by Barthes and Metz, but it's like a foundation you lay down and build things on top of.[14] You don't see the theory in an obvious way within my work. But it helps me think about what I'm doing. Men's work has influenced me, too. John Cassavetes, definitely. And Martin Scorsese is the best filmmaker in the United States today. They care about storytelling, the material of film, and how to manipulate that material to get across what they need to say.

So many women I've interviewed have apologized for naming men who've influenced them.
I don't know where that comes from. Men have been important. When I started, there were no women. I took two film classes when I was in graduate school, a Super 8 class and a 16mm class. There were twenty-five students with only one other woman, the same woman, in each class. She's a film director now, Bette Gordon.

Did you have any other women as role models?
My role model was my grandmother. I grew up in a multigenerational family—three generations living in the same house. In the '50s that was peculiar. Everybody else was shifting into nuclear families in the suburbs. Mine was a working-class, matriarchal, Jewish family, ruled by my grandmother. She controlled everything. I grew up in a family with strong women, and I was my grandmother's favorite. She worked in a factory. It's not like we're talking about upper-class power here. But she was strong. She groomed me to take over, but it was subtle.

Film School

Can we talk about women in film school?
I started teaching when I got my doctorate at the age of twenty-five. I was such a young teacher for so many years.

What's different now about teaching in film school and what hasn't changed?
There's a lot more women teaching. I've taught at three universities: Temple, Grand Valley State University, and Northwestern. At Temple and

Northwestern, I was the first woman in the department. That situation created intense problems. For my first job teaching at Temple University, the department chair who interviewed me took me to lunch, drank a lot of Scotch, and put his hand under the table where he slipped it up my skirt between my legs. I'm twenty-five years old, I'm terrified, I'm almost choking, and I can't say anything to him. I just smile and think, "Well, I'll get this job." And I did. It wasn't until we had an analysis, a theory, a politics that I could understand that horrific moment.

Faculty composition, in terms of gender, has changed dramatically. But the composition of the students hasn't changed. I started teaching in 1974 at Temple University, and I'm now, in 1996, at Northwestern. In the freshman class, 50 percent of the students are men and 50 percent are women. In the senior class, when I teach advanced directing, I'm lucky if I have two women out of fifteen.

I teach in a department with six faculty in production; all but two are women. So it's not about role models. It's surprising. I know that many young women go into television because they see that medium as more flexible, more mobile. They can readily become producers in television. They can conceptualize themselves succeeding in corporate America. Film is still too much like an art, and women can't imagine a place there. It's disturbing to me. They don't see themselves as film directors. Most of the experimental work today is done in video, not film. When people talk about an independent filmmaker nowadays, they mean someone who wants to make their "indie" feature as a calling card to get a three-picture studio deal.

The field has changed in twenty years, just look at the proliferation of film schools. When I went into film, a woman was an outsider. There was no way I could imagine ever going to Hollywood. There were only two women directors: Ida Lupino and Dorothy Arzner.[15] In the '70s, there were a few more: Agnes Varda and other European women.[16] But still, to go into film was to make a choice to be an artist, an outsider. Teaching, being an academic, softens my outsider status some. But for students today, it's different. Video, maybe, still has that outsider status. Film doesn't. Do you know why there aren't any women?

No. I've thought about it. I think it has to do with . . .
Money?

Technology. Women's relationship to their own source of power. Why is it always in film classes that men want to be directors, and women are doing the behind-the-scenes work?
But the other women directors you've interviewed haven't made that choice.

MEGAN CUNNINGHAM (associate producer): *What do you think about women being more involved with video than with film?*

I've always thought of video as more "feminine" and film as more "masculine," which is why I like film. Video is more process-oriented. I did make a film, *Parthenogenesis,* which I shot on video. I would shoot every morning, with two women musicians, and then in the afternoons we would watch the tape and talk about it. The process of video is so different from that of film. When you direct a movie, you are directing a small army. It's about taking authority. It's about possibly firing people and about saying, "Not today," and "Give me this shot," and "I have no time for this now." It's no different from running a university department. Video, because you can play it back to your subject immediately, is a very different process.

▶ ───

Obstacles

What obstacles did you face?

I faced the obstacles of my family, who didn't think that a woman should go to college. I put myself through college by washing test tubes with hydrochloric acid for thirty hours a week. My family, for all the strength they gave me, also created tremendous blocks that propelled me to succeed. And obviously, so did the culture. When I see a barrier, it raises the hair on my neck and I want to tear it down. And whatever insecurity or sense of insufficiency I have about myself is more about class than about being a woman.

And we live in a society that doesn't understand class. We can't even talk about it, but we can at least be verbal about gender.

Right. The ways in which I trip myself up have more to do with class than with being a woman. Now I feel barriers connected to age. I've tried to get funding for a number of films, but I'm not a twenty-seven-year-old boy—or girl. It's hard to get films made.

What are the age barriers you're experiencing?

Film, as it's construed now in this culture—meaning the Hollywood, indie culture—is young, exciting. It's a generational thing. The older you are, the harder it is to raise money. Because of the political climate, there's no more public funding. I've been doing performance for the past four years. That's really satisfying, but it leaves me with nothing tangible to hold.

What will be the longer-term impact of how much we value the fresh voice?

I've been watching these lesbian features. They're mainly coming-out stories where you get ninety minutes of foreplay and then a weak sex scene. Maybe people like that if they're twenty-four years old. It doesn't speak to my life experiences.

We're living in a society that devalues that knowledge.
Well, I'm writing a book. I would love to make another film, but I have many ways to express myself. I'm an artist, not just a film director. If there is a barrier, I'll move in another direction.

Film is the voice that most people can hear, but it's so expensive that a lot of us decide to speak another way. However, I did just produce a feature film, The Watermelon Woman.
Congratulations!

I'll tell you about it later. I won't do it again—the amount of time and energy that it takes is really stupid. A hundred people could have made $1,000 videos with that money.
It's very complicated. One of my scripts has been optioned. It's not like I haven't had confirmation that the work is good. It's just hard to get the film produced. It's been easier to write a book: just me and my computer.

▶ ───────────────────────────────────────

A Footnote in History

What do you think is your place in the history of feminist film?
Daughter Rite is an important film. I joke that it's the movie that will not die. It said something, in terms of feminism and film, about borders and permeable boundaries, and about crossing them. I feel wonderful to have made a work that spoke to as many people as it has and affected people's lives. The most rewarding thing about making art or teaching is that you touch someone. That sounds so corny, but that's what we are all after. That's why we have conversations. I know that because *Daughter Rite* is an important film, I will always have a footnote in history. But that's not why I made the movie. It's hard for me to talk about this. I feel self-conscious.

It's hard for women to talk about it.
It's funny. When I go to the university and talk to my dean about a raise, I have no trouble pushing myself. At those times I can say, "I'm one of the most important women in film of my generation. They're just about to publish this huge book in Europe about my work." But that's when I'm pushing for something. It's harder when I am having a more intimate conversation, if I'm not hustling.

Earlier we were asking why there aren't women film directors. Maybe one reason is this difficulty women have with saying, "I'm important." One of the secondary purposes of this project is hearing women talk about why they're valuable.

I like the power I get from being a filmmaker. When a woman stands up after seeing my film and talks about her relationship with her mother, I know I have somehow enabled that. That feels strong to me, and it's absolutely about power. It's different from being in a film history book, which helps me get a raise.

What do we owe you?

Five dollars. Five thousand dollars. I don't know. I made a space. Someone sent me a book, an anthology of Illinois poets, and there's a poem in it that was written for *Daughter Rite*. I don't know the woman who wrote it. But something I cared about rippled out and affected someone I never met. I opened up a space where another artist could write a poem.

I struggled intensely to open that space for myself. And because my life as a woman at this moment in history is similar to that of other women, when I open it up for myself, I open it up for others. It's a struggle because every time I make a film or create, I get anxious and scared. It's as if I'm telling a secret that nobody is supposed to know. I have to trick myself to finish the project. I say, I'm just doing this for myself, I don't have to show it to anyone.

Most women trick themselves to get past the anxiety of expression.

It's about exposure and vulnerability. Good art, even if it's not personal, always creates a vulnerability for the artist who makes it. That's what is scary. I don't like to be vulnerable, even though I understand the rewards of vulnerability. This is not a safe culture for women to be vulnerable in: we get fucked, raped, battered.

I think you're right, in that when a man puts himself out there, he's not going to be hurt in the same way.

Part of what I'm writing about is autobiographical film, like Ross McElwee's *Sherman's March* (1985). The reviews said this male filmmaker was courageous. Men get applauded for their confessions. Women don't, because women say things that people don't want to hear. Women talk about being raped or being abused as children. Society doesn't want to hear those things.

When women do autobiography, it's confessional, but when men do it, it's courageous.

MC: *What did you get from your work that kept you on a straightforward career path?*
Daughter Rite is so visible that I can't disappear. I'm going to Austria in about three weeks because of that film. And I'm intensely ambitious. I started running when I was eight years old and I never stopped. Well, that's not quite true. I'm not a workaholic like I used to be.

Don't romanticize my life or have any illusions about it. I haven't made a film since 1983. I spent five years, in the '80s, with $100,000 for film development, making a film that fell apart when I got ill. That film and the $100,000 are gone, and there is only a fifteen-minute reel to show for all that money, time, and energy. I spent a lot of years feeling like a failure because I hadn't made a film in so long. Even though I will make art, no matter what—and I do hope that this book will be as important as *Daughter Rite*—I spent years feeling terrible. The shift to performance and writing is easy to talk about now that it's happened. But for years I would wake up at three o'clock in the morning and feel anxious, as though I had peaked too early and had nothing left to say. I felt wretched because my ego is very involved in my work as an artist. It's hard. I was in that place for about seven years. But I'm not there now. I sound like I have it all together, but who knows what next year will be like?

Films

1973   *Self-Defense*, 16mm, 4 min.
1974   *Integration*, 16mm, 8 min.
1975   *Parthenogenesis*, 16mm, 25 min.
1976   *Birth Tapes*, video, five at 30 min. each
1978   *Daughter Rite*, 16mm, 55 min.
1983   *What You Take for Granted*, 16mm, 75 min.
1983   *Mother Right*, video, 25 min.
1988   *Great Expectations*, 16mm, 15 min.
1999   *As American as Apple Pie*, CD

Plays, Performance, and Publications

1991   *Pandora*, play
1992   *Speaking the Unspeakable: How We Talk when Words Fail*, performance
1993   *The Simple Act of Seeing*, performance
1999   *Home Movies and Other Necessary Fictions* (Minneapolis: University of Minnesota Press)

Distribution and Contact Information

Women Make Movies, 462 Broadway, #500, New York, NY 10013; (212) 925-0606

Michelle Citron, www.rtvf.nwu.edu/faculty/citron

[8] *Vanalyne Green*

Vanalyne Green, a videomaker and associate chair of the Film and Video Department at the School of the Art Institute of Chicago (SAIC), is best known for a series of videos she produced in the 1980s: Trick or Drink, A Spy in the House that Ruth Built, *and* What Happens to You? *I have taught* Trick or Drink *in several different college classes focusing on a range of feminist topics from women's illnesses to feminist autobiography. This tape's masterful conjoining of familial drama (her parents' alcoholism), autobiography (Green's dieting, bulimia, and similarly obsessive relationships to men: she wants to eat them up), and the broader culture makes it one of those exceptional works of feminist art that speaks both to its core communities (children of alcoholics, women with eating disorders) and to viewers who have not directly encountered these particular experiences. In a feminist classroom, especially where there are men or resistant "post-feminists," educational tools like this are key because Green's deeply autobiographical work ends up also speaking broader and more accessible truths. The personal is the political.*

Green came to video through a feminist art education at the Feminist Design Program at Cal Arts (California Institute of the Arts) in the early '70s. Her first video was a collaborative piece on menstruation made for Sheila Levrant de Bretteville's program. According to Cecelia Dougherty, the new feminist art education in Los Angeles was based on a critique of traditional art education. Until this time, art school (and the art world) was for most women an insurmountable fortress built on ideals of male genius and artistic virility, and an old boys' network. The Feminist Art Program supported a politically based art production and pedagogy that believed that women should learn from each other: "There was an underlying radicalism, a hybrid of personal transformation therapy, a sprinkling of Maoist ideology (criticism/self-criticism), and a lot of sexual exploration and feminist cultural production."[1] At the Feminist Art Program, women's work was central and women's experience core. The radical education offered there involved incorporating consciousness-raising into art classes taught by and for women where "women discussed not only their work, but also their lives, dreams, memories, desires and possibilities for the future" (Dougherty, 9).

Judy Chicago originally founded the Feminist Art Program at Fresno State College in 1969.[2] "Chicago's purpose was to allow women to come together in a safe place—that is, outside the framework of male-dominated culture—to experience themselves more authentically as women, to raise each other's consciousnesses, and then to use these experiences as a source from which to make art."[3] In 1970, the program moved to Cal Arts, a new art school. Miriam Shapiro was on the faculty and codirected the program there. In 1971 Arlene Raven and Sheila Levrant de Bretteville were added to its faculty.[4] In 1973, de Bretteville, Chicago, and Raven established the Women's Building, a now infamous structure that housed an amazing array of artistic and political functions all run by and for women, including a public center for women's culture. This center, the Feminist Studio Workshop, offered an alternative space for feminist studies and the making and exhibiting of art. The Women's Building closed its doors in the '90s.

Green, a product of an education that valorized video, explains that it is always "the Ellis Island of art forms": cheap, easy to learn, and unencumbered by already threatening histories of male, hierarchical power and prestige. In her history of early feminist video art, JoAnn Hanley explains: "Without the burdens of tradition linked with other media, women video artists were freer to concentrate on process, often using video to explore the body and the self through the genres of history, autobiography, and examinations of gender identity."[5] Green suggests that she has recently become less confident about speaking from a purely autobiographical position because this method seems stale after decades of feminist use. Yet neither does she champion a return to formalism, evidenced in the direction of the work of many of her students. Her latest video, Saddle Sores, attempts to integrate both approaches while still maintaining feminist content in its quest to understand why even feminists (who know better) do not practice safer sex when overwhelmed by heterosexual desire.

Green's ruminations about her many conflicting feminist influences are of great interest to me. Her relationship with her parents plays a significant role in her work, but so does her place within a cohort of video artists, her status as a feminist student, and her professional life as a feminist teacher. For instance, Green recounts that what originally drew her to the Feminist Art Program—Judy Chicago's central, dominating personality and drive, not to mention Chicago's need to get away from her own mother—ultimately resulted in pushing Green away from Chicago and to another role model, Sheila Levrant de Bretteville. Green's experience with her own mother, then Chicago, then de Bretteville, and now as a feminist video professor herself highlights a formidable conflict raised again and again in these interviews and the history they sketch—a deep, abiding, and nearly universal generational ambivalence. How do we feel about our mothers and other older women? What do we owe them? What do they owe us? What about when we become the older women? And it doesn't end there. Green's personal journey, like my own, from student to teacher is marked by another contradiction: what Green felt she needed as a feminist student is not proving to be the same for the later generations of women whom she now teaches; and what her students seem to need is certainly not what Green feels she herself desires as a feminist teacher. "It's like blood transfusions with different blood types." Younger generations of women are not reborn in your image but come to school as people already in response to your generation's image. There is both sadness and joy in engaging with a generation so like and unlike you.

Green's observations on feminist teaching reflect another major issue defining feminist media: it is hard to support oneself as an artist, especially in a society that continues to defund arts granting (and other supportive) institutions; therefore, many feminist artists support themselves by teaching. One of the serious catch-22s of this profession is that while women often choose to teach to facilitate their own creative work, most of their time gets spent facilitating the work of others. Green calls teaching "service provision," being "an emotional and intellectual prostitute." She associates it with many similar feminized sectors of our current economy—not to mention that least-valued of occupations, mothering. She identifies a sometimes greedy, demanding, consumer base that believes that it is purchasing everything a teacher possibly has to offer. "What's happening with teaching is what's happening with every sector of the labor force; there's a greater discrepancy between rich and poor." And feminist teachers are saddled with further work obligations in that many maintain a political or personal connection to their feminist students on top of already significant workloads. Only recently have academics, like Green, begun to question publicly their rights and practices as laborers within an institution.[6] Green's discussion of her ambivalence about teaching underscores the precarious economic existence experienced by most women artists who have very few other options. Given such constraints (not to mention the personal and political obstacles women face), Green testifies to the courage of feminist artists who demand their practice even as necessary support systems wax and wane.

The Feminist Art Program

I was nine units away from my degree in psychology at Fresno State College. In my last year, I decided to take art classes because I'd been good at art in high school, and I thought it would be fun. Originally, I hadn't majored in art, because my mother told me that it was too competitive. I signed up for a figure drawing [class] and a sculpture class, and I thought I would pick the one that I liked the best. The teacher of the sculpture class was Judy Chicago, then known as Judy Garowitz. She strutted and swaggered across the room and said, "I moved two thousand miles to get away from my mother." Well, I had ambivalent feelings about my mother, too. But here was someone who talked about it, and a professor, no less. I knew that she was the teacher for me. Judy asked us to go around the room and talk about our ideas for art projects. I wanted to take a female mannequin and suspend it from a hook attached to a mechanical device that would make it go around in circles. She said, "Do you know that is a woman's image?" I lied and said, "Yes." I knew nothing.

The sculpture course lasted a semester and included doing performance art in the nude up in the hills of the Sierra Nevadas. Then she interviewed women for the new program she was starting, also at Fresno State, but just for women students. I really wanted to be in it; Judy was very dynamic. One of the things she did was have us call each other if a student couldn't make it to class. Of course, a good portion of the time we were just slacking off and we were caught. But getting a call from her or another student asking if we needed a ride to class or help in any other way was quite astonishing at that time. It still would be, I suppose. It translated into a feeling that I was accountable and couldn't get away with the usual passivity I was accustomed to performing in a class.

After my interview, she accepted me into her new women's art program but told me I'd have problems. She was right. How to say this? In some ways, Judy was a bit of a fascist. She called the one-year program "personality reconstruction," and it was. It was probably the closest thing to EST I'll ever experience. We had weekly dinners that usually ended in a systematic confrontation of one of us. At one of the meals, when it was my turn to be "confronted," Judy picked up a wine bottle and threw it across the room in response to her frustration with me. By the end of three months, I was clearly in a group of women with whom I didn't fit in. I'm sure she wanted me to drop out, but I didn't. Many of the other students were seemingly more radical than I was. I felt rejected in a program that was supposed to be about nurturing young women students.

It took me a lot of years to pick up the pieces. I did that by working with Sheila de Bretteville, whose teaching style was as profound but less confrontational. Not coincidentally, they were both red diaper babies and deeply committed to mobilizing students to participate in the aesthetic and social concerns of the day. Still, they had different methodologies. Sheila let me incubate. I worked with her for a year in the Women's Design Program at California Institute of the Arts [Cal Arts]. This was one of the most exciting periods of my student life. During that time at Cal Arts I wasn't even officially registered. Suzanne Lacy talked Sheila into letting me come into the program, without paying and officially registering, as long as I participated fully. Later I was able to get credit for that time in spite of the fact that I hadn't been a paying student. It makes me sad. As chair of the video department here, I'm a cop in the sense of enforcing rules like, "You don't get to use equipment unless you pay for it and blah, blah." But I was nurtured in a more generous and forgiving time period.

Later, when I was in the Women's Building, I was part of a group called Feminist Art Workers (with Nancy Angelo, Laurel Klick, and Cherrie Gaulke). Suzanne Lacy, Bia Lowe, and Susan Mogul were in that scene also. Nancy and I made a tape about how women work together called *On the Road*. Part of it holds up over time and part of it doesn't. We shot it in one take; Nancy Buchanan was the cameraperson. Two footprints, representing each of us, go through various obstacles together as a way of revealing how we (as women) handled collaboration, competition, and envy. I loved working with Nancy. She's one of the overlooked and signal people of that time on the West Coast. Her tape *Why I Went to the Convent* is an unforgettable piece.

Can you think of other influences on your development?
In terms of filmmakers, Su Freidrich was important to me, particularly in the way she divides and organizes her films conceptually.[7] I was inspired by her when I did the baseball tape *[A Spy in the House That Ruth Built]*.

MEGAN CUNNINGHAM (associate producer): *So what happened with Judy Chicago?*
There was a real fundamentalist streak in the group. One day, for example, I hung a goofy painting I'd made to hang on a diagonal, and Judy said, "It doesn't go that way." Well, it was my painting, wasn't it? This is one little example I give to demonstrate the contradictions of creating a program to help women find their "own voice" and yet at the same time teaching those voices that they have to be discovered in only certain approved ways.

Teaching

Many women artists have a moment when they feel that permission to be an artist was granted. I'm not sure that men even think about that. What do you think about that, especially now that you're a teacher?

I came to SAIC wanting to impose my feminist agenda on young women (sound familiar?), and then I needed to step back from that, especially with young students who were raised by feminists. They really needed to define that territory for themselves. This was hard. It was like blood transfusions with different blood types: what was important to me did not translate for my students. I felt that I had a life-changing gift to give them, but they didn't want it.

Another issue: in a classroom, I often find it easier to give young men more attention than my women students. The men seem more comfortable with not knowing and still feeling they have a right to be there. I have to be very conscious of my teaching to encourage women students. They know too well how to be in the background.

I had a breakthrough in a class one day. A woman was talking about "PMSing." I loved that she used premenstrual syndrome as a verb. All the women in the class woke up. We talked about how it's illegal in the U.S. to advertise sanitary napkins using the color red. It was amazing how the guys in class became so subdued in such a loud way. They didn't know how to step back. Somehow, their silence was deafening to me. Women students can be silent in a way in which they become invisible.

I haven't figured out how to teach well and make my own work. I feel as though being an artist is being a professional supplicant—a professional taker—and that being a teacher is closer to being an emotional and intellectual prostitute. The things you give to students can't be quantified; they pay money—a concrete amount—and you provide services in an unquantifiable amount. I'm like a sex worker, except my services are emotional, social, and intellectual.

Do you teach as a way to support your work or because teaching is important to you?

Teaching is good for growing up. I'm always interested in learning social and psychological skills and find the challenges of the classroom compelling. But being a copy editor was better for my work because I could more easily detach. When I teach, I feel as if I'm giving one and a half of me. At the end of the day, there's just a half left.

John Hanhardt [senior curator of film, video, and new media at the Guggenheim Museum] said that he had begun to think that the time of fruitful connection between the academy and artists had passed. I've had students say, "I can call you at home because I didn't meet with you this week and you owe it to me." What's happening with teaching is happening with every sector of the labor force in the United States. Everyone's anxious to get their money's worth.

▶

We've Been Here Before

What specific ideas did the younger women reject?
I went in assuming that my women students would want to read what had been inspiring to me—*The Mermaid and the Minotaur, The Bonds of Love, The Dialectic of Sex,* for instance[8]—that they would want to be in a study group; that they would identify with the idea of working among themselves in some situations without male students; and that they would want to know the history of the feminist movement. I don't find those things to be true, generally speaking.

Do we still need consciousness-raising? Students feel they don't.
Since there still is discrimination against women, I think there still is a need for young women to meet with each other and have consciousness about social, racial, and class differences.

As a woman, I often engage in overcompensatory teaching. Students in high school are not given access to great portions of this history. For example, they come to SAIC without much exposure to other types of art making besides the Great Masters narrative, and teachers have to work against the idea of the individual artist and for collaboration, among other styles. I tell my women students that they might want to look at women artists, say, Susan Mogul, Suzanne Lacy, Leslie Labowitz, Lee Lozano, or Claude Cahun. But many students don't want to look at that work. They're still invested in the ideas of purity, pure inspiration, and the preciousness of that. It's difficult to say, "Actually, we've been here before."

Is it that they don't care, or is there a way that as feminist teachers or historians we haven't made that accessible to our students?
You're right. We can do much more. I think it's an uphill battle. There's nothing in the culture to encourage them to look at that work. They're not getting it in the earlier stages of their education. Maybe women historians and artists aren't doing enough, but it's not easy.

Video

Why video?

After my parents died, I went and house-sat in Palm Beach. I was going to do a piece about my family and their alcoholism. I spent three months worrying about it and two weeks writing the script. Originally, I performed the script because that's what I did—I was a performance artist. People who saw the performance said that it would make a good video. As it turned out, my boyfriend, Matthew Price, was a professional sound technician and a frustrated artist. We were a good pair because of his ability to guide me and teach me certain things. For my part, I was able to give him some thrills and the sense of how you put something together that begins in an amorphous state—the psychological stuff. So we would go into the BBC (where he worked) and shoot and edit at night.

But I'm less sure what video means now. In my class "Film/Video: What's the Difference?" the video students tell me that they're taking the course so that they can have an intelligent argument when film students ask them "Why video instead of film?" The technology is so much in flux that we have to think past comparing one with the other. At the same time, video has always represented something that I love: it was the lab space for experimenters crossing over into different media. Video came out of sculpture, performance, happenings. It was fertile. For me, video had to do with Judy's attitude that you must put women into nontraditional art forms. That way, she said, we would be able to say something interesting without being inhibited by "Masteritus."

When my tapes started playing at mainstream venues, such as the Rotterdam Film Festival, I was shocked. Women makers were peripheral. The experience of women as equals was natural for me because of my education. But at Rotterdam, I couldn't help but think, "Oh my God, this is totally patriarchal! Why would a woman in her right mind go into film?" I don't understand why more women don't stand up and fight for this more economical form—video—that has had really interesting moments in the community, instead of looking at art as social power. Why do women defect to film? Why not legitimate this thing that is so much more politically interesting? In that sense, I've always been kind of hardcore about video because it's been the Ellis Island for women, African Americans, poor people. Why haven't more people fought to legitimate it? That's really sad.

You made a clear statement, but you prefaced it by saying, "I don't know." You do know. Why don't they do it?

They don't want to be marginalized. Video is marginal. How that's going to change, given that all these things are collapsing, I don't know.

▶ _____

Autobiography

I was just talking this morning to my friend Doug Ischar, who thinks that the time to do autobiographical art, such as feminist narrative, is over. I'm working on a tape now about getting a nonlethal sexually transmitted disease from, I think, a cowboy with whom I had an affair *[Saddle Sores]*. I've been trying for four years to figure out how to work with the material so that it doesn't default into bathos or "heterosexual woman gets victimized."

Perhaps the problem is that the criticisms of society women artists registered in the '70s and '80s still prevail in many ways. We have to invent new strategies to discuss the same persistent inequalities without being accused of being negative and self-indulgent.

Why do you or your friend Doug think that autobiography is dead for feminists, or even in general?
I don't think it is, exactly. I do think that there are certain tropes—the close-up of the eye in the pixel-vision camera, or "This is a story about . . ." or irony and pathos—that we've seen before. I'm as interested as anyone else about saying things in a fresh way. Some of the subject matter has been explored in earlier work, but it's not like those problems have been resolved in society or in an interior psychological way. So how do you say it in a way that isn't troped out?

I've talked to several women today who are committed to decidedly autobiographical work. It's probably true that most of those women are people of color and/or lesbians. I think the experience of white, straight feminists is underlying what you're saying.
It reminds me of that article that Jane Gaines wrote, "Politically Incorrect Claims of Heterosexuality." She used my piece *A Spy in the House* and Bette Gordon's piece *Variety* [1982] as examples of the dilemmas. Maybe the work reads as retro, but there's something there to which we still need to pay attention. Gregg Bordowitz's *Fast Trip Long Drop* [1994] addresses the ways in which, even in gay and lesbian work, some things get clichéd. His tape, for me, is a turning point in that we can go back and look at certain aspects of gay culture and say, "Enough already. We have to find new ways to say these things. We have a history."

One could say that Bordowitz's tape is a metavideo about AIDS video history. It was once a fresh art form; now that history is a burden. I think that's why a lot of students don't want to go to history, because they don't want to take responsibility for knowing that twenty years ago another artist already did this.

I agree. These are bad times. There isn't much of a crossover between art and politics; there is not enough to drive people in overt and exciting ways, so makers are rehearsing formalist exercises.

▶ ───

Feminist Video History

How would you define your place in feminist film and video history?
I've had this amazing history. To be part of these moments, working with these various groups of women—I wonder how it happened to me. I stumbled into things that changed my life. Maybe I would've found them on my own or maybe I'm not giving myself enough credit. I did things that other women around me couldn't or didn't do. I articulated some things that were important and found ways to be funny and inclusive. In talking about women's sexuality, I was able to find some crossover audiences, particularly in the baseball tape [*A Spy in the House*] and the tape about my parents' alcoholism [*Trick or Drink*]. I looked for audiences outside of feminism and I found them. With *What Happens to You*? I have seen other women learn from my mistakes in terms of how to do a tape about depression, how to do work about interior states. I've been happy to see other women use that tape to see what you can and can't do.

What do we owe you?
I have two answers to that. One is you owe me nothing. The other is what a curator once said, "I've been looking at work, and I can see your influence." You owe me nothing but something.

I'm interested in what you're doing here. How are you going to use these interviews? How are you planning to tell this history?

It's an absurdly large project, and yet also it needs to be done. This history hasn't been told, it's not archived, it's not passed on.
I remember that day at the roundtable [preproduction research meeting held at the John D. and Catherine T. MacArthur Foundation in Chicago]: everyone, young and old women, felt as if they owned this history. It was so sad and precious and cute. I remember talking with Kate Horsfield about why I agreed to do this interview today. I told Kate that I agreed to

do this out of vanity. And the next reason was I've lived this history, and it's not really articulated that much now. And I suppose I have a sense of ownership.

Everyone does own this history—it's completely alive—and twenty years is hardly "history." I've talked to 150 people who all own a version of it. What can I do in the face of that? It seems absurd that they won't share some of it and true that they can't tell it all. That's why I said, "Tell me your story," instead of other things I could ask. That's what you own, that's what you have. I did this rather than involving you in a debate with other women about whose version of the history is correct.

▶ ─────────────────────────────────────

The Loss of Community

It's interesting to have come out of that rich, fertile ground at the Women's Building, where we were so excited to be giving each other support and doing things. We really had goodwill toward one another. I realized how far things had deteriorated when I attended a conference on women and video at Hunter College in the '80s. Every woman I knew was not speaking to at least one other woman there. It was a switch from "Oh, isn't it wonderful and exciting? We're discovering new things" to "Some of us are getting ahead and some of us aren't." In real terms, things aren't equal. That was the nadir of the women's movement in the media community. I had lived in New York for ten years at that point. Almost all of my women friends were painters or writers. It was too dangerous to have women friends in media; people were too beaten up.

Is competition the explanation for that community breakdown? And where are we now in terms of a women's media community?
For sure, backlash is part of the explanation. I remember that Sheila de Bretteville, who is now the chair of the design department at Yale, said in 1978 that we'll see a backlash, and it will be more than we can imagine. And it was. I was living in New York in the '80s, the bull market era. It was inconceivable that *Roe v. Wade* would be contested the way it was. That had an effect, and so did the way there wasn't a women's community but various communities. The sex conference at Barnard—that was a signal moment of the division in terms of the different directions the movement would take.[9] Those differences were key with regard to why women turned on each other. Experientially, it felt scary. There was no support there and a need to get it elsewhere.

What do you feel the situation is now in 1996?
Women say they don't want to be feminist artists. Having cut my teeth with Judy Chicago, that's so sad. What is feminism but behavior that's in support of women's rights and acknowledging that some things are discriminatory or unfair? What's to argue about? What's not to be a feminist about?

◆——————————————————————————————————

VANALYNE GREEN

Videos

1984	*Trick or Drink,* ¾" video, 20 min.
1989	*A Spy in the House That Ruth Built,* ¾" video, 29:30 min.
1991	*What Happens to You?,* ¾" video, 35 min.
1998	*Saddle Sores,* BETA, 20 min.

Distribution and Contact Information

Video Data Bank, 112 South Michigan Ave., #312, Chicago, IL 60603; (312) 345-3550

Or through the artist, SAIC, Video Dept., 112 South Michigan Ave., Chicago, IL 60603; (312) 345-3540

[9]   *Constance Penley*

Constance Penley is the author or editor of eight books and countless articles, a founding coeditor of Camera Obscura: A Journal of Feminism and Film Theory *(as well as an associate editor of the earlier journal* Women and Film*), and the chair of the Film Studies Department at the University of California, Santa Barbara. Her focus has shifted, quite dramatically at first look, from initially writing about avant-garde, formally challenging feminist film to considering mainstream feminist popular cultural production such as prime-time soap operas, pornography, and female fan culture. In the '80s and '90s, Penley edited anthologies and authored her own work on feminism and science fiction, feminism and new technology, and feminism and pornography, including* Close Encounters: Film, Feminism, and Science Fiction *(1990),* Technoculture *(1991), and* NASA/TREK: Popular Science and Sex in America *(1997). Penley states that these shifts are not so radical if one considers that the goals that underlie her studies do not change: a commitment "to make feminism popular culture." Penley currently finds that there is less need for her to focus on alternative feminist cultural production because a great deal of feminist action now occurs closer to the centers where power actually lies: for instance, in television, feminist pornography, and other cultural forms where women's strong role as makers, viewers, and subject matter is undeniable.*

Penley's scholarly interests also mirror the shift from margin to center in the careers of many filmmakers (and scholars) already detailed in this study. To explain, she posits a contradiction that defines much of the current feminist landscape. Whereas a great deal of "feminism" is perceived to be alienating to average women, many women and the cultural productions that they nevertheless enjoy evidence the values and ideals championed by the women's movement: "I looked at the issues women in fan culture deal with in their stories and in the videos they make. Not a one would call herself a feminist. . . . I set out to learn why this particular group of women couldn't identify with feminism. I discovered that they believed that all feminists are antipornography, antisex, antimen, and antipleasure." So now she finds feminist culture in places that might not be self-described as such.

Penley's concerns and opinions about feminism, film, television, and cultural studies have contributed to the changing shape, and the increasing institutionalization, of these fields. As is true for all of her contemporaries—women who fought against the entrenched sexism of the academy to create new fields of study that propose both feminist subject matter and method-ology (e.g., cinema studies, women's studies, black studies, chicano/a studies, Asian American studies, queer studies)—Penley connects intellectual work to political goals. "Producing, critiquing, interpreting, and teaching (litera-ture) were often perceived as front-line activities in the 1970s,"[1] explains Lisa Maria Hogeland in her study of '70s feminist cultural productions. Energized, and in some manner authorized, by the burgeoning discourses of "critical theory," many scholars founded their careers on an understand-ing that discursive systems like film and teaching were arenas where change can occur. Within film studies, it was and is feminist work to seek to change the traditional language and content of films, as well as the language and content of academic teaching and writing, so that they no longer replicate the commonsense concerns, compulsions, and power structures that were the basis of more traditional systems. This politicized understanding of scholarship and teaching provided the fuel for the "p.c. debates" of the late '80s and early '90s, where some scholars and politicians argued that dis-tanced, objective, traditional (male) approaches to knowledge—approaches, they believed, that were at the very foundation of this and other Western cultures—were being threatened by a more committed, partisan, personal pedagogy, this to the society's certain doom.

When I interviewed Penley, one of my scholarly role models, I also became more clear about a difficult phenomenon that I confronted on several occasions during the research for this project. As one of a relatively small number of women who were the first-generation pioneers of my scholarly field, cinema studies, Penley and her cohort are now middle-aged women, perhaps not even yet at the height of their academic careers. They do not perceive themselves as firmly entrenched, because they have fought precariously for every gain and toehold that they have won. And yet so they seem to the two, ten-year generations of feminist film scholars who follow them. Younger female scholars study the first generation's writing for comprehensive exams and then establish their own feminist position in relation *to those of these pioneers (see interviews with Welbon, Negrón-Muntaner, Oishi). While the scholars who created this field feel they are simply living their lives and doing their work, younger feminist scholars perceive this work to be already part of* history. *And while the women who created the field perceive their places as something for which they struggled, younger scholars see them as developed sites on the intellectual map. Penley jokes: "It seems funny to me when young women come to me and ask, 'How did you get to be a feminist film theorist? Where did you go to school to study feminist film theory?' In the '70s, there weren't any schools in which to study feminist film theory, there weren't any programs."*

Only those formally schooled within feminist film scholarship can take for granted that it has been around for approximately twenty years. But isn't that okay? This study raises again and again the question, what does the next generation owe to those who preceded it, those who made the field in which younger women now work? Yet Penley raises an important flip side to this conundrum: what does any one woman owe to her culture, her generation, and those who follow? She ends her interview by invoking the "'60s principle" of struggle on many fronts. I think that this is an apt way to describe her career thus far and the legacy she leaves behind. Younger feminist scholars can learn from the way that Penley demonstrates the adaptability and flexibility of one woman's intellectual work, struggling on different fronts across the span of a committed career.

▶ ───

Why Film?

I'm not someone who came into film because I had a passion for the art form, although I certainly did develop that passion later. Growing up, all I saw were films like *The Mole People* at Saturday matinees or *Thunder Road* at the drive-in. I didn't get hooked on film until 1967 when I saw my first Godard film in the Student Union at the University of Florida. I remember stumbling out of the screening of *Pierrot le fou* completely flabbergasted, asking myself: "How in the world is what I just saw up there on the screen a *film*?" But even after I figured out the answer to that question, I was never satisfied with just acquiring the expertise to appreciate all that formal complexity—the art of film, if you will. I was also drawn to film because it was a popular medium, and as a feminist I was looking for a medium that could convey feminist ideas to large numbers of people. As it turned out, I think that popular feminist medium was television, and not film, certainly not Hollywood or so-called independent film.

Please talk about your own history within feminist film scholarship.
It seems funny to me when young women come to me and ask, "How did you get to be a feminist film theorist? Where did you go to school to study feminist film theory?" In the '70s there weren't any schools in which to study feminist film theory, there weren't any programs. We had to make it up as we went along, in the journals that we started, in the festivals we organized, in the conferences we put on. It took a long time to bring this work into the university. Most of us, in the '70s, led two lives. There was the work we were doing toward our graduate degrees (almost none of them in film departments, by the way) and there was the work that we were doing outside the university.

It tells you a lot that the word *feminism* appears nowhere in my very formalistic UC-Berkeley dissertation. I remember my thesis adviser telling me that I could have a brilliant career if I would just lose the feminist stuff: "*Camera Obscura* will be an albatross around your neck," he said. When I gave the speech at his retirement party, I thanked him for his patience in not minding that I had never taken any of his advice. He just laughed and said, "I have three daughters. I'm used to it."

One of the reasons that I wanted to work in film was that it was such a new field, with many more opportunities for women than in the more established humanities disciplines. From early on, it seemed that half the people in the field were women. They were not only creating feminist film criticism but also charting the direction for film studies itself. This is still true today. Think about all of the energy around the Console-ing Passions conference, which was started by a small group of women back in '92 who felt that there wasn't enough space within Society for Cinema Studies to present all the new feminist work on television and video. Now it's the most vibrant international media studies conference that we have.

▶

Women and Film and Camera Obscura

Can you talk about some journals from that period?
My origin story begins with an epiphanic moment of walking into Cody's bookstore on Telegraph Avenue and discovering that there was a magazine that brought together women and film. It's a good origin story because it emphasizes just how stunning that discovery was. Remember, we barely had feminist literary criticism in the early '70's, much less film criticism. But rather than tell that story again, I'd like to talk about what I think were some of our successes and failures over the (Oh my god, you're going to make me say it) nearly thirty years of feminist writing about film.

The *Women and Film* that Saunie Salyer and Siew-Hwa Beh created in 1972 in Los Angeles was completely new and original. Not only did it publish the first feminist critiques of Hollywood film, it also tried to find films that represented an alternative to "dominant cinema," as we called it then, such as films by Godard, Kaplan, and Makavejev. It also began a much-needed excavation of film history to uncover women's contributions to that history. Ida Lupino and Dorothy Arzner were two early archaeological finds.

The original *Women and Film* editors saw the project of developing a feminist analysis of film as central to the aims of the women's movement, especially the Marxist-feminist-anarchist strand of it with which they were allied. For this interview, I went back to read the editorial in the very first issue of *Women and Film*. It was a sobering experience. The editorial identified six immediate problems that needed to be addressed: a closed and sexist industry; "false" images of women on the screen even in supposedly "liberal" films; the publicity packaging of women as sex objects, victims, or vampires; the auteur theory that valorizes individual genius, almost always male; the elitist hierarchy and vicious competitiveness of the cinematic system itself; and, finally, the prejudice and discrimination that prevent women from being on the faculties of film departments or in production programs. Do you see why I said "sobering"? It's been almost three decades now, and we've solved one of the six "immediate problems"—the last one—or maybe just half of it because women are still not adequately represented in film production programs or in the jobs that follow from them.

Just because we didn't make a dent in the Hollywood system doesn't mean that we shouldn't respect the successes we did have in academia. No other humanities discipline has been so shaped by feminism. And the insights of feminist film theory have been highly influential on other disciplines, from English and art history to sociology. For those of us who experience teaching as closer to being in the trenches than living in the ivory tower, it means a lot that we've been able to introduce so many students to feminist analyses of media and culture.

But our failure to make a dent in the Hollywood system (and the horrible realization that things may have gotten worse!) sure has pushed me to think about what other areas of media culture might be more open to feminist intervention.

Can you talk about the reasons why four of the Women and Film *editors broke off to start* Camera Obscura?
Well, according to Ruby Rich in her recent *Chick Flicks,* the four of us (myself, Janet Bergstrom, Sandy Flitterman, and Elisabeth Lyon) went over to

the Dark Side. We proceeded to destroy *Women and Film* and then viciously and opportunistically build *Camera Obscura* on the still-warm ashes of our worthier predecessor. But I was there, and I don't remember having a Darth Vader moment! I remember two reasons for wanting to start a new journal.

The first, and at the time the most important, was that we wanted to work collectively, which had been promised to us when we first came on to *Women and Film*. It became clear that this was never going to happen, even after we went through a lengthy and emotionally draining mediation process supervised by a therapist who specialized in working with troubled progressive groups. (Is this Berkeley-in-the-'70s enough for you?)

The second reason for breaking off, which I can now see directly followed from the first, was that the four of us were beginning to believe that we needed to expand our theoretical understanding of how films work and how they work in relation to spectators, but we had little say in the direction of the magazine, even though by that time we were doing the majority of the research and writing. We felt increasingly that if we wanted to find true alternatives to dominant cinema, we had to know in great detail precisely how it functioned. We thought that the analytical tools of structuralism, semiotics, and psychoanalysis could help us give a better description and explanation of the cinematic system that we wanted to counter. What and how much do you have to change in that system to produce a truly different kind of film?

As you can see from the first issue from 1976 of *Camera Obscura* (now a collector's item, available on eBay, I'm sure!), we continued *Women and Film*'s efforts to critique dominant cinema, but in a much more theoretical way by translating and publishing "The Apparatus," Jean-Louis Baudry's groundbreaking essay on the impression of reality in the cinema. And alongside the Baudry analysis we published two studies of films made by women that we felt meticulously deconstructed the Hollywood system on the way to creating a feminist narrative, Jackie Raynal's *Deux Fois* (1970) and Yvonne Rainer's *Lives of Performers* (1972) and *Film about a Woman Who . . .* (1974). *Camera Obscura* continued that dual focus for much of its history (2001 will be its twenty-fifth anniversary), even after taking a cultural studies turn in the '90s toward a wider range of visual culture, including everything from television and video to noncinematic imaging technologies such as X-rays, sonograms, and mammography. It was during this period that the new generation of editors changed the undertitle from *A Journal of Feminism and Film Theory* to *Feminism, Culture, and Media Studies.*

Subversive Strategies

If our critique of dominant cinema managed to describe the system but not change it, our attempt to find a truly alternative feminist cinema foundered too, or at least had to take new directions. The *Camera Obscura* project deliberately focused on avant-garde filmmaking practices as the best source of strategies to subvert the dominant Hollywood system. We paid little attention to feminist documentaries because we felt that they reproduced the standard talking-heads-speaking-the-truth style of traditional documentary. They simply weren't self-reflexive enough for us at the time. But my own teaching and research on documentary over the years has really changed my mind. One of my favorite courses to teach is Experimental Documentary, in which I try to show that documentary filmmaking is, by necessity, the most experimental filmmaking of all. Some of my favorite early feminist documentaries that were in fact very experimental are Valeria Sarmiento's *A Man When He Is a Man* (1982), Sara Gomez's *One Way or Another* (1974), and Trinh T. Minh-ha's *Reassemblage* (1982).

Our early focus, then, was on the kinds of films that seemed constructed to refute, subvert, or transgress Hollywood film styles. Besides Raynal's *Deux Fois* and Rainer's *Lives of Performers* and *Film about a Woman Who . . .,* we looked at the films of Marguerite Duras and Chantal Akerman.[2] We felt that we could see certain common strategies used by these filmmakers to frame the woman differently, to reposition her in the narrative, and to enunciate an active woman's desire. In other words, we wanted to identify how they were attempting to overturn or reconfigure the fixed dichotomies of Laura Mulvey's famous concepts of the "male gaze" and "female to-be-looked-at-ness." A number of these filmmakers put the woman's whole body into a static frame so that the body would not be fetishistically cut up. They didn't use classical cinema's system of shot-reverse-shot, which, as film theorist Raymond Bellour demonstrated, tends to set up a system that subtly privileges male agency at every level of framing, voice, and action. And in these films the woman looked straight into the camera; so much for being reduced to pure "to-be-looked-at-ness." When we were making the argument for the subversiveness of these common strategies, we were in no way trying to come up with an essential feminine or feminist style. We were pretty strict constructionists!

But then our work on the feminist avant-garde ran into a big problem: there's never been a lot of funding in the United States for experimental filmmaking, but the situation got even worse with cutbacks in federal funding for the arts, the total disinterest of institutions like the AFI [American Film

Institute], Sundance, PBS, and the Independent Television Service in truly experimental work, and the disappearance of venues for showing it. Of course, women artists and filmmakers kept on making experimental film— you have only to think of Su Friedrich, Leslie Thornton, Sadie Benning, and Abigail Child to name a few—but they were screened mainly in cinema- theques in a few urban centers or in our classrooms.

Right around this time, when we were realizing that avant-garde filmmaking was being culturally marginalized, I was very influenced by something my parents said to me. Here were these two old crackers from Florida (see my "Crackers and Whackers" piece in Wray and Newitz's *White Trash* for the whole juicy story) dutifully perusing the latest issue of *Camera Obscura.* They said, "This is all very nice, but why don't you write about things that people really watch instead of these films that we've never heard of?" Boy, did they live to rue the day they said that to me. Five years later they were saying, "Why do you always have to write about such embarrassing things? We can't even show this to our friends." I've never left my love of the avant-garde, but my homegrown populism started popping out all over the place, no pun intended.

▶

TV and Fan Culture

Because we were so focused on the project of critiquing Hollywood and dis- covering experimental alternatives to it, I think we missed seeing that where it was really happening was television. Right at the moment of a supposed backlash against feminism, you have a top-rated show like *Roseanne,* which embodied a '70s-style radical and socialist feminism. Every episode of the 1992 season was devoted to showing the disintegration of the American family under the policies of Reagan and Bush. And Roseanne did it with such humor and intelligence. Whatever the inadequacies or contradictions of shows like *China Beach, Cybil,* or *Ellen,* or the Lifetime programming, or the Oprah empire, it became clear that women rule on television.

Fortunately for *Camera Obscura,* the second generation of editors included some young television scholars who would go on, again, not only to create feminist television studies but also to shape the field of television studies itself. The 1990 special issue on "Television and the Female Con- sumer," edited by Denise Mann and Lynn Spigel, was an important mile- stone for us. And it's significant that it was at the moment of publishing the special issue on Lifetime, edited by Julie D'Acci, that the *Camera Obscura* editors chose to change the undertitle to reflect the turn toward other media besides film and an expanded range of critical methods.

My own interest in television and television audiences came about in a strange and wonderful way. In the mid-'80s we were putting together one of my all-time favorite issues, on "Science Fiction and Sexual Difference." In the course of researching possible material for the issue, I came across a couple of articles about "slash" fiction, one by Patricia Frazer Lamb and Diana Veith, and the other by feminist sf writer Joanna Russ. I wasn't able to get any of these authors to contribute to the special issue, but their writing on small groups of women fans who rewrote *Star Trek* to turn the Kirk/Spock relationship (that's where the slash comes from) into a homoerotic, pornographic romance intrigued me, to say the least. I began buying slash fanzines through the mail and continued to be intrigued and then astonished by the quality of the writing (the first porn I'd ever really responded to) and the subversiveness of the way the slashers rewrote popular television shows. They rewrote them to make them more answerable to their sexual and social desires for a more tolerant, diverse, and egalitarian world. And did I mention that this stuff was hot? I jumped at the chance to attend a slash convention when I got an invitation in 1986. And the rest is (my) history. I learned so much from the slashers about women and popular culture consumption (and continue to have a good time doing so!), but I also learned some lessons about feminism, pornography, and popular culture that have influenced everything I've done in the past decade.

Porn

So here I was, hanging out with these fabulous women pornographers whose work I loved, and I realized that not one of the slashers would call herself a feminist. They sure seemed liked feminists to me, in both their political opinions and the decisions they made about how to lead their domestic and work lives. In talking to them, I discovered that they were only rejecting feminism before feminism rejected them. They, like the rest of America in the '80s and on into the '90s, believed that feminism and the antiporn movement were one and the same, which meant that to be feminist you had to be antisex and antimen, in which case the slashers hardly qualified! They were also pretty sure that feminists—in their view mostly upper-middle-class professsional women—would disdain them for their love of television.

Inspired by the slashers, or, rather, challenged by them, and realizing that I needed to know a lot more about pornography—and women's relation to it—I started teaching a course in 1993 on pornography as a popular film genre. With a teaching collection of films from the teens through the "golden age" of the '70s, supplied by the Institute for the Advanced Study of Human Sexuality in San Francisco, I created a genre course just like any other genre course. In the class we track the themes, contents, styles, modes of production, and viewing venues through the decades. To teach the video and digital era of porn, from the '80s on, I have guest lecturers from the adult industry ranging from John Stagliano ("Buttman"), and the great gay/straight crossover director/producer Gino Colbert, to such feminist power-houses as Nina Hartley, Veronica Hart, Candida Royalle, and Sharon Mitchell.

A fascinating sexual dynamic unfolds in my porn classroom, but probably not in the way that you might think. One of the things I was worried about when I was first thinking about teaching such a course was that the women students would feel even more silenced than usual. All feminist teachers are pained by the fact that women are still less aggressive about speaking up in the classroom than men. And we know about those fright-ening studies that show that even women teachers, including feminist pro-fessors, call on the men more and grant them greater authority. So here I was, planning to teach a class in which the men probably had far greater knowledge of the genre than the women did and would therefore be even more dominant in class discussions! What happened, though, and I've taught the class five times now, is that the women take over the class. The men sit there, not able to open their mouths. I discovered that there's no way that men can speak in public about porn without denouncing it, es-pecially not in the space of a university class equally populated by women and taught by a professor they know to be a feminist. And the women, when the idea of porn that has been such a bogeyman in their lives is dis-pelled, feel completely free to talk about it and analyze it openly. [Catharine] MacKinnon and [Andrea] Dworkin have been telling women for years that living in a world where porn exists means living in a constant state of ter-ror of imminent violence. It's liberating for the women students to realize that most porn films, when placed in the spectrum of other forms of popu-lar culture, are no more and no less violent than *America's Funniest Home Videos, Mad Magazine,* or the WWF [World Wrestling Federation]. The women also become a bit contemptuous of the men after seeing a historical survey of films that have until recently been made by men for men. "This is it?" they say. "This is the limit of your sexual imagination?" There's much more to say about this, obviously, but I hope to do so in a book that Linda Williams, Susie Bright, and I are editing on teaching porn. We want it to be a how-to book—everything you need to know to teach pornography to undergraduates.

I had another reason for wanting to teach a class on pornography, other than wanting to contribute some actual film scholarship to the porn debates. I knew that my course would get a lot of attention, and it did. I had learned from the slashers that one of the chief causes of feminism's unpopularity was its near-total identification with the antiporn movement. If I had to say what my overall project is, beyond media criticism, beyond feminist theory, it's to make feminism popular. That's what I appreciated so much about *Roseanne*. It was feminism as popular culture, popular culture as feminism. So I wanted to teach the porn class to get a different picture of feminism out there circulating in the media and the public eye, a picture of a pro-sex, anticensorship feminist engaged in research, not spouting bitter, empty polemics that divided women and put people off feminism.

I believe that I've succeeded in making the study of pornography a necessary and normal part of a media studies curriculum and in making feminism more popular (with a little help from my friends, of course, especially Linda Williams, Laura Kipnis, Susie Bright, Anne McClintock, Eithne Johnson, and Jane Juffer). I can now sometimes count on reporters to tell this news: there's a much greater range of feminist opinion on sexual representation than has generally been granted, and there are more feminists like me in academia than feminists like Catharine MacKinnon and Andrea Dworkin. I hope that I've made it at least difficult to portray feminism as having degenerated, as in the nineteenth century, into a public decency or moral hygiene movement that is hateful to most women and men alike.

One of the things that I hated most about antiporn feminism was that it drove a wedge between feminists and also divided feminists from women who could have been feminists. I hope that I've helped to create a sense that there is a continuum of feminists working in academia, porn, fan culture, television, and experimental film and video. This is perhaps the '60s idea of struggle on many fronts. It's also my idea of utopia.

Socialism

It's hard to describe my feminist politics now because we can't say the s-word anymore. Socialism has just dropped off the map. We all know about the triumph of capitalism, we know about the "Free World," and no one has any way to talk about a more just distribution of wealth. I've always thought of myself as a democratic socialist and as a feminist. Those two have always been pretty equal for me, with democratic socialism reminding feminism of class issues, and feminism making democratic socialism more attentive to issues of gender and class, as well as race. That's hard to talk about now.

I was just described in a Hollywood documentary film that's being made about the current state of the porn industry. The filmmakers are good, smart people. They sent me a copy of the script, and I looked at how they described me. They portray me as a pioneer in the teaching of pornography as an American film genre. They say, "Professor Penley is a liberal feminist in her thirties, bravely taking on mainstream feminism." As much as I hate giving up this very flattering portrait of myself as a young sex radical, a heroine, and a pioneer, I had to set the record straight. I want a more accurate picture of feminist media politics. I had to write and tell them that I am not in my thirties, I'm the same age as Catharine MacKinnon and Andrea Dworkin, and this is not a generational issue. It's not young sex radicals against those old, dried-up, antisex feminists. It's a political difference. I also wanted them to know that I'm closer to what they characterized as mainstream feminism than they realized, and that my course on pornographic film got interest and support from feminists. However, when it comes to this Hollywood documentary, which its makers are hoping will be the *Hoop Dreams* of porn, I couldn't begin to tell them why I wasn't a "liberal." I left the description of democratic socialism to another day and another draft that I'm hoping to write at some later time.

▶ ──

A Career in Film

Who gave you permission to have a career as a film critic?
Nobody gave me permission to have a career in anything. No one in my family had ever gone to college. It was quite an improbable thing to do. I guess I just read too many *Mad* magazines, too many Jane Austen novels, so I decided I wanted to go to college.

When I was thinking back on some formative childhood moments, a media event that strongly influenced me was repeated every Sunday morning. My father would turn on Oral Roberts's televangelism show. I figured that he did it to torture me because he knew I hated Oral Roberts and he knew—or at least I thought he knew—that it horrified me that my father would be so taken in by this televangelist. Many years later, by the time I'd gone off to college, I asked my father, "Why did you do that to me? Why did you put me through that every Sunday morning? Why did you like Oral Roberts?" He looked at me in astonishment and said, "I hated Oral Roberts! I was watching him to figure out what in the world his power was over people." He said, "Don't you know the story of my grandfather? He had this big farm in central Florida. He was going to give it to his three sons, but they were all battling each other. So he got frustrated one day and just sold the farm for $40,000. It was where Disney World is now. But he just sold it and went up to North Carolina, walked into a tent revival, and gave away the money." He said, "I watched that show to try and figure out why in the world my grandfather could have done that." So this taught me that whatever you think people are doing when they are watching a movie or a television show, you are probably wrong. And you might do well to try and ask them what they are doing when they are consuming that film or show. The memory of that event has taken me from the very necessary early work of doing close analysis of film and video—textual, stylistic, narrative, and institutional analysis—to looking at how film and video figure in people's lives, what they make of it, what it means to them.

▶

My Particular Trajectory

Here's what my cultural chain of being looks like now: Hollywood film is elite popular culture; television is popular culture; and pornography is *very* popular culture. It doesn't surprise me that a good deal of current feminist experimental film and video is looking to television and porn for ideas and images, which is a widespread practice among contemporary artists in general.

My methods for doing a feminist analysis of culture and my objects of study have changed over time, but I like to think that I'm always building on what I've done before. I began with the close analysis of individual film texts carried out within a semiotic and psychoanalytic theoretical model, a model that also tried to account for the subjectivity of the spectator. When I first worked on a television text—*Pee Wee's Playhouse*!—which was also the first time I worked directly on masculinity, I was forced to pay attention not only to the text but to the whole televisual flow, including ads and other shows. And I also had to study the children's advertising industry and network politics. But it wasn't until I worked on slash fan culture that I addressed audiences rather than the spectator. And, very importantly, the slashers gave me a much larger and more porous idea of "the" text and the relation that a fan or critic could have to it.

Now, instead of just writing about texts or flows or institutions, I try to enter them, to join in a process of rewriting them from the inside. That's what I tried to do with NASA in my *NASA/TREK* book [1997], which documents my efforts to get myself and other women into space (note the slash in the title). Working as a member of the GALA Committee, I got inside Aaron Spelling's prime-time soap opera *Melrose Place*, where we were able to collaborate with the cast and crew to turn the show into our big old art video, now being beamed around the world on Rupert Murdoch's satellite systems. If you don't believe me, check out www.arts.ucsb.edu/mpart.

Most recently, I started the Oxygen Media Research Project with my colleagues Anna Everett and Lisa Parks. We're proposing to track the development of the Internet/cable network for women founded by the most powerful women in television, most notably Oprah Winfrey, Geraldine Laybourne, and Marcy Carsey. We're studying the programs and Web sites (and their interaction); the viewers and fans; the industry and press coverage (comparing it to the coverage of that other, all-guy, media triumvirate Dreamworks SKG); and the project's place in the history of women's efforts to gain a powerful media voice. And finally, we want to study the day-to-day work of decision making and production through participant-observation in the offices and on the sets of Oxygen Media. We're employing all of these different research methods (textual/ideological, historical, ethnographic) to see if we can devise a way of doing feminist media research that can keep up with the speed of capital. Even though the old socialist in me wants to barf at the thought of corporate feminism, I think that Oxygen Media is too large and unprecedented for feminist media critics to simply ignore or disdain.

As you can tell from the trajectory that I've laid out for you, I want feminist media criticism to matter, to make a difference, to help democratize our mass-mediated culture. And to do that, I'm willing to risk the charge of being too populist, too impure, too utopian, or my favorite, too ludic.

Journals

1973–74	*Women and Film,* associate editor
1974 to present	*Camera Obscura: A Journal of Feminism and Film Theory,* cofounder and editor
1982–86	*m/f,* advisory editor
1995 to present	*Journal for the Psychoanalysis of Culture and Society,* advisory editor
1996 to present	*Sexualities,* advisory editor
1999 to present	*Technologies,* consulting editor for the book series (Athlone Press)

Books

1988	*Feminism and Film Theory* (editor), Routledge, Chapman & Hall
1989	*The Future of an Illusion: Film, Feminism, and Psycho-analysis,* University of Minnesota Press
1990	*Close Encounters: Film, Feminism and Science Fiction* (editor with Elisabeth Lyon, Lynne Spigel, and Janet Bergstrom), University of Minnesota Press
1991	*Technoculture* (editor with Andrew Ross), University of Minnesota Press
1992	*Male Trouble* (editor with Sharon Willis), University of Minnesota Press
1997	*NASA/TREK: Popular Science and Sex in America,* Verso
1998	*The Visible Woman: Imaging Technologies, Gender, and Science* (editor with Paula Treichler and Lisa Cartwright), New York University Press
2000	*The Analysis of Film* (editor) by Raymond Bellour, Indiana University Press

Creative Project

1996 to present	*Art on Primetime by the GALA Committee*: www.arts.ucsb.edu/mpart

[10]   *Susan Mogul*

Susan Mogul is a Los Angeles videomaker whose twenty-five years of artis-
tic production evidence an unyielding fascination about the video camera
as a tool for deciphering herself, her world, and those around her. In her
autobiographical, experimental documentaries, Mogul wages an investiga-
tion into the everyday world of regular people (including herself), an artistic
preoccupation originally introduced to her by her professors at the Feminist
Art Program at Cal Arts in the '70s. The idea that lived experience was the
stuff of art, already prominent in the art world through "movements" like
Fluxus, performance art, happenings, process art, conceptual art, and earth-
works, was enriched and expanded by a feminist analysis that also found
beauty, meaning, and politics in personal experience. Theories and strategies
from the women's movement coincided with the changing focus in the art
world to allow for a distinct amalgam of form, content, and process in femi-
nist video that has had lasting effects on art. Ann-Sargent Wooster writes
about early feminist video art: "The innovations in subject matter intro-
duced by women artists—language and personal narrative, discussion of
the self, sexuality, women's experience in the world, and the presence of
everyday life—have now become part of general art practice. These video-
tapes by women are the fulcrum between modernism and post-modernism."[1]

The video camera, newly available to consumers, provided these devel-
oping feminist artists with the perfect tool with which to document every-
day spaces and activities with a depth, openness, and immediacy that the
overly expensive, overly technological, less-mobile, and more-distancing
film camera could never permit. Says Mogul, "There was so much going
on that was about developing relationships with the camera, with col-
leagues, with people in the everyday world. I was learning all those ways
of working—performing and observing and self-examination, which is
what consciousness-raising was about—that have all stayed with me."

Mogul's early work, shot on a portapak and unedited, displays herself en-
acting "private" performances to and for the camera. In Dressing Up *(1973)*
she performs a reverse striptease, starting naked and dressing in clothes
that she and her mother bought while bargain shopping. Take Off *(1974)*
records Mogul discussing how she learned to use a vibrator, here making
intimate acts into public performance. In the '80s, in videos like The Last
Jew in America *(1984), Mogul continued to use her own life as her subject,*
always combining humor with the pathos of day-to-day existence. In two
*videotapes from the '90s—*Everyday Echo Street: A Summer Diary *(1993)*
and I Stare at You and Dream *(1997)—Mogul began to experiment with*
new video technologies in her continuing pursuit of personal exploration.
With a light(er), cheap(er), and professional-quality Hi-8 camera, Mogul's
work adapted into a series of narrative-diary documentaries.

While Mogul still finds the possibility of an inexpensive and approach-
able artistic medium intoxicating, video did not maintain its position as
darling of the art world for long, perhaps because so many women found
their voice and position through this medium. Although there remains a
tradition of art video within an art-world context (most commonly as video
installation but sometimes as single-channel video sidebars to thematic
shows), the medium is now most commonly perceived as an illegitimate
stepchild to high or avant-garde art. This shift in status over its very brief
history has everything to do with the very qualities of the medium that
initially made it so exciting and that still connect it to feminism: its accessi-
bility, its inability to be commodified, its close likeness to the mass art of
television.

Mogul and others in this study have been directly affected by video's
precarious position in the art world. Since there is little money or status
to be made through video (there are only a few distributors of art tapes—
Video Data Bank, Electronic Arts Intermix, V-Tape, Artcom—and the mar-
ket is almost exclusively to academics like myself), its makers must choose
to make financial and other kinds of sacrifices to continue at this work. In
her interview, Mogul discusses an economically tenuous existence that is
standard for most women artists, especially those, like Mogul, who do not
gain the economic stability of full-time teaching. While Mogul has sought
employment as a teacher, she believes that her work does not fit academia's
rigid set of theoretical or political prescriptions. In the past few years, how-
ever, she has found some financial stability through a reconceptualization
of her audience, namely, to that of public television. Enabled by the even
more accessible technology of Hi-8 video (first available to consumers in
the 1990s), well funded by ITVS (Independent Television Service), then

aired on public television, Mogul's work shifted from the rarefied gallery and museum into the "real world" (of television) that has always been her subject. As "art," her work had a limited viewership and an even more limited earning power; as "television" her video—for 1995 at least—serves to support itself and Mogul.

Equally significant to Mogul's sense of her work and life (as is true for every woman discussed thus far) is the contradiction of two related experiences: living through the heady, exuberant, communal, interactive spirit of the women's movement in the early-to-mid-'70s, and then living through the almost entire absence of such spirit in the following decades. In some ways, Mogul represents the stereotypical artist: a person who has to make her art at whatever cost: "Art comes out of a need. I know it sounds so romantic." But she is not just any run-of-the-mill, romantic artist, but perhaps more like one version of the classic feminist *artist—trained in, focused on, and motivated by feminism, even as feminism changes.*

▶ ──

One's Career/One's Work

Please narrate to us your career in video.
I believe that there's a distinction between one's career and making work. A career has to do with shows, recognition, teaching, credentials—all those things that one puts on the résumé. Certain things are good: getting a grant furthers your career. It's prestigious to be able to say you've gotten a grant to do a project because that affords you the chance to fund another project. Or if you have taught at one place, it affords you the opportunity to teach elsewhere. If someone bought a piece of your work for his or her collection, that has to do with prestige. All those things make up your career, your professional record. Then there's your body of work. It's part of your career, but it's something more discrete. That's why you're an artist to begin with: to make that work.

I don't see them as so distinct, because your "career" allows you to make your work.
But someone might say, "Well, my work is going well right now, but my career sucks, because I can't get a job."

I've learned that this history is as much a history of the career as of the work. The hard part is making the career: getting the necessary grants, getting the necessary shows. I see the history of the career and its work being a social, economic, and political history.

An Artist Doing Videotapes

I consider myself very lucky because I was trained as an artist. I still think of myself as an artist, and the way that has evolved is that I'm now an artist doing videotapes. I come from a history of doing live performances, video, documentary photography, and some installation and the through-line in my work has always been autobiographical.

I started college in the late '60s. Ten weeks after I got to Madison, Wisconsin, I was demonstrating in the streets against Dow Chemical being on campus. Then a few years later, I was living in Boston, going to Boston Museum School, and I was involved with the women's movement there. I was already very committed to being an artist. That seemed to be the thing I did well. I had feminist friends, but feminism and art seemed to be very separate.

I found out about the Feminist Art Program at Cal Arts because there was an article in *Time* or *Newsweek* about Judy Chicago and Miriam Shapiro's WomanHouse. So I thought, "Oh! Feminist art!" I was lucky when I came to Los Angeles to go to Cal Arts because of the Feminist Art Program. People were just starting to make video with portapaks. There was a blossoming feminist art movement. The personal was political. Women's diaries were being celebrated; the everyday, the mundane was being celebrated. Also, storytelling was something I had never before realized that I liked to do and had a flair for. Lynda Bengalis was a visiting instructor; she thought everyone should make videotapes. Judy Chicago was my mentor, and she thought that everyone should divulge his or her private life to her. Alan Kaprow was at Cal Arts; he saw the everyday as performance. We had a performance class in which performances were done without an audience. They were more conceptually based, focused on the everyday, little things that one doesn't usually think about.

These things all came together for me. A year or so later, David Ross became the video curator at the Long Beach Museum, where we're filming this. He created a show called Southland Video Anthology, which was very democratic. It had big artists like John Baldessari and Eleanor Antin and baby artists like me. I was twenty-three, twenty-four years old at the time. This was a medium that a lot of people were getting into for the first time. There weren't those hierarchies of the more experienced ones and the lesser ones. I was lucky. Soon after making my first tapes, I was getting them shown, and that was exciting.

My early works, like Valerie Soe's, only cost a few dollars to make. One work that got a lot of attention, which was called *Take Off* and is now known more commonly as the *Vibrator Tape,* is a satire on a Vito Acconci piece, *Undertone* (1973). It's now part of the history of video art and is included in feminist studies. It's probably shown more now in the '90s than when it was made in '74. *Take Off* is a ten-minute videotape that shows me talking about my vibrator. At that time Acconci was showing quite a bit and was quite well known as an artist. *Undertone* is a tape of him masturbating under a table. I wanted to respond to him because I liked his work a lot. I liked his weird sense of poetry. My work is autobiographical, and a lot of it is in response to others. Responding to *Undertone* was a way for me to talk about learning to masturbate with a vibrator. I used Acconci's format and structure to also comment on how a man dealt with his masturbatory experiences. I was able to reveal something of myself while revealing some of my ideas about the male artist.

▶

Feminist Art Education

When I think about video at the Feminist Studio Workshop at the Women's Building, mostly I remember the place as a whole. There were a lot of conferences. We had a design conference and a performance conference. We had a summer arts program, run by the people who were students in the winter. I taught in that. We designed a whole program and solicited students from all over the country. There was a film and video conference. We used to go out and lecture. That was the other thing that Judy Chicago was so good at doing. She would say, "Okay, I'll do this speaking engagement if two of my students can present their work, too." During one of the years in which I was at the Women's Building, I wrote to an art school back East and told them, "I can give a lecture for you about the women's movement on the West Coast, and I'll charge you $250," and they wrote back and said, "Yes!" I was in shock. I was twenty-four and giving my first lecture. I put together a whole slide show. We were encouraged to be very public. There wasn't this concept of waiting until you were ready when your work was polished. Being in the Feminist Studio Workshop was all about moving out into the world.

The first video that I made while I was at Cal Arts and that got a certain amount of attention was a piece called *Dressing Up* in which I do a reverse striptease. I start naked and wind up putting on clothes. But there's a reason for it. I'm not trying to titillate you: I'm doing it as a way to talk subversively about my mother. I talk about each item of clothing in terms of the bargains that "we" got. It's this repetitive activity of talking about bargains and munching on corn nuts. It's about this obsession that my mother passed to me. So I'm eating these corn nuts as an "undertone"—the name of that Vito Acconci piece. And I'm just talking to the camera. It was an unedited piece. Much to my surprise, people thought I was funny. I had never thought of myself as funny, or having a sense of humor, or being a storyteller. These were things that I discovered through the camera and through being part of this movement.

Another meaningful thing about being in the Feminist Art Program at Cal Arts was that everyone else drove and I didn't. When I came here in 1973, all these women were driving and they said, "We're tired of picking you up and driving you around," because we were a very close-knit group that was collaborating and doing stuff together. And one of them volunteered to teach me to drive. And I said, "Okay, you can teach me, but I'm going to pay you because I want you to be committed." And so, after six months in Los Angeles, I got my driver's license. Going home that summer to my family and being able to say "I'm a driver" symbolized the beginning of my work. I was able to create a new identity in the Los Angeles landscape. So I made this postcard that I sent to everyone, including my driver's ed teacher. It says: "Mogul is Mobile." The visual image is of me flying over Los Angeles. This work begins to set the tone for the body of my work that followed. My work has always been about "Where and how do I fit in?" It's been about myself as an individual and my relationship to my culture, my family, identity, about beginning again, and using my name.

I was doing work at that time, between January and June of 1973, that set the stage for all my work that followed. I was doing a photo essay on a beauty parlor in Newhall, and that was about observation of everyday activity and about female community. I was also part of another female community that was the Feminist Art Program itself. I was both observing and performing for the camera. I was in consciousness-raising groups. There was so much going on that was about developing relationships with the camera, with colleagues, with people in the everyday world. I was learning all those ways of working—performing and observing and self-examination, which is what consciousness-raising was about—that have all stayed with me.

The other thing about the Feminist Art Program was the way we were a tight group and very supportive of one another. There was a sense of excitement and exploration. We were finding something new. For the first time, a teacher, other than my high school chemistry teacher who liked me even though I wasn't good at chemistry, said, "I can identify with you." Judy Chicago said, "I can understand you." When she was telling me that, she was sitting on one toilet in the basement of Cal Arts in the ladies' room and I was on another. Tears were streaming down my face. Now, that's not an exact quote, but there was something very powerful about an instructor ten years my senior saying that she identified with me. It was extremely moving, overwhelming.

There were other people who thought I was special, like Sheila de Bretteville, who was a graphic designer at the Women's Building. She took an interest in me. Here I am twenty-three, twenty-four years old, a young adult, and it's the first time I feel as though my mentors and instructors really value me. I don't think I had a horribly low self-image, but I never had a teacher think I had something special to offer. That was probably one of the most significant things about the feminist movement: there were people who said, "You're talented, you're unique." I had never thought of myself that way.

It took a three-thousand-mile trip to learn how to drive and find all these things out about myself. So I identify with the personal is political. I think politics is important. But you have to start from yourself. I try to do that when I teach. I try to network for my students like Judy Chicago did for me. She was the one who said to David Ross, "You have to see Susan Mogul's work." I never identified much with Judy's work, but what I appreciated about her is the fact that she was always trying to network people together. She would say, "You and Suzanne Lacy should be doing a project together. Do it!"

It's such a different way to relate, a way of assuming the best of you. That ought to be how any educational situation is. That's where I get my strongest marks in teaching. I get bad marks because I digress too much, or I'm weird, or I'm odd. But I'm enthusiastic, and there's a certain amount of caring. I learned how important it is to be encouraged and supported.

▶────────────────────────────────

Feminist Art

How, or does, being a woman and a feminist nuance your experience as an artist?
My work comes out of my life. I'm odd. I live alone. I've never been married, never lived with a man. I don't have children. That's weird. There are many, many women in this country who live without a man, but they're mothers. It's strange for a woman not to be a mother. Without trying, I'm coming from a different perspective. I'm engaged in asking, "Why am I like this? Why have I chosen this path?" So the work is, by default, probably having some feminist perspective.[2]

People have never known quite what to do with me. I never fit neatly into definitions of a feminist artist, but I'm not neatly defined as a mainstream artist either. I've been hurt because in the late '70s and early '80s, people were beginning to write books about feminist art, and I wasn't getting included. I decided that I wouldn't be a feminist artist anymore, because the definition had become very small. One's work had to be strictly political. People were no longer seeing how documenting women's mundane experiences could be feminist.

What had been exciting about the women's movement when I first came here was its expansiveness. I guess what happens to any movement is that in the beginning it's very open, anything goes, and then people want to codify it, make it more narrow. At Cal Arts, the Feminist Art Program was in the basement. That reflected the attitude at school about the Feminist Art Program. It was like the fourth floor in high school—that's where the slow kids went, where they hid people away. If you were in the Feminist Art Program, you were considered an incompetent artist. You didn't fit into the cool John Baldessari, David Salle set. So it's funny to me that now, in the '80s and '90s, feminist theory has been codified and has an academic cache. The work of certain feminist artists is being shown in fancy galleries. That doesn't really affect me, though.

What do you mean, it doesn't affect you?
Right now, I'm starting to show my work on public television. I make tapes that are hybrids: narrative-diary documentaries. They're not made for galleries, but for screenings or to be shown on TV. The gallery scene doesn't really have any bearing on my work.

▶ ───

Everyday Echo Street

Why that shift from the gallery to the television? And can you give an example of a piece that reflects that shift?
I didn't expect my last piece to get on television. I was very lucky to get a commission from Peter Sellars's Los Angeles Festival in 1993. They were looking for artists to do community-specific projects. I had already done such work. For a year, I was an artist-in-residence, teaching photography at a home for abused children. I had also worked with children in a hospital [*Five East,* 1990, video portraits of seriously ill children]. I decided that it was time for me to do something in my own neighborhood. I had lived in a working-class, Latino neighborhood in Los Angeles for fourteen years. The work was constructed around asking questions like, "Why am I here, living alone, in this neighborhood?" The tape [*Everyday Echo Street*] was made in the neighborhood, and it premiered in a neighborhood restaurant.

A year later Claire Aguilar saw it and wanted to show it on KCET. I had never shown anything on television before. It's a phenomenal thing. Claire told me, "We're going to show it at 10:30 on Monday night. I hope you get a good rating." I called her up afterward and asked how the rating was. She said, "Oh, Susan, it was only a Share 1." I asked what that meant. She said, "Only thirty thousand people saw your piece last night." I laughed. I told her, "*Only* thirty thousand people? In my whole career, thirty thousand people have not seen my work!" I got fan letters. Strangers were calling me on the phone because it was shown in Los Angeles and people could tell from the piece that I live in L.A. I had no sense of what it would mean to be on television. Because of that one show, I started getting recognized on the street outside of my neighborhood. I got some very touching responses. Men were calling me trying to get a date. Women were calling because they could identify.

Everyday Echo Street was the first piece I made that had popular appeal. Because my work is humorous and not theoretical and because it deals with everyday stuff, a lot of people are able to enjoy it. However, in the past it was shown in art spaces like LACE [Los Angeles Contemporary Exhibitions]. The KCET airing was the first time my work was shown to a more general audience. I have had work shown in local libraries and high schools, but this was the first time that I'd had a piece shown under circumstances that enabled a working-class Latino to respond to it for his set of reasons while, across town, a middle-aged, white woman responded to it for hers.

Money

How do you support yourself?
This year, from September of '95 to September of '96, was the first year in my life in which I made a middle-class salary. I'm forty-six, and don't think I don't have guilt. [Laughter.] I have a middle-class background, but after all these years I developed a poverty mentality.

Luckily, I haven't had a shit job since '87. Since then, I've been juggling stuff, like artist-in-residence grants, semesters teaching, collecting unemployment, and selling a few tapes to Michael Renov at USC. Usually, I make $15,000 a year. I pay $400 a month for my place. I live frugally. Ninety-four was a really, really bad year. But this year [1995], I have a production agreement from ITVS. So this is a good year.

What do you get in return for giving up middle-class wages?
I make the rules. I get to examine my life and other people's lives. I keep learning. That's why I make work. It's a combination of the satisfaction in making something and the process. Making *Echo Street* was a process of discovery. I learned more about myself, and in turn the people I filmed felt validated. They got to be on TV, too. Rosie Sanchez, from Armando's Restaurant, and I become closer friends, and now she's in a new piece I'm making called *I Stare at You and Dream.* Now I'm able to pay her for being in the work. I'm focusing on her life. In the process of validating my life, I validate her life and her family's. I'm learning more about myself through her, and she's learning more about herself through me.

For me, making art is a process of discovery about yourself and other people and how things work. I would love to make a fictional piece, but I don't think that I ever will, because I don't like that idea of knowing how something's going to turn out ahead of time. I'm engaged by this process, this examination of myself and others. That's what feeds me and makes me feel sane. There's this constant fascination with how people cope, how people fit in, and how people survive. The other people who are central characters in this new work are all working class. It's about how different people overcome or compensate for their past, or their generosity. Why are people the way they are?

I liked what Valerie Soe said about making work. Now that I have this funding, I may have a broadcast-quality piece, but I've been making work for twenty years. If you want to use your own voice, then you find a way to do it. I have a hard time with people who are "waiting for their funding." Especially now, when you can buy a cheap camera. When I was coming up, I knew an artist who sold a car in order to buy a portapak.

ELAYNE ZALIS [Long Beach Museum of Art Video Annex]: *Could you talk about the Long Beach Museum of Art's Video Annex [where the interview is being shot]?*[3]
Echo Street was on-lined here, at the Video Annex. It was shot on Hi-8, and it was on-lined here on Betacam SP.[4] I would not have been able to finish my work if it wasn't for the Video Annex. Money and/or access do allow you to do certain things. I did not have funds to do an on-line in a Hollywood postproduction place. I could do it here. Not only was I able to afford the facilities, Joe Leonardi was the editor, and he was also great with sound, so the quality of the piece was quite extraordinary. People have remarked about it. Also, the Long Beach Museum has all along shown and collected my work. They even agreed to make copies of all my work, so if there's an

earthquake that damages my place, the annex will have copies. It's great to have a supportive institution. I don't take that lightly.

▶ ──────────────────────────────────

Making Art

Making art comes out of a real, core need for me. That's why I'm willing to live in a frugal manner. I don't crave a lot of things. I would like to have a bigger apartment. But art comes out of a need. I know it sounds so romantic. I wasn't one of those people who had a desire to be an artist when I was young. I wanted to be an actress. [Laughter.] You can imagine the parts I would have gotten. I would have been a real neurotic. Worse than this. Making work makes me feel balanced and more a part of society, even though, as an artist, you're an outsider, observing.

You've been making video for a long time. You've been an artist since 1973. What do we owe you for your work? What have you given us?
[Laughter.] I'm too hard on myself. I don't think anyone owes me anything. What have I given? Anything I might say in response to that question would seem self-serving.

It's meant to be self-celebrating, not self-serving.
All artists want to be recognized for their work. I feel lucky this year because I'm being fully supported. This is unusual. I don't know what will happen next year. What do you think? What have I given and what do you owe me?

I think that this project comes out of a sense that we owe a lot to the women who came before us. We don't value the lives of these extraordinary people, making difficult choices and struggling so that the generation that follows doesn't have the same struggles around the same things. We owe them a recording of their voices; we owe them the maintenance of their legacy; we owe them thanks for holding a space in society, so that it's available for us. Your invention of a life for yourself as a woman artist, as an unmarried woman who doesn't have children, creates a space for the next woman who decides to do that.
I try to get people to appreciate the beauty of ordinary people and to celebrate the everyday, the humor and pathos you can see right outside your window. And to be aware of how rich people's lives are, including those people whom you might not think have interesting lives.

Videos

1973	*Dressing Up*, 7 min.
1974	*Take Off*, 10 min.
1980	*Waiting at the Soda Fountain*, 28 min.
1984	*The Last Jew in America*, 22 min.
1988	*Dear Dennis*, 4 min.
1990	*Five East*, 15 min.
1991	*Prosaic Portraits, Ironies and Other Intimacies*, 46 min.
1993	*Everyday Echo Street: A Summer Diary*, 30 min.
1997	*Home Safe Home*, 6 min.
1997	*I Stare at You and Dream*, 60 min.
2000	*Sing, O Barren Woman*, 11 min.

Distribution and Contact Information

Videos available from the artist: SusanMogul@aol.com

[11] *Carol Leigh*

Carol Leigh is a sex worker and activist videomaker whose vast body of
work focuses on human rights issues involving sex workers, AIDS, and the
San Francisco counterculture. She was a founding member of ACT UP/San
Francisco, was seated on San Francisco's Board of Supervisor's Task Force
on Prostitution, currently volunteers at a women's site food program that
operates a needle exchange program, and curates the San Francisco Sex
Worker Film and Video Festival. A "life artist," Carol Leigh is the first
artist in this study whose political video career was initiated by cable access
and the technological advances in cable, video, and television that occurred
in the mid-to-late-'80s. She also points to sex work as the thematic center
of and inspiration for her work.

Cable access has a politicized understanding of the media at its core:
"Congress had intended public access cable to . . . be 'the video equivalent
of the speaker's soap box or the electronic parallel to the printed leaflet.'
Public access' mandate is thus linked to the implications of the First Amend-
ment: if it works, it is a public forum, a facilitator of public discussion and
action."[1] When a community has cable access, it is usually the direct result
of local activism by media makers who hold cable networks responsible for
their once-legal mandate to provide services to the local communities that
support them. In 1975, the FCC adopted rules requiring any cable system
with 3,500 or more subscribers to provide equipment and training in cable
production as well as the facilities to air community programming.[2] As
these rules were chipped away in the '80s, media activists had to take on
the role of watchdog, monitoring and maintaining cable access. In a limit-
ed number of American cities (perhaps 15 percent of cable systems nation-
wide),[3] this has meant that cable companies fund and operate local centers
where television production is taught to community members for low to
no cost, and then local television is produced and aired. Leigh learned video

production in one such flourishing center in Tucson, Arizona. In the '90s, the rapid affordability of consumer camcorders, and then computer editing, has allowed Leigh to continue to produce video outside the facilitating structure of cable access.

Although Leigh credits feminism as her greatest artistic influence, as a working prostitute she has spent most of her career on feminism's fringes. Her outsider status to this already marginal field has allowed her to focus her humorous camera on feminism's hypocrisy. She pushes at a political movement that only embraces the experiences and interests of some of its constituents. In 1992, Leigh's video Outlaw Poverty, Not Prostitutes was censored by students and professors at the University of Michigan Law School, and Leigh was later awarded a settlement when she was represented by the Arts Censorship Project of the ACLU. "It is sad to me that mainstream feminism demonizes women who are sexual and women who are sex workers. I still prioritize women's experience, and compassion, so I still embrace feminism," explains Leigh. "I hope that I can contribute to a change in the concept of feminism because that would certainly be something new."

In videos like Pope Don't Preach (I'm Terminating My Pregnancy), Bad Laws, and Safe Sex Slut, Leigh makes her personal contribution to changing the face of feminism by rewriting and remaking music videos to espouse and enact radical lyrics and sexual politics. Given that the majority of her work plays on TV through her cable access program, she has also reworked other genres: the sitcom (Elaine's, about a leftist waitress who espouses positions on sexual health, homelessness, domestic violence), the PSA (public service announcement; her series of Mom videos record a Jewish mother's rapid-fire advice about everything from safe sex to domestic abuse), the news magazine (Whore in the Gulf, in which reedited footage expresses Leigh's interpretation of the war), and the biopic (Mother's Mink, in which Leigh introduces us to her working-class, Jewish upbringing in New York). She uses familiar televisual form but infuses her brand of TV with new messages. Mixing humor, street theater, and civil disobedience in her videos, Leigh performs the role of outrageous, voluptuous, sex-positive warrior and invites anyone so inclined to join her.

I first learned of Carol Leigh when I was making an AIDS activist video about prostitutes and AIDS in the late '80s. At the time, prostitutes, Haitians, and bisexuals were being scapegoated for the spread of HIV to "the general public," and I understood this to be a feminist issue. Jean Carlomusto—the producer of the Living with AIDS Show, a weekly public access cable program produced by the Gay Men's Health Crisis and airing in New York City—told me about a woman named Scarlot Harlot (a.k.a.

Carol Leigh), a prostitutes' rights, AIDS, and video activist from San Francisco. I called Leigh up and asked to see some of her work and ended up using a great deal of her video in my video (It's Not What You Do, It's How You Do What You Do: Prostitutes, Risk and AIDS, 1988). A year or so later, I was editing another AIDS video at DCTV (Downtown Community Television Center)—one of a number of community media organizations that play a central place in this history—and there was Carol Leigh, in the flesh (I'd see more of that later), and in residence, completing her latest tape.

When I became a film and women's studies professor at Swarthmore College the following year, I began teaching Leigh's work, as well as that of other outrageous and provocative feminist videomakers who deal explicitly with sex from a feminist and pro-sex position (e.g., Maria Beatty, Annie Sprinkle, House of Chicks, Jocelyn Taylor, Shu Lea Cheang).[4] I was intrigued to find how well Leigh spoke to college students (living in a sexual world that for their generation had been defined by AIDS and sexual nervousness) who were particularly moved to see a woman who was flamboyantly and also humorously in control of her own body and sexuality, not despite but taking account of AIDS. One of my students, Petra Janopaul, ended up interning for Leigh the following summer (and for me the summer after that), which propelled Janopaul's own education in down-and-dirty, by-the-seat-of-your-pants, political videomaking.

Yet even as Leigh serves as a role model for many young women, her own experience within feminism has mostly lacked mentors. She explains that the sexual moralism at the heart of much first- and second-wave mainstream feminism has left women like Leigh feeling abandoned and even demonized. Needless to say, this is not to deny that there is an equally strong tradition of sex-affirmative feminism that is embodied by Leigh's and others' lives and work (see Schneemann, Hammer, Penley, Negrón-Muntaner, and Dunye interviews). Even so, Leigh believes that she has been situated outside of mainstream feminism, and to compound this, that she also resides on the margins of more "mainstream" video culture. Working from a political and pragmatic position, making work that needs to be made with whatever—cheap—means necessary, Leigh explains that she is ensconced in neither the art nor academic worlds where most video is discussed, given attention, given value. Although her work has certainly interfaced with these milieus on numerous occasions, she sometimes feels that her work is unresponded to and underappreciated.

As one of a small number of scholars who has written about and taught Leigh's work, I need to think seriously about what her feelings of marginalization express about the field of feminist video. People like Leigh make video for contradictory reasons, themselves definitive of the medium: it is a form of inexpensive and marginal culture that can mimic expensive and mainstream culture. Video allows for a radical critique from a marginal position but in a dominant form. One makes video to speak to oneself, one's community, and the whole damn world, all at the same time. Thus, while it seems a precondition of Leigh's feminist pro-sex video practice that almost nobody *would* see her cheap, radical, sexual videos, it is also a precondition that nearly everybody *could* and *should*.

However, there are no neat pipelines established between marginal culture and the academic or art world professionals who could or should write about it. Most feminist film professors know little more about activist video than does anyone else in the society. Activist video circulates, for the most part, in the few remaining radical or avant-garde art establishments of America's larger cities. Since the vast majority of feminist professors have little access to this work, they focus instead on mainstream film and television culture. This focus can be explained in other ways as well: many feminists have a political or intellectual commitment to understanding dominant culture and therefore "real" power; have a personal predilection for mainstream culture (mainstream media works can be beautiful, compelling, and professionalized products); most feminist critics are working within relatively conservative departments that do not readily take to contemporary or alternative forms. Given video's marginal status within the arts and academia, it is risky for people who are attempting to speak to their profession (and thus get jobs, tenure, promotions) to discuss this field. Jennie Klein explains: "Resistant to the traditional art historical narrative of great artists, 'greater art,' and male-generated innovations, video art and criticism remains on the fringes of that discourse in spite of efforts to the contrary."[5]

Leigh's sense of her own distance from the art world and academy—themselves terrain that are more often than not distinct—speaks to another complex dynamic that underwrites this history. The field of feminist film and video is situated in museums and art galleries, within community and political groups, in books and classrooms, at movie theaters, video stores, on television, and in for-profit and nonprofit organizations like festivals, distribution companies, and funding organizations. These fields depend on each other, influence each other, but are not particularly organized or even networked and are sometimes even in opposition. While this immense diversity of form, content, venue, funding, audience, and intention is what makes feminist film and video so dynamic, it is also a great liability.

Although it may be experienced as painful, there is something productive about distance from "real" power and authority. In Leigh's case, it allows her to make her decidedly personal and very political videos. Yes, they *are on a small scale; yes, they are not widely distributed. Yet when they are seen, it is Leigh's marginal, funny, and personal voice that makes her message of "acceptance, human variety, [and] control of our bodies" so powerful.*

Video

Please tell us about your career in video.
I've worked in a variety of media. I knew after seeing Shirley Temple when I was four years old that I wanted to be an actress. When I was a teenager, I started writing poetry. I went to Boston University to study with Anne Sexton. She killed herself during the semester I got there. I moved to San Francisco, where I've been tackling one genre at a time. I write music, I sing, I've painted. Video is my final frontier. It really combines all the other media.

Why video? When I was younger, there was no concept of a woman having a video career, or a filmmaking career, but my father was a television repairman. When I was a child, my parents had the television shop in the bedroom. The room where I was suckled was lined with television carcasses. I think this was how video, somehow, came to me. I was always waiting to do video. In college, while all my friend had stereos, I was the only one who could plug in the RCA jacks in the back. I just gravitated toward that.

What does video allow you to do that other media don't make possible?
I think of myself as a life artist. I'm a prostitute. I'm Scarlot Harlot. I live this life and document it. Video is the best medium with which to document my life in its totality. It allows me to give a little publicity to the counter-culture. As a teenager, I saw news shows about hippies in San Francisco, and I always wanted to live there, in some kind of subculture. When I started making video, I would go to demonstrations with a camera and show what people were doing. I'm a propagandist for various subcultures.

What propaganda have you done?
I've covered gay church resistance and spiritual warfare. *Die Yuppie Scum* is about the Anarchists' Conference in San Francisco. *Take Back the Night* is about sex workers' response to a Take Back the Night march. I've covered reproductive rights marches. My video *Sun Reich, Sun Set Up* is about the Gulf War, and it features Barbara Bush. During the war, I had a weekly TV show, and I created a series called *Whore in the Gulf*. I took CNN and demonstration footage and put out my own news about the war. That was one of my most powerful experiences. I've had a public access show since 1988. I was trained in public access, and I teach in public access now. I was

trained to take the public vision seriously and let it loose somewhere. Luckily, we had our own little oasis.

This is one of the major stories of my life: when the AIDS crisis hit, I had been producing a one-woman theatrical show, *The Adventures of Scarlot Harlot*. My play was about how stigma affected me as a prostitute. Once the AIDS crisis hit, stigma was no longer the issue; health issues became more important. I didn't know how to deal with that. Sexual health had not been my forte. I could talk about condoms, but it was hard to really, really know the specifics of how to use them. I wanted to leave San Francisco and cast my fate to the wind. I couldn't stand to see every day on the news more claims that prostitutes and gay people were spreading AIDS. I intended to go to another city to form TWAT, Texas Whores and Tricks. But my car broke down in Tucson. I met someone there immediately, the producer of TWIT, Tucson Western International Television. Tucson has one of the largest grants in the country for public access TV. This producer, David Bukunus, who was gay, understood my issues about AIDS. He took me under his wing.

I was voracious about video. I would just stay up all night and edit. It was totally free in Tucson. My first work was *War and Pizza in the Global Village*. We were a techno-performance ensemble. We all edited and shot. It was a unique video community. As you might imagine, in Tucson there was little else to do. I worked with TWIT, then got a grant to produce an episodic situation comedy called *Elaine's,* based on a female who owns a restaurant. She was a bleeding heart liberal, according to Tucson's standards. We had episodes about sexual health, homelessness, domestic violence—all sorts of interesting issues. This was my apprenticeship.

▶

Influences

Who gave you permission?
I was fortunate as a child because my parents didn't tell me that I had to do only women's things. They were amused when I did anything boys could do, so I was encouraged in that direction. My father was a TV repairman, so of course I developed an affinity with that medium. My father invented television. Yes, someone else had invented it, but we had an oscilloscope at home, and he reinvented it for us. So television was always a part of my life.

My parents were socialists, and I grew up with the feeling that I wanted to have an influence on the world, that I should contribute and reach as wide an audience as possible. I didn't want to reach any kind of esoteric milieu; I wanted to get out there and do what the people were watching. Video is accessible. Before, I was writing poetry. I found that the response to my videos was better than the response to my poetry.

Maybe it was Shirley Temple. Maybe she's my role model.

Starting with Shirley Temple, have any other figures been important to you?
I worked with Suzanne Lacy on a piece called *Freeze Frame.* That influenced my career as a feminist maker. For the first time, I was involved with a broader production based on organizational skills. I saw how to organize women and that organization is a part of the work of producing. Woody Allen has been an enormous influence. My last piece, *Mother's Mink,* was about a Jewish character, me, who has certain mishaps, goals, successes, and failures.

▶ ─────────────────────────────────

Prostitution Pays the Bills

How do you finance your work?
I've created about seventy-five videos. I do have a cable access show, so I have to create a weekly piece. Some of it's more trash video, but I've funded my life and training by doing sex work. I didn't make a lot of money, but I work as little as possible at sex work, so I've had time to do video. Prostitution has also been an inspiration to me. This was a choice in my career early on as an artist: to live an adventurous life and to document it.

There is more to the financial aspect of this. Fifteen years ago I became a sex worker. I'm lucky that I ended up doing video. Now I don't have to suck dick to make money; I live by editing other people's pieces. I found an artistic medium from which I can make money. Since I have expertise around sex, I've gravitated toward graphic or explicit material. Most of the esoteric sex teachers in San Francisco have hired me: I've done a visionary penis massage movie, and an interesting work about anal fisting. I'm doing this for money. My clients love this stuff. I'm developing porno in new directions. I'm looking forward to my next piece, *Genitals, the Comedy.*

▶ ─────────────────────────────────

Video Themes and Thrills

I have a central theme, a woman's right to control her body. My early music video *Pope Don't Preach (I'm Terminating My Pregnancy)* encapsulates what I was trying to say about my ownership of my body. I like to be naked in all my movies. I usually appear in some state of undress. I like to do it outside. I make it a political statement: "You don't like me here, naked like this? Too bad."

Would you like to get naked here? We could do it now, later, whenever you want.
I would, definitely, like to do that. Most recently, I've masturbated on the American flag. That was one of the most thrilling things I've done on video. Every time I time I see that shot of my vulva superimposed on the flag, I get a deep thrill and I know that I want to take it further.

Was masturbating on the flag part of a larger work?
Yes. Recently, I've become a feminist porn artist. I've been documenting women masturbating. It's about self-representation and sex. Annie Sprinkle, feminist porn artist, is in that movie. The women tell stories about what masturbation means to them and they masturbate. There are close-ups of vulvas. The vulvas are exalted, you see them in a new light. I'm very excited about this video. I love editing it. Editing has been my specialty. I'm proud to be a technician, and I love to sit in front of the editing machine and work for hours. To do that, working on juicy vulvas, creating positive, playful images of women's sexuality, has been some of my favorite time ever spent in front of those editing decks.

Carolee Schneemann said her legacy was the vulva. What is your legacy?
I hope that young women watching this documentary become sex workers and document their lives. But that's a felony to say. . . . It's hard to say what I want to give women. I'd love to influence them to take the camera on to the front line. Currently, I'm taking the video camera to the stroll district where we do outreach to prostitutes. We have a hidden camera and we watch for police violations of prostitutes' rights. That's my latest project, and that's a great use of video.

▶───────────────────────────────────────

Think Big

Can you talk about how hard it is to be a woman artist in this society?
I had a romantic concept of being an artist. I never had money; my parents couldn't support me. I've never had the exact body to be discovered as an actress. That's why I wanted to go into video: I was an actress and I knew I wouldn't be discovered as some svelte Madonna. I would make my own pieces. I would be a character in my own work, since I would not fit into any stereotypical female look. . . . It was a romantic choice. I put relation-

ships secondary. I am a love-addict type. I meet someone and want to get involved and forget my work. So I deprioritized relationships. I knew I wouldn't have children. I had to give up everything else to prioritize that work and to be an artist.

Being a prostitute is part of that: "I'll do anything for my art, even suck cock." And it worked. I did it like Gloria Steinem became a Playboy Bunny. She was going to do an exposé, checking it out. The difference for me was that I went in there and I was interested. I knew it would be my central theme as well as the way to support myself. Hemingway went to the front lines, and when I was a young feminist I read *Amazon Odyssey* by Ti-Grace Atkinson, and she said that prostitutes were on the front line of the battle of the sexes.[6] So I said, "All right, I'll go out there and be a prostitute."

How has your work been received?
I'm so lucky and grateful that it has been received as well as it has. But sometimes, I think about all the other artists who have been received better than I have and I get really jealous. In fact, I'm totally obsessed with that. In fact, Madonna drives me crazy. And then sometimes I think about how successful I am in relation to other artists.

Do you lose anything in the process?
I wish I had tried even harder. I wish I had never slept. I wish—and women don't do this enough—I had thought big. Invest in big productions and take big risks. And that's one of my obstacles: to think big and plan big projects.

Why is that hard?
Like many women, well, I'm only a nice little poet like Edna St. Vincent Millay, like Emily Dickinson—a creative, sensitive woman expressing myself.

But this form costs tons of money.
No. No. I can do everything cheap, for no money. People let me do things for free, I do trades, I get small grants.

Has there been a video you wanted to make that you haven't been able to because you couldn't? Say, because of the money?
When there's something I can't make, I'll make it later. I'm forty-five years old, and I wonder how many videos I can make. I better start really thinking: what can I make? I only want to make features now. I'm tired of festivals. I don't understand the advantage. I don't get distribution. I like awards, but then what? They're not shown on TV. I need to make something commercial.

How do you distribute?
I distribute myself. Art Com does some of it. Now the porn I make is with House of Chicks. The esoteric sex teachers have their own audience.

What do you like about the idea of a larger audience?
I want to have a mainstream audience, I want to influence the public in general. I could show people that the weird people in San Francisco aren't so weird, or entice some to move to San Francisco to join us and help us.

▶————————————————————————————————

I Still Embrace Feminism

Tell me about your relationship to the feminist movement.
I got involved with feminism between 1970 and 1971. It really meant a lot to me. It explained my childhood: why my father was oppressive to my mother, why my mother couldn't defend us. It explained my psychology and my family history. I like women because they are compassionate, nice, good. My mother was good, my father was bad. I understood I could pull out of the negative influences in my life. Compassion has been important to me and being open-minded and being forgiving. That was the center of my politics. I know they call it essentialist these days. But I still love being a feminist because I can promote feminine virtues, feminine values—nurturing, compassion. The whore with the heart of gold: that is still the central image in my work.

Have other movements been important to you?
Feminism has been my central artistic influence. I've been involved in protesting the Vietnam War, peace movements, reproductive rights. My politics stem from wanting to be compassionate and to teach people to accept people's diversity. In my work, I show how people are different but we all are human beings and can love, get along, and respect each other. That's what motivated me and is my strong political mission.

Can you talk about feminist censorship?
My video *Outlaw Poverty not Prostitutes* was censored at the University of Michigan Law School by students of Catharine MacKinnon, who teaches at the university. She was sponsoring a conference called "Prostitutes from Activism to Academia." No proud or out working prostitutes were invited. However, there was an art event in conjunction with the conference where my work was included. During the course of the conference, the students closed down the exhibit. They stole the videos from the exhibit. There was no sex in my video. Someone said "fuck" once. I was furious when it was censored. The ACLU represented the case from the Art Censorship Project.

That's one way to tell the story. But when you are censored, you are also more famous. I'm not too worried about being censored these days. I'm worried about being demonized. There are lies going around about what people like me are promoting—like child sexual abuse. That frightens me.

In my work I'm talking about two important things: people promoting acceptance despite differences and control over our own bodies. I think of myself as a neofeminist. The women's movement has been protectionist. The new vision says we don't need to stay in our bedroom to protect ourselves from date rape. We can be free and display our sexuality publicly. Yet for some women my freedom may be the rope with which to hang herself.

Is there anything else you want to say?
In the '70s I became a feminist. My sexuality was not in keeping with politically correct feminism. I was bisexual, I was chastised, I never fit in. For me, being a feminist was talking about the compassionate woman. But I was disenchanted because women were very cruel to me, made me feel like an outcast. Through my rejection, sexually, I was catapulted into prostitution; it expressed my rejection and my feminist angst about my sexuality. All the antiporn writing made me gravitate toward the center of it. It is sad to me that mainstream feminism demonizes women who are sexual and women who are sex workers. I still prioritize women's experience, and compassion, so I still embrace feminism. It's sad. I hope that I can contribute to a change in the concept of feminism because that would certainly be something new.

So many of my students want so desperately to experiment with their own sexuality, their own sexual self-confidence and persona, and yet they feel that feminism has told them that is not appropriate. They have that struggle embodied within them. But there has always been another voice in feminism, those women who applaud sexuality, not just those who deride it.
Historically, feminism gave us the right to vote, the temperance movement, and the criminalization of prostitution. Recent feminist history has been protectionist and antisex. Young women might feel that feminism controls their sexuality. People need permission to be bad. It's not that I feel prostitution is the greatest thing, but there's so much ambiguity. We need freedom to try to deconstruct prostitution, sex work, and our roles. We won't do that by staying at home and feeling we have to protect ourselves from being sexual.

▶ ───────────────────────────────────

A Figure Alone

Where's your place in feminist video history?
It's about doing guerrilla work and feeling like you can go out there with your camera and live the life you feel like, and if people tell you women

can't or it's bad to be too sexual, you do it. My figure is a figure alone. Sometimes you do have to go out there on your own.

You answer in such a self-mocking way, but your work is so important to people.
People see my work, but I don't hear back from them. It's out there. I'm constantly working. I put out material but receive no feedback. I have no concept of my place in video, or how people are receiving it. I want to know what it means to people.

Is that lack of exposure something about video?
I'm not in an academic context. I go to meetings with social workers or politicians. My work is outside academia and the art world. I put my energy where it is most needed. That's why I'm not seeing feedback.

MEGAN CUNNINGHAM (associate producer): *With your interest in a mainstream audience, what would you hope young girls to get, and why would you want them to join you?*
We need more street-fighting women out there doing sex work and writing about it, making pieces. There aren't enough images of big women, of fat women, in the media. The older I get, the more I like taking off my clothes. I can't wait to be older and fatter and taking my clothes off in more places. We need to know about human variety. My messages are clear: acceptance, human variety, control of our bodies. I embody the goddess. I am the big woman, the great goddess. When I am naked and righteous, then women are naked and righteous. And I don't mind that role.

Anything else you want to say?
I have a dual personality: Carol Leigh and Scarlot Harlot. It's like Clark Kent and Superman. That's my symbolism.

This has been so good for me. I feel far away from being a maker. The studio where I worked was closed down. I don't have the kind of access I once had. I haven't started a major piece for awhile. I need to do something big. I know what I want to do, too. [Carol Leigh takes off her clothes.]

Selected Videos

1984	*War and Pizza in the Global Village,* 40 min.
1985	*Elaine's,* 6 episodes, 30 min. each
1987	*Bad Laws,* 5 min.
1987	*Mom PSAs,* 30 sec. each
1987	*Pope Don't Preach (I'm Terminating My Pregnancy),* 5 min.
1987	*Safe Sex Slut,* 30-min. compilation, 4-min. song
1989	*Die Yuppie Scum,* 28 min.
1990	*Take Back the Night,* 28 min.
1990	*Yes Means Yes, No Means No,* 8 min.
1991	*Sun Reich, Sun Set Up,* 5 min.
1991	*Whore in the Gulf,* 6 episodes, 30 min. each
1992	*Outlaw Poverty, Not Prostitutes,* 20 min.
1994	*Mother's Mink,* 15 min.
1998	*Blind Eye to Justice: HIV Positive Women in California Prisons,* 34 min.

Distribution and Contact Information

Videos available from the artist at her e-mail addresses (info@bayswan.org or swfest@bayswon.org) or her Web site (http://www.bayswan.org/penet.html)

[12] Juanita Mohammed

Juanita Mohammed is a community video artist and activist. She uses inexpensive camcorder video technology to respond to the needs of those who matter to her. In her work at the Gay Men's Health Crisis (GMHC) in New York City, Mohammed makes educational videos for and about the AIDS community. In her personal video work, she looks to her friends and neighbors to find stories that are not typically represented in the media. Discussing the political implications of "community media" in an article about its ethics, Frances Negrón-Muntaner says: "Despite our often casual and imprecise use of the term 'community,' it is no accident that we tend to choose the word when speaking about groups with an unempowered relationship to dominant power structures. Thus we refer to the black community, the Latino community, the gay community, and the women's community. We never say the men's community."[1] Mohammed works with just such a politicized understanding of both community and media to give voice to the people she knows. In so doing, she joins another community: those who make radical use of camcorder technology. Camcorder activists "narrowcast" targeted information to the usually underserved communities who need it most, while at the same time refashioning cultural power by reestablishing who has the knowledge and authority to speak publicly. Ellen Spiro, an AIDS activist videomaker, preaches in her "Camcordist Manifesto" (1991): "Camcorder footage contributes to a broader analysis of an event by offering an alternative to broadcast media's centrist view. It has the power to add a dimension to the chorus of voices heard, providing a platform for seasoned activists and concerned community members, rather than the same old authoritative experts giving the same old scripted rants."[2]

Deirdre Boyle sees AIDS activist video as a direct descendant of the guerrilla TV of the '70s. A working-class, black mother of two who had been forced to terminate her college education in film due to financial and other constraints, Mohammed came into video in the '90s through just this ideological legacy when I invited her to join an AIDS activist video collective. I am also a product of the sector of the media community that believes that political and personal growth can be facilitated through media access. I learned video production in the '80s at progressive media arts centers in New York City. I took classes, received grants, and rented equipment from several organizations founded in the '70s that had maintained their commitment to community media empowerment: Downtown Community Television (DCTV), Global Village, Film/Video Arts.[3] Meanwhile, I was also studying about the history of media activism in graduate school. As I learned about organizations like George Stoney's 1960s Challenge for Change Program in Canada, which allowed local communities to make television about issues that concerned them, or Third World Newsreel, which became committed to educating people of color in media production in the '60s and then distributing this work, I believed that similar work could contribute to activism around the AIDS crisis.[4]

I invited Mohammed to join the Women's AIDS Video Enterprise, a project that I organized in 1990 to facilitate the production of community-produced, community-specific AIDS educational video.[5] Already a talented and committed community activist and a political artist, Mohammed was mentored into her current full-time career in video by several feminist teachers including myself (also Jean Carlomusto and Alisa Lebow, both colleagues of Mohammed at GMHC). An eager student, Mohammed had already been self-educating, keeping her eyes open for feminist film role models wherever she could find them. She first found Mae West, was later moved by the work of Barbra Streisand, and then by Barbara Hammer. In the '80s, Mohammed was making the art she could afford to make— particularly poetry—even though her love was for film. What she needed was access to the expensive technologies that record moving images in time. And then, suddenly, there were camcorders, VCRs, video rental stores. The significance of the rapid affordability of these technologies in the '90s cannot be overstated. Whereas communities of color have had but a limited role in the history of film and video due to structures of access, Mohammed foreshadows the next period in media history where levels of wealth, education, or even proximity to major arts centers will not impede expressive people from representing their ideas and lives with that most dominant of media, television.

Given her primary political commitment to AIDS, Mohammed uses television to show PWAs (persons with AIDS) who are women, people of color, drug users, and gay men; her subjects speak for themselves and discuss lives in which AIDS plays a central role. Sexuality is one aspect of this life;

safe sex is a major component of this life; racism, poverty, addiction, and violence play a large share. For instance, A Part of Me *introduces the viewer to Lilly Gonzalez, a lesbian, former IV drug user, who is now a safer-sex educator.* Two Men and a Baby *tells the story of two working-class, black gay men who adopt an HIV-positive relative. And* Homosexuality: One Child's Point of View *is just that: Juanita's daughter, Jazzy, relating her open views on sexual freedom and identity.*

Even though all of her video work is about and for her community, in her interview Mohammed explains that it is her role of mother that most inspires her career. She wants to leave a legacy for her daughter. Of the twenty women whom I interviewed, only four (Mohammed plus Bowser, Reichert, and Vesna) referred, if only in passing, to their children. The vast majority of my interview subjects do not have children—an uncommon situation for American women. The choice or consequence of childlessness for women artists, even as the theme of mothering and foremothering is so central, was rarely referred to directly in the interviews. Carol Leigh was the exception to this rule. Leigh explains how she self-consciously chose not to have children to best facilitate her career as an artist. More commonly, women spoke of their own mothers, or their teachers, students, friends, or role models. While the challenge for many contemporary women (feminists or no) seems to be the balancing of child and career, the immense challenge of claiming *a media career, in its own right, seems as much as most women in this study could bear.*

As Mohammed continues to make work for her children and her community, that community changes, grows, and shifts because she has entered into a larger world through her videomaking. That is a significant explanation for why so many of us accept the risks and sacrifices involved with making activist video: making feminist art is also about fashioning a better self, making relationships, affecting one's community, striving to make a better world, and in so doing entering that world as an engaged participant.

▶ ———————————————————————————————

A Tool to Educate

Could you talk about the role of video in the communities where you work?
Video is a tool to educate. It's especially valuable in communities of color because children and their parents look at TV incessantly. A family might not have money to save up for a vacation, but every weekend they'll find enough to go to the movies or pay to have cable TV. A lot of the things they look at are for entertainment, not learning. But they *are* learning something,

even though they don't realize it. A lot of videos give out stereotypes that people accept automatically.

In communities of color, we don't get education in our schools about making or criticizing film or video. In my school there was one little film class. The teacher showed us films. I was the only student interested in film as an educational tool. For everyone else, it was entertainment. When I told the teacher I wanted to be a director and producer, she said, "Oh, that's good." She really didn't think that this little black girl would ever get there. The librarian was black, and she gave me all the books on film in the library. I think it was more to get rid of the books, or to get rid of me, than out of a belief that this little girl was really going to be a filmmaker.

Where do you place yourself in the history of feminist film and video?
I think that in the history of women feminist filmmakers, I am one of the forerunners of the community video movement. Even though I went to film school for one year, I didn't get that formal training. I haven't done that much reading, or attended many workshops, or hung around with theorists or formal filmmakers. I'm an educator. I go to community groups that don't have cameras. I give women who live in shelters, and prostitutes, and women at home being mothers a chance to videotape their stories. I'm coming from a land where finding cameras and shooting are hard and where we're not shooting from what the theory says but from what we see and what we believe in.

▶───

Film Education

When I went to college for one year at the School of Visual Arts, everyone had money. There were three other black people, and they had money, too. And then there was me. Everybody was rich, school was expensive, nobody took time out to help me. That was probably because I didn't ask, but when I did, the response was really fast. It was like, "Well, this is how to do this." But nobody saw that this girl lives in Brooklyn, a poor community. It was like, "She'll get by, don't worry about it." They were always saying, "I just saw this film or went to this workshop," but I'd never been to those places and wasn't going to go to those places, because I didn't have the money. A lot of times people would ask, "Did you see this film?" and I'd go, "Not yet," and they'd get into all these issues about it and I'd be sitting there lost.

When I would come back to my own community, there was no one to talk to about it. If I tried to talk to my mother, she'd say, "Get a real job, be a secretary." I want my own children to be filmmakers, even though

I know my daughter will be something like a lawyer and my son a policeman. But film will give them a way of looking at the world from the outside and also the knowledge that they are inside that world. And when they look at television and see something stereotypical, they will realize that's not true and that there are other ideas and other points of view.

Where did you find the resources you needed to develop into the professional you are today?

The places I looked to for resources, so that I could self-educate and become a video maker, were TV and movies. I would see somebody like Mildred Pierce work her way up from waitress to manager. Or in *Gone with the Wind* Scarlett went up and down and never gave up. That would push me. By the time I got to high school, I wanted a camera. I saved up my money and my stepfather helped me. I bought a camera. I had never read a book about how to use a camera. I didn't know anything about documentaries. I just knew that people write scripts and you make films from them. So I would get in the house with my little camera and force my brother and sister to be in my movie. Luckily, they were hams. I would say, "Okay, you are the stars." There were no character actors in my movies.

I was always the director, never inside the film. It was a power thing. I would show the movies on the projector to my mother and aunts. And then they would be placed in a box and forgotten. As I got older, I wanted my films to be shown. No one wanted to see them. Nobody thought they had anything to say. They thought, "She's just playing with the camera." From the time when I was sixteen to when I was twenty, I had four cameras. They would get stolen, and I would get a new camera.

▶ ———————————————————————————————

The Women's AIDS Video Enterprise

Eventually, I stopped going to school. I started working construction and gave up on ever being a filmmaker. I got involved in a little activism because that was when women were first starting in construction, and I worked with some groups. I would sit and listen to the white girls talking about working on this or that issue. I was always included when it came to doing the work, like putting up banners, but when it came to the educational part where there were discussions about what to do, I wasn't included. I did absorb some activism during that time. I went into Housing Preservation and Development and became an inspector. The agency had five women and two hundred men. I felt like a strong, independent woman. I would tell my mother that constantly, and she would say constantly, "Be a secretary."

I was making $14 an hour. Secretaries were making seven. We would go to houses to inspect, and the inspectors always knew if the guy in the bed had AIDS. They could be quite insulting. I felt so guilty for working with those people, that I called up Brooklyn AIDS Task Force (BATF) and started volunteering.

Finally, Alex Juhasz came to BATF. She wanted to make a video with women who were involved with AIDS. I said, "This is me. Perfect!" I almost ran over to the woman who told me about the job. The group met. There were about six women, and we were really different. I was thinking, "Hmm, I don't belong with these women." Some of them were married; they were low-income. At the time, I thought I wasn't low-income. I was a housing inspector; we made money.

And we made a video. I really thought, "Okay, this isn't going to be *our* video, it'll be this little white girl's video." The first time she said, "You can take the camera home," I thought, "Really? Is she crazy? It'll get stolen, and besides, I don't know how to use this camera." I took it home and didn't sleep all night thinking the camera was going to get killed. But I was up for the next two days, just filming away. The power came back. I realized that I can hide behind this camera and I can make people do anything I want. When we were three-quarters of the way into the project, it came time to interview other people. Insecurities came back. Interview people on the outside? I had been on the inside, filming the kids and stuff. I was scared, but I took the camera out. First, I went into my own neighborhood and interviewed people. Then some drug dealer started telling people not to do the interview. That really pissed me off. I said, "Who are you talking to? I live in this neighborhood; I'll do what I want. I can interview anyone I feel like." The video finally got finished [*We Care: A Video for Care Providers of People Affected by AIDS*, 1990]. It was the first video I had worked on, and people liked it. I was in shock. We did it. We all did. People still ask about it.

Video

Why do you make video?
I make video because it's cheaper than film, because there's stories to tell and video is the easiest means by which to get them out to people in different communities. Everyone doesn't read or doesn't have the time to read. People can look at a video when they get it or a year from now. They can stop and start it when they feel like it. And anyone can make a video. You don't have to go to school; you can be a child and make a video. And they

are learning tools for the person who is making them. When you shoot video, you see a different facet of a situation, things you didn't notice, and you learn from that. Video provides power to get out information.

Please talk about some of the videos that you've worked on.
I do two types of videos: those I do where I work, at GMHC, and those I do for Mother/Daughter Productions, which are for myself. The videos for GMHC include *Two Men and a Baby, Iris House, A Normal Life,* and *A Part of Me.* My work at GMHC is about people with AIDS and the issues surrounding them. In the past two years I've made about twenty videos, each up to twelve minutes long. I like the ones I make about women, and I like making videos with people I work with. A lot of times, my mind is set on one approach, but they point me in different ways. I'm more trusting of them than I am of myself.

I made *A Normal Life* with my cameraperson, Gary Winter. We had to go to the Bronx, which I despise. I got sicker than a dog. Five shoots, and I kept getting sick. But Gary never gets tired. If I say, "Let's do this," he doesn't question me, so I get to be really free on those kinds of shoots. The video was about a home with ninety-nine family members where there were people who were HIV-positive. It was based on the story of two girls who met in the shelter, fell in love, and moved out. They're together with one of the girls' little daughter. They became a family. I felt a lot of their stuff was in me. I called them two days ago. A lot of times, I'm afraid to call people I've already shot because I think, "Oh, my God, one of them will probably be dead." Both of them were still alive. They left me a message in return saying, "Thanks for calling, Juanita, we love you, too."

Please talk about some of the work that you do on your own.
That work is based more on community stuff. For four years, I've been doing a video on my neighborhood, Bushwick. There was this newspaper article that came out six or seven years ago. It said Bushwick was the worst place in the world. They interviewed the family of a kid who was out mugging people. They went into every bad thing that anyone in his family had ever done. There wasn't a single good thing. There was a line in the piece about how everyone in Bushwick is on welfare or poor or on drugs. I got so pissed off. I wanted to write in to the newspaper, but I never did. So I decided, "I've got to show the good parts of Bushwick." I've been shooting families at graduations, the parades we have against drugs. The neighborhood community people and politicians are not helpful, because I'm not doing this video for them or in the way they want me to. I've had problems with drug dealers who don't want me to film them. But the people are really

forthcoming. So it will eventually get made. I hope it gets made before I move out of Bushwick.

I'm doing a video about a man who has cancer. I'm also doing a video about one of my neighbors, who is fifty and a lesbian. She's never been really involved with the lesbian population, but suddenly she has a new girlfriend, and now she's all, "Oh my God, I'm a lesbian!" I shoot a lot of videos for drug groups and for the police. The police were going to Florida to help some hurricane victims, so I shot a little video for that. I shoot church groups that have some kind of organization that they want people to see. I shoot for free because I have no sense. I like filming in the community. I do a lot of videos with my children. I'm doing a video with my son now because in school he's supposed to be a "behavior problem." They want him in a horrible school where only the most troubled kids are. We don't see it, so me and him talk about it in the video, and he's always just dying to be interviewed.

The first video I ever made was a collaboration between my daughter and me. It was called *Homosexuality: One Child's Point of View*. At the time, my daughter was eight. There was going to be a film festival at Downtown Community Television Center. I told Jazzy, "I'm going to enter a film festival about gay people. Do you want to make a video?" And Jazzy said, "I don't want to make a video with you. I want to make a video by myself!" So I was helping her, doing some of her camera work and some of her sound. It was horrible working with her. She was eight, and she'd tell me what to do. I would set up the camera a certain way and explain why and she'd say, "No! I want it over here. It's *my* video!" It was a six-month process. When we got up to the editing room, after two minutes, she was playing. The video premiered at a film festival. She was Miss "I Made the Video, I Did the Editing."

I think that I worked with her mostly because I was scared to make films. I was behind her. I could say, "The little kid made all the mistakes." I'll say it now: "I made it." It was a cute little video. A lot of it had to do with me wanting Jahanara to not be insecure, to grow up to be a feminist. Maybe it's bypassed me, but I can mold her to be a woman who doesn't take crap from men or anyone. And she's actually emerged into that person.

▶──

Two Men and a Baby

What is important to you about how you make your work?
When I make a video, I'm trying to show real people. The video that really expressed the message of the people who were in it was *Two Men and a*

Baby. Two Men got started because two young guys I know who are lovers came to me one day, and one of them said that his sister, who was HIV-positive, had a baby and they wanted to keep that baby. I was amazed because they were so young, and one of them was slow, with a lot of health problems. The other was using drugs. I thought, "They want that responsibility, and they're smart enough to come to me and ask about it?"

So I told them what to do, and they got hooked up with an AIDS agency. They got the baby, and I started to see that, as they lived with the baby, they began to mature. I wanted to make a video to show how they had changed and how dealing with an HIV-positive baby made them grow and brought them into a community that they had been on the fringes of.

So I told them, "I want to make a video about you." They said, "Sure! We're going to be stars!" So I went to their house with two other people. When we first arrived at their place and got out of the car, I said, "I hope we won't get robbed or mugged." The crew probably thought I was joking. I wasn't joking. When I come to my neighborhood with people who don't live there, I want them to know that the neighborhood is good, but I also want them to know that you can be in a dangerous situation. Now, usually these guys were the most big-mouthed people in the world. I had filmed them at parties and stuff and they were like, "Blah blah blah." But when the film crew came out and turned on that light, the only person talking was the kid, who was then about two years old. We got to editing, and we thought they didn't say anything valuable. But it came out excellently. It only ran about seven little minutes. That video was in twelve international festivals and finally last year was shown in this country, too. We didn't send it to the film festivals. People would see it in one place and call for it.

And now we're making *Part 2*, and it's such a difference. The guys have separated. I did the shoot with Ray first, and he was his usual droll self. But when I asked questions, he was more articulate and knew about more issues. When I interviewed Tyrone, he analyzed the situation, something he had not done before. He was articulate. While he was analyzing what I was saying, he was also analyzing their relationship and what they do with Eric, the baby. I stay in touch with them, and I've seen changes. They show the video. They started with showing it to their families and then showed it to friends, and now Tyrone takes the video around to different organizations. The biggest thing that video did was getting them incorporated into the gay community. Before the video, all they knew about was going to the Christopher Street Pier. They didn't know there was a lesbian/gay center, or lesbian/gay film festivals, or restaurants. They were tourists: "Saturday we'll be gay. Monday, we won't know gays in other parts of the community." Now they go to the center, they go to AIDS workshops, and they go to restaurants.

A feminist video?

I think that *Two Men and a Baby* is a feminist video because it shows people empowering themselves. They have a problem, and they don't wait for other people to help them. They do what feminists do: they are caregivers. They had to take care of Eric when, for a long time, they were not taking care of themselves. After making the video, they realized, "We have to take care of ourselves. No one else is going to do it." Women have always taken care of everyone else and saved themselves for last. Now women are saying, "I'll put me first and then take care of the rest of you."

Obstacles

What obstacles do you face?
My own insecurities. I don't think I'm a videomaker. I always think that somebody else can do it better. When someone offers me a big project, I kind of shy away: "Let someone else do it." I won't do a big project, because I think, "That needs someone with talent, or someone who's really good with the camera or machinery."

Where does the insecurity come from?
I think that my insecurity comes from my peers and family. Not my video peers, but the people I live with in my neighborhood. I don't want to move away from them, but I don't think that those people believe that I'm a videomaker. It's like, "She gots a camera, and she works for those people, but she's not a *real* video person."

Is that a feminist issue? Is that an issue about race, about class?
It's race, class, sexism—all of those together. When I see black male videomakers from my community, they're more self-assured. The guys are like, "Yo, man, you made a video, good for you!" When I make a video, they're like, "Oh, really? That's nice." When I make videos, my neighbors assume there's black people in the video. If I say there's not, I get that look like, "Why? You don't think we're good enough? You don't like your own people?"

Influences

I'm interested in your influences. How were you introduced to feminism?
The first films I liked starred Mae West. I didn't know she was a director or
producer. But she was a powerful star. She was a woman who laid men out.
If she wanted sex, she had sex; if she wanted sex with more than one person,
she had it. She wasn't scared to tell anybody what to do. You never saw her
in the kitchen. I tried to walk and talk and act like Mae West. When I was
thirteen, I read that she was a filmmaker, a producer, and a director. Oh,
wow! That's when I started wanting to make films.

I cooled down until I was sixteen. I knew that the movies I was looking at were made by men, but it wasn't wrong to me until I hit sixteen. A
teacher showed *Joyce at 34* by Joyce Chopra (1972). I was like, "She directed it? Wow!" I remembered that Mae West directed—women can direct
films! I was thrilled by that film. She has a baby in the course of the film,
and it turned me off to having kids. I decided that I wouldn't have a baby,
or if I ever did, it wouldn't be by natural childbirth. (I have two kids, both
cesareans.)

I started looking for women filmmakers. I saw that Barbra Streisand is
committed to her work and is powerful in her films. I went to a film festival
and saw a Barbara Hammer film. It was the weirdest thing I'd ever seen in
my life. I liked it. I sensed the power and compassion behind that film, *Superdyke* [1975]. I realized you don't have to make a film where people talk all
the time: there can be movement. The camera can be upside down. I had
wanted to make stuff weird. That film gave me the freedom to mess with
the camera: upside down, sideways, things out of order. That gave me a big
sense of power. I can play with the camera; I can place the people where I
want. If that actor, my sister, had hair in her eyes, I could leave it that way.
That's where realness came from. If I make a mistake and think it's cute, it
can stay in there.

*Whom do you owe for creating the conditions that allowed you to take
your place in video history?*
My mother. I wouldn't have said it a few years ago, but she gave me inde-
pendence. Not purposefully, but I saw her around the house fixing stuff,
taking care of three kids by herself. She taught me to be strong-willed and
do what I want. My aunt was religious. She instilled in me the value of
helping other people. That pushes me to make videos that are worthwhile,
not just for money. And Alex Juhasz—she gave me the freedom to work
and wanted my ideas. Without that, I would still be in construction, not in

video. And Jean Carlomusto—she let me work at GMHC and she let me produce. She let me make mistakes. And Alisa Lebow [AIDS activist video-maker]—she pushes me. I want to be lazy. Alisa asks, "Why? What does this mean?" I want to do it, but I'm scared. She pushes me, and I do it right.

Oops, I almost forgot, and my daughter. I get angry at her, but she's always there for me. If I'm down, she pushes me up; she makes me remember who I am. I'm doing this so that one day she can say, "I am the way I am because my mother pushed me. I respect her, and she left stuff behind that's useful."

JUANITA MOHAMMED

Selected Videos

1995 to present	Segments for GMHC's *Living with AIDS Show*
1995	*Iris House,* ¾" video, 15 min.
1995	*Two Men and a Baby,* ¾" video, 7 min.
1995	*Iris de la Cruz Family,* ¾" video, 26 min.
1996	*Binkowitz Family,* ¾" video, 10 min.
1996	*Lavender Light,* ¾" video, 7 min.
1997	*A Part of Me,* ¾" video, 15 min.
1997	*A Normal Life,* ¾" video, 28 min.

For Mother/Daughter Productions and Other Groups

1990	*We Care: A Video for Care Providers of People Affected by AIDS* (with Women's AIDS Video Enterprise), VHS, 30 min.
1992	*Bushwick: A Viable Part of the City,* VHS, 10 min.
1992	*House of Hope Homeless Center,* VHS, 20 min.
1993	*Homosexuality: One Child's Point of View* (with Jahanara Mohammed), VHS, 5 min.

Distribution and Contact Information

Gay Men's Health Crisis, 119 West 24th Street, 9th Floor, New York, NY 10011; (212) 367-1208

[13] Wendy Quinn

*When I interviewed her, Wendy Quinn was the program director of
Chicago's Women in the Director's Chair (WIDC). WIDC stages one of
the few remaining women's festivals in the United States; there is also a
festival in Denver, Seattle, New York City, and San Francisco. Quinn's
work with WIDC is dedicated to media education and empowerment
through expanding channels of access, distribution, and exhibition. She
believes that unlike the hierarchical model of fiction filmmaking taught to
her in film school, feminist film distribution and education are a last bastion
in the media world that is rooted in the egalitarian, communal spirit she
cherishes from the '70s women's movement. "That's why I ended up with
a group like WIDC: it operates by the feminist principle that the process is
as important as the product," Quinn explains. Needless to say, although
the few remaining feminist organizations dedicated to distribution and exhibition struggle to maintain such values, this has not led to fiscal solvency
or institutional stability. Burnout, lack of fiscal support, diminishing societal
enthusiasm for feminism, and waning understanding about or interest in
alternative culture are only partial explanations for the current dearth of
women's film festivals.*

*The fact that distribution and exhibition are consistently a weak link
in the feminist film and video cycle—which moves from conception, to
funding, to production, to distribution and exhibition, to audience and
critical response—is by no means a testament to feminists' lack of trying.
In fact, much of the history of feminist film and video has been both fueled
and hindered by feminists' politicized commitment to "getting the work
out" through feminist distribution companies, festivals, and scholarship
and film criticism. It is one of the definitive features of committed media
practice that distribution—in all its uncelebrated, grassroots, hands-on
glory—takes on a central role. This is because personal power gained by*

the filmmaker is not the only, or even the most important, goal. Equally important is the potential empowerment of other women who can be moved by filmmakers' work and also a commitment to altering the very landscape of the culture by making sure that alternative viewpoints are expressed.

And yet film and video are shadowed by the distribution models of Hollywood film and broadcast television, two of history's most successful systems for getting a standardized product quickly to a hungry consumer. With this as the rule, it is no wonder that most feminist filmmakers and distributors become frustrated with the limited exposure and revenues that define the alternative distribution market. Quinn argues that there would need to be real social change, along a number of fronts, before such frustration about distribution could be truly appeased. For instance, she believes that we would need to begin with a greater commitment to public arts education. You need an audience who feels educated and interested in viewing experimental art before you can hope to sell it to them. And she also suggests that a general decrease in political consciousness affects alternative distribution because you first need a culture where people feel capable to participate in political debate in order to have an audience eager to view politicized art work. During the heyday of the women's movement there was a ready and organized audience for such work through women's clubs, consciousness-raising groups, women's centers, women's organizations, and the decade's institutions for feminist art. And in the not-so-distant past we had significant arts funding in America, which meant that art was not dependent on supporting its own production costs through sales, rentals, or exhibition. Many other societies still utilize state-supported arts funding models where the distribution of art need not be profit driven.

Beyond these structural limitations, radical distribution is usually a pretty thankless task, the much-deserved celebration of Women Make Movies' twenty-fifth anniversary notwithstanding.[1] This is compounded by the explosion of home video, which led to alternative theaters and screening venues closing down in the '90s, leaving the academy and the art establishment as the two remaining viable outlets for radical film culture in this society. As a direct consequence, more and more feminist artists choose to go mainstream because even if they espouse a radical agenda, there are fewer and fewer networks through which to get this agenda out to a significant audience. Meanwhile, feminist distribution organizations have been forced to take up the more corporate organizational structure now demanded of nonprofits.

Even though Quinn has a degree in film production, like many of the women interviewed in this study, she feels more comfortable defining herself

*as an activist, not an artist. Working on this project, I have been inspired
to learn how various women draw their own interrelations between film
or video in its many aspects: as an aesthetic and expressive mode, a tool
to critique our society, and a forum from which to enact a commitment to
social change. Given that we live in a time where we are rarely allowed to
hear people speaking about motivations other than the accumulation of
wealth, power, or prestige, I find interviews like Quinn's to be especially
moving: "The media can point toward positive changes. If you can see in
media that something is being done somewhere, that gives you a connection
and points toward action you yourself can take. That can help you to feel
power, to feel that it is possible to step in and take charge of your own life,
or to organize with others and make change."*

▶

Women in the Director's Chair

I would like you to talk about your work in film and video.
My work in film and video is as program director for Women in the Director's Chair, which is a not-for-profit media arts organization based in
Chicago. The largest work that WIDC does, and the largest work that I
do with them, is to help to put on an international film and video festival,
which showcases work by women directors from all over the world. We
also have several other year-round programs. The festival is the well from
which all the other programs spring. We have a national touring program;
we have a prison program where videos, videomakers, and peer educators
go into prisons in Illinois; we have a youth media outreach program where
we teach basic video production and media literacy at alternative and some
public high schools; we have an archive, which continues to grow, and is
available to prisons, community groups, film- and videomakers, curators,
and researchers. So I am someone who works in all of those areas with a
large group of volunteers who are not only in film and video but also community organizing.

How did you get to where you are?
I graduated three years ago, in the '90s, from film school. Growing up,
I really identified with film characters but didn't think about the process
through which films are made. So I wanted to touch cameras and touch
lights and all that techno stuff. There's an element of both fear and desire
involved in the process of thinking about, Can I do this, can I not do this?
So I went to film school, and the elements of being afraid and wanting to

make work did continue. But film school was really male-oriented then, which I think it still is. That's why WIDC focuses on work by women exclusively because even though it's not stated that women are not going to be able to work with these particular implements, the sentiments are still there.

▶───

Film and Video

How did you get to where you are now in film/video?
I went to college in the sort of traditional, eighteen-going-to-college mode, but it didn't take at that point, probably because of personal confusion. I took a long break from higher education. I was always interested in film, from when I was a young child. But I viewed it as something that was not real, because I was watching Hollywood movies and TV. My take on it was that it was a fantasy thing. I had no connection with the process, with how these things came to be made. They were just there.

So I took a long time off. I worked in music, and I like music because it's really visceral, the most moving art. It misses the intellect and enters your psyche and soul bypassing the intellect. And film can be that way, too. I didn't think film school or making films was something that I could do, a viable life choice. So I didn't pursue it for a long time. But I got to a certain age, and I thought there was no reason not to do it, especially if it was something I wanted to do. Even if I wouldn't be successful. Also, coming from a family of attorneys, there may have been an element of rebellion against the family business. So I went to film school to try to make films.

Tell me about your film practice.
I'm not working on anything now, and if I did another project, I'd want to use video. Video is more attractive to me now because it's more democratic, less expensive, and easier to use. I've worked mostly on small productions. I did work on a well-known film made in Chicago called *Go Fish* (Rose Troche, 1994). It was interesting in terms of how people work together and why they do the work they do. *Go Fish* started out at the level of a student production. It continued through the course of several years, got a general release, and is now well known and written about. *Go Fish* was a project people worked on without pay, over a long period of time, because they thought it was an important thing to do. Working on an all-female crew was a revelation to me because of what I learned in film school about power issues concerning who's "the king" and how people relate.

Power with Responsibility

Do you consider yourself an artist?
I don't think that I would say I'm an artist. I'm an activist. I'm not working on anything of my own. I've shifted into a different mode. I think I have doubts about whether my work is the most important work to spend time on or to make sure people see.

What are the social movements, or artistic movements, or theoretical movements, which have been influential to your career?
The women's movement. I was a teenager in the late '70s: that was a time of such ferment and movement. All kinds of ideas were formed then that inform me and how I live my life now. That's why I ended up with a group like WIDC: it operates by the feminist principle that the process is as important as the product. The way you arrive is as important as what you have at the end. That's not how things are done generally. That was not my experience in film school.

Columbia College exists to produce people who can get commercial jobs. They teach how to use equipment well, and they teach the narrative structures of mainstream TV and movies. They teach how to work together as a crew: it is a hierarchical structure where the director is "God." That's why people want to be directors! It's the only place where you can be the "King" or "Queen," and no one disputes it. *You* are the one, and the people are there to serve you. That's sexy. That kind of autocratic power is wild.

That made me uncomfortable, actually. There's a responsibility with that. When you are the King or Queen, you have a responsibility to your subjects, to take care of them. As a woman, I focused on that: do people have enough to eat? It's important. They're busting their asses for you. There's not enough emphasis on ideas like, "Everyone has an opinion and it is valid," and "Decisions should be reached by consensus." That was what I liked about CR groups. Everybody has an opinion and a voice, and they are all equally important. So going to film school was alienating; it went against the grain of my beliefs.

KATIE BOWMAN (production assistant, Chicago): *Another interviewee put much more emphasis on the upside of power.*
Power, yes, but with responsibility. That's important to me. The more power you have, the more responsibility you have. How you use it is important. To have a lot of power, and knowing you have a responsibility with it, is frightening. It's also attractive. Who doesn't want to be the one calling the shots?

▶

Women's Film Festivals

In the '70s there was a large number of women's film festivals in this country. In 1996, there's only one?
Also one in Boston and Seattle and New York.

How can it be true that once there were so many film festivals for women and now so few?
What is the nature of history? Is it linear? Are there permanent gains made in progressive ideas? Currently, there's a backlash against equal rights for women, a repeal of affirmative action laws. It's a reactionary time that we're living in related to the pendulum swing of history. (I also think that twenty years is not a long time, really.) And who controls things? The day-to-day operation of an organization like WIDC is that we have two paid staff and the rest of the work is done either by a board of directors, which is pretty large, or by volunteers. And it's a tremendous amount of work, and people are doing that work because they think it's important. And they're not being particularly well paid. And they're working hard!

That's the reality of women's film festivals. Women don't control large amounts of money. Movies are very expensive to make and distribute, at least the kinds of movies we see in multiplexes. To put forward work by women or special festivals—black, Asian, Latino festivals—people do it because they think it's important and they love the work, but not because they're making money. I think frequent burnout goes with those circumstances.

Why do you think the work of running a women's film festival is important?
I believe that the media is a strong tool to form people. Americans are constantly exposed to TV and movies. They're such a huge presence in the lives of Americans. They form people, they form your psyche, your ideas about who you are and what it's possible for you to do; what you can have, who you can meet, who you can talk to, what you can talk about.

The structure of our lives is changing. The institutions that form people, like families, school, church, are influenced a great deal by the media, so it's important that there be a diversity of voices and opinions available. For an example, look at the ways in which people are stereotyped on TV and the words that are used that define experiences for people that they don't really have, the way that young black men are the scapegoat of the moment. People in Iowa or South Dakota may have no experiences of black teenagers, but they see plenty of images of them in TV and movies. Their ideas may not be from experiences they've had themselves but from what they've seen on TV. Who's telling it? Whose story is it? Who benefits from the telling? The old feminist idea: every woman has a story, and everyone should tell her own, and no stories have more credence.

▶

Money Is Always Important

Can you be specific about the impact of a backlash?
It is increasingly important—as control of media is concentrated more and more in the hands of smaller numbers of people—that we enable people to tell their own stories. There's a direct correlation between the NEA or NAMAC having their funding cut, and independent artists having less money, so they make less work, and then we have fewer entries. It's frightening when you think about it. We see the fallout immediately in the numbers of entries each year to the festival.

Economics are important when you consider an expensive medium like film or video where the implements for your product are expensive. Money is always important. Who has the money? Government has a lot of money. Who gets the money? The backlash against the NEA is used to justify cuts to the NEA. Unpopular points of view, or "illegitimate" points of view—like those of homosexuals, people who are not legitimate—in this logic shouldn't be allowed to speak. The media is focusing attention on people or groups who won't be able to respond or fight back in the media arena, because they don't have access. Because, of course, it is large companies that own and control the means of distribution of messages, of words, and ideas.

▶

Community Activism

WIDC does a festival but also more "political" or "educational" media projects as well. Why community activism as well as the festival?
Media is incredibly powerful. There's real power in being able to speak—to speak your voice, to speak your mind. That's why people want to be humiliated on TV talk shows. People want to be heard. They want to feel like what they're saying is important. TV confers legitimacy on people, makes you visible. People hear you. People are willing to be humiliated in order to get that.

Getting back to community activism, WIDC exists to provide exhibition and promotion for independent voices of women and to provide access to people and to ideas and forms that are pushed into the margins. In terms of the festival, we show work by women, we show experimental work, short work, work by beginners. We are always running up against the ideas of "quality." We are so used to seeing a high degree of technical proficiency in TV and movies. We hope to be able to disrupt that, the ways that people have of consuming because it's palatable, because we're used to it.

It's important to disrupt how people think, so that they'll think more. We try to provide information to people who don't have it. How can people not have this information? We, people in media, have access. Everyone doesn't have access. If you don't have access to basic information about health or whatever, you'll be left out in important ways. WIDC wants to use independent media as a tool to provide information and access to groups that don't have access.

WIDC hopes to point toward action of some kind—the idea that it's possible to take action to make your life better. TV and movies are so much about consumption and not about action. It is inherently passive to sit and watch. But what you can do afterward is something else again. There is a responsibility for media to point toward something beyond consumption or the passive idea of being informed. "I'm informed, I know about that." So what are you going to do? We would be proud to call ourselves an activist organization.

▶────────────────────────────────────

Distribution

What is the importance of distribution in the creative cycle?
If you have something to say but you can't get it heard, then what impact do you have? TV and mainstream movies are closed. Not many people can get their work into that incredible distribution line. To have your work being shown on two thousand screens around the country—what does that mean? Ultimately, does it mean anything? So then what would happen?

I guess, maybe, it's a revolution to see a little movie like *Go Fish* on thousands of screens. A movie like that presents possibilities of a way of living to people who wouldn't be able to live that life, because they're not in a city or a place that would tolerate it. For these people, it wouldn't be possible to live in a group of openly lesbian friends. There is power in getting what you have to say out to different people. A young person sees that movie and says, "It's okay for me to be a lesbian. There are people doing it and I'm seeing a movie about it." That makes it legitimate in a way that it's not in daily life. So the film points to a possibility and a sense of not being alone.

Distribution is one of the paramount factors in changing attitudes and ideas. Distribution determines who sees media, who gets to think about it, talk about it. WIDC exists as an alternative mode of exhibition and distribution. We're small, but important.

Do you have anything to say that I didn't ask about?
WIDC started fifteen years ago as an organization that existed to provide exhibition and promotion for work by women, and it was also promoting women in the media through professional networking. In the past six or seven years, a slight ideological shift has occurred. The thinking is more about supporting women *through* media, not *in* media. The media are powerful tools through which people can see themselves in different ways, see new possibilities for living or working. The media can point toward positive changes. If you can see in media that something is being done somewhere, that gives you a connection and points toward action you yourself can take. That can help you to feel power, to feel that it is possible to step in and take charge of your own life or to organize with others and make change.

♦——————————————————————————————

WENDY QUINN

Program Director
1995–97   Women in the Director's Chair, Chicago

Operations Manager
1993–95   Women in the Director's Chair, Chicago

Assistant Director
1993   *Go Fish,* feature film, Chicago

Location/Production Manager
1992   *Back to Front,* feature film, Chicago

[14] *Victoria Vesna*

Victoria Vesna is important to this study because she undertakes her feminist work in a new medium. She is a feminist computer artist who has an extensive art practice in digital imaging, dynamic Web design, online multi-user environments, CD-ROM production, video production, installation, and performance. Vesna is one of a handful of women who is self- and formally educated in both the hands-on (programming) and theoretical aspects of this still "male" field. She is currently completing a Ph.D. in Interactive Arts with a dissertation titled "Online Public Places," and she serves as the chair of the Design Department at UCLA. She has been making feminist projects on the Web since 1995, video installation since 1986, and single-channel video since 1982 (video that plays exclusively on a television monitor without an associated, constructed, artistic environment to house it). In computer-based interactive installations like Another Day in Paradise *(1992, 1995) and* Virtual Concrete *(1995) she investigates the relations between feminism, art, science, and technology as she juxtaposes computers and video screens against "natural" objects like trees, cigars, or women's bodies. "That became my interest," she explains. "How to combine the tactile with the electronic, how the two worlds connect, and how the body connects to the intangible." With World Wide Web interactive installations like* Datamining Bodies *(2000),* Dublin Bodies *(1998), and* Bodies© INCorporated *(1997), Vesna moves her practice fully into cyberspace and stakes a feminist presence in this enormous and virtually uncharted cultural arena.*

Vesna entered the feminist art world in the '80s, after the peak of the women's movement and feminist art. Her art education was in Yugoslavia in a high-powered, high-art tradition. When she arrived in the United States, she immediately entered into the performance/video scene in New York City. At this time, the very idea of being a woman artist—singer, videomaker, computer artist—was not the anomaly it had seemed only ten years previously to an earlier generation. Because of mentoring by feminist teachers and colleagues, Vesna's early art career seemed a legitimate possibility. Although her art school education in Yugoslavia had been structured through the same kind of male-centered elitism that defines art education in the United States, Vesna also acknowledges that whenever she sought female role models, she found them, including Carolee Schneemann, who became a colleague and friend after a chance meeting in the '80s. Vesna's video portrait of Schneemann, Vesper's Stampede to My Holy Mouth, is the result of collaboration between them.

I found it interesting, in the process of doing these interviews, that while one woman understands her life and career—no matter the actual number of successes, prizes, conquests or failures—as a narrative of obstacles, disappointments, and inequities, another, like Vesna, may look at a similar landscape and relate her movement through it as a steady, difficult, but rewarding journey. Certainly to some extent a matter of personal temperament as well as self-presentation, this attitude is also clearly dependent on where, when, and under what conditions a woman engages in her career in the media. The significant majority of the women whose careers began in the '80s or later narrated their life stories with little emphasis placed on the difficulty of claiming the role of feminist artist, or finding the necessary resources (educational, institutional, interpersonal) to do so. Although younger women had some level of self-consciousness about how the relative ease of their experiences had been enabled in part by the women before them (all of the younger women have at least one mentor whom they acknowledge in their interviews), they seemed to be less self-conscious about how their experiences differed from those of the women who came before them. I observed that women from the '70s and before claimed their very careers with pride and difficulty, whereas for post-'70s artists like Vesna, this one claim, at least, could be taken for granted.

The relative ease of Vesna's early career—one that seemed to have had its gears greased in part by the previous generation—enables her to move boldly into a field completely dominated by men. There, she insists on founding a feminist practice and pedagogy with the plan of greasing the wheels so that younger women can follow her into the world of computers. In her interview, this notion raises a related contradiction: she herself feels enabled to work in this "male" field in part because of her feminist teachers, and yet she has difficulty passing this confidence on to her female students. The pattern that I identified above—that the work of one generation eases the struggle for the next—does not seem to hold true, at least for this new *medium. Vesna argues that this has more to do with women's relationship to technology, a new and different hurdle, than with women's relationship to their own professionalism. Yet she also identifies (as do many other interviewees) a postfeminist backlash demonstrated in the unexpected guise of a generation of students less radical, less active, less angry than the one before them. Even so, in her work as feminist scholar, artist, and teacher, Vesna remembers how women facilitated her career, and she remains committed to enabling the careers of other women: "As a feminist and an artist, I have a strong feeling of responsibility. As I progress and become more active and visible, it's important that I be conscious of myself as a role model and not forget how hard it is to get there, and actually help others. . . . In my head, artist equals responsibility." While this credo is admirable, Vesna discusses how hard it can be to fulfill.*

▶──

A Career as an Artist

Can you narrate your career?
The narrative of my career probably starts when an elementary school-teacher told me I should go to art school. I came to New York from Yugo-slavia and went to the High School of Art and Design, and I got into fashion design right away. After New York, we went back to Belgrade, where I was admitted to the Academy of Fine Arts. It was a tough school to get into. Out of three thousand candidates, maybe three hundred are screened, and then thirty finally get in.

In a class of thirteen, there were twelve men and myself. I was sixteen, and the youngest person after me was twenty-eight. They all had beards. On the first day of class, the main professor, who was around ninety years old, came in and looked around and said, "Only one of you will be a real artist." I knew it would be me because I was the only woman. The school was actually an excellent, very European academy with years of anatomy and the technology of painting. It was a five-year school, and after three years I'd had enough. I wanted to forget about art. I rebelled big time. I actually went to the dean and signed out. It was the most radical moment that I'd experienced, leaving a school that was so hard to get into. I went to New York and within a year formed an experimental band. It was experimental, and my idea was that it was antiart. I never went to galleries; they were horrendous to me. I have to admit that I still don't relate well to the art establishment. I'm repelled by gallery openings, art circles. That's why I'm in the media I'm in. I feel so much more at home with intangible, interdisciplinary work.

But I was doing art, in a way, doing performance with my band, experimenting with slide shows, and we cut a few records. I decided in 1981, in the East Village of New York City, to produce a video for the band. I went to my friend's house to do a music video, and that was the second important moment. I was so impressed with the speed with which we edited that tape—which was probably amplified because he was on coke—but, anyway, I was impressed. I took the tape, it was called *4 Minutes to Midnight,* and ran off to Danceteria, where we had played a few times, went straight to the deejay and said, "Here's my tape." He said, knowing how unpredictable we were, "Wait until it clears out a little bit." At 4 A.M., we put in the tape that I had just finished that night on this huge screen, one of the first huge, high-res screens in a dance club.

Seeing what we did a few hours ago up on that screen, I decided, "This is it. This is what I want to do." I very quickly dissolved the band and went back to Yugoslavia to finish my degree at the art academy. I was readmitted to the school because my professor, who happened to be a woman, really wanted me to complete my studies. She came up to me at one point and said, "Look, I don't understand at all what you're doing, but I believe in you and I want you to finish this. So you'll have a huge studio, you can do whatever you want—just finish. You'll need a diploma." I'm very grateful to her, and also to my mother, who really wanted me to finish. Obviously, I wouldn't be teaching today if I didn't do what she said.

At that time, I fell immediately into video, performance, and a whole wonderfully active atmosphere that existed in Europe. Another mentor appeared—Biljana Tomic. She really helped me understand my place and purpose in the art context. Biljana included my work in many important shows. From then on, it's been very active. I haven't had too much trouble with showing. I've been quite lucky. I attribute some of that to the fact that I don't like the art world, so they accept me. It's a very strange situation. Right out of school, I exhibited at the Museum of Twentieth Century Feminist Video Show. There was no transition. I never felt a struggle, so I can't say that I've had a problem with putting my work out. The problems were in different places, with doing the work, being accepted, and becoming part of the economy. But showing, getting tapped on the shoulder? No problem.

▶ _____

Money

Can you talk about your problems with becoming "part of the economy"?
I've pretty much figured out my own way of dealing with resources from the start. When I came back from Europe, the film supply house, Rafik,

where I had worked had become a video production place. I came back as they were setting up. I got hired again and worked for them during the day. At night I had access to the equipment and did my own tapes. After a while, I realized that I was actually editing, and one of the most empowering things for me was that I made an effort to learn hands-on and be independent in the production process. A lot of it happened by default because I was working and I learned little by little. I would probably have been intimidated if I had been told, "This is the equipment, and this is how you're going to do it."

In the beginning I never got grants. It's only recently that there's a certain established feeling about what I'm doing. For the first ten years I financed my own work through industry work, freelance work, and willpower. When I started working with computers and installations, I would go directly to a company and pitch a project and ask them to lend me equipment and give me access. I gave up on applying for grants at one point because my collection of refusals became too depressing, so I decided to just figure out a way around it, and I'm still doing that. Now, I get grants.

▶——————————————————————————————

Influences

Are there role models or other women who succeeded before you whose examples allowed you to do your work?
There are always these little moments when something clicks. When I went back to school and started doing performance, I was looking at a book and saw this great picture of Carolee Schneemann with a snake on her belly. I zoomed in on it and thought, this is the kind of female power in which I'm interested, where you don't deny your sexuality, you don't deny the fact that you're erotic, that you're fabulous. When I returned to New York, I was a VJ for a cable program, *Videowaves,* with artists and musicians. I saw Carolee Schneemann talking at Donell Library. I was floored by her guts and the work she does and the way she could stand up there and be so articulate about it and so strong. I went to her and asked if she would do an interview. She was very gracious and asked, "What is your name?" and I gave her my card. She looked at the card and said, "You know, I'm doing a piece called Venus Vectors. Would you help me work on it?"

A really nice relationship developed, and we continue to have a special bond. When I first saw her photo, she was a mythic personality to me, and now she is a real person in my life. She's been so incredibly special as an artist and as a woman, an amazing, inspiring force. Carolee represents one of the women who has made a path possible for me. I have it easier, thanks to her.

I started to do the interview with her, and it became a portrait. We wound up collaborating on this piece about her. It became a strong feminist statement called *Vesper's Stampede to My Holy Mouth*, attacking a taboo that nobody touches: she kisses her cat and exhibits an erotic animal-human relationship. I was trying to figure out how to represent in half an hour a woman who has twenty-five' years worth of a huge body of work. She works so much with her dreams, and I don't usually, but while I was working with her, the dreams came to me. I learned a lot about her and about myself. In my dream I had the idea to represent her through the cat. We had long discussions about the taboo against even using the word *feminist,* about how it cuts off a huge audience because it's become such a negative word, and why. I also learned the importance of loving men, which is an unusual feminist approach. She feels very protective of feminist men and feels that it is critical to support them. This was an important lesson for me.

▶ ──

Feminist Art

Do you consider yourself a feminist artist? And, as you create your work and career, how does feminism matter to you?
By default of being a woman, if you're conscious of yourself, you're "a feminist." I don't take it so very seriously, but I am aware of what I am doing. I feel responsible to make a statement and to be strong about it as a woman. However, I feel the strongest statements are those in which you don't necessarily focus on feminism but manage to project that message through the work.

I do have occasions when I focus on it. For instance, I did a piece that took me about three years to complete called *Sometimes a Cigar Is Only a Cigar (Freud).* I had a studio in Soho in the basement of a cigar factory across the street from Castelli Gallery. When you walked in, it was as if you walked into the seventeenth century. The laborers were all women, paid maybe $3 or $4 an hour. They all smoke cigars in that musty, dark atmosphere with a boss who keeps track of what they're doing. I had to pass the cigar factory daily to get to my studio and eventually became obsessed with this space that existed in parallel with an elite art world right outside. I started making friends with the women there and began to think that I would do a documentary about the place. Instead, it became a piece about the feminine power of Latin women, and the matriarchs who helped the slaves in Cuba survive through rituals using cigars. The project became an installation that was exhibited at the alternative art space, PS 1, and an artist book. It consisted of six large objects: two triangles, one square, and three pillars with video monitors embedded inside. The room smelled like tobacco, yet there was an electronic element to it. From that point on I explore how to combine the tactile with the electronic, how the two worlds connect, and how the body connects to the intangible.

▶

Another Day in Paradise

I've had a fascination with computers since 1985, when I did one of my last music videos with a band. I had an opportunity to experiment with computer graphics, and it was a moment of epiphany, just as with my first video. I wanted to get my hands on it. In L.A., I found a mom-and-pop operation that wanted an artist to learn animation and computer graphics. I signed a deal with them that was actually pretty thankless. For each hour of learning, I owed ten hours of work. Because I was so hungry for knowledge, I did maybe fifty to sixty hours of study and had this huge amount of hours that I owed them. Finally, the woman in charge, Stephanie Slade, came up to me and said she had a wild idea of connecting artists from around the world by computer and having them work together on a kind of collage. I said, "I'll do that. I know artists from all over. That's how I'll pay off my hours." This experiment in 1992 had a profound effect on me. I was introduced to the networking technology and became fascinated with a network as a creative space.

At that stage, I met Kathy Brew and Sean Kilcoyne, with whom I started a project. Living in Irvine, I decided to do a piece with palm trees, *Another Day in Paradise*. When we landed at the John Wayne Airport in Irvine, I was confronted with a John Wayne statue surrounded by palm trees, and I was absolutely fascinated by this Stalinistic image of him. It was like Eastern Europe, but completely right wing. I noticed that the trees look fake, look real, feel fake, feel real. I couldn't figure it out. I was scratching at one of the trees, and a woman who was a guard said, "You know, those trees are preserved with silicone." Here was this fabulous atrium, light pouring in, and they're preserving trees with silicone!

After doing some research, I tracked down the company in Carlsbad that made those trees and said to them, "I'll do a commercial promo for you, and in return I want you to build me three trees with video monitors inside." And they agreed. It was a nice subversive thing, but then it kind of turned on me because I really was promoting them as well as getting material for my own work. At the same time, I met this young Vietnamese man, Vi Vuong, at a computer lab who wanted me to be his mentor as an artist. He told me about the time he ran away from Vietnam on a boat and how he finally landed at John Wayne Airport. Vi became the central character of this piece.

Of course, the project is about displacement of people and nature, and the silicone in our bodies. I thought of the silicone palm trees, housing developments, and how we already live in a virtual environment—we don't need to put on the goggles, it's here. So I created these three trees, one of which was shaped a little bit like a woman. That was the "video tree" in which you viewed the Irvine landscape, the development, and if you took the time to sit down and put earphones on, you heard the very tragic story of how this young man ran away from Vietnam. The second tree was a surveillance camera with about a quarter-inch lens, so you did not see it but yourself. My message there was about how we're all a part of this and you can't really separate yourself from this fake, simulated environment. The third tree had an interactive touch screen. That's where Sean Kilcoyne and Kathy Brew helped me with getting materials. Kathy provided material on Vietnam War widows, on both sides. Sean, as a Vietnam vet, dealt with the issue of reclaiming humanity after doing horrendous things. It's a kind of virtual palm tree place. If you go in, you find out what's swept under the rug, and it's not very pretty.

▶

Virtual Concrete and Bodies© INCorporated

That tree project led me to think about silicon a lot. This was during the Northridge earthquake, when people were isolated and communicating through silicon. I realized that it is silicon as an element, silicon in concrete and in chips, that propels the information superhighway. So I was still investigating the idea of the virtual and the concrete, and also the body and the disembodied, how we relate to this duality we're brought up with. I decided to create a concrete path that you could walk on, on top of which were images of a male and a female body, eight feet long. I found out a way to take an electrostatic print and remove the paper so that only the paper is concrete. The digital becomes the concrete. But that didn't go far enough as a connection to the intangible, so I decided to put in a video camera looking at the path so that as you step on these bodies you're connected to the Internet and the rest of us can look at who's walking on the bodies. I had sensors on both sides of the concrete path with six channels.

Images of the bodies on concrete were thus captured in a photograph, converted into digits, manipulated, printed, and placed onto concrete. Once concretized, the bodies—now granted physicality—could be accepted by the art world and entered into the gallery or museum space, a space where the object is usually considered sacred and untouchable. I wanted the audience to walk on the bodies in pure irreverence, to trespass as they moved on the piece that uncannily resembled the "sacred" fresco. I must confess that the concrete was also a tongue-in-cheek statement about the digital artist working within the confines of the museum.

The interactivity with the physical piece was successful: people walked, crawled on the concrete, sparked off sounds, and stared at the camera. On the Web, however, I felt that watching the activity of people in the gallery through the camera was not enough. Since the core idea of the project was that of a "real" and "virtual" body in cyberspace, I decided that a good way to extend the interactivity would be for the audience to create a body at a distance. Therefore, I put a simple questionnaire on the same page on which the video of the installation was being projected and asked participants to give us a name for their body, assign it a gender, and make a statement about what the body meant to them. To my surprise, there were more than a thousand bodies on order in two weeks—and before long, people were asking to "see" the bodies they had "ordered." This demand persisted and made me reconsider the meaning of online identity. So that's my latest work, dealing with the whole issue of the evidence of the body.

Bodies© INCorporated was conceived as a response to the need of the *Virtual Concrete* online audience to see their bodies, and it was informed by my research of MOOs, multiuser worlds, cyborgs, and avatars. I did not want to simply send back what was demanded but answer in a way that would prompt the audience to consider their relationship to the Internet and the meaning of online representation.

When I uploaded the questionnaire in *Virtual Concrete* asking the audience to "order" their imaginary body, it never crossed my mind to take it much further from the conceptual realm. But I was intrigued by the need to be represented graphically and further to have these bodies somehow enact a life of their own. This fantasy is one that could easily be manipulated into a convenient way to gather personal data for other purposes. And, in fact, large corporations do use this seemingly democratic space; as we become incorporated into it, we also enter a collective state that could mean the loss of identity. It is a marketplace; it is an imaginary space.

The title *Bodies© INCorporated* is a play on words. *Bodies* is accompanied by a copyright symbol and *INCorporated* draws on the *corpus* root while alluding to a corporation: bodies are incorporated into the Internet and their information is copyrighted. The logo of the project is a bronze head with a copyright sign on its third eye, signifying the inherent contradiction of efforts to control information flow. Once the participants enter the project, they click through a series of legal notifications. My goal was to create a controlling space where the signing of legal documents and inputting of personal data become an emotional experience. These legal announcements were taken from the Disney Web site and edited to suit our needs. The assumption is that no one is reading these documents, despite the fact that they take away all rights—a tactic designed to alert participants about the legal issues attached to their navigation through information space.

Upon entering the main site, participants are invited to create their own bodies and become "members." They have a choice of twelve textures with attached meanings, which are a combination of alchemical properties and marketing strategies. The body parts are female, male, and infantile, left and right legs and arms, torso and head. The bodies themselves are wire frames that were donated by Viewpoint Datalabs, three-dimensional scans that are used for medical imaging. It is fascinating to track how people play with gender and to notice that most decide to be their opposite, or transgendered.

▶ ——————————————————————————

Women in Technology

In several of the pieces you described, silicone is an important compound. Can you talk about that and also the issue of feminist production on the Internet?
My initial connection to silicone is with implants, particularly with how it's put into the breasts of women. It's mostly women who wind up with silicone inside them. I believe that the treatment of nature runs parallel to the treatment of women.

I'm very keenly aware that there are so few women in technology. It's very sad. I find myself working with only men all the time. I don't mind working with men—I have nothing against men—but I have a problem with the situation. So it's my responsibility to try to change it. I deal with issues of women and technology, as an educator, on a daily basis. On the Internet there's now a pretty good percentage of women, so there's also real hope. Nonlinear thinking is easy for us. So even though the technology, from hardware to software, is foreign to us, as it becomes more user-friendly, we can work well with it.

As an educator, I try to pass on my knowledge. It's difficult. As we get to an advanced level, women start dropping out. It's hard to pull them back in, to have them go against their nature. In order to be effective in this medium, you have to be able to work with it deeply, not just on the surface level with the software. You have to go inside and program. This is foreign territory to us; we're not conditioned to do this work. Physically, spatially, we're not programmed to think this way. What I have to tell them is, "You're a feminist, you *have* to go against your nature just to survive in the world we're in and try to make a difference." We're living in an age of anomaly. Hundreds of years from now people will look back at us and say, "They did try, at one point." But it's pretty grim, if you look at it realistically. I look at who's in power, at how many men are really in the top echelons making decisions. It's really their world more than our world.

I'm afraid of the Bill Viola syndrome in which one person becomes representative of the entire field.[1] All the women who have been working in video since the beginning have been submerged. Who knows where they are? I'm afraid this will happen with digital technology. Right now, there's a window. There's nothing established in the field, particularly in the art world. But the art world is very similar to the computer industry. It's 90 percent male. And once art and industry merge, our survival will be questionable.

I am grateful to all of the women who have allowed me to have this feeling of self-confidence and power. I'm also careful and conscious of the young women coming up now who are actually becoming backward about feminism, and I'm trying to bring them up-to-date. I don't know where it's coming from, but that backward turn is very prevalent—it's like they're living in the '50s. It's a strange time because many women who are more progressive are actually older, and often it's younger women who are more conservative. It will be interesting to see how these ideological oppositions are resolved.

▶───────────────────────────────────────

Artist Equals Responsibility

How do you see your role as an academic combining with your role as an artist?
It is crucial for women to learn this technology, especially hands-on. I started out thinking that I was a role model, but this was clearly not enough. So I decided that I really have to pay attention to the fact that women do get intimidated by this technology. So, obviously, knowledge is power. If I'm in a position to pass on the knowledge and create this power in women, I have the ability to perform a very important task. Connecting academia with industry is important to me because in my field women may end up in industry rather than the art world, and I want them to be conscious of their role and power there.
Where do you see your place in the history of feminist film and video?
I'm hoping that I'm in the generation of women who can break through the glass ceiling. In my work with technology, I find myself working more

and more with industry. Also, I'm in a university setting that, like the computer industry, has its own hierarchy that needs to be redefined. I am a kind of bridge between two worlds and each has that ceiling. My hope is to use the small window of opportunity that is given with this new medium to pass through the crack and create more space for other women to fully participate. We haven't done it yet, but it's possible and I'm hopeful. I hope I can be one of the women who can reach the top and not forget to create opportunities for the women who come after.

Please talk about being an artist. Why, since you hate art, are you an artist, and what does it mean to you to be a feminist artist?
I have a love-hate relationship with the idea of myself as an artist. It's a matter of established ideas of what an artist is. I'm repelled by it and have to find the will to destroy that idea and create another image. The guy with a beret in front of an easel: that's not me. As a feminist and an artist, I have a strong feeling of responsibility. As I progress and become more active and visible, it's important that I be conscious of myself as a role model and not forget how hard it is to get there and actually help others. The people who have helped me were largely women. I don't want to forget that or start believing press releases and hype. I want to be in a place within the art world where I can help to redefine what it stands for and what the image of an artist is. In my head, artist equals responsibility.

Media Work

1982	*Four Minutes to Midnight*, video
1984, 1985	*Red Angel*, performance and video/environmental installation
1984, 1985	*Thunderbolt*, performance and video
1986, 1987	*Sictransitgloriamundi*, installation/performance
1989	*Crnica*, Installation
1990	*Sometimes a Cigar Is Only a Cigar (Freud)*, performance-image
1992	*Vesper's Stampede to My Holy Mouth*, ¾" video (with Carolee Schneemann)
1992, 1995	*Another Day in Paradise*, interactive installation
1995	*Virtual Concrete*, networked installation
1997	*Bodies© INCorporated*, WWW interactive installation
1997	*Life in the Universe with Stephen Hawking*, CD-ROM/WWW
1998	*Dublin Bodies*, WWW interactive installation
1999	*ZKM Bodies*, WWW interactive installation
2000	*Datamining Bodies*, WWW interactive installation

Distribution and Contact information

Work available from the artist's Web site: http://vv.arts.ucla.edu

[15] *Valerie Soe*

*Valerie Soe received her BA from UCLA and her MFA from the School
of the Art Institute of Chicago (SAIC) in the 1980s. She is the product of
Asian American studies and activism at UCLA, a student of Kate Horsfield
and Lyn Blumenthal at SAIC, and is currently a teacher of high school and
college students, as well as an accomplished and prolific videomaker. In
single-channel videos and video installations, Soe explores the experience
of Asian American women in American culture. For instance, her first
video, "ALL ORIENTALS LOOK THE SAME" (1986), takes this common mis-
perception and turns it on its head by showing, in quick flashes, the distinct and diverse faces of countless people of Asian heritage. In* Picturing
Oriental Girls *(1992) Soe catalogues a visual compendium of orientalist
and exoticizing representations of Asian women snatched from American
film and television. And* Mixed Blood *(1992) presents a personal view of
interracial relationships in the Asian American community.*

*Yet even as she was producing these and other works exploring con-
temporary identity, Soe acknowledges that she was at the same time a cultural heir to Reagan- and other Republican-sponsored initiatives that
systematically threatened and dismantled the very progressive arts and cultural institutions (affirmative action, the NEA, the Corporation for Public
Broadcasting, abortion rights) that had allowed her this lively, youthful,
feminist career—a schizophrenic position to be sure. Added to this, Soe
explains that she is heir to '80s "multiculturalism," another you-win-some-
you-lose-some type of proposition. While a newfound cultural commitment
to ethnic diversity facilitated certain aspects of Soe's career, as she was consistently supported to make work about her Chinese American identity, it
has also limited her in that her fascination with formalism has been forced
to take a backseat to her more easily fundable "identity" work. However,
the subsequent backlash against multiculturalism, felt particularly hard in*

California, has created another schizophrenic impasse where Soe's "identity" is at once celebrated and demonized by different factions within the same broader culture.

As is true for many of the women in this study, Soe lives a hand-to-mouth artist's existence by cobbling together what she calls "contract work." She teaches video production at institutions like California State Summer School for the Arts and San Francisco State University, she receives grants and commissions to make new work, she writes film criticism for independent film magazines, and she follows in her parents' footsteps and lives frugally. Perhaps as a function of her age (Soe is in her mid-thirties), while she admits to a certain amount of anxiety about paying the bills, she interprets her choice to live in this manner in much the same spirit as did the women "on the edge" who began this study: as a snub to the values that drive bourgeois capitalism. While most of the women discussed previously seem to have risen to a relatively stable middle-class income and lifestyle (mostly as a consequence of taking teaching positions, and in a few instances due to winning grants or through film/video sales/rentals), Soe seems set for now in her economically marginal, if artistically productive, existence. She makes her work "by any means necessary," adapting her ideas and goals to the technological systems her budget will afford.

This is by no means to say that her life or career has been easy, although she readily acknowledges that the cogs were greased by the earlier feminists and others who created the art video community in which Soe currently works. For she also speaks of a profound sadness and even apathy that underline her sense of her life and career. She feels a deep nostalgia for the purported community, social progress, and political consciousness of the '60s, which was so quickly lost to the individualism, greed, and indifference that defines her experience of the '80s and '90s. Contradiction infuses Soe's situation. She makes her work as a way to ensure her agency even as the very mechanisms that made it easier for an Asian American woman to be an artist are systematically dismantled. Her work self-consciously continues the legacy of her teachers and role models even as the broader culture depicts a vision of culture devoid of such commitments. Like many of the women who precede her in this study, Soe lives by a social/economic critique of corporate American society that privileges personal and societal growth over individual financial gain. She says that her life as an artist is organized around the "'60s values" she learned from her teachers. But the intellectual and political climate that supported this analysis has been replaced by a new economy, even as traces of the '60s and '70s remain. Michelle Sidler highlights the contradictions of economic possibility and impossibility that mark the careers of third-wave feminists like Soe: "Second wave feminism's identity

politics gave twentysomething women the opportunity to enter the work-
force and empowered us to create our own agenda, but with the rise of class
instability we face a new playing field complicated by facets such as un-
employment, debt, and technology. In short, third wave feminism needs
a new economy." [1]

▶ _____

Video

Will you tell me about your history with video?
When I was an undergraduate, almost fifteen years ago at UCLA, I was really involved with the Asian American community there, and I was also interested in journalism. But UCLA had neither a journalism department nor an
Asian American studies department, so I couldn't major in either of those
things. They do have a film school, but the film school was impacted. You
couldn't get in unless you had a really good grade point average. Actually,
that turned out to be just as well because I found out that they had video
cameras in the art department. I figured, "I'll learn how to use the video
cameras over there, and then I'll make movies, right?" So then I became an
art student. Then I found out that the video cameras in the art department—
this was around 1981—were those black-and-white things they use in banks
for surveillance cameras. That kind of dashed my hopes for feature filmmaking. But it turned out really well because I found that I liked being in the
art department more than I would have liked the film department because it
was more experimental. You didn't have to stick to strict forms. So I started
to make really short videos. I could bring my political beliefs into my work.
I could make videos about the stuff I was doing with the Asian American
community, about racism, and all that stuff. So it worked out well. I haven't
gone back to trying to make feature films, and I'm really glad.

So you started at UCLA, and you were making videos with little surveillance
cameras. What were they like and what did you do after that?
Mostly the work started out being autobiographical, and a couple of the
pieces that I made there are still in circulation. *"ALL ORIENTALS LOOK THE*
SAME" is one of the first videos I ever made. It was done with two slide
projectors and a dissolve unit and a camera that was set up pointing at the
wall, and that's why it looks more filmic than most videos. And then the
autobiographical stuff was easy because when you're twenty-one years old,
you don't have a lot of worldly experience outside your own little life. So
that's what I started to talk about.

Also, I knew as a Chinese American that the images of Asian Americans that I saw on television and in mainstream films were nothing like the people I knew in my family and my community. They were really stereotyped. So it was a way for me to bring a little truth of representation into what was being shown. And I think that has stayed with me—trying to counteract some of the incredible ignorance and stupidity that's in mainstream film and television, especially when it comes to people of color.

▶ ──

A More Realistic View

Can you talk about how you do that?
I'm trying to present a more realistic view, not necessarily a "positive image." I'm not interested in heroic figures. With them you're just substituting one stereotype for another, right? I really like having people with personalities and interesting stories in my work, like my weird family and my weird background. Growing up in suburbia as this Chinese American kid is a contrast in itself to those one-dimensional things you see on TV.

Can you talk more specifically about a work in which you did that?
One of the first really autobiographical pieces that I did was *New Year,* which is in two parts. It was actually an installation in which I had two monitors running at the same time, which is something I still do sometimes for the hell of it. On one of the monitors was found footage, recontextualized images from mainstream film and television that contained stereotypes of Asians and Asian Americans. It was some really great stuff: from Charlie Chan, Mr. Moto, Kung Foo—what's that guy?—Rambo, shooting down the Vietnamese. That was all edited together so you get this barrage of horrifying stereotypes that you usually see only in little snips. You see a weird image in a movie, and you forget about it. But when you put it all together, it's more disconcerting, especially if you're Asian American.

I wanted to do that because it reminded me of when I would go to a movie and I'd be really enjoying myself. Like you're watching *Breakfast at Tiffany's* or something. And all of a sudden this hideous caricature comes on, like Mickey Rooney playing this Japanese guy with these fake teeth, and it totally destroys any kind of pleasure in the film. And you feel really uncomfortable and attacked and personally reviled. Just this sensation of, "Oh, my God, I'm being treated in this foul and horrible way by people who don't even know that they're being offensive."

Tell me about your experiences after college. Where did you go and what did you do?

After college I went to grad school at the Art Institute in Chicago. I got my master's in photography and in video. I decided after that, that I didn't ever want to live in the Midwest again. I had come straight from Los Angeles and had lived on the West Coast all my life. So to go to the Midwest, where it was cold and much more monocultural—well, it was very cold. So I went back to San Francisco, even though I didn't have any kind of job prospects. My parents lived there. I actually stayed at my parents' house for three months until I found a job. I just knew that I would much rather be unemployed in San Francisco than working in some other part of the country where I didn't feel there was a culture that I could relate to. I'm not enough of a pioneer to go out there and forge ahead into unknown territory.

Did you find then, or do you find now, influences from feminist film theory or production?

Yeah. Anytime you deal with images from media, you need to think about representation and the male gaze. I took classes with Lyn Blumenthal and Kate Horsfield. They team-taught back then. They were good at talking about how videomaking came out of a social movement. It was part of the antiwar movement, the civil rights movement. It had that '60s sensibility of trying to change the system through the use of media technology. It wasn't just something you'd do for yourself. That teaching was really useful. It tied in with what I'd done at UCLA.

I was a student at the same time. I think we were a sort of a second generation.

I do think it's a second-generation kind of thing. I definitely wasn't part of the first wave. I also wasn't just in video; I did work in the other visual arts. Postmodernism was very important at that time; the idea that there is no such thing as the original image was very resonant in my work. If there was a conflict with the previous generation, it was in the fact that there wasn't much work specifically about racial issues. It was much more like white people talking about this stuff, and usually middle-class white people. Well, definitely middle-class. There weren't that many people of color making work that I saw then.

Do you consider yourself a feminist videomaker?
Yeah. That means having political consciousness of how art, politics, social
change, media, representation, and all that stuff go together. There's no way
in which you can avoid dealing with feminism . . . unless you're Phyllis
Schlafly. What it means is that the work is made about women's experiences by a woman. It means trying to affect or reflect the social milieu it
comes from. To work for social change. To have an awareness of connections to other aspects of the world besides the art world. To have a holistic
worldview, I guess, which is a '6os term. To know that what I do affects
other people besides myself, and sometimes only in subtle ways.

What provided the groundwork for you to become a feminist?
Well, the women's movement, of course, the civil rights movement, the antiwar movement, the '6os. My family letting me do what I was doing instead
of sending me to pharmaceutical school. Just being lucky enough to grow up
in a time where women could decide what they wanted to do. Also growing
up in a time during which there was enough economic prosperity in this
country and I didn't have to think so much about making a living. I could
be a bit more cavalier. Do you want me to talk about Ronald Reagan now?

Sure! I'm waiting for you to throw him in!
I love feminism. I think it's really great! But when I hear older women who
were involved with feminism in the '7os talk about things like consciousness-
raising groups and the joy of learning to empower themselves for the first
time, then I think that I'm very lucky because I don't have to think about
not having that choice. But at the same time I think that my life has been
ruled less by hope than by despair. It's a general despair about the shrink-
ing possibilities for myself and the world. The environment is going to hell.
The Republicans are taking all the money away from everybody. People are
becoming more paranoid and selfish—or being told to be more paranoid
and selfish.

A lot of that comes from coming of age during the Reagan administration. Growing up as a child in the '6os and '7os, I remember this as an incredibly optimistic period. People thought that they could be whatever they
wanted—you know, a potter, a sculptor—nobody wanted to be a banker in
the '7os. Then in the '8os, *everybody* wanted to be a banker. So all the gains
and promises of social progress that came about in the '6os and '7os have
been reversed. For me, it's been depressing to see how people have been
forced to think more about survival rather than being allowed to expand
their idea of what they want to do, to dream about something besides just
making a living and having children, or making car payments. It's like we've
gone back to the basic sustenance level.

▶

Money

I have anxiety, too. I'm living hand to mouth in a much more prosperous way than someone on the street is, but I'm still wondering where that next paycheck is coming from. I'm being distracted by basic survival issues. In my paranoid moments I think that's what multinationals and the Republicans want. They want you to be so preoccupied by thinking about how you're going to make a living that you can't think about things like social justice, freedom, art, equality, or anything like that, because you're too busy trying to put food on the table. It's an insidious strategy that we all know about because we're all conspiracy theorists, right?

What kind of work did you do after you finished grad school?
I had a regular job for a couple years. I worked at a postproduction house. I worked there and saved my money, and then I quit right after the earthquake. I started to do whatever I had to do in order to make money. I had a couple of part-time teaching jobs, teaching kids art at a private school and teaching senior citizens to use video, so my students covered a span of years. And then I was doing apartment building management and writing art reviews for different magazines. Gradually, I started to get more teaching jobs at the university level. Right now, I do contract work. Next semester, I have no idea what I'm going to do. It's been a matter of patching together a living. But, as I said, it's much better to be where I am than to be someplace where I'd be cut off from cultural stimulation.

So why do you patch together a living instead of doing what most Americans do, which is run out and find a living wage? I ask because in this documentary often the idea of women's video and film falls away and the idea of being independent women doing their work rises. It's rare that we hear of that.
Why do I do it? It's really stressful, but you have the freedom to do whatever you want. If you need to take a month off to work on a project, you don't have to explain it to anybody. You don't get paid for it, but you're making your work, and that eventually pays off in some way or another. You have the satisfaction of doing something besides a nine-to-five job that's meaningless to you. Why else? I do it because I can. Because I've been privileged enough to get jobs that allow me to work part-time and make enough money to pay the rent. Because I like to sleep late. I don't know—attention deficit disorder? Because there's no such thing as real jobs anymore. Why spend your life working for a company that you don't like, if they're going to fire

you? Also, because I don't want to support the corporate economy, because I think it's disgusting. Mainly, because I can.

How do you fund your work?

When I was in school, and throughout the rest of my film career, access to equipment has always been questionable. I don't have a "real" teaching job where I might have access to an editing studio, where I can use the same edit system over and over again, or the same camera. So I try to make my work as concept driven as I can. Not relying so much on technology and not killing myself if I can't get it. If I can't afford to use Betacam, then I just use Hi-8 or whatever—VHS for all I care.

The economic crisis in this country has been bad for funding work. Right-wing paranoia—backlash—is a big obstacle. I was really, really anxious about a year ago, in the mid-'90s, because things were so bad out there for making work. In the early '90s it seemed as though there were so many opportunities for funding one's work and for exhibition. People were seeing stuff; there was a dialogue going on. Now that seems to have been systematically shut down. We've had the NEA [National Endowment for the Arts] problems, the ITVS [Independent Television Service], CPB [Corporation for Public Broadcasting]—all these things being threatened. People are getting more and more paranoid. California's Proposition 187 was an example of that.[2] People are panicking about something—or being incited to panic by the powers that be. Too much unity among us working-class stiffs is not a good thing for the ruling class.

My mom and dad are frugal. They clip coupons and stuff. I really learned growing up that a penny saved is a penny earned. I drove with my dad to L.A. to install my last show. Six hours in the car with your dad, right? So, he's telling me, "You've got to go to the stores and look for the specials on beef," or whatever. And "Look for two-for-one coupons!" I think that's really been imbued in me, the idea that you need to make the most of what you have. I try to be as realistic as I can about what kind of expectations I can have with my technology.

▶

Identity Politics

I've made close to a dozen pieces, and most of them are in distribution. The ones that are most popular—and I'm not sure if distributors pick them up because they think they're the better pieces or because they're the ones that will sell the most—are the ones that deal with identity issues, such as *Mixed Blood* and *Picturing Oriental Girls*. The ones about broader topics don't get picked up as much. I don't know if that's because when people think about Asian American makers, they think that they have to do stuff about identity politics. I want to expand what identity politics can encompass.

People who oppose multiculturalism call it reverse discrimination. That's untrue. Ninety-seven percent of upper-management positions are held by straight white men. That's a lot! It's the same thing in colleges with regard to management and professorships: huge percentages of those in power are white men. The fact that some people are becoming so paranoid when there's tiny incursions or attempts to rectify these imbalances is inexplicable to me. It's like, "What are you guys talking about? I'm not making out that much from this!" Other people I know are not. At the same time, being an Asian American woman has been useful because people are aware that they need to diversify. That can be seen as a really simplistic solution, but I know that when I talk to Asian American students or other nonwhite students and they see my work, they're so amazed. They say things like, "I've never seen anything like this before that I can relate to so personally." To me, that makes all the difference in the world.

I had an experience with one of my tapes, *Black Sheep,* about my uncle who had a nervous breakdown. It's basically just talking heads, me talking about my bizarre family and their various strangenesses. Anyway, this tape aired on a local PBS station at something like 11:30 on a Sunday night. The next day, my Aunt Vivian called my mom. She said, "I saw Valerie on television last night. She was talking about Joe!" She was really excited. She said, "I was just flipping the channel and I saw a Chinese face, and it was so different from what I've seen before, and then I realized it was my niece." But the main thing she was excited about was that the Asian face on TV didn't have an accent, was not doing kung fu, and was not wearing a kimono. So it's not just about me blabbing about my personal life.

Another response I received about that same screening was from a friend of mine, a white male, who said, "Why are you always making these projects about yourself? Why are you always talking about yourself?" He doesn't realize that seeing someone on television who looks like you, if you're not him, if you're not a white male, is so revolutionary, so amazing, that you will stop flipping the channels and watch it. That's one of the reasons that I enjoy making this kind of work. There are a lot of people out there who don't have the ability or the opportunity to tell their own stories. If I can make my story clear enough or make it relate to them in some way, then they'll feel a little bit better about themselves; they'll understand that they exist. They're vindicated by being on TV.

What are you working on now?

There's a project that I'm supposed to be working on, called the *House of Ong,* for which I actually got pretty good support. It's a continuation of the piece about my crazy uncle, except that it's now about my entire crazy family. They are these Chinese people who live in Phoenix, Arizona, and they really like it there. And Phoenix is not the best place in the world to live. It's really hot, it's really flat, it's ugly suburban sprawl, really hideous. But for some reason, my grandfather moved out there at the turn of the century and planted his family, and they've thrived.

What has happened is a cross-cultural hybrid. My uncles all speak Spanish, and Chinese, and English, and Spanish was the first language a lot of them learned. My aunts heat up tamales in the rice cooker and my grandmother used to make really excellent flour tortillas. They listen to country music and wear those little bolo ties. Southwestern Chinese people. . . . So I want to talk about that a little bit, this culture that exists completely outside of the black/white dichotomy, which seems to be the only way that some people can think about race relations in this country. Or the white/other dichotomy that fills up the rest of the world. This is an Asian/Latino or Asian/Native American kind of culture.

What kind of critical response has your work received?

Pretty good, I think, because it kind of caught the wave when a lot of people were interested in multiculturalism, and I think they still are. Younger people seem to like it a lot because it talks about stuff they want to talk about like identity issues. It's as though I had made a coming-out tape if I were gay. Establishing a reputation on that level is allowing me to move off to other stuff. I want to do Stan Brakhage kind of stuff, like drawing on film stock or something. Just to see what kind of response it'll get from people who are used to seeing me talking about issues with a big *I.* Actually, I adore formalism.

Influences and Advice

What was it like studying with Lyn Blumenthal and Kate Horsfield? Did you have any other role models?

They led by example. They weren't overtly dogmatic. Well, yes, they were. They were running the Data Bank, they were teaching feminist history, and they were really strong, together people. They were dedicated to their craft, their community, to changing the world, to being an alternative to the mainstream. I think that just having role models like that was exciting.

What were the politics they presented?
I can't remember. Just all of the above. They had short hair and groovy clothes. I think that my mom was a strong role model, too. She's a career woman. My father does all the cooking, and my mother goes out and makes money. Actually, my dad works, too. But having two other strong role models was nice. It kind of fit in my head. I guess I'm from a matriarchy.

I love Marlon Riggs. He was a brilliant technician, and he was also a brilliant theorist. And he could make engaging work from personal experience that other people could relate to. And he also broke down boundaries. He was not just a black man. He was a diva, a filmmaker, a political activist, a writer—all of these different things. I think his work is an incredible legacy, and his loss was one of the worst things to happen to this field in a long time. It's devastating to see someone so bright and prolific, taken. I think that all the rest of them are men, I'm afraid.

Why would you tell a young girl to be an artist?
The act of creation is satisfying and rewarding, and coupled with that is the feeling that you're contributing to society at large, that you're somehow acting to advance the human race. You're not just a victim of the horrible things in our society. You feel as though you're doing something useful and having fun, too.

Video Work

1986	*"ALL ORIENTALS LOOK THE SAME,"* ¾" video, 1:30 min.
1987	*New Year, Parts I and II,* two-channel video installation
1990	*Black Sheep,* VHS, 6 min.
1990	*Diversity,* three-channel video installation
1991	*Destiny,* VHS, 6 min.
1992	*Picturing Oriental Girls: A (re) Educational Videotape,* VHS, 12 min.
1992	*Heart of the City,* site-specific video installation
1992	*Mixed Blood,* Betacam, 20 min.
1992	*Twenty Questions* (with Lawrence Andrews), two-channel video installation
1994	*Walking the Mountain,* SVHS, 2:30 min.
1995	*Binge* (with Amy Moom), video installation
1997	*Beyond Asiaphilia,* digital Betacam, 14 min.
1998	*La Vida Povera De San Pancho* (with Erika Olsen-Hannes), video installation

Distribution and Contact Information

NAATA Distribution, 346 Ninth St., San Francisco, CA 94103; www.naatanet.org; (415) 552-9550

Video Data Bank, 112 South Michigan Avenue, #312, Chicago, IL 60603; (312) 345-3550

Women Make Movies, 462 Broadway, #500, New York, NY 10013; (212) 925-0606

Or from the artist's Web site: www.sirius.com/~sstark/mkr/vs/vs-bio1.html

[16] Yvonne Welbon

Yvonne Welbon is completing her Ph.D. in film from Northwestern University. At the same time, she also makes autobiographical art videos, produces narrative film through her company, Our Film Works, makes more traditional educational documentaries, and writes about African American women and film. In this diverse practice, one focus becomes particularly clear: Welbon's dedication to researching and passing on the experiences of African American women, particularly African American lesbians. With many of the same goals as those that underlie this project, Welbon documents and analyzes the underrecognized contributions of black women in this society by writing, filming interviews with her fore-mothers and sisters, and recording her own experiences on video. "You have to have a sense of who came before you, and what they were doing so you can understand yourself and where you fit in," she believes. Thus, her current documentary, Sisters in the Cinema, *offers a historical overview of the lives and films of African American women. Another project,* Living with Pride: Ruth C. Ellis @ 100, *tells the story of the oldest-known living African American lesbian. Videos like* Remembering Wei Yi-fang, Remembering Myself . . . *(1995),* Missing Relations *(1994), and* Monique *(1991) use autobiography to envision a coming-to-terms with race and racism, culture and migration, denial and celebration.*

An entrepreneur by constitution, Welbon moves from field to field, medium to medium, situating herself wherever to best accomplish her immediate goals. For example, her documentary videomaking, academic scholarship, and popular writing about Julie Dash look at Dash's career from a variety of perspectives: professional, personal, inspirational. Welbon wrote her MFA thesis on the making, marketing, exhibition, and distribution of Dash's feature film Daughters of the Dust, *and she produced a documentary portrait of the artist in her video* The Cinematic Jazz of Julie

Dash *(1992–93)*. Meanwhile, as a curator Welbon makes sure that audiences in Chicago can see films by and about black women, in their diverse voices. And as a segment producer for Split Screen, *broadcast on the cable station Bravo and the Independent Film Channel, Welbon gets out her messages about independent media to an ever-broader audience. Her career marks a correction to some of my earlier observations. Where I had suggested that the fields of art, academia, business, and the "industry," were distinct and often isolated, Welbon points to a generation that may change independent media by attempting to destroy these artificial and limiting boundaries.*

Welbon suggests that you can and must tell a history of work that has never, or has only recently, been made by speaking of the conditions that initially disallowed its telling. For instance, the history of African American lesbian cinema does not become visible *until the '80s. In her articles on black lesbians in film and video, Welbon documents the stories of the African American lesbians who can only now make their work and claim their place.*[1] *According to Welbon, the significant number of out African American lesbian media artists is a direct product of their being raised after the important gains of the civil rights, women's rights, and gay and lesbian rights movements. Yet even as Welbon writes about this newly visible generation of women, she claims and makes visible the* invisible *foremothers who are also her legacy: invisible in that their lives are undocumented; invisible in that they were not able to document their own lives; invisible in that there was not always an available vocabulary to speak proudly about the complexity of racial, sexual, gender, and national identities. In videos like* Sisters in the Life: First Love *(1993), Welbon makes such invisible stories visible by speaking her own stories, those of her ancestors, and those of her sisters.*

Welbon suggests that the recent but marked presence of African American lesbians in media can also be seen as a consequence of the institutionalization of feminist filmmaking, teaching, and scholarship. For most of the women Welbon studies benefited from a higher education that was itself peopled by feminist professors of film. The steady entrenchment of women into film and art schools notwithstanding, Welbon was the first black woman in her master's program in film and video at the School of the Art Institute of Chicago. Thus, she is motivated by creating a visual, scholarly, and personal legacy about and on media—placing herself and other black women in the media into the picture—so that black women who follow her will have that tradition in place from which to build. In this respect, she adds to the work of many other feminists in the media who attempt to remember those women who worked in the past so as to expand options in the future. As Judith Redding and Victoria Brownworth write in their study of independent women directors:

There has been a conscious manipulation of historical fact in an effort to ex-
cise women from the cinematic picture, just as they have been edited out of so
much other history. And leaving women out of the history of filmmaking contributes to the problems women directors continue to have in achieving their
filmmaking goals, making it that much easier to restrict women's roles in filmmaking today: if no precedent exists for women's place in the directorial (or
cinematographic, producing, management, etc.) oeuvre, then each new female
director (cinematographer, producer, studio head, etc.) looks like the *only* one.[2]

*Welbon works with memory, writing, filmmaking, and curating to
ensure that others know that she is not "the only one," not the only African
American lesbian in film.*

▶━━━━━━━━━━━━━━━━━

Everything across the Board

Please discuss the various things that you do related to film and video.
I am a filmmaker and a video artist. I am also a curator and a film scholar,
and I also work on other peoples' films in producing capacities. So I do
pretty much everything across the board when it comes to the whole film/
video arena.

Why film and video, and then, why everything?
I became interested in film and video in the late '80s. This grew out of a
literary form that I was trying to develop called "imaging." I was trying
to write in a way where people could read and relate through their senses:
a tactile way, auditory, or to feel what I was saying. I moved to Taiwan in
1984, and my primary language was Chinese. By 1985, I was publishing
an arts and leisure magazine there. I felt that language could divide people,
but that basically people were similar: they had the same feelings and
emotions, but language could get in the way. I was trying to develop a kind
of writing form dealing on an emotional or intuitive plane; I hoped that I
could bring people together. It didn't work when I was trying to do it on
paper.

   In 1989, I went to a publishing conference in Bangkok, and everyone
was talking about video—at a print publishing conference! And when I got
back to Taipei, my photographer said, "You should put the magazine on
video." At that time I had a managing editor who had done cable access
work in Austin, Texas, and a new volunteer who was an associate producer for 20/20. (He had moved to Taiwan to learn about his wife's culture.)
So he was free. And I put together this whole video format for my publication. I never got to realize it, because I was in a motorcycle accident, and it

took me five months to recover. When I recovered, I decided to come back to America and go to film school. I came back to the States in 1990, and I took a filmmaking class, "Film I," at the School of the Art Institute of Chicago (SAIC). I loved it and I made my first film. I did what I was trying to do with imaging in that first film called *Monique*.

Monique is an autobiographical piece that deals with my first experience with racism as a child. I shot the piece all in shadows. The shadows were little-girl images represented by paper doll cutouts. With shadows, the images weren't so literal. Because they were shadows, individuals could put themselves in that space because it was just an outline, not a literal being. The piece was my first, and it is really rough. In a way that lent to the piece, the footage seems almost bruised. On a formal level you feel what I was going through as a child having this encounter with racism.

It's 1990, you're in film school, and suddenly six years later, here you are, you do everything.

Well, I took that first class in 1990, and I decided to get a master's degree. In 1991, I started working on an MFA at SAIC. There had never been a black woman in their master's program in film. So on some level, some of my concerns were never really thought about, because there had never been someone like me there before. For instance, when I was an undergraduate I studied history. You have to have a sense of who came before you, and what they were doing, so you can understand yourself and where you fit in. When I started school at SAIC, I wanted to find the African American alumnae. I wanted to know what they had gone through. I wanted to see their work. There was nothing here at all. I had to go outside of the institution to find out what I felt I needed to know: to see works by other black woman filmmakers and to meet other black women filmmakers. The situation has changed since then at the Art Institute; the school has actually bought films by black women artists for their collection. It's not so bad now. But when I came here, it was.

▶———————————————————————————

Curating, Collecting, Writing

I started getting involved in a curatorial way in a lot of different organizations here in Chicago. One of the organizations was Women in the Director's Chair. I began by volunteering, and then I was asked to join the board. They had a special program called "Mosaic in Black" for which I was one of the curators. It highlighted the works of black women filmmakers in the 1992 festival. It was really important for me that I got to be involved in curating that program. I was able to see *Losing Ground* by Kathleen Collins (1982). I had heard about it, but I'd never gotten to see it, because you have to rent it on 16mm film and project it. It's not available on video. At that time I thought it was the first feature film by a black woman, and I wanted to see it. As a curator you can program to make sure things happen; you can see hard-to-find work with an audience.

I also got involved with ETA, an arts organization here in Chicago on the South Side, which started the African American Women in the Arts Festival. The festival focused on all the arts, including film and video, and I joined that committee and participated for three years. We had the only African American women's film festival in the country. We would get lots of work in. It was one way I could see the work and meet the women filmmakers.

What is the significance of your statement "the only African American women's film festival" to you, the community in Chicago, and nationally? When I started graduate school, I knew the name of one black woman filmmaker, and her name was Julie Dash. And I did not know any other black women filmmakers; there weren't any at the school. It was really odd; it didn't feel right. I knew I wasn't the only black woman who was interested in studying or making film. It's not good for people to work in isolation. It's not healthy.

I started looking for other black women because I knew that I wasn't by myself. It is so important for people to know we exist because we do exist and we are doing things. So I started a database. I started collecting all the information I could find about black women filmmakers. It was really obscure and really hard to get. That year I found about sixty names and 120 works. That was the year I got involved with ETA, and we held the first African American women in the arts competition that we knew about. That first year we received about forty films and videos. I got to see everything. It was incredible to see that amount of work, to find another black lesbian filmmaker. That's when I found Cheryl Dunye. She sent her stuff in. And I didn't even know she existed. Here I was, a black lesbian filmmaker, and I didn't know there were any other black lesbian filmmakers.

When I started collecting this information and found out how obscure it was, it made me think I also needed to write because there just wasn't a lot of stuff written about black women filmmakers. This is really important because it's almost like we don't exist. If you don't have a presence, people don't know you exist. It was hard for me because it was like I was invisible, right? Even though I was here, existing, I didn't see any reflections of myself anywhere. I'm a pretty strong person. I went to Vassar College. As a Vassar woman, there's nothing you can't do. My mother raised me to believe

"Don't say can't." But another young black girl might not think of being a filmmaker, because she doesn't see any image of a black woman as a film-maker. I wanted to do something about that. Sometimes that's what some-one needs to even believe it's possible for her to do something.

▶————————————————————————————————————

Remembering Wei Yi-fang, Remembering Myself . . .

Your work is around individual empowerment in relation to invisibility, both for you and young girls coming up. Can you talk about how questions of visibility and invisibility are important on a larger ideological or political landscape?
Even though all of my work so far has been basically autobiographical, I am really interested in having more images of African American women reach American TV and movie screens. It's important because sometimes the images of African American women that do reach these screens are stereotypical and not representative. In the last piece I did, *Remembering Wei Yi-fang, Remembering Myself . . .*, I focus on the six years I spent in Taiwan. I did this because people acted like it was really weird that I went there: "You lived in Taiwan for six years!" I said there were a whole bunch of other black women there when I was there. I wasn't the only one who thought of doing this.

It's odd. People don't think that black women *do* these things. I left America when I was twenty-two and moved to Taiwan. In *Remembering* I present a parallel story about my grandmother who left Honduras when she was twenty-two and immigrated to America. I show two images of African American women in this tape. And I also show how when we leave home, things happen. The tape focuses on identity and how we be-came racialized in our new homes. My grandmother became "black" and learned a lot of new words like "nigger." For me, leaving America was different. I had an opportunity to live in a way where I was respected for starting a magazine at the age of twenty-three. I would be respected for that here, too, but I didn't face the daily racism in Taiwan that I did here. So this tape accomplishes a lot of things. It shows two black women you don't usually get a chance to see on TV: my immigrant grandma and me.

AJ: *It will be on* POV *and reach a national audience. How does that feel?*
It's important for all artists to think about where they want their work to be shown and to think about that in preproduction and in developing the idea. When I started working on *Remembering* I saw it as a general-audience film. In my mind that meant PBS. And I thought it would be on *POV.*

What do you hope to accomplish from a general public seeing those two stories?

I hope that people will watch this tape and that they'll look to the left and look to the right and look at people they see and won't always assume, "That's a black woman and I bet xyz thing," but instead they will look at her and see her. I'm showing two black women in one family. We're really different, yet we're from the same family. I hope that a viewer will see this and think more broadly about black women and realize there is a range of black women. I don't think a lot of people who aren't black women think about black women very often. Perhaps this will encourage the general population to think of black women as individuals instead of as stereotypes or statistics.

When you say the "general public," it sounds to me like you are referring to white people. Is there a black audience in the general population? And for an audience of color, as part of that general public, what do they get from your film being on POV?

Most of America is white. The general population is very white in my mind. It's like 70 percent of the country. So that's the general public. It includes everyone, but it's mostly white. In my heart this film is really for black women. I think they will love it. So far, the response has been really wonderful. Also a lot of Taiwanese people have seen it. They are having a lot of interesting internal dilemmas right now around identity. This tape is interesting for them, too. I talk about Taiwan and Taiwan's identity. The piece has a political structure, too. I, as a black woman, relate myself and my life to the Taiwan political situation. Any immigrant, particularly listening to Grandma's story entering this country, will enjoy this piece. African Americans, African American women in particular, African American children, Asian Americans, and Latinos will actually relate to this tape. All of those cultures intersect within this tape. So I think a lot of people will relate.

▶ ────────────────────────────────────

Success

The story you've told of your work has been one of successes. It's been easy for you. You've done all this incredible stuff. Have there been obstacles for you?

You have to remember that at twenty-three I started the first English language arts and leisure magazine of its kind in Taiwan. I did this in Chinese. I had to navigate a culture and a structure that didn't make much sense. Nothing after that is difficult. I had this particular experience of struggle in another country. So the fact I can do everything in English, with clear guidelines and rules to follow when I apply for things, I can't tell you how easy it seems by comparison. My experience is really unusual. Yes, all my work has been funded and won awards. Yes, I haven't had problems and I don't plan to. I don't. I'm not planning to. I plan to do things so that I don't have problems.

Where are you going with your career? What are your goals?
I am finishing a Ph.D. I have started a production company, Our Film Works, to produce and consult on films. This might have come out of running my business before in Taiwan, but I like being the boss and I like the business side of film. I learned everything about making a film—lighting, directing—but what I really enjoy is the business side: figuring out the money, putting it together, doing the budget. That's the part of it that I love. I'm really fortunate. I believe that I can do anything I want. Since producing is what I like, that's what I'll focus on.

Then, going back to my scholarly work, as part of my Ph.D., I'm getting a certificate in telecommunication policy, management, and science. I'm focusing on new technologies. I'm most interested in distribution and exhibition. You can make a film, but if you can't get it to an audience, forget it. So what I am focusing on in the dissertation is the way new technologies will be used in the marketing, exhibition, and distribution of black women's work. I'm focusing on how African American women's work will travel this information highway. And hopefully my dissertation will be actually realized as a book.

▶ ─────────────────────────────────

Community

SIMON POOLIO (cameraperson, Chicago shoot): *Could you tell us your thoughts about new technology?*
I'm thinking about how new technology will be used to distribute, exhibit, and market our work. There are so many possibilities on the horizon. What is problematic is that we don't own it. The Telecommunication Act of 1996 will make it even less possible for us to own it. It's scary. But I'm not totally pessimistic. I did a study of the marketing of lesbian feature films on the Internet. I found that what's being established are cybervillages. Those communities act just like regular communities. Information is spread through word of mouth. This method of promotion works really well for independent films.

I did a survey on Sistanet, a black lesbian list-serv. I found that the women on Sistanet feel a responsibility because they have this privilege, this access. They believe they get information faster. They feel they have a responsibility to take back what they get from their cybercommunities to their actual communities. Sistanetters are in Canada, America, Africa — all over the world. That is a really positive, inexpensive way to speed up information dissemination. These women also want to help fund work so that more work can be made. They have used Sistanet and cyberspace to help support the work of black lesbian film and video artists.

Whose work has influenced yours?
Last week Julie Dash was here, and I found her visit incredibly inspiring. She just finished her first novel, which is tentatively titled *Tales of Daughters of the Dust*. And it follows characters from the movie into the 1920s. She has another book half-written. She has three features in development hell. She's just done a women's erotic program with Showtime and is working with HBO. She also just did a Tracy Chapman video, and she's producing projects where other black women directors will be involved. That's great. She says, "I can always teach: I do have three film degrees." And I can always teach, too; I'll have two film degrees when I finish. That's great to me. Then you, you've got your book out, you're making your work, you're producing. Lots of women are out there and are busy and are not necessarily part of Hollywood or the powers that be. I'm interested in people who work outside the box.

▶ ───

Sisters in the Life

Do you consider yourself a feminist filmmaker?
I wrote a whole article about black lesbian film- and videomakers as feminists. And I talked to a lot of black lesbian filmmakers, and everyone was stepping around that term. Even though I did that piece, I'm still not sure how I feel about it. It seems, from the little bit I know about early feminism, it wasn't very inclusive of black women. And then, what I know of black women's history is that we were always feminists. We were always doing stuff, from before early suffrage. Black women were doing a lot of things, and white women didn't want to include them. In theory, yes, I have to be a feminist, but I've never really used that word to describe myself.

MEGAN CUNNINGHAM (associate producer): *I'm interested in your article. Could you mention some works or pieces that you write about?*
The article is called "Black Lesbian Film and Video Art."[3] I look at about twenty-two black lesbian film and video artists and seventy of their films,

videos, and interactive computer work. I look at what brought these women into existence after 1990. I look in depth at a couple of women who have broken a lot of new ground. They include Cheryl Dunye, Jocelyn Taylor, Pamela Jennings, and Ann Marie Jane Bryant, who is an African American lesbian and the first deaf woman to get a degree at NYU film school. I focus on the makers' work. I look at who influences them. For instance, I consider how Jocelyn Taylor is interested in the body and sexuality. She also deals with the family and how her family relates to her. I examine the works of many different women in the piece.

In the preproduction research meeting you explained some of the conditions that allowed a movement of black lesbian film and video production to start in the '90s. What conditions were in place?
The black lesbian makers discussed were born in the '60s (except for H. Lyn Keller, who is in her forties) and came of age after civil rights and after Stonewall. For instance, I asked Cheryl, "How did you come out?" She told me, "There was a poster on the bus about a gay teens' hot line," and she called it and started attending meetings. There were things in place when we came of age and became aware of our sexuality. The women's movement made a lot of things possible. Almost all of us studied with women filmmakers who had learned their craft throughout the '70s. Our instructors were women. We didn't have to go through those struggles: "There are no women here. They don't even want me here." That obstacle wasn't there. And technology—consumer camcorders became so affordable.

In my article, I look at Cyrille Phipps, who has her activist grassroots background in Not Channel Zero, a camcorder activist collective, and Jocelyn Taylor coming out of ACT UP and DIVA TV, an AIDS video activist collective. All of these movements influenced us. So it doesn't occur to us to be closeted. There's a whole group of black women filmmakers from the '70s who are still closeted. I also look at class. We come from a wide range of class backgrounds: working class to upper class. But one of the things that was prevalent was that almost everyone went to East Coast, higher-tier, competitive, undergraduate schools. Everyone attended college, almost everyone graduated, and a really high percentage of us went to graduate school. We are an unusual subset of the American population.

Let's say I include you in my definition of feminist film practice. Where do you see yourself or your role in that history?
I think it's important that I'm choosing to do this writing about black women filmmakers, and I think it will be significant as time goes on. There is no basic introductory article on black lesbian film and video art except

for my "Sisters in the Life." I'm setting up a theoretical framework to look at work, to analyze work. I place it within a context.

It's important because when teachers show black lesbian work in their classes, they say, "This is black lesbian week." But the way I set it up, you could focus on a number of themes when presenting the work. This way, our work may be shown with other works that deal with those issues or themes. So I'm trying to show that it isn't just that a black lesbian made it, although I think that's important. That does lend to the aesthetic. I'm stressing that one doesn't have to ghettoize this work. It can be integrated into larger discussions where we are looking at intersections of race, class, sexual orientation. A lot of intersections, not just "Black Lesbian Day." That's important, and I've noticed that I have created a framework where it's up to us. By this I mean if black lesbians are really concerned about the way our work is talked about, written about, discussed, we need to lead the discussion. I'm doing this writing, Margaret Daniel is out and doing writing, and so are Jackie Goldsby, Jocelyn Taylor, and Jacqueline Woodson. We need to take the lead.

KATHY KIERNAN (associate producer): *What do you want to pass on? What is your inspiration to younger feminist, black, lesbian women?*
That's really hard. Everyone is so different. I'm interested in producing black girls' coming-of-age stories. I think it is important for young girls to see themselves on the screen. Perhaps it will make them think about making films themselves. Having the information out there helps to create the possibility for young girls to think about being filmmakers. There's a lot, comparatively, of black women out there—making work, producing, directing, writing—and I think that will encourage more work being made and more work reaching audiences. This will hopefully make it possible for a young girl to think about being a director of photography or a gaffer or a writer or a producer.

Film and Video

1991	*Monique,* 16mm, 3 min.
1992–93	*The Cinematic Jazz of Julie Dash,* ¾" video, 24 min.
1993	*Sisters in the Life: First Love,* video, 23 min.
1994	*Missing Relations,* 16mm, 12 min.
1995	*Remembering Wei Yi-fang, Remembering Myself . . . ,* 16mm, Super 8 film and Hi-8 video, 30 min.
1997 to the present	*Split Screen,* segment producer
1999	*Living with Pride: Ruth C. Ellis @ 100,* digital video, 16mm, 60 min.
In progress	*Sisters in Cinema,* digital video

Publications

1991	"Interview with Julie Dash," *The Black Screenwriter* (September)
1992	"Calling the Shots: Black Women Directors Take the Helm," *The Independent* (March)
1992	"Left in the Dust: Lesbians Become More Visible on Screen . . . Sort Of," *Windy City Times* (December)
1995	"Black Lesbian Film and Video Art," *P-Form* (Spring)
1996	"Daughters of the Dust," *Take Two Quarterly*

Distribution and Contact Information

http://www.sistersincinema.com

[17]   *Frances Negrón-Muntaner*

Like Welbon and myself, Frances Negrón-Muntaner is a scholar as well as a media maker. She completed a Ph.D. in comparative/Caribbean literatures and cultures at Rutgers University in 2000 and has, concurrent with her scholarly education, made a large body of work in film and video confronting issues from AIDS to lesbian identity within the Puerto Rican diaspora to feminist history. She is completing a feature documentary on the Spanish-American War and its aftermath, The Splendid Little War, *and has recently completed both* Puerto Rican ID *about Puerto Rican viewers' relationships to American TV and her experimental autobiography,* Brincando el Charco: Portrait of a Puerto Rican. *She is the author of a book of her own collected poems,* Anatomy of a Smile, *as well as the editor of two books, one rethinking nationalism and colonialism,* Puerto Rican Jam, *and the other, a collection of poetry by Latino poets in Philadelphia.*[1]

Her aim to both make and theorize culture is a direct consequence of the intellectual activism of the generation who taught us: the women (and men) who began to insist that work within cultural production—making and thinking about art—is political. Whereas traditional film education has separated theory and praxis, more and more students—tutored in a tradition that emphasizes the value of engaged scholarship—think critically about what they and others make, and then also make critical media about the real-world issues in which they are engaged. The institutions of higher education that instruct us are slower to follow than may be the demands placed on them, but institutions do change, especially when people like Negrón-Muntaner bend them to her liking. Before her Ph.D., Negrón-Muntaner also received an MFA in film as well as an MA in visual anthropology. No one program met all of her educational needs, so she devised a route of study that would satisfy her. Perhaps this will prove to be another example of my generation's contribution to infrastructure building: the revamping of media education. It is currently too soon to tell, as we are only recently landing full-time jobs, but if our training and output are any indication, more educational programs will be organized like my own at Pitzer College, where undergraduates incorporate film and video's written and visual history into their academic writing and critical image making.

A feminist film- and videomaker whose graduate education in feminist film theory made her think that feminist film theory was dead, a "textual feminism," "an artifact in a museum," Negrón-Muntaner made it come to life by infusing her own story, community, and desires into the pictures she made. Negrón-Muntaner insists that Laura Mulvey's "Visual Pleasure and Narrative Cinema" had a significant impact on her education, even if this was through counterdistinction. She explains that while the article did not describe her experiences with the cinema, it did provide the cornerstone for almost all feminist film scholarship that followed it, including Negrón-Muntaner's.

Mulvey used Lacanian psychoanalysis to describe a cinema "organized to the tune of male desire," where women were objectified by the camera, director, narrative, and male spectator through either a too-loving (fetishistic) or too-violent (sadistic) gaze. Negrón-Muntaner found that such a description did not adequately explain all of the aspects of the cinema that she experienced. This allowed her to understand how, for her at least, the pleasures of cinema were largely contextual—derived from the situation in which she watched a film: with a best girlfriend as an illicit adventure, surrounded by other Puerto Ricans at a community screening. Further, as a lesbian who found herself desiring women on the screen differently from the misogynistic way that Mulvey had postulated the desiring male gaze of cinema, Negrón-Muntaner knew she had to seek other models in order to understand and then represent her own experiences. Two feminist critical traditions that developed in the '80s and '90s helped Negrón-Muntaner speak to the blind spots of earlier feminist scholarship: women-of-color feminism and queer theory. Both traditions sometimes criticized, but always also augmented, earlier feminist theory to establish that a spectator's identifications (or a woman's identity or social position) is influenced by conditions both including and other than gender. Thus, Negrón-Muntaner explains that the work of gay male filmmakers has been as influential to her work, if not more so, than has been the work of her feminist or lesbian foremothers. In so saying, Negrón-Muntaner evidences a kind of feminism that does not isolate gender from the other conditions that create identity, community, and political allegiance: race, class, sexuality, nationality. In fact, Negrón-Muntaner posits a theory of identity that is, like her theory of film spectatorship, almost entirely contextual. She is a feminist in certain *circumstances and for certain reasons, a lesbian in others, or a Puerto Rican lesbian when it is necessary or urgent to be so: "The bottom line here is practices and effects, not 'identities.'"*

▶ _____

Early Influences

I'm interested in hearing you talk about how you make, what you've made, what have been your influences, what has allowed you to have a career.

It was possible for me to conceive of becoming a professional filmmaker because of my grandfather, who was a frustrated commercial director. He had studied film at the University of Miami during the '40s and returned to Puerto Rico a few years later without completing his degree. Although my grandfather was passionate about making feature films in Puerto Rico, he seemed to have been routinely ripped off by industry sharks. This led him to eventually close a studio-for-rent he had built behind his house. After abandoning features, he became a medical photographer and slowly began to lend me the tools of his trade. When I was around ten, he gave me a Super 8 camera, which I used extensively to record my everyday life and environment including my block, my sisters, my parents, myself. I also experimented with imitations of mainstream cinema and television shows like *Planet of the Apes* and *I Dream of Jeannie*.

However, after I graduated with a BA in sociology, I was bound for a career in academia. My parents were pressuring me in that direction, and I gave in. I went to the University of Massachusetts at Amherst, set up an apartment in Northampton before classes began, and I immediately felt uncomfortable. The town was supposed to be an American lesbian haven, but I felt the whole scene was extremely superficial, white, and privileged. I agonized a bit over this seemingly strange contradiction and then told myself: "No, no, no, no. I'm leaving." I came to New York for a few months. After that, a friend from Philadelphia invited me to visit.

Once I settled in Philadelphia, I began to have a series of intellectual dilemmas. I was coming from a social science background with its faith in science, objectivity, and truth. But everywhere I looked, all of these concepts were being radically challenged. Since I no longer believed in the tenets of science as a way to relate to the world, I needed to find another mode. What's the best epistemological alternative to objectivity? The answer for me was film: the illusion of objectivity.

What other conditions were in place that allowed you the possibility to imagine yourself as an artist, as a professional woman?

I come from a middle-class, academic family, where both of my parents have Ph.D.'s, and so do my uncles. The older women in my family are also educated. My paternal grandmother is a lawyer, while my maternal grandmother had close to a master's degree in English. And we're talking about a period when women weren't usually educated at all. So by the time my sister and I were born, it was a given that we'd both have academic or professional careers of some sort. Due to my many interests and conflicts with academia, however, I ended up with an M.A. in anthropological film, an MFA in film and video, and a Ph.D. in comparative literature. Ultimately, however, my public location is more as a filmmaker or a writer than an academic per se. But I do interventions in that arena as well.

▶

Feminism

I'd like to hear about your relationship to feminism. Your first contact. How much has the women's movement affected your having a career?

The whole process of modernization in Puerto Rico created both a middle class and unprecedented opportunities for women to join the labor force as professionals. Many among my parents' generation became solidly middle class and found niches in academia and in other professions. Because of this relative stability, I think my generation felt they could take some risks. To talk about the women's movement in Puerto Rico is another thing. There have been feminist claims on the state since the beginning of the twentieth century. Some of these demands have been appropriated or honored in some ways, but feminist groups have rarely constituted a massive movement or political force.

My first meaningful encounter with feminism was through the women with whom I became sexually involved during the early 1980s. I gravitated around a group of women who were ten years my senior and who were also pioneers of the second wave of feminist practice in Puerto Rico: the women who were the core militants of the feminist groups during the '70s. I was introduced to feminist history through the experiences of these women and later through the books to which they often referred. In this sense, feminism for me has always been linked to lesbian communities and struggles. At the same time, my attraction to feminism as an "identity" was also connected to my disenchantment with the political left (a grand metanarrative) in Puerto Rico. Once I joined these groups, however—and this was a harsh thing for a young idealistic person to deal with—I witnessed all the same kind of power dynamics present in the larger society, but without any reflexivity. Socialist-Feminist Truth was the only truth.

Coming to the United States and entering into a film school gave me another space to interact with feminism. This was no longer the middle-class, political-pressure groups of my very recent activist past, but the academy. At that juncture, I interacted with feminism in a different way since feminism was a *textual* history that you read in books, one that had occurred in the not-too-distant past. Since feminism was a one-class topic in a crowded curriculum, the message to me as a young student was that feminist film and video practices were dead, that they had become artifacts in a museum or library. And just as with a museum artifact, you can look at these canonical films, jot down their historical importance or innovations, and move on. At the same time, there were other considerations. For a whole generation of students entering the academy, feminist history was beginning to be repositioned by the work of women of color. So canonical "feminist film and video," mostly produced by white women, could be read as not only passé, but also exclusionary.

▶

Spectatorship

AJ: *Talk about the women-of-color feminist textual work. Who are you reading? How does that make you feel?*
Less than specific theorists, the issue is about spectatorship. For example, perhaps because of my feminist history or my own personal obsessions, I was influenced by Laura Mulvey's article "Visual Pleasure and the Narrative Cinema."[2] What was impressive to me was not so much what the essay proposes, but the tensions it unleashes. The possibility of signifying plea-sure as negative or politically suspect was potent. In Puerto Rican culture, women are available everywhere as "pleasurable" objects and representa-tions. A theory of spectatorship that negates these "mainstream" pleasures seemed to ignore the specificity of viewing: who is looking at this woman/object/representation, in what context, and with what effects.

Remembering my own history of transgressive film moments, I have to recall when I was fifteen and snuck out of my house to see *Doña Flor and Her Two Husbands* (Bruno Barreto, 1976) featuring Sonia Braga as the ultimate hot sex object. I recall this as a transgressive moment because I took a risk in my "defiance" of paternal authority. Once I was in the the-ater, I felt my imagination challenged both the heterosexual sexual econo-my as well as the Hollywood representation because I was determined to enjoy this image, *my way.* Not only was Sonia Braga a "woman," she was a mulatta (not white), she was petite (not tall), she was from Brazil (not Los Angeles), she could communicate with the dead, and she felt torn by a tension between her most radical desires and her well-being. Although I may now chuckle at my teenage naïveté, my identification took place along several axes. Most feminist writing (to this day) fails to account for this.

Are there other works that have inspired you, particularly works by women filmmakers?

In Puerto Rico, I had no access to any work that could be called "feminist" either by the intention of the maker, its textuality, and/or its reception. The only film that I could identify as feminist due to its context of reception was *Lianna* by John Sayles (1983), which I saw during an "underground" gay and lesbian activist screening when I was eighteen or nineteen. It was not until I came to the United States that I had a context, a body of texts, and the institutional spaces to watch films as a "feminist" spectator. Within that process, I recall two feminist films that had an impact on me. The first was *The Mothers of the Plaza de Mayo* by Lourdes Portillo and Susana Muñoz (1985). I remember seeing that film about ten times. It was probably the first time I saw a "Latin American subject" in a documentary from a feminist oppositional point of view, and Susana Muñoz was the first Latina filmmaker that I ever saw in the flesh. I was thrilled. The second film that had an impact on me, and I have returned to many times later, is *La Operación* by Ana María García (1982). Although the film was made in the early '80s, I never saw that film in Puerto Rico, but in the context of a Latina health conference that took place in Philadelphia.

At the same time, I have to say that many of the films that impacted me while I was at film school were not feminist films. I was profoundly affected by films like *Man with a Movie Camera* (1929) by Dziga Vertov and most importantly, *Chronicle of a Summer* (1961), directed by Edgar Morin and Jean Rouch. The reason that those films were so challenging and impressive to me was that they incorporated a reflection on spectatorship: how is looking possible? How do I see what I see? In sum, the films that could be labeled feminist and that influenced me were not the ones I saw in film school, but the films I tended to see within the context of community organizations and community events. I'm referring to Latino communities, lesbian feminist communities. In this sense, the moment of reception, a crowded theater with people eager for dialogue, was key.

Which brings me to the whole experience of engaging in a dialogue with a film. For example, when I went to see *Thelma and Louise* (Ridley

Scott, 1991), I saw it in a theater. The audience was 98 percent women. We can argue whether the film is a feminist narrative or not. But what I experienced in the theater was, if not feminist, a similar gut response toward what we were seeing. People were screaming at the screen. It was very participatory. Yet this is not the only time I have felt this way. For instance, I once went to see *Terminator II* at a theater where the audience was predominantly African American and young. There is a scene where the Terminator kills his first victim, and it is an African American man. A couple of young men behind me started talking back to the screen: "Why did you have to kill the brother first?" I was having a similar thought, which begs the question of interpolation in relation to allegedly stable categories like gender, race, and sexuality.

Support

Why do you make work? Why are you a filmmaker, videomaker, artist? What do you want to do with your work, and why film?
If I was going to rationalize my involvement in film, I would say it is because there is such a vacuum of films made by Puerto Rican women. That fact has had a lot to do with my ability to make films, in the form of opportunities and support.

By whom? By what?
After *AIDS in the Barrio* was completed, I found Latina women, some Puerto Rican, some not, who invested in my development. I was nurtured and invited into a community by people like Lillian Jimenez, Blanca Vazquez, Beni Matias: women who are interested in media, had made media in the past, and/or who are pioneers in the field.[3] This support was invaluable since I had to grasp what being a U.S. Puerto Rican meant, what kinds of possibilities and limitations came with the package. These women were responsible for getting me, to some extent, to where I am. They helped me to acquire a certain knowledge and reflexivity about my position in this long history, what happened before, where I came in, and how we could work together. After *Brincando el Charco*, I experienced a similar process in Puerto Rico, where women like Ana María García, Teresa Previdi, and Sonia Fritz were very nurturing to me.

To what else do you owe your success? Perhaps success is not a word you want to use to describe your career. I don't know . . .
. . . the ability to make stuff . . .

... *the ability to make stuff. It's successful as far as most women's careers are concerned. Most women don't get to make work, and you have been able to.* Given the fact that Puerto Rican women have been making films for less than thirty years, I feel success is simply hanging in there. Making the work. Stirring discussion. *Never* giving up. At this point, when I am interested in making more ambitious projects, success is more relative and elusive.

Yes, I am taken in by people who have been doing this for a long time, and I am nurtured and walked through. I recall when my second film was going to be produced and my grant application went to the Paul Robeson Fund for Film and Video (which no longer gives money for production), and I got a call rather than a letter from their director, Lillian Jimenez, saying, "You'll get this amount for this film." That was my first grant. And that played a major role in the conditions of possibility, that I was able to hook into a community that nurtured me. Mind you, I'm nineteen years old, and I decided I want to make film. I have no history here; I have no network, no resources. Nothing.

AJ: *In the interview that we shot before with Carolee Schneemann, the feeling of the interview was that she has never been fully recognized, she's always at the wrong place at the wrong time. Her work is recognized fifteen years later. Earlier, it is censored. It is remarkable to experience your interviews up against each other.*

Let me talk about context. In the United States my work is generally well received. In Puerto Rico, the situation is more complex. I make my work from the United States precisely because I can take more risks. If I were to live in Puerto Rico, there would not only be resource constraints but issues of self-censorship. With *Brincando el Charco,* I've had polarized responses to the film. For instance, I showed it as part of a conference at Berkeley. There were people who just hated my guts and others who applauded it as a new cinema opening up possibilities, rarely any responses in between. In sum, in the United States, I have an uncomfortable fit into different narratives of alternative film, ethnic cinema, queer cinema. In Puerto Rico, I am the ultimate other as a diasporic, postnationalist, queer filmmaker. Yet it is perhaps among Puerto Ricans that the work will always be experienced as charged.

▶

Feminist Film

Are you a feminist filmmaker?
I don't consider myself a feminist filmmaker, at least not exclusively. I often identify as a queer filmmaker—and I privilege queer over lesbian in the sense

that *queer* allows me a location beyond the gay/straight dichotomy and to assume a critical position in relation to dominant culture (which is, of course, another dichotomy, but much more ambiguous and relative). In other contexts, I am a diasporic filmmaker and feel most at home with other displaced peoples, since migration probably defines my adult life more than any other single process. I've had to reinvent myself not only in relation to sexual communities and practices but in every aspect of daily existence.

I relate to feminist work and I incorporate feminist concerns into my work. But as an identity, it tends to exclude other concerns that have to do with migration (for instance, my diasporic sensibility), and being located at the intersections of power relations. In that sense, I think of my work as a cinema that is trying to challenge, or seduce into challenge, the audience in a multiplicity of ways that don't necessarily place issues of gender at the center.

But, then, what's so interesting is that when I say, "You are a feminist film-maker," you say, "Well, yes and no."
Right.

But your work has a place in feminist film history.
Right.

Different question.
Right.

How do you define feminist film/video? Can you?
In my own work, I operate with two definitions of feminist film and video. The first is mediated by my relationship with strategies, institutions, and discourses associated with this social movement, as it emerged at a particular point and place in history. For example, one of my films is distributed by Women Make Movies, an institution I consider to be feminist. In this sense, my generation has been able to enjoy the fruits of previous struggles. The fact that a number of institutions exist today makes it easier for younger women to turn their attention elsewhere or to attempt to expand or challenge the orthodoxies of feminism. The second way I relate to feminism is less as a history of texts, people, rhetorics, and/or specific institutions than as an oppositional politics within particular fields where gender is privileged. And this second way is more akin to my own history as a feminist spectator and filmmaker. When I am showing a film in a context that is hostile to discussing issues affecting women or giving women a voice, I have no problem deploying feminist discourse and strategies, regardless if it is labeled "feminist" or not. The bottom line here is practices and effects, not "identities."

Lesbian Film

ERIN CRAMER (associate producer): *Could you tell us about how you fix yourself in relationship to lesbian film and video? Because you've talked about several films and they weren't actually lesbian.*

At the same time that I can say that I saw feminist films at a relatively late period of my formation as a filmmaker, I saw lesbian films, of any kind, way after my formative years. Hence, these films didn't have the impact on me that Mexican popular cinema or even the early work of film/video collectives from Britain had. For instance, I first saw a series of Barbara Hammer's early films when I was twenty-seven years old. And by the time I saw these films, my viewing was mediated by more than two decades of other work and critiques. And I think that to some extent, just as the AIDS movement brought gay men and lesbian women to work together in ways that were unprecedented for some, I've watched gay men's films, both in quantity and quality, much more than I've seen lesbian films.

At the same time, I also think that some of the proposals found in gay men's films, in the areas of sexuality, for example, have always been much more provocative to me than most of the lesbian work that I've been able to see, until very recently. In this tendency, there is both an issue of cultural affinity to gay male subcultures and the fact that lesbian work is less available.

One concrete instance of conscious borrowing from queer men came when I decided to design an erotic scene for *Brincando el Charco*. Toward the end of the film's production, I was faced with the question of whether I was practicing self-censorship by not representing lesbian sex. By ignoring sex, was I implying that sexuality is not important to Puerto Rican lesbians? Or was I censoring myself because this is a film that has public television funding and, arguably, my parents were going to watch it at some point? At the same time, does every single film with a lesbian as a main protagonist need sex? I wavered on that issue. But the idea, the thought, the horror that there had never been a film by a Puerto Rican woman representing lesbian sex—or any sex!—as an enjoyable representation won me over.

The sex sequence is actually a fantasy involving three couples. While I was designing the sequence visually, I watched other films for inspiration. What did I get from the video store? *Sammy and Rosy Got Laid* (Stephen Frears, 1987), *Looking for Langston* (Isaac Julien, 1989), *My Beautiful Laundrette* (Stephen Frears, 1986). Those were the films where I found the sensibility and sensuality I was looking for. Since men are likely to feel comfortable with the notion that desire without objectification, even fetishism, is impossible, I was able to locate an analogous structure of feeling in that work.

Apart from the gay male work, the other model I could have studied was pornography aimed at heterosexual men. For a substantial number of viewers, their only access to lesbian sexual representation is through porn. This state of affairs presented me with a specifically feminist discourse that has often portrayed pornography as exploitation and violence against women. I tried to find ways I can have my cake and eat it, too. Not because I oppose pornography, but because it is such a complex issue. Hence, I used several devices in order to address the possibility of facile appropriation. These included intertitles, black-and-white photography, and a fantasy landscape.

Despite these efforts, some people come up to me and say, "That scene is too tame" or "All I see is breasts." My mother, for instance, told me that the only aspect of the film she was critical of was the sex sequence because it looked like a "jeans commercial." In this sense, there is a certain level of self-censorship. Some parts of the body are acceptable for TV and others are not. Other spectators suggested that the use of the intertitles demonstrated that I was uncomfortable with my own sexuality since I "joked" about it. I don't think that's accurate. Regardless, in my new film, *Tropical Depression Dolores* (coauthored by Paul Seligmann) I am exploring objectification and seduction to its ultimate, and sometimes dangerous, consequences.

What place does your work have in the history of feminist film/video?
I want to clarify something. The identity that I may claim for myself—which depends on the audience, what the piece is about, and what concern of mine is on the table—doesn't mean that I would not take on a feminist, lesbian, national, or ethnic identity if that's what it takes at a particular juncture. To me, it's not about unchanging and absolute identities but ways to contest power and open up options. Also, how I choose to represent myself— as a queer, or diasporic, or cyborgian creature—may not be the way I am represented by others or how others receive me. So self-identification is only a part of the equation. It's more complex than anyone's volition. I have no doubt that when I walk into a Latino context of a certain kind, I may be perceived as a feminist or as a lesbian filmmaker. Just as when I walk into a white, gay, or lesbian context, I am immediately marked first as an ethnic filmmaker. Hence, I think that there may be versions of American feminist film history that would have a place for my work, but it would not exhaust my work's readability. In Latino film history, works dealing with sexuality tend to be accentuated more than those addressing "mainstream" topics such as representation or homelessness. In other words, I can claim and be

claimed by many different discourses and communities that may even be in contradiction, or totally oblivious of each other. But that only speaks to the multiplicity of meanings that can be read into anybody's work.

◆━━━━━━━━━━━━━━━━━━━━━━━━━━━━━━━━━━━━━

FRANCES NEGRÓN-MUNTANER

Work in Media

1989	*AIDS in the Barrio: Eso no me pasa a mí*, 16mm, 29 min.
1991	*Third World, USA: Philadelphia, First Stop*, Hi-8 audio, 13 min.
1994	*Brincando el charco: Portrait of a Puerto Rican*, 16mm film, 56:30 min.
1995	*Puerto Rican ID*, BETA-SP, 5:17 min.
1996	*Homeless Diaries*, Hi-8 video, Super 8 film, 50 min.

Selected Publications

1993	"Of Lonesome Stars and Broken Hearts: Puerto Rican Film/Video Making," *Jump Cut* 38
1994	*Shouting in a Whisper/The Limits of Silence: Latino Poets in Philadelphia*, Asterion Press and Pennsylvania Council on the Arts
1996	"Drama Queens: Latino Gay and Lesbian Independent Media," in *The Ethnic Eye*, ed. Chon Noriega and Ana López, University of Minnesota Press
1997	*Puerto Rican Jam: Rethinking Nationalism and Colonialism*, ed. (with Ramón Grosfoguel), University of Minnesota Press
1998	"No Woman Is an Island" (with Chris Borja), *Wide Angle*, special issue, twenty-fifth anniversary of Women Make Movies
Forthcoming	*Anatomy of a Smile: Collected Poems (1988–1994)*, Third Woman Press
Forthcoming	"Feeling Pretty: West Side Story and Puerto Rican-American Identity," *Social Text*

Distribution and Contact Information

Women Make Movies, 462 Broadway, #500, New York, NY 10013; (212) 925-0606

Cinema Guild, 1697 Broadway, Suite 506, New York, NY 10019-5904; (212) 246-5522

Or from the artist, Polymorphous Pictures, (305) 531-1349; Bikbaporub@aol.com

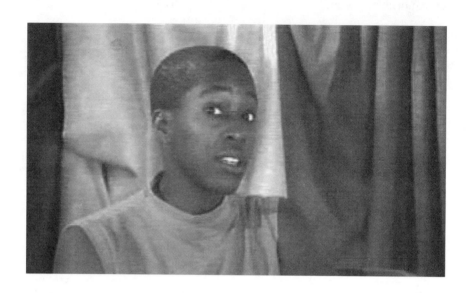

[18] Cheryl Dunye

Cheryl Dunye says she has invented a unique style of film- and videomaking, the Dunyementary, *which is a hybrid of narrative, documentary, comedy, and autobiography. A celebrated artist who has only recently turned thirty, Dunye has made a number of films and videos about and from her position as an African American lesbian. These have circulated foremost within the academy and art world. However, with the limited theatrical distribution of her first feature film (which I produced),* The Watermelon Woman, *her unique take on the world has entered more broadly into, if not the mainstream, at least the art-house milieu. Hotly debated on the floor of Congress because it received $30,500 of federal funding from the NEA and briefly depicted lesbian sex,* The Watermelon Woman *is actually a complex experimental narrative about the relationship between missing precedence and contemporary identity. The "Cheryl" character, played by Dunye, wants to be a filmmaker but feels she needs to know about the lives of her foremothers before she can fully claim this identity and voice for herself. Because the lives of black women in film, let alone black lesbians, were never considered worthy of historical record—so were never documented—the Cheryl character has a hard time finding authorities who will do their job and authorize the existence of black lesbians from the past. This is when Dunye (the filmmaker) decides to entirely fabricate the life of a woman who did not but could have existed, Fae "the Watermelon Woman" Richards, a black, lesbian actress who worked in Hollywood and race movies from the 1920s to 1940s. The movie follows "Cheryl" as she unearths Fae's history: a story that fuels Cheryl the character and Dunye the filmmaker.*

The student of feminist videomakers like Martha Rosler, the heir to lesbian experimental filmmakers like Barbara Hammer, and the friend of black, feminist mentors like Michelle Parkerson and Ada Gay Griffin, Dunye nevertheless broke new ground when she pushed the boundaries of traditional documentary form so as to push the representation of traditional identity.[1] She explains that by merely articulating her personal position—as black, female, lesbian, artist, intellectual, middle-class, Liberian, American, Philadelphian—she creates a new kind of political art practice based on the complexity and humor of identity. She puts herself into her work, then laughs at her own trials and tribulations as she seeks for meaning and romance in her life. In her earlier quasi-autobiographical, fictive, documentary-esque art videos like Janine (1990), She Don't Fade (1991), Vanilla Sex (1992), and The Potluck and the Passion (1993), self-ridicule mixed with self-interrogation creates easy openings for the audience to consider the complexity of their own identities, even though the subject under consideration (Dunye) may not be "like them." As is true for Negrón-Muntaner and Oishi, Dunye considers identity to be playful, funny, and fluid, even as others have punitively invoked a fixed and damning interpretation of her identity (the very public NEA controversy, for instance). She unleashes her interpretation of her life as a black lesbian artist living in the (post)-modern world into a society that would as readily like to pretend that she did not exist.

Dunye explains in her interview, "If I am being honest, I am being theoretical." Thus, she and her generation add to the familiar feminist adage the following twist: the personal is the political is the theoretical. Writing on what distinguishes third- from second-wave feminists, Nancy Miller emphasizes how theory has become a given for the younger generation due largely to their feminist-inflected education: "If one of the original premises of '70s feminism (emerging out of '60s slogans) was the 'the personal is the political,' '80s feminism has made it possible to see that the personal is also the theoretical: the personal is part of theory's material. Put another way, what may distinguish contemporary feminism from other postmodern thought is the expansion in the definition of cultural material."[2] Dunye's voice is mobilized through a conjoining of postmodern theory (which marks the end of identity) and identity politics founded on her race and sexuality (which insist on identity's relevance in a bigoted society that continues to reward and punish individuals in the name of identity). While she acknowledges that her graduate education helped her form this unique orientation, she says she is equally influenced by her investment in both popular and alternative cultures.

Dunye is less ready to embrace "feminism" as an influence. She perceives feminism or the women's movement to be the ancient, unresponsive tradition of older white women—a common perception shared by many of the younger women interviewed in this study. This, in part, because feminism became institutionalized and was taught from books to students like

Dunye by tenured female faculty at respected universities. Miller sees the same phenomenon as one of academic feminism's biggest successes: "It has become possible to teach feminist criticism from books: real objects that *appear on bookstore order lists, and not the eternal handouts and home-made anthologies . . . to simplify, let's say that by normative academic standards, feminist criticism now exists" (58). These competing interpretations of the meaning of institutionalized feminist education signal key gaps of perception among feminists.*

Yet feminism certainly does exist in Dunye's work—unnamed as such but certainly present—as evidenced by a responsive vocabulary with which to understand and claim the legitimacy of her own life and work as African American lesbian filmmaker. Perhaps this points to another of feminism's adaptabilities and strengths: its capacity to be an influence but not a dogma for younger women.

▶

Film and Video

I will ask you about your position within feminist film and video history. We will focus on the importance, at this moment in your career, in moving from independent video to feature film. What videos and films have you made?
I've made five videos and one film. I made my first video as my senior BA thesis, called *Wild Thing.* It was an experimentation with a poem by Sapphire, the black lesbian poet. She presented it at Columbia University. I taped her reading it and then did a montage onto that. That got me into a style, or form, and doing the montage was really creative for me. And it was a good base to identify someone whose work I liked. I was able to have a spirit for it. So it was something about being close to my subject, or liking my subject.

My second tape was *Janine,* which is a talking-head, cathartic video where I tell a story about this woman who I had a crush on in high school named Janine. And I just lay out the whole canvas of our relationship. And I made a montage on top of that, but instead of somebody else's pictures that would refer to it, I used my own. So I become my own text. Then I made *She Don't Fade,* a twenty-plus-minute video made with the girl gang from Philadelphia, where I'm from. We just had fun. I guess it's the hip-hop, lesbian, Godardian *Masculin-Feminin,* where I play a character who is looking for love and does a video talking-head presentation throughout the tape that drives you forward and gets you into the character. I show these vignettes and have these stop points that lead you through it like a silent film: these title cards.

Then after that I did a short video for a project that Shu Lea Cheang was producing, an installation called *Those Fluttering Objects of Desire* (1992). She contacted twenty women-of-color artists to talk about interracial desire, and I did a short video for that called *Vanilla Sex*. Then I immediately did *The Potluck and the Passion*, which is another twenty-minute girl gang video. I call them "Dancing Girl Productions" because I consider myself a dancing girl. It was the continuation of the kind of experimentation I was doing with *She Don't Fade*, where a character drives you through it, as does title cards. Then I did a short video called *An Untitled Portrait* for a show in Philadelphia at the Institute for Contemporary Art at the University of Pennsylvania. I did a four-minute video about my brother, who I never really thought I'd make work about. He wasn't around, so I had to conceive a tape with what memories, or footage, were around of my brother. So I used our family archives, Super 8 film, and put that together and told stories about my brother. And then in 1994, I did a short on 16mm film called *Greetings from Africa*. It was a kind of conglomeration of all the video work into a short, eight-minute film where I have a talking head: there's lots of humor, and there's a black lesbian subject. I talk about issues. I drive you through a condensed story. It's about lesbian dating in the '90s.

What are some films or video that you haven't made? You wanted to make and couldn't make . . .
I was born in Liberia, and my father has passed away, and he was from Liberia. I'd like to make a film about looking for my father. I'd like to experiment with genre. I'd like to do remakes of genres that have a relationship to my own media history—sitcom or horror or sci-fi—to put my twist on it, sign my name on it. I'd like to continually work with humor because I think it is a powerful political tool. Those projects aren't really defined yet. And of course, I want to make *The Watermelon Woman*, my feature film.

▶

My Own Personal Identity Politics

What issues do you think are most commonly addressed in your work?
My own personal identity politics. Which is also a political identity politics, or the way that identity politics gets talked about in the populace. This is about me dealing with who I am as an individual, as an identity, as identities plural, which is a battle between race, class, and sexuality. And I put myself in my work, and I usually put humor in my work.

Janine was my first piece. It's the fall of 1990. I'm a first-year MFA student at Rutgers University in New Brunswick at Mason Gross School of the Arts. I'm trying to keep up with the transition from being in a BA program that was more traditionally in a communications department, to being in an MFA studio art program with painters and sculptors and other artists. So I'm trying to put twists on my work. I am sitting at midnight taping pictures from a book on African American women artists onto the wall. I was going to do a documentary and ask the question, "Why are there so few African Americans women artists?" I had recently talked to this chip on my shoulder, Janine, from high school, who I had a big crush on and came out around. A big light bulb came above my head, and I decided to sit down and rip the pictures off the wall and sit in front of the camera and tell this story that was burning inside of me. I wanted to get out all these issues that were burning in me, not just the crush, but that she was a white woman and came from a different class background. We were both in school together, and my mother had values and I was angry at them in that she wanted the best for her daughter, and put me into this kind of institution. . . . I went to a private Catholic school. I was a young black girl in love with this white girl.

So I really wanted to talk about that. It was two takes. I sat down in front of the camera and told the story. It started coming out like sweat. "Why don't I pick up some candles and blow them out and they represent both of us and our relationship?" "Why don't I put my own pictures on the wall?" Not a soapbox but a project that talks about the constructive and not the deconstructive side of art making. I think all those elements—talking about issues, my own truth, using my own self in the work, physically or through my own pictures, and making myself real, empowering myself—are something that I did in this work, and something I try to do throughout my whole career.

Money

How has your video been funded?
I was at Rutgers in their MFA program. They had a small amount of video equipment there. The standard half-inch camera and lights, and that's enough for me. Hi-8 was just made commercial, but it wasn't accessible for me at this time. So I focused on half-inch, traditional VHS format, something that's very accessible, very proletariat. Something people can get their hands on, that can be shipped anywhere. Something I could afford. How I made my work talked about my means. I had Rutgers, their equipment, and

$5 to buy videotape. And I had "our gang" of girls who wanted to get involved in the work. So I put them to work. Let's all get empowered.

Many things are significant about this work: how I make it, who my audience is, what goes into it. At the time I had some friends, limitations financially, and half-inch video equipment. Yet while I was at Rutgers, I made four tapes: *Janine, She Don't Fade, The Potluck and the Passion,* and *Vanilla Sex.* A lot of my video came from that MFA moment. Without that, I wouldn't have been able to do that work. I also received a few grants. A Frameline grant. An Astraea grant. An ArtMatters grant. No significant grant—it was about being creative with what I had. I was also able to submit the work to a completion awards program with a PBS station in Philly, WHYY TV12. If your work is selected for their local film festival, they either buy your work or give you the services or resources for completing it. That's really how a lot of my videos got done. I've gone through a rough struggle. It's been difficult to do work without money, in the sense of ideas, problems, growing. My work has been about using what means I have and also wanting to do different things. There's been a roller-coaster rhythm to what I'm doing.

ERIN CRAMER (associate producer): *Will you talk about the NEA?*
Oh, the NEA grant, I forgot about that.

EC: *You just got this major grant . . .*
In my career within the film and video community I have received a few larger grants. I received a MARMAF [Mid-Atlantic Regional Arts Media Fellowship] grant for makers in Pennsylvania. And I just recently received an NEA, which I'm amazed at, and I keep forgetting because it doesn't seem real because I haven't received it yet. I've just received the letter. It's hard to believe that after so many makers of color who are lesbian and gay, like Marlon Riggs, have been bashed by the Congress and others for getting an NEA grant, they then give money to a black, lesbian feature. I'm just waiting to see the check.

I don't know what to say until I receive it. Upon receiving the check, I'll get my nails done (just kidding), and I think I will actually speak out about the problems of grants. Up until the moment I got this letter, I was on the verge of writing an article about making work without grants because we don't have grants anymore. We don't have a structure to make or fund work. We have to be inventive and creative about how to make work in the twenty-first century. There won't be grants. I'm one of the last recipients of these NEA grants. I don't want to think about that.

I want to think about how to continue to make work. It has nothing to do with grants but, rather, with a lot of speaking out to institutions that are actually making work, like Miramax and Fineline. These Hollywood companies are running around buying up the low-budget, no-budget world. They should put their money where their mouth is and put out seed-money grants or fellowships for independent makers to get their work off the ground. I think they owe us. We run around and jump through hoops of fire to get work done, jump off cliffs with cameras to be creative and different, and they will buy our work, and we don't get money in the process. Usually, we get it screened. "Crossover." That doesn't mean survival, or the next work.

Look at Shu Lea Cheang, who is caught in this well of distribution hell with her film *Fresh Kill* [1994], or Rose Troche, who made the big crossover lesbian hit *Go Fish* and is still struggling to make her next work. Or Nicole Conn who made *Claire of the Moon* [1992]. That film wasn't a crossover, perhaps, but after *Claire of the Moon* is she making another film? No. It takes so long, especially for lesbian work, for the writer or director to see another project made. The companies that distribute these works need to put their toilet-paper money right into a fund.

Also, I've had other creative strategies. *The Watermelon Woman* involves creating a photographic archive. So I put the pictures up for sale (currently available as the book *The Fae Richards Photo Archive*).[3] I believe firmly in the Camille Billops School of Filmmaking: "Do you have a T-shirt, a button, a poster, a mailing list?"[4] That's a way to get money. One problem about media: we create work for an audience as if they are just out there. We have to start identifying our audience and making them active viewers, make them supportive viewers of work. "Send a dollar in for every independent." I'm trying to mobilize audiences, too.

▶
_____

Audience(s)

You're professionalizing—that means you haven't made anything in a few years. Why have you stopped making cheap half-inch videos and are trying to make a transition to film?

One thing about my work is about audience. Who watches it. Having so many inexpensive videos out there that are fun and cute and talk about issues, a lot of people can see my work, but the people screening it aren't necessarily black lesbians or people of color. I have a problem with that. Black audiences are into media that is more clean; it is about them having access to work. They're not running to lesbian and gay festivals to see it. It takes a lot for somebody of my mother's generation, or from a working-class or middle-class black background, it takes a lot for them to go to see work at some avant-garde house. I want to see how my issues play out in the black context. That's one reason why I'm working on a feature, so I can see how my story affects this black audience.

Of course, a lot of people have seen my work. There are black lesbians who have seen my work and a mass of white lesbians and gay men who have seen my work. That's about 30 percent of the audience. And then there's the academy. My work has been consumed by the academy. It comes from me being a thinker, an intellectual, dipping from the same cultural well. Some of the ideas in my work fit in with certain academic discourse. My work is like a sample tape for it. The academy: that's been my survival. My distributors ship those tapes right off to the academy. In one sense, I've never left school. And then there are moments when my work gets to interesting, diverse communities. Communities of color. Gay and lesbian communities of color. Foreign communities. Communities through advocacy. To low-income or no-income communities, to older people. My work has been in the Whitney Biennial and in various museums. My work has been broadcast. So sometimes I find a sixty-five-year-old woman like my mother who says she's heard of me, and I make "those movies." I like that, even though it's "video" and not "movies," and I don't know what "those" means. I like the times my work touches those who don't usually see it.

Whom in the academy are you talking about? Who specifically supports your work? White feminists, feminists of color, some gay men . . . What does the academy like about your work?
I am from the academy. Most of us have received some sort of academic training and know what are hot issues in popular culture: identity politics, multiculturalism, issues dealing with race, sex, class. My life story as an individual, I realized at some point along the line, is all about that. I am my own text. So I talk about myself, and that becomes interesting. If I'm honest, I'm being theoretical.

▶───────────────────────────────────────

There Is No Word for the -Ism That I Live From

Is feminist film theory one of the theories that you use?
I don't necessarily consider myself a feminist per se. I must say that I've been empowered by feminist issues, and I've been empowered by African American issues, and by other political battles, anarchist movement issues. A whole bunch of those things have become who I am. But there is no word for the -ism that I live from. Yet feminism is a part of that. I don't know if that's answering your question. But I do think that the feminist movement

was about a certain kind of liberation and focus on putting issues around sex, or sexism, or sexual difference, on the table. That has something to do with what I believe are the problems, or what's wrong with the world. Women are people, too. Coming from my feminist genes—or whatever I have in me, "jeans" or "genes"—I deal with some of the issues that feminists deal with. Feminist academics see that and can dip into it. I am not going to say I am feminist or I am not feminist. I am as much feminist as I am black as I am a tennis player as I am a dog owner. It's a shifting identity. We have to embody all that in order to really "be."

That's why contemporary academic feminists like you.
Because I say I'm not a feminist?

The conversation has gone one step farther. People are not interested in identity in isolation. Your work starts imagining more complex identities, identities that are informed by many of the liberation movements from generations before and are not stuck in one.
If you look at that from an African American point of view, I am the bad black girl who is not dealing with being black, or I am the bad woman not being a feminist. I'm not believing in one thing, but believing in too many things. And that becomes a problem for certain people. When it comes down to it, is it a problem for me? No. Is it a problem for the rest of the world and how I deal with it? Sometimes.

▶ ──

Influences

What have been some of your inspirations? Do you have any feminist inspirations?
Let me go back to the feminist point. Feminism has inspired me. A lot of my coming-to-voice, coming-to-tongue, becoming empowered, has to do feminism. There was a significant moment in the mid-'80s for me, but it actually took place in the '70s, where media work was being done by feminists who were women of color and white women. I got to see that media in the '80s when I was in college, and that inspired me.

But I also saw other stuff: Chantal Akerman. The most powerful work for me was done by a straight white man, Jim McBride. The film was called *David Holtzman's Diary* [1967]. It made my work all that. I was also empowered by Joyce Chopra's *Joyce at 34* [1972]. It is funny that Juanita Mohammed also talked about it. Woody Allen. *The Brady Bunch. The Addams Family.* I'm a TV-generation person. Every bit of media has an effect on me. The most powerful: *Killer of Sheep* [1977], by Charles Burnett.

She's Gotta Have It [1986], in one scary way, by Spike Lee. A variety of things. I'm trying to think of something that is feminist or is not feminist. Godard, *Masculin-Feminin* [1966]. Michelle Citron, *Daughter Rite*.

I like work that is not just talking about issues but is doing something with the form to push the issues. That's why I make media, to push it one step farther. I'm not just having something interesting to say, but I'm seeing how those ideas seep into an experimentation or exploration of building new ways to talk about these things or change these things. So many people in the academy's work is about rhetoric. When I was exploring feminism, it was a bunch of *books* that made you a feminist. There was no movement that I, as a young black woman, could run into. It was about a lot of reading and feeling uncomfortable and standing around people I didn't like who said they were feminists.

EC: *Is there someone whose work you see as continuing?*
Barbara Hammer. Everyone has mentioned Barbara Hammer, and I mention Barbara Hammer, too. She is someone who just makes her work and continually makes her work because she knows how important it is to make work, and how important it is to get work out there, and how important it is to grow. And by making more work, you will grow. So I can relate to her vibe, even though we work in different genres and styles. I feel connected to that constant exploration, and not having boundaries about what goes into my work. The feature I am working on now is a mixture of three different mediums: Super 8 film, Hi-8 video, and 16mm film. I'd put 35mm there if I could afford it. Why I use all media is because I can't afford 16mm. I build work that really talks about not having access to a complete 16mm production. That kind of creative thinking—not just thinking about a political identity—is about a lot of things.

▶

Obstacles and Opportunities

What obstacles have you faced, in the spectrum from Frances Negrón-Muntaner to Carolee Schneemann?
What kind of spectrum is that?

Do you see yourself as someone who has had everything available? Is it a career of obstacles? Or a career of opportunities?
I feel like odd girl out in the art world, in that I do have a presence but I don't feel it. Or I don't want to feel it. Or if I were able to walk around in the head of feeling it, then I wouldn't be the artist that I am. I feel safe and most productive in the margins of the art world, or the media world, or the

feminist film and video world. I don't ever want to be an insider. I want to be looking in or looking out. It keeps me alive, it keeps me vibrant. If I were to say I am or am not a feminist, then I wouldn't be.

Who paved the way for the first black lesbian feature film? Whom do you owe?
I owe Michelle Parkerson a lot. She is the mama, to me, of black lesbian work. She works in film, she works in documentary. She just made a documentary with Ada Gay Griffin called *A Litany for Survival: The Life and Work of Audre Lorde* [1997]. The whole project, the people involved with it, and who they made it on, Audre—it's just all about energy and power. I owe a lot to all three of those women. It took them ten years to make that feature. It shouldn't take that long to talk about the work and life of someone so important.

I owe it to their ten years. That's making my two to three years real. So I owe it to those women and my colleagues, those other black lesbians out there making work: Yvonne Welbon, Jocelyn Taylor, Dawn Suggs, Shari Frilot, Aaron Birch, Michelle Crenshaw, my director of photography.[5] And a mess of others who I'm missing. Okay, not a mess, five more people. . . . I owe it to my colleagues because we are constantly supporting each other. I owe it to Marlon Riggs, a black gay man who died of AIDS last year. He constantly made his own work. I owe it to all the people who've made work regardless of the circumstances because they wanted to make it and had something to say, all the way back to Leni Riefenstahl.[6] She made work. I probably ruined your documentary by saying *Leni Riefenstahl,* but she was a mover and a shaker in many successful and sad ways.

▶━━━━━━━━━━━━━━━━━━━━━━━━━━━━━━━━━━━

Crossing Over

Let's talk about the transition into feature filmmaking. Are you making a "crossover" film?
I am making a crossover film and I'm not making a crossover film. I can never give you a definitive answer. I don't know. Is that a genre? The crossover film genre? I'm making my own work. The historical moment that we live in might have a space for that to reach a large audience. If it does, yes, it will be a crossover, and if it doesn't, it'll be an academic hit. And I know I've won the academy over, with all the feminists and all the queer theorists, and all the performance theorists, and all the theorist theorists.

So I feel that my work has slowly but surely found its way into an academic setting. And my constant production will have its place in the academy, and the academy is starting to affect the public, and my work is starting to reach the pages of the *Village Voice* or the *New York Times*. So maybe through these means some new audience will be found for my work. If that happens in a successful way, it will be a crossover, or if it is marketed and packaged, it will be a crossover, or if I am edited out of the film, and put a wig on and have a nail job and some nice outfit and change my name to Channelle, I'll be a crossover hit.

Why are you making a feature film?
Because everyone else is? . . . No, really, I'm making a feature because I've been working in half-hour segments, and it hasn't been enough time to explore everything I want to. So why not put it in the guise of a feature film? My feature film is not modeling itself after traditional feature-film narrative or format or structure. Yes, girl meets girl, but they do not get along, and all these other things happen in that context. So it's not girl meets girl, girl has problem with girl, and then they get together—it's dealing with more. I'm challenging myself as an artist to make a feature film. Shu Lea did that in *Fresh Kill.* Camille Billops does it constantly, and Yvonne Rainer. Barbara Hammer challenges herself in her recent feature-length work.

I'd also like to reach more audience, have that crossover audience, not just the audience of the converted, but a new audience. I've converted a lot of people but want to go one step further. I don't want to look like the one woman of color star of the moment, "Oh, you look like Dionne Farris." Or when I had dreads, "You look like Whoopi Goldberg." As Josephine Baker said, when she walks down the street, people said, "Oh, Josephine." I want people to see me. I want them to say, "Cheryl," and pronounce my last name right, too.

If you make your crossover film, and it's a big success and you go to Cannes or whatever, would you make a Hollywood film?
Under an alias. You'd never know, would you? Maybe. I might consider it. It depends on what issues are on the table. Would I direct, write, produce, star in it? What would Hollywood want me to do? In this project now, *The Watermelon Woman,* I write, direct, produce, star. First, I'd have to figure out what Hollywood wanted me to do, and looking at the black lesbian presence in Hollywood, I don't think I'd be doing much.

Under the Kitchen

You've been working on this project as one of the videographers, and as my girlfriend you've seen me working on it for the past year. Does that give you some information to think differently about your own place in this history?

I'm learning about all the places you can't work on this project. You're dealing with something that's so precious and significant to so many different people and a history that's different to so many individuals. I'm learning from how you are empowering and making everyone valid and making every history real. The strategy of having interviewees sit down and interpret the history of feminist film and video through their own experience— it makes everyone historical. It doesn't leave anyone out of the mix. We all fit into it differently.

I enjoy meeting these women whose work has influenced my own. Meeting Carolee Schneemann and hearing her talk about what the world owes her. As a white, straight, avant-garde artist, her set of issues seems remarkably similar to what is owed to me as a black, lesbian filmmaker. There are so many stories, so many connections. Hearing our goddesses and mentors in the feminist film world tell us their stories, you feel like, "Wow, I'm right on track. I haven't received my grants for xyz years, and I'm stuck in a hole with new ideas, and I'm reading Proust to my girlfriend at night." They're so humble. They're not this faraway thing.

Where do you see yourself in this history?

In the kitchen. Making drinks. Making sure everyone is happy. *Under* the kitchen. That was a project that didn't get made: *Under the Kitchen.* Black women are usually in the kitchen. And black lesbians are under the kitchen. Actually, to tell you the truth, I do see myself as a significant part of this history in that I have been trying to spit out black lesbian work for the past five years. It's found its place. And I have inspired others to make work who aren't black lesbians, and that's when I know I've found my place.

Videos and Films

1990	*Janine,* VHS video, 10 min.
1991	*She Don't Fade,* video, 24 min.
1992	*Vanilla Sex,* Hi-8 video, 4 min.
1993	*The Potluck and the Passion,* VHS video, 30 min.
1993	*An Untitled Portrait,* Hi-8 video, 3 min.
1994	*Greetings from Africa,* 16mm, 8 min.
1996	*The Watermelon Woman,* 16mm, 90 min.

Distribution and Contact Information

First Run Features, 153 Waverly Place, New York, NY 10014;
(212) 243-0600

Video Data Bank, 112 South Michigan Ave., #312, Chicago, IL 60603;
(312) 345-3550

Third World Newsreel, twn@twn.org

Women Make Movies, 462 Broadway, #500, New York, NY 10013;
(212) 925-0606

Eve Oishi

*Eve Oishi is an assistant professor of women's studies at California State
University, Long Beach. Her scholarly work is concerned with Asian American women's representation in film and literature, particularly as filtered
through the concepts of authenticity and fakeness. She has written on new
media by queer Asian American artists and the uses of the erotic in lesbian
film and video. As a curator of experimental film and video by queers
of color, she has organized screenings titled "Bad Asians" and "Exiles,
Aliens, and Tourists." Oishi's career is a testament to the hard-fought intellectual and political traditions that were set in place before she entered
college in the mid-'80s. Most of her scholarly positions, in fact, are in
direct response and sometimes in contradiction to that of the generation
that set the terms for the fields in which she works: Asian American studies,
women's studies, queer studies, and feminist media.*

*Although she was classically educated in feminist film (an oxymoron?)
by one of the field's founders, Sandy Flitterman-Lewis, Oishi says she learned
a great deal from, but then ultimately also rejected, many of the field's
founding principles, especially about women's pleasure and spectatorship.
Oishi, like many who are critical of traditional feminist film theory, insists
that there is room for her desire in film and television, a great deal of this
informed by viewing context. Whereas an earlier tradition proclaimed that
there was no place for female desire, or even a female viewing position in
traditional cinema, Oishi insists on claiming and describing her own pleasures in viewing. She found feminist role models in images that her mentors would have deemed patriarchal and sexist, like* Charlie's Angels *and*
Wonder Woman. *She found access to her identity and history in narratives
about male virility: samurai films and action-thrillers. She was excited by
whatever was* not *allowed to her: violence, guns, uncensored desire. "My
love of film had to do with illicitness, voyeurism. It had to do with fantasy.*

And fantasy that was often violent and that was often forbidden." When I was discussing this project with Laura Mulvey (one of my professors in graduate school), she insisted that her generation was simply not ready to analyze their own "erotic charge" as they unveiled dominant systems. However, she admits that they certainly set the stage for later scholars to do so. Feminist theory has a difficult time understanding women's sexuality in general, not to mention the sexuality of feminist film critics.

Oishi's sense of herself and work as a biracial, queer, feminist scholar is enabled by recent trends in political action and thought that forefront the fluidity, flexibility, and construction of the once seemingly stable entities of identity, race, sexuality, and gender. For Oishi and our generation, the identity of "feminist" itself becomes stable enough to serve as both fluid core and bedrock from which to build or play with a more adaptive sense of identity. Further, the enormous importance of women-of-color feminism and gay and lesbian studies, which altered the stakes and terms of women's studies in the '80s and '90s, respectively, has made it nearly impossible for any feminist scholar not to think through the interconnections of race, class, sexuality, desire, and gender in her own life and her life's work. Oishi chooses to complement her feminism with other rich sets of traditions because her feminism is as adaptive as her ideas about gender.

This understanding of feminism—so certain as to be mutable—is another result of '70s feminism, one that can be considered either dangerous or liberatory. When this flexibility is called "postfeminism," especially in the mainstream press, a dangerous argument is waged, explaining that some women no longer identify as feminists, because they don't need to, because this work has already been done. In its more liberatory aspect, Oishi claims that she need not be forced to privilege any aspect of her identity, including her gender, unless she so chooses to mobilize it. Her feminism complements her daily existence as well as her work, but often in ways unclaimed and unnamed. "I think this is precisely because what is valuable about feminism is its looseness and its ability to adapt itself to different needs and to different people's experiences. It's an analytical tool, not necessarily an object or something static."

▶

Authenticity and Fakeness

What is your scholarly work in film studies?
My scholarly work is about contemporary Asian American fiction and independent film and video by women. I am dealing with the question of authenticity and fakeness in this work. There are all kinds of debates about

who is an authentic Asian or Asian American, who can speak for that experience, and who's a fake. A lot of those questions revolve around anxieties about gender and class, about national identity, generations, who is closer to some kind of "original" Asian history or identity.

Can you name some of the tapes or films that are interesting for your work, and describe them briefly?
One of the key film texts is Rea Tajiri's *History and Memory* [1991], which is a re-creation of her mother's experience being interned as a Japanese American in World War II, and her mother can't remember this experience. The film is an attempt to re-create and remember this experience for her. A lot of the experience was blocked out because of fear, or anxiety, or the conditions in which she was interned, so Tajiri has to re-create a lot of these herself. For example, she re-creates the train ride from the city out to the camps. She films the view out to the camps. And this is a view that her mother would not have seen, since they drew the shades of the train to not allow the Japanese Americans to see where they were going. So in fact, this is a memory her mother never would have had. But to re-create it in this way, and to "fake it," using her own and newsreel footage and Hollywood films, comments on the conditions under which experiences are forgotten as well as remembered.

There is an independent film called *Fresh Kill* by Shu Lea Cheang. It's an experimental narrative. Unfortunately, it has only had a limited distribution, so not many people have seen it. It's a very postmodern, futuristic narrative about two women, who are lovers, and their daughter living in New York City, and all the members of this extended family are played by people of different races. It's commenting on the place the nuclear family has played in a lot of these texts by Asian Americans because the nuclear family is a very important unit to define identity, ethnic experience, and national experience. There's a film called *Two Lies* [1989] by Pam Tom, which is about a mother and her two daughters. She's a Chinese American woman who's had eyelid surgery to make her Asian eyes appear less "Oriental." The film raises tensions about sexuality and race between the mother and daughters and about fakeness as well as authenticity.

When were the films made that have influenced your study?
The contemporary work that I'm looking at owes a lot to earlier film that was being done in the late '60s, mostly in California. There was a lot of activist work, documentary work, by Asian Americans who were located around universities like Berkeley. And I'm not looking specifically at that work, but that work made this later work possible.

Is it also enabled by feminist history?
The work that I'm interested in definitely comes in fairly late in what is a traditional history of feminist film and video. And this is because it takes up these issues of fakeness and authenticity. This may be oversimplifying, but there are two strains of media history that come together in a lot of the work that I'm looking at: a history of Asian American media activism in the '60s, and feminist film and video, which is primarily by white women, where issues of race were not worked through at the expense of investigations about gender. And a lot of these debates about authenticity and fakeness are debates about gender.

What happens when there is a claim for authenticity in Asian American literature or cultural studies is that it often happens at the expense of investigations of gender. Asian American women who write about or represent misogyny in Asian American or Asian culture are accused of betraying Asian American men, of figuratively sleeping with a white male establishment that is going to publish them or get them promoted. They are not allowed to be "authentically" Asian and also have a sophisticated analysis of gender. So the women artists that I look at, who specifically take on questions of authenticity, are speaking to traditions that have not allowed them to investigate both sides of their experiences at the same time. Really, the only way to do it is to embrace a kind of fakeness, if you will. To be an authentic woman means that you do not have a race, or you can't think about questions of race, while to be an authentic person of color, you can't really think about questions of gender.

Influences

What feminist scholarly work has influenced your work?
The forces that led me to become a feminist film scholar had very little to do with feminism, film, or scholarship. [Laughs.] So it's an interesting history. My family scorned television. And we didn't really go to the movies much. We'd been living in Germany for several years. I came back to the United States in 1976, and I discovered American television for the first time—television that I could understand. It was exciting.

The kinds of shows that I was watching obsessively were shows in which there were strong women running around after criminals. For example, *Charlie's Angels* and *The Bionic Woman*. I had this incredible cathexis for cyborg women and women without bras with big hair running around with huge guns. Somehow the pleasure of watching these images melded with my little, adolescent, protofeminist consciousness and taught me something about where I was getting my pleasures from in the media. At the same time that I was watching those things, I was watching samurai movies with my father. He loved to watch both Westerns and Miomoto Misatchi's samurai films that he had watched as a child. There was something very ritualistic about these programs with a lot of violence, but that all had a kind of predictable formula, that I would watch with my father. And that was a way that I was able to be the sort of son I always wanted to be for him and share in a cultural heritage that I wasn't really aware of.

And then in high school I first discovered film, as separate from the movies, that is art film and what's taught in film school. In high school, I'd go to the movies with my friend Nancy and I would spend the night, and we would take the bus into the city where I wasn't supposed to go. We would see these double features, and they were always sort of black-and-white art films, and in my mind they became kind of horrific and extremely erotic because they were forbidden. I remember watching *Nosferatu* and *The Elephant Man* in a double feature. That's where I remember seeing my first Hitchcock films. There was a kind of charged eroticism about watching the spectacle that I wasn't allowed to see.

Then in the '80s, I discovered Arnold Schwarzenegger and action films that I would later watch with my father as a way of bonding, again, because it was what my mother didn't want us to see. We discovered John Woo together and Hong Kong action films and then Jean-Claude van Damme films. When I got to graduate school and started taking courses in film theory, the work that was given to me as feminist film I never found particularly compelling, until I started working in African American literature and Asian American literature. I wanted to find film equivalents for that kind of fictional work. And of course, I could only go to independent film because that's all that existed, in terms of feminist work. So I saw Julie Dash's *Daughters of the Dust* [1991], and that was really transformational.[1] I began to seek out work at film festivals, independent work by women of color, and I began to know filmmakers and better understand how films are made.

What was striking to me was that this history of me as a feminist film critic had very little to do with feminism and had a lot more to do with how I understood the kind of charged pleasure that I got in watching different kinds of spectacles and the context in which I saw them. If I saw them with a girlfriend and we were sneaking out to the movies, or if I saw them with my father, that was very much part of the whole experience.

Is there a difference between your feminism inside and outside the academy?
In the classroom, I can't necessarily call a John Woo film or Arnold Schwarzenegger film in which all the women are being bludgeoned to death or blown away a "feminist film," even though in my particular complicated history it has everything to do with me being a feminist and my feminist fantasies. But I can't really do that when I'm working with eighteen- and nineteen-year-olds, because it's too personal and complicated. So I think it's a different kind of feminism.

▶ ─────────────────────────────────

Feminist Film Theory

It's interesting: you keep self-naming yourself a feminist, which has not been true of many of the interviewees thus far, and yet you have presented a history where feminism has had very little part. So where does the feminism come from in your identification as a feminist film scholar?
Well, when I was looking back and trying to trace the path through which I became a feminist film scholar, or a feminist, it was interesting that I found all of these roundabout histories that weren't traditionally feminist. They had to do more with trying to understand what my racial identity was, what my relationship to my Japanese American father was, what my relationship to American culture was, as someone who spent some of her childhood abroad and felt like a foreigner in that culture. And my relationship to popular culture, my relation to violence, and power, and my relation to technology.

And I think one of the reasons that I don't claim a traditional '70s feminist film history as one of my major influences is that I wasn't exposed to it during the formative years in which my feminism developed. And because the history I'm tracing has so much to do with other elements besides being a woman, a lot of that work feels limited to me. So that when I was first seeing Laura Mulvey's *Riddles of the Sphinx* (1976), for example, or *Daughter Rite*, or a lot of those films that are studied in feminist film courses, I couldn't respond, because it didn't have the same sort of erotic charge that I came to need in work that I studied. Because for me, my love of film had to do with illicitness, voyeurism. It had to do with fantasy and fantasy that was often violent and that was often forbidden. And that was the work I wanted to keep pressing.

The work from the '70s that I saw didn't have that charge, because it was so self-conscious and so self-consciously correct. I don't want to use the word *politically correct*, because I'm suspect of it, but there was no

transgression. Except for in Chantal Akerman's *Jeanne Dielman* [1975].
That was a big film for me. I had a reaction to *Jeanne Dielman* in a way
that I didn't have to a lot of films that I saw in feminist film courses. That
had to do with the dissonance that was working in the film between the
violence of it and its everyday domestic ritual. That was really effective.

*Can you talk about your vision of the history of how feminism, or feminist
film theory, has been institutionalized in the academy? How has it been
taught to the following generation of scholars?*
I think that the kind of film work that is embraced by the academy and that
has been forwarded by the academy is work that is very theoretically self-
conscious, and in it the theory is very easily discernible and therefore easily
teachable. It is also really easy to write about this work. And it has been
much more difficult to find work that is more disturbing politically or that
isn't necessarily interested in taking up its own terms of production or existence. And so what has happened has been that there's a kind of canon that
has been developed, and a lot of it is around French film theory and classic
French and Italian filmmakers and Hitchcock, for example. And then there's
a feminist film theory canon that begins with Laura Mulvey. But a lot of
the work that has been left out is work that wasn't claiming itself in a theoretical way as feminist.

*Cheryl Dunye's interview expresses how her work is embraced by the
academy. You talk about the academy as if you're not a part of it. Yet your
work is what's defining the next generation. Your work is creating interest
in Cheryl's and Shu Lea's work. Their work is beginning to be institutionalized. So what is feminist film theory doing today, and how is it related to
the work of women ten and twenty years ago?*
Well, I certainly would not be able to do the kind of work I do today if feminist film in the '70s had not been embraced by the academy in the way that
it was. And if French theory had not been embraced by the academy in the
way that it was. I also owe a lot to the institutionalization of theories of
race, to gender studies as opposed feminism as opposed to women studies,
to lesbian and gay studies or queer studies. All of those trends came into
the academy separately yet piggybacked on each other and had a lot to do
with particular institutional politics and what was happening in the world
at the time as well. They're all coming together now and making possible
what I think is a more complex, richer understanding of the role that media
and film and video play in the art world.

   The genealogy is no longer just feminism, feminist film, feminist theory
to feminist film theory; it's being fed by all these other tributaries. And I
think that trend is going to continue. It has to do with the academy being

more able to deal with interdisciplinary work. The borders of disciplines are seeming to break down a little bit, becoming more porous. Different disciplines can inform each other now. Different political histories can inform each other in a way they might not have been able to before.

The Feminist Film Canon

It's so interesting to me the way that the first generation of feminist film scholarship has been characterized in many of our interviews: it's something that's dry, it's in a book, it's completely distanced from lived experience. It's about this intellectualization of politics, right? And everyone who's taught it is like, "Euhk!"—this bad, dry object.
I think that the reason that people tend to think about the canon, the '70s feminist film canon, as kind of dry and purely theoretical, as having no pleasure, is because of the way it's been packaged by the academy. We teach the aspects of the work that are easily extracted as theory, the aspects that can be talked about and written about in a certain, very specified language. And what gets lost in that are the aspects of the work that may have had a charge or were more radical in other ways—visually, politically, even theoretically.

For this reason, feminist film theory has to look more at the experience of spectators, of film- and videomakers, as well as what's happening in the film itself, on the screen. Because the politics, as I said before, the feminism and the politics of the work are always flitting back and forth between those things. It sort of lives in that murky realm between the different parts of that piece of work. And that's what gets erased by a lot of academic work. It sort of flattens it out and looks only at what's "theoretical." And it seems like that was probably happening as a lot of the French theory was getting translated and imported into the American academy. Theory had a kind of currency at that time that made it very valuable but also tended to value the theory over the aesthetics, for example.

The Women's Movement

Do you have a relationship to the women's movement?
Absolutely. I have a very intense relationship to the women's movement. I acknowledge it, I claim it, I put myself in its history. I may sound like I'm disavowing a certain strain of artistic history of the women's movement, but the political history was very important for my own consciousness. The activism around pro-choice issues, around consciousness-raising, and

women's liberation—I needed that very much when I was in college. I first began to think of myself as a feminist in the late 1980s, which seems pretty late. It had never occurred to me to use that term before. Political activism in the women's movement enabled me to do so.

What do you feel about that term now? Feminism? *Does it trouble you?*
It doesn't trouble me at all, even though I would have difficulty defining it. I would have difficulty, for example, defining what is feminist film and video. Or even what is the feminist or women's movement. I could not give you an answer for that. And yet I have no problem claiming myself as a feminist at all. I think this is precisely because what is valuable about feminism is its looseness and its ability to adapt itself to different needs and to different people's experiences. It's an analytical tool, not necessarily an object or something static. And so you can trace strains of feminism, feminist politics, through all kinds of complicated histories that may not be identifiable as *feminist* to many people. But it is also a way of looking back at history, of revising history, or revisioning history, as Adrienne Rich would say. And seeing how those different strains, whether they be about race, or about class, or about national identity, can form a contemporary feminist consciousness and politics.

▶

Academic Work

What do you think that academics' positions are in the history of feminist film and video?
Well, as I said before, I think that academics and the academy played a fairly large role in early feminist film and video because there was a kind of marriage between academia and feminist filmmakers. And I think we're at a really exciting point right now in the academy. The proliferation of independent film and video is making a lot of scholars look at that work. And usually scholars are the ones who write about work, and get it publicized, and get it shown to college students, or get it shown in the academy. There's a possibility for a new kind of union between those two arenas.

Much of this history is about lack of access, but you suggest that now we have more opportunities to see work.
I think what's really key about this work being more accessible in the academy is the *video* part of the feminist media title of your project. Because I think that video, which is cheaper to make, easier to distribute and circulate, really has allowed a lot of people who normally wouldn't see this work to

get it, to watch it in their homes, to see it on television, and to teach it in their classes.

As a young scholar embarking on your career in the academy, what do you want to do with it? What do you hope for your work?
What I really hope for my work is to be able to break down the barriers between the way that academics have talked about film in the past and the kind of work being done by contemporary artists. The academy is an amazing institution in that there are all kinds of freedom to bring in scholars and artists and to introduce them in original ways, in how you organize a syllabus or an event—you can do all kinds of theoretical work that way. You can comment on the work itself in radically new ways. I would like to see my career as being both a teacher and curator, to straddle the line between the academy and the art world and bring both sides of those worlds to each other.

▶

An Asian American Feminist Aesthetic

SUH KYUNG YOON (project assistant): *Do you find an Asian American feminist aesthetic?*
The work I've found has a particular aesthetic in that Asian American women working in the media are working against hundreds of years of stereotypes of Asian women as docile, exotic butterflies. Feminist work often tends to destroy that quite deliberately and with a kind of glee that I enjoy. I have a fascination with guns that is also shared by Asian women with whom I go to movies. There's a kind of violence that draws me to specific kinds of work, not an overt violence, but there's an awareness that there's violence being done to past images, stereotypes, and cultural expectations, representational expectations about the body, voice, beauty, that are being shattered in radical, exciting, beautiful ways. That's the work I'm drawn to by Asian American women.

TRUC HA (project assistant): *I'm interested in why you, who claims multiple identities as an Asian American woman, a queer woman, an academic, why you can call yourself a feminist, but then you can't define it?*
One of the reasons I have so much trouble defining feminism, but it's still so useful and powerful as a political tool, is that it is able to incorporate and to recognize all the different strains within my experience and my identity. The fact that I am a woman is relatively low down in defining who I am. Much higher up is the fact that I am middle-class, academic, biracial, the fact that I'm queer, I live in a city. Those things often take precedence

over my gender identity, but feminism has consistently allowed me to understand those parts of me as separate but also collaborating to form who
I am and my experience, and to speak from that fractured experience and
identity. That place where nothing seems to fit together. I still have a political voice, and I can do political work, through feminism. It's adaptable in
that way. It's large.

◆————————————————————————————————

EVE OISHI

1997 to present   Assistant professor of women's studies, California State
                   University, Long Beach

Publications

1994   "Uses of the Erotic: Sexuality and Difference in Lesbian
                   Film and Video," *Art Papers* (November/December)
1998   Introduction for *Miss Nume of Japan* by Onoto Watanna,
                   John Hopkins University Press
Forthcoming   "Bad Asians: New Media by Queer Asian American
                   Artists," in *COUNTERVISIONS: Asian American Film
                   Criticism,* ed., Darrell Hamamoto and Sandra Liu,
                   Temple University Press
Forthcoming   "Virtual White: Generating Race in New Media," *Annals
                   of Scholarship: Art Practices and the Human Sciences in
                   a Global Culture*

Curating Work

1995   "Close Encounters: Exiles, Aliens, and Tourists," MIX:
                   New York Lesbian and Gay Experimental Film/Video
                   Festival
1997   Short film and video programmer, Philadelphia
                   International Gay and Lesbian Film Festival
1998   "Bad Asians," Outfest: Los Angeles Gay and Lesbian Film
                   Festival

Presentations

1994   "White Lies: The Alien in American Cinema"
1996   "Fictioning Asian America"
1998   "Visual Perversions: Race, Sex, and Visual Pleasure"

[20] Megan Cunningham

Megan Cunningham has been a producing partner on Women of Vision
*from its genesis in 1993 when I was leaving Swarthmore College for more
receptive pastures. She became my student during the first semester of her
freshman year when she took my introductory English and women's studies class, "Visible Symptoms," about the history of representing "female
disorders." At Swarthmore, she worked with me on two collaborative,
educational video projects, one on college women's ideas about feminism
(*Excited, Angry, Active, Vocal: Women Out Loud, 1991)*, and the other
about college students' ideas about safer sex (*Safer and Sexier: A College
Student's Guide to Safer Sex, 1992)*, and she became a feminist videomaker,
seeking to put her interpretations of female experience into the world.
Since college, she has worked in digital postproduction, as a film research
editor, and as a postproduction researcher and assistant. She now owns
a documentary postproduction and foreign sales company.*

*Vividly aware of how her personal video production functions differ-
ently from that of the generations that precede her because she has worked
so closely on this project, Cunningham speaks of working outside of any
organized movement or even community of women and making private
work for herself and her friends. Her position exemplifies the odd state of
contemporary feminism: quieted and hidden due to backlash and also formative and continuing in the private world of individual young women.*

*This said, Cunningham has also participated in all aspects of this very
public and communal video project. She shot and helped organize many of
the five research meetings. She edited clips from the meetings so we could
present what had already occurred to later gatherings, and she shot many
of the twenty-one interviews. Throughout the long process, she contributed
ideas and encouragement.*

This feminist video project—underfunded but brimming over with commitment from students, friends, and colleagues—is itself a direct consequence of a particular sort of feminist/selfish pedagogy: passing on in order to be able to receive. In Cunningham's invaluable participation in this project, and in her developing career as a feminist editor, videomaker, and producer, I hope is evidenced the fundamental goals and perhaps even value of my work: the search for history, for foremothers, necessitates the commitment to foremother oneself, perhaps the best way for the women's movement to actually move.

▶

Women of Vision

Why are you working on this project?
I began working on the project because I saw it as a great opportunity to learn more about feminist film and video history, which I had just touched on in college in women's studies and in film studies. I also saw it as an opportunity to meet makers whose work I respected. I was curious to see what the people behind the images that entertained and inspired me were like, what made them tick. It was an intellectual curiosity. As it evolved, my motivations changed. I began to see the project as something I couldn't *not* do.

I feel as though the anecdotes and details of people's career histories have been so much more useful than anything I've learned from my study of film history or in the little film classes I've pursued as preparation for working in the industry. The personal stories, the autobiographies of filmmakers have been more educational as I acquire my own strategies for managing my career. I'm addicted to learning more about filmmakers and why people make the work they do. The allegiances I have to working in film and television, the set of ideals are championed by a very select group, and those people happen to call themselves feminists. I didn't find myself in feminism and then begin making video. I came upon them at the same time.

What are your goals for this project? What role do you want it to play in the world?
My hope is that everyone who watches it will say, as I have said on numerous occasions while shooting this project, "Oh, I had no idea!"

"I had no idea . . ." what?
For example, I had no idea that feminism looks so different today than the '60s. I had no idea that a woman who works in Hollywood could consider herself a feminist, that so many kinds of success have been achieved by women. I had no idea that people who only showcase their work to their

daughters are as valid participants in this history as are world-renowned critics and academics.

Feminism

What ideals do feminists champion that you also champion?
It's about why they do what they do; it's about a gratification that comes from defining success along their own personal line. When I was first learning about film history, it was this foreign thing. I went to film history to find film- and videomakers whose careers sounded like something that I might want to model. Instead, what I found in film books were things that were much more distant from my life than I had intended. I had intended to find people who were just breaking in and had all these anxieties or stories of happenstance meetings that turned out to be points of success in their career.

And then I met some feminist filmmakers in this project, and their stories sounded like what I had expected to learn from film history. It was like a revelation I had when I was a girl and sort of trying out womanhood. My friends and I realized that our bodies were not women's bodies. People would buy a bra or a girdle with hopes of achieving this womanly hourglass figure. When I tried those things on, they were so uncomfortable and constricting. That was how film history was for me. I was so disappointed with the record that was there. Coming across feminist film history that was not in the books, speaking with feminist filmmakers, was so much more on target. I looked in that mirror and felt inspired, felt that this is something I can do, this is someone I can *become*.

Generation

Please be specific about some of the anecdotes that registered for you.
Cauleen Smith. At the San Francisco research meeting, there was a selected group of young filmmakers, just three or four I think, and the rest of the people in the room were women filmmakers and academics and critics from the '60s and '70s who had lived through a whole different history. Their careers were about an older kind of feminism. Early on, they were the loudest voices at the meeting, and I thought that this was almost the kind of foreignness I had experienced in film history, where I could understand the words and languages, but the experiences did not hold much meaning for me. They told fascinating tales, but they described a time and place that I had never visited.

When younger women, such as Cauleen Smith and Valerie Soe, began to speak up, their stories about coming into film and video in the '80s when Reagan was elected, their acceptance of disappointment and limited expectations, the bleakness, the dismal atmosphere and mood into which they entered, made more sense to me. It was already a downward spiral. They talked about a hard time in which there wasn't much of a movement. There wasn't that coalition that the women of the '60s and '70s described. Nor was there that spirit of leftist politics being almost mainstream. In fact, there was a fear of expressing liberal thought. Anyone who spoke out against the Gulf War was seen as absurd.

It made sense to me that you would make your own little video in your room and show it to your friends because this was your own little personal crusade. It had nothing to do with launching a career or a larger political movement. It wasn't about joining forces; it was about surviving. Those were the stories that made sense to me. Stories about watching MTV, for what it's worth, going to sources like that for experimental images, for something different.

Whom do you owe?

I owe a number of people. I owe Jodie Foster for doing things in Hollywood that no man or woman has ever been able to do, for securing deals and figuring out innovative ways to make the films that she wants to make, and for making innovative films for a mass audience and bringing them to the screen with their integrity intact. I owe many foreign filmmakers for creative visual strategies that Americans have not been able to create. I owe a handful of female producers I've met in New York. They've all been so generous in sharing professional insights out of their own regret at not having a female role model. I owe the academic world for validating alternative media, for writing about it, thinking about it, and inviting me to do the same. I owe the producer of this project for being the most consistent, encouraging force in my life in ways that I can't even remember, for being there at the earliest moment in my career when I was making videos just for myself and thinking that didn't mean much, and for convincing me that it did.

▶

Film and Video

You speak of a sense of nihilism and a lack of a movement. And yet you're not a negative person. Does your career in film and video come from that nihilism or somewhere more complicated?

No matter what I do for a day job, I'll make film and video. I entered into film- and videomaking from a commitment to writing and photography. It was a melding of those two arts. Eventually, it became something larger: an exploration of interiority, about clarifying and expressing an internal reality that made sense to me and that I didn't see expressed on television or from Hollywood.

I think that I come to this medium in almost a utopian way: entering into this project, and through other resources at college, and supportive friends, and being surrounded by strong women like a mother who invited me to risk expressing myself. I've had numerous sets of privilege that work to my advantage and make it possible for me to have access to a career like this. I've also worked really hard. The reasons for what I do have changed with each project. Through the validating process of coming across these women in feminist film and video history, I can say I am a feminist maker.

When I turn on the camera during the weekend, it's something different. It's more of a diary. It's more about establishing an internal reality, about an experiment, wanting to see something made that I don't see being made elsewhere. I want to envision something in a way that's tangible, that can be projected and debated, in a way that's provocative or offensive, that launches dialogue.

Please tell us about some of your own work and some of the work that you've done in the industry.
I've worked in video documentary for the majority of the time during the past four years. My first project, called *Food and Body Image,* was for a class. It's a documentary about women, by women, for women who range in their healthiness regarding their eating habits and feelings about their bodies. The second tape is called *Women Out Loud.* It features a collective of twelve women who got together to represent young feminist thought. Then I made a tape called *Safer and Sexier.* It was also created by a collective. In that work, I collaborated with AIDS educators who were creating a document that had never before been contextualized for a college-age audience. The tape played in colleges and universities throughout the country and won many awards. Most recently in television, I've worked on a documentary feature about an AIDS education theater troupe that travels to high-risk neighborhoods in New York City. Following that, I worked on an image tape about the history of television to be used to sell a new channel that Nickelodeon is launching. Currently, I'm working on an episode of *The American Experience* about a Hawaiian Queen in the 1850s through the 1890s. It traces her history as America decides whether or not to become an imperialist power.

What have you learned from working on this project?

The greatest hope I have for this project is that it will awaken a sensitivity in people who come in contact with feminist film- and videomakers. That they'll be able to work with a female editor and not condescend to her knowledge of technology. I've learned that the kind of success that I hope to have, in this industry and with my own career, takes the same kind of consideration that I have about my political, personal, and moral life. It's an intimate thing to make those decisions. It's not about these superficial kinds of success that the myth would have you try for. For instance, if the ultimate moment in television is to become a network mogul, it does not seem as attractive if you don't have access to the kind of creative power that I hope to have, or to direct influence over what an audience believes to be true at the end of a show. If you make all kinds of compromises along the way of getting to that point, then that's not success at all. That's what the dominant culture would have you believe to be success, but it's not rewarding in the ways that I hope my career will be rewarding.

◆————————————————————————————

MEGAN CUNNINGHAM

| 1997–98 | Director of business development, Virtual Media Communications, Inc. |
| 1999 to present | Principal, Magnet Media, LLC |

Production

1991	*Excited, Angry, Active, Vocal: Women Out Loud,* 30 min. video, crew
1992	*Safer and Sexier: A College Student's Guide to Safer Sex,* video, 26 min., editor
1994 to present	*Women of Vision,* coproducer
1995	The American Experience, postproduction researcher
1996	The Image Bank, editor

For Magnet Media

1997 to present	*Starting Out,* director/producer
	Girls of Gold, coproducer
	Collectors, associate producer
	A House Divided, producer's representative
	Family Secrets, producer's representative

Contact Information

c/o Magnet Media, 535 Eighth Avenue, 19th Floor, New York, NY 10018; (212) 477-2625; MC@Magnetmediafilms.com

Afterword

*Origin stories about the women's movement are interested
stories, all of them. They construct the present moment, and
a political position in it, by invoking a point in time out of
which that present moment unfolds—if not inevitably, then
at least with a certain coherence.*
    :: Katie King, *Theory in Its Feminist Travels*

Working on this project has let me better understand my own interest in
stories about both the '70s and contemporary feminism and, more important, their possible interrelations. While I set out to make work for my students and others like them, I admit I had selfish interests as well. I needed
to remedy my own confusion about being a feminist in an ever more conservative present, about being a progressive woman who lives haunted by
an almost-lived, immortalized, recent, politically vibrant past embodied in
the writings, images, institutions, and actual bodies of women only slightly
older than I. While I agree with King that the process of creating my own
(and enabling others') "interested stories" about feminist history often led
me back to origins in the '70s, I am less certain that this also created the
coherent present she theorizes. As there really is no neat road back to the
'70s, even if we would want one, our current path into the next century
also seems rocky at best. When I show the documentary, the discussions
afterward try to make sense of our current and future decades—confusing
and uncertain times for feminists and other political people. "Instead of
working with a sense of certainty and urgent zeal toward a clear goal, we
find ourselves taking steps that only lead to the next uncertain juncture,"
respond third-wavers AnnJanette Rosga and Meg Satterthwaite to the
memoirs of the '70s collected in *The Feminist Memoir Project*. "Perhaps
we young Anglo-American feminists are the inheritors of the grief that

came from these authors' lost center: postmodern children of our modernist mothers."[1]

Grief, apathy, or nihilism are some legitimate responses for postmodern children, but then, so are productivity and possibility. For I have found that while younger women, including myself, try to make sense of our less-than-political present (especially by comparing this to a recent past that is remembered so differently), *we still make our work,* as do those from the generations that precede us. This book—like my subjects' ceaseless outpouring of writing, and videos, films, festivals, classes, and words—demonstrates not a giving up on feminism but a continuing will to contribute to its existence and to its even better future. Feminist media work is always an act of resistance, both defensive and righteous.

MEGAN CUNNINGHAM: *If this is a history of resistance, and a record of resistance, what are you resisting as a documentary videomaker?*

ALEX JUHASZ: In seeking to document, preserve, and pass on the lives and work of women who have, in whatever way they can, sought to live precariously on the edge of their culture—because they are independent, because they are vocal, because they value what is inside their own heads and hearts—I am resisting the common enterprise of condescending to, ridiculing, or violating women who choose to live in this way, pushing them to the edges, or treating them like they don't matter, as if they are deviants. I resist the society's ongoing work to marginalize these lives, and I resist the simplification of the work and lives of women who are feminists into some kind of prepackaged, inane, simple vision of who we are and what we believe in.

I don't say this against radical, lesbian, separatist feminists, whose work I adore, but our society has simplified the range of things that we fight for as independent women by turning us into the society's worst nightmare: man-hating, unshaven-legged, angry, militant separatists. Again, I cherish women like that, but not every feminist is that woman. And not all the women I interviewed live lives like that. I resist that simplification of the lives and work of feminists.

So I attempt to make work that broadens the representation of who we are, what has mattered to us, what we fight for. We fight for social justice, we fight for economic freedom, for control of our own bodies; we fight against war, against racism, we fight to get better health care. We fight for so many different things in so many different ways with so many different voices. I resist simplifying who feminists are and what we fight for.

Instead, I demand that my viewers see our differences. See the difference between the forty-year-old lesbian filmmaker whose work is about representing the unrepresented. See how her work is different from a twenty-year-old Latina lesbian filmmaker whose work has been celebrated. See the differences among us. But with these twenty-one histories, see how we speak to each other. See how we are related. See how the basic questions that we struggle with as feminists remain consistent: the demand for the integrity of our work; the demand for control of our bodies; the demand to live complex, rich, intellectual, creative lives; the demand to help other women or people. I resist the reduction of our demands, our agency, and our voice.

Because, finally, this piece is less about film or video and more about what it is to live the life of an artistic, intellectual, political woman in this society who finds herself compelled to speak to others, or speak from herself out into the world, onto a medium that records movement and sound in real time, and that holds it there permanently. So that's what these women's histories have in common: they make use of similar platforms on which many, many women have decided they can best speak what matters to them and put it out into the world. And many, many women have then said, "I can hear you, and myself, in your images and words and sounds," which is what the media records, makes permanent, and makes into history.

Notes

Introduction

1. Before the second wave of the organized women's movement, some feminists did work with film, although usually in isolation. In their films they publicly and aesthetically articulated their visions of female experience, anger, or power. See, for example, Lauren Rabinovitz, *Points of Resistance: Women, Power, and Politics in the New York Avant-Garde Cinema, 1943–71* (Chicago: University of Illinois Press, 1991).

2. *Women of Vision: Eighteen Histories in Feminist Film and Video* (Alexandra Juhasz, 1998). Available from the Cinema Guild.

3. In Andrea Juno and V. Vale, *Angry Women* (San Francisco: Re/Search Publications, 1991), 69.

4. Elaine Showalter, *A Literature of Their Own* (Princeton, N.J.: University of Princeton Press, 1977), 10.

5. Ellen Willis, "Forward," in *Daring to Be Bad: Radical Feminism in America, 1967–1975*, Alice Echols (Minneapolis: University of Minnesota Press, 1987), vii.

6. My interviewees are also all American. I eagerly await other studies that will give us more of the feminist media world, but I was sufficiently overwhelmed by the complexity of U.S. history to know that I could not take on more.

7. Leslie Heywood and Jennifer Drake, *Third Wave Agenda: Being Feminist, Doing Feminism* (Minneapolis: University of Minnesota Press, 1997), 3.

8. Mona Narain, "Shifting Locations: Third World Feminists and Institutional Aporias," in *Generations: Academic Feminists in Dialogue*, ed. Devoney Looser and E. Ann Kaplan (Minneapolis: University of Minnesota Press, 1997), 155.

9. Nancy Whittier, *Feminist Generations: The Persistence of the Radical Women's Movement* (Philadelphia: Temple University Press, 1995), 25.

10. Patricia Zimmermann, "Flaherty's Midwives," in *Feminism and Documentary*, ed. Janet Walker and Diane Waldman (Minneapolis: University of Minnesota Press, 1999).

11. There are notable exceptions. For instance, one of the early aims of feminist media scholarship was to identify women who currently or had previously made media. Since then, there have been several publications that list, interview, or discuss the work of female (but only sometimes "feminist") filmmakers: Sharon Smith, *Women Who Make Movies* (New York: Hopkinson and Blake, 1975); Jeanne Betancourt, *Women in Focus* (Cincinnati: Pflaun Publishing, 1975); Bonnie Dawson, *Women's Films in Print* (San Francisco: Booklegger Press, 1975); Barbara Koenig Quart, *Women Directors: The Emergence of a New Cinema* (New York: Praeger, 1988); Annette Kuhn, *Women in Film: An International Encyclopedia* (New York: Fawcett Columbine, 1990); Ally Acker, *Reel Women: Pioneers of the Cinema 1896 to the Present* (New York: Continuum Publishing, 1991); Gwendolyn Audrey Foster, *Women Film Directors: An International Bio-Critical Dictionary* (Westport, Conn.: Greenwood Press, 1995); Judith Redding and Victoria Brownworth, *Film Fatales: Independent Women Directors* (Seattle: Seal Press, 1997); Gwendolyn Audrey Foster, *Women Filmmakers of the African and Asian Diaspora: Decolonizing the Gaze, Locating Subjectivity* (Carbondale: University of Southern Illinois Press, 1997); Jacqueline Bobo, ed., *Black Women Film and Video Artists* (New York: Routledge, 1998); Christina Lane, *Feminist Hollywood: From "Born in Flames" to "Point Break"* (Detroit: Wayne State University Press, 2000). Jan Rosenberg's thesis manuscript, *Women's Reflections: The Feminist Film Movement* (Ann Arbor: UMI Research Press, 1979), provides an early examination of feminist film written while this "movement" was still forming. Some scholarly books have been published on

distinct periods within feminist media history, most notably Lauren Rabinovitz's *Points of Resistance* and E. Ann Kaplan's *Women and Film: Both Sides of the Camera* (New York: Methuen, 1983). In *A Fine Romance: Five Ages of Film Criticism* (Philadelphia: Temple University Press, 1995), Patricia Mellencamp periodizes women's representation in and with film through a theoretical/historical grid of her design, and in *Shot/Countershot* Lucy Fischer contrasts male and female authored films (Princeton, N.J.: Princeton University Press, 1989).

12. For example, in the trade press, Myrian Miedzian and Akisa Malinovich, *Generations: A Century of Women Speak about Their Lives* (New York: Atlantic Monthly Press, 1997); Rachel DuPlessis and Ann Snitow, eds., *The Feminist Memoir Project* (New York: Three Rivers Press, 1998); Anna Bondoc and Meg Daly, eds., *Letters of Intent: Women Cross the Generations to Talk about Family, Work, Sex, Love and the Future of Feminism* (New York: Free Press, 1999). And from academic women, Looser and Kaplan's *Generations*; Nancy K. Miller, *Getting Personal: Feminist Occasions and Other Autobiographical Acts* (New York: Routledge, 1991); Jane Gallop, *Around 1981: Academic Feminist Literary Theory* (New York: Routledge, 1992); Gayle Greene and Coppélia Kahn, eds., *Changing Subjects: The Making of Feminist Literary Criticism* (New York: Routledge, 1993); Diane Elam and Robyn Wiegman, eds., *Feminism beside Itself* (New York: Routledge, 1995).

13. B. Ruby Rich, *Chick Flicks: Theories and Memories of the Feminist Film Movement* (Chapel Hill, N.C.: Duke University Press, 1998); Michelle Citron, *Home Movies and Other Necessary Fictions* (Minneapolis: University of Minnesota Press, 1998); *Camera Obscura* 20–21 (1989); Janet Walker and Diane Waldman, eds., *Feminism and Documentary* (Minneapolis: University of Minnesota Press, 1999).

14. Gloria Hull, "History/My History," in Greene and Kahn, 62.

15. Quoted in Gayle Greene, "Looking at History," in Greene and Kahn, 11.

16. Susan Stanford Friedman, "Making History: Reflections on Feminism, Narrative, and Desire," in Elam and Wiegman, *Feminism beside Itself*, 32.

17. Deborah McDowell, "Transferences: Black Feminist Discourse: The 'Practice' of 'Theory,'" in Elam and Wiegman, *Feminism beside Itself*, 104.

18. Echols, *Daring to Be Bad*, 16.

19. Radical feminism is one sector of a women's movement composed of groups that understand differently patriarchy and women's oppression within it. Radical feminists seek to alter fundamentally the very structures and assumptions of society.

20. John Hess and Chuck Kleinhans, "U.S. Film Periodicals," *Jump Cut* 38 (1993): 105.

21. For example, the Worker's Film and Photo League of the 1920s, Frontier Films of the 1930s, the Film Arts Society of the 1950s, and the Film-Makers Cooperative of the 1960s. See John Downing, *Radical Media: The Political Experience of Alternative Communication* (Boston: South End Press, 1984).

22. For example, the Museum of Modern Art's Film Collection, the Pacific Film Archive, Anthology Film Archives, the Video Data Bank, and Electronic Arts Intermix. See Film Arts Foundation, *Alternative Exhibition Information of the Universe* (San Francisco: Film Arts Foundation, 1998) for descriptions of and contact information for hundreds of American alternative exhibition programs.

23. For example, the Association of Independent Video and Filmmakers, the Society for Cinema Studies, the University Film and Video Association, the National Association of Media Arts Centers, the National Asian American Telecommunications Association, the National Black Programming Consortium, the National Latino Communications Center, the Native American Public Broadcasting Consortium, and Pacific Islanders in Communications. See Ilisa Barbash and Lucien Taylor, *Cross-Cultural Filmmaking* (Berkeley and Los Angeles: University of California Press, 1997) for an extremely useful appendix providing contact information for these and other media service organizations.

24. The Robert Flaherty Seminar, for instance, is not run by a professional organization. For more on its history and contributions to independent media, see Patricia Zimmermann, "Flaherty's Midwives."

25. The Edinburgh Women's Event in 1972 and the Edinburgh Film Festival in 1979 hosted two meetings where foundational, if contentious, discussion was produced. These and other early feminist film festivals are discussed in detail in Rich's *Chick Flicks*.

26. For example, Newsreel (which later became Third World Newsreel), Women Make Movies, the Boston Women's Film Co-op, Cinewomen, Kartemquin Films, Film/Video Arts, and Paper Tiger. For a history and analysis of Newsreel, see Downing, *Radical Media*. For a history of and other writings about Women Make Movies, see the twenty-fifth-anniversary special issue of *Wide Angle* 20:4 (Spring 1999).

27. For example, Global Village, Downtown Community Television, Appalshop, Film Arts Foundation, Scribe Video, the Community Film Workshop, Visual Communications, Asian CineVision, the Bay Area Video Coalition, Educational Video Center, New Orleans Video Access Center, and Pittsburgh Filmmakers. See Bay Area Video Coalition, *Mediamaker Handbook* (Berkeley, Calif.: BAVAC, 1999) for contact information for these and other media organizations. Also see Barbash and Taylor, *Cross-Cultural Filmmaking*; and Film Arts Foundation, *Alternative Exhibition Information*.

28. For a comprehensive list of international gay and lesbian film festivals, see PopcornQ at http://www.popcornq.com or call (415) 547–2800.
29. Hess and Kleinhans, "U.S. Film Periodicals," 105.
30. Molly Haskell, *From Reverence to Rape* (New York: Holt, Rinehart & Winston, 1973); Marjorie Rosen, *Popcorn Venus: Movies and the American Dream* (New York: Coward, McCann and Geohagan, 1973); Joan Mellen, *Women and Their Sexuality in the New Film* (New York: Horizon Press, 1973).
31. Claire Johnston, "Women's Cinema as Counter Cinema," in *Notes on Women's Cinema*, ed. Claire Johnston (London: Society for Education in Film and Television, 1973), 24–31; Laura Mulvey, "Visual Pleasure and Narrative Cinema," *Screen* 16:3 (1975): 6–18.
32. From written notes provided to me by Lesage, one of the readers of the manuscript for the University of Minnesota Press.
33. For instance, the now defunct Film Fund, and the still-viable Astraea National Lesbian Action Foundation for Women, the Paul Robeson Fund, or the recently mandated and nationally funded Independent Television Service (ITVS). See Barbash and Taylor, *Cross-Cultural Filmmaking* for a short guide to media funding.
34. See Rabinovitz, *Points of Resistance*.
35. Deirdre Boyle, *Subject to Change: Guerrilla Television Revisited* (New York: Oxford University Press, 1997), viii.
36. Ibid.
37. See my own *AIDS TV: Identity, Community, and Alternative Video* (Chapel Hill, N.C.: Duke University Press, 1995).
38. Thomas Waugh, *"Show Us Life": Toward a History and Aesthetics of the Committed Documentary* (Metuchen, N.J.: Scarecrow Press, 1984), xxiv.
39. Chela Sandoval quoted in Elizabeth Larsen, "Our Bodies/Our Camcorders: Video and Reproductive Rights," *The Independent* (March 1992), 26.
40. Rosenberg, *Women's Reflections*, 12–19.
41. Lisa Maria Hogeland, *Feminism and Its Fictions: The Consciousness-Raising Novel and the Women's Liberation Movement* (Philadelphia: University of Pennsylvania Press, 1998), 5.
42. Betty Friedan, *The Feminine Mystique* (New York: Norton, 1963).
43. For example, Alice Embree, "Media Images 1: Madison Avenue Brainwashing—The Fact," and Florika, "Media Images 2: Body Odor and Social Order," in *Sisterhood Is Powerful*, ed. Robin Morgan (New York: Vintage Books, 1970).
44. Rosenberg, *Women's Reflections*, 12.
45. Tommy Lott, "A No-Theory of Black Cinema," in *Representing Blackness: Issues in Film and Video*, ed. Valerie Smith (New Brunswick, N.J.: Rutgers University Press, 1997), 93.
46. Barbara Christian, "Being 'The Subjected Subject of Discourse,'" *differences* 2:3 (1990): 58.
47. John Hess, Chuck Kleinhans, and Julia Lesage, "Some Politics of Editing: *Jump Cut*'s First Twenty Years," *Jump Cut* 39 (1994): 133.
48. Laura Mulvey, "British Feminist Film Theory's Female Spectators: Presence and Absence," *Camera Obscura* 20–21 (1989): 69.
49. Judith Mayne, "Feminist Film Theory and Criticism," in *Multiple Voices in Feminist Film Criticism*, ed. Diane Carson, Linda Dittmar, and Janice Welsch (Minneapolis: University of Minnesota Press, 1994), 49.
50. Rich, *Chick Flicks*, 2.
51. Mulvey, "British Feminist Film Theory's Female Spectators," 77.
52. Rosenberg, *Women's Reflections*, 7.
53. Barbara Smith, "'Feisty Characters' and 'Other People's Causes': Memories of White Racism and U.S. Feminism," in DuPlessis and Snitow, *Feminist Memoir Project*, 481.
54. Janet Walker and Diane Waldman, "Introduction," in *Feminism and Documentary*, 13.
55. For instance, *Living with AIDS: Women and AIDS* (1987), *Prostitutes, Risk and AIDS* (1988), *WE CARE: A Documentary for Care Providers of People Affected by AIDS* (1990), and *Safer and Sexier: A College Student's Guide to Safer Sex* (1992). See Catherine Saalfield's videography in *AIDS TV* for distribution information for these and other AIDS activist videos.
56. Hull, "History/My History," 60.
57. Bonnie Zimmerman, "In Academia, and Out: The Experience of a Lesbian Feminist Literary Critic," in Greene and Kahn, 120.
58. Nina Felshin, "Introduction," in *But Is It Art? The Spirit of Art as Activism*, ed. Nina Felshin (Seattle: Bay Press, 1995), 17.
59. Jeff Kelley, "The Body Politics of Suzanne Lacy," in Felshin, *But Is It Art?*, 223–24.
60. Boyle, *Subject to Change*, 33.
61. Chon Noriega, "Imagined Borders: Locating Chicano Cinema in America/América," in *The Ethnic Eye: Latino Media Arts*, ed. Chon A. Noriega and Ana M. López (Minneapolis: University of Minnesota Press, 1996), 8.

62. Community building is usually not a criterion for arts or humanities funding. For instance, a program officer at the NEH told me that PBS only supported documentaries that told "both sides of a story." A State Humanities program officer from Illinois told me that my work was too much like "advocacy" and not enough like "scholarship."

63. My documentary was funded in two ways: through the small yearly research budget I received as a full-time, and then tenure-track professor at Swarthmore, Bryn Mawr, and Pitzer Colleges, respectively (funds intended for the costs of written, scholarly research, not video production); and through trades and other in-kind support from the under- and defunded organizations that themselves play a central role in this history (Film/Video Arts, the Philadelphia Independent Film and Video Association, Women Make Movies, Women in the Director's Chair Film Festival, the School of the Art Institute of Chicago, the John D. and Catherine T. MacArthur Foundation, the Film Arts Foundation, and the Video Annex of the Long Beach Museum of Art). I did receive two outright grants: a $750 preproduction research grant from the California Council for the Humanities and a $2,000 postproduction grant from the Astraea National Lesbian Action Foundation.

64. *Women of Vision* currently airs on the nationally satellited community access program *Free Speech TV.*

65. Miller, *Getting Personal*, xv.

66. Barbash and Taylor, *Cross-Cultural Filmmaking*, 2.

67. Felshin, *But Is It Art?*, 12.

68. For more on Stoney, see Erik Barnouw, *Documentary* (New York: Oxford University Press, 1983).

69. Barbara Halpern Martineau, "'Talking About Our Lives and Experiences': Some Thoughts on Feminism, Documentary and 'Talking Heads,'" in Waugh, *"Show Us Life,"* 254.

70. Julia Lesage, "Feminist Documentary: Aesthetics and Politics," in Waugh, *"Show Us Life,"* 231.

71. Hogeland, *Feminism and Its Fictions*, xi.

72. Hull, "History/My History," 54.

73. Katie King, *Theory in Its Feminist Travels: Conversations in the U.S. Women's Movement* (Bloomington: Indiana University Press, 1994), 127.

74. Ellen Willis, "My Memoir Problem," in DuPlessis and Snitow, *Feminist Memoir Project*, 484.

75. Judith Roof, "Generational Difficulties; or, The Fear of a Barren History," in Looser and Kaplan, *Generations*.

76. Joan Scott, "Conference Call," *differences* 2:3 (1990): 83.

77. Noriega and López, *The Ethnic Eye*, xiv.

78. Devoney Looser, "Introduction," in Looser and Kaplan, *Generations*, 34.

79. Shirley Nelson Garner, "Mentoring Lessons," *Women's Studies Quarterly* 1 and 2 (1994): 9.

80. Christian, "Being 'The Subjected Subject of Discourse,'" 58.

81. Diane Elam, "Sisters Are Doing It for Themselves," in Devoney and Kaplan, *Generations*, 64.

1. Pearl Bowser

1. Foster, *Women Filmmakers of the African and Asian Diaspora*, 1.

2. Thanks to Yvonne Welbon for this thorough list: Ruby Oliver, *Leola: Love Your Mama* (1989); Julie Dash, *Daughters of the Dust* (1991); Ayoka Chenzira, *Alma's Rainbow* (1992); Leslie Harris, *Just Another Girl on the IRT* (1993); Darnell Martin, *I Like It Like That* (1994); Bridgett Davis, *Naked Acts* (1995); Cheryl Dunye, *The Watermelon Woman* (1996); Kasi Lemmons, *Eve's Bayou* (1997); Maya Angelou, *Down in the Delta* (1998); Cauleen Smith, *Drylongso* (1998); Gina Price Blythewood, *Love and Basketball* (2000). See Foster, *Women Filmmakers*, and Bobo, *Black Women Film and Video Artists* for more on the careers of these and other women-of-color filmmakers.

3. According to Bowser's research, the Walker Theater in Indianapolis, built by the millionaire Madame C. J. Walker, still stands as a monument to the entrepreneur of cosmetics for black women. Mrs. Loula T. Williams was the proprietor of a movie house in Tulsa, Oklahoma. And on occasion Mrs. Sherman Dudley, the wife of a renowned vaudevillian and theater owner, even functioned as a distributor and agent.

4. Combahee River Collective, "A Black Feminist Statement," in *This Bridge Called My Back: Writing by Radical Women of Color*, ed. Cherríe Moraga and Gloria Anzaldúa (New York: Kitchen Table Press, 1983), 210.

5. Ada Gay Griffin, "Seizing the Moving Image: Reflections of a Black Independent Producer," in *Black Popular Culture*, ed. Gina Dent (New York: Dia Center for the Arts, 1992), 231.

6. Richard Leacock is one of the central figures in a significant American documentary film movement of the 1960s—direct cinema. See Barnouw's *Documentary*.

7. For more on Oscar Micheaux, the most prolific, and many would argue, talented director of race films, see Bowser, *In Search of Oscar Micheaux* (with Louise Spence), forthcoming from Rutgers University Press; and *Oscar Micheaux and His Circle* (with Jane Gaines and Charles Musser), forthcoming from Smithsonian Press.

8. For more on this film, see Julie Dash, *Daughters of the Dust* (New York: New Press, 1992).
9. For more on Marlon Riggs, see Kobena Mercer, "Dark and Lovely Too: Black Gay Men in Independent Film," in *Queer Looks: Perspectives on Lesbian and Gay Film and Video*, ed. Martha Gever, John Greyson, and Pratibha Parmar (New York: Routledge, 1993); and David Van Leer, "Visible Silence: Spectatorship in Black Gay and Lesbian Film," in Valerie Smith's *Representing Blackness*.
10. For more on Cathy Collins, Ayoka Chenzira, Maya Angelou, Zeinabu irene Davis, Alile Sharon Larkin, and other African American women filmmakers, see Foster, *Women Filmmakers of the African and Asian Diaspora*; Acker, *Reel Women*; Redding and Brownworth, *Film Fatales*. Also see Alile Sharon Larkin, "Black Women Film-Makers Defining Ourselves," in *Female Spectators: Looking at Film and Television*, ed. E. Deirdre Pribaum (London: Verso, 1988).

2. Carolee Schneemann

1. Carolee Schneemann, "Brief Biography," personal papers, 1998.
2. Rich, *Chick Flicks*, 21.
3. Rabinovitz, *Points of Resistance*, 3.
4. Two major publications are forthcoming: *Imaging Her Erotics* (MIT Press), and her collected letters, edited by Kristine Stiles (Johns Hopkins University Press).
5. Juno and Vale, *Angry Women*.
6. Maya Deren is America's most heralded female filmmaker and is considered the "mother of the Underground Film." Until recently, she was typically the only woman taught in film studies classes. She was a major force in the organization of independent film production and distribution in the '50s and '60s. She made *Meshes of the Afternoon* (1943), *At Land* (1944), and *Ritual in Transfigured Time* (1946). See Acker, *Reel Women*; P. Adams Sitney, *Visionary Film* (New York: Oxford University Press, 1974); Vèvè Clark, Millicent Hodson, and Catrina Neiman, *The Legend of Maya Deren: A Documentary Biography and Collected Works* (New York: Anthology Film Archives, 1984).
7. Rabinovitz, *Points of Resistance*, 3–6.
8. See Sally Banes, *Democracy's Body: Judson Dance Theater, 1962–64* (Durham, N.C.: Duke University Press, 1993).
9. For more on Stan Brakhage and other experimental filmmakers, see David James, *Allegories of Cinema* (Princeton, N.J.: Princeton University Press, 1989).
10. Kate Millett wrote the central feminist text *Sexual Politics* (Garden City, N.J.: Doubleday, 1970).
11. See James, *Allegories of Cinema* for more on these major figures in American avant-garde cinema. See Rabinovitz, *Points of Resistance* for a discussion of women's role in the American avant-garde cinema.

3. Barbara Hammer

1. Redding and Brownworth, *Film Fatales*, 77.
2. Mary Ann Doane, Patricia Mellencamp, Linda Williams, "Feminist Film Criticism: An Introduction," in *Re-Vision: Essays in Feminist Film Criticism*, ed. Mary Ann Doane et al. (Los Angeles: American Film Institute, 1984), 5.
3. Ibid., 8.
4. Rich, *Chick Flicks*, 287.
5. Vsevolod Pudovkin's *Mother* (1926) is a loose adaptation of Maksim Gorky's novel about a downtrodden woman who transforms into a sacrificial heroine of the revolutionary movement of 1905–6.
6. Barbara Hammer, "The Politics of Abstraction," in Gever et al., *Queer Looks*.
7. See Christian Metz, *The Imaginary Signifier: Psychoanalysis and the Cinema* (Bloomington: Indiana University Press, 1982).
8. For more on Shirley Clarke, see Louise Heck-Rabi, *Women Filmmakers: A Critical Reception* (Metuchen, N.J.: Scarecrow Press, 1984); Rabinovitz, *Points of Resistance*.
9. *Cinema News* 6/1 (1980–81).
10. See Trinh T. Minh-ha, *Woman, Native, Other* (Bloomington: Indiana University Press, 1989). For more on Yvonne Rainer, see Yvonne Rainer, *The Films of Yvonne Rainer* (Bloomington: Indiana University Press, 1989).
11. For more on Su Friedrich, see Chris Holmlund, "When Autobiography Meets Ethnography and Girl Meets Girl: The 'Dyke Docs' of Sadie Benning and Su Friedrich," in *Between the Sheets, in the Streets: Queer, Lesbian, Gay Documentary*, ed. Chris Holmlund and Cynthia Fuchs (Minneapolis: University of Minnesota, 1997).

4. Kate Horsfield

1. Boyle, *Subject to Change*, 4.
2. For more on the relation between feminism and video, see Martha Gever, "The Feminism Factor:

Video and Its Relation to Feminism," in *Illuminating Video*, ed. Doug Hall and Sally Jo Fifer (New York: Aperture, 1990).

3. JoAnn Hanley, *The First Generation: Women and Video: 1970–75* (New York: Independent Curators, Inc., 1993), 14–15 (program guide). Hanley is quoting Martha Gever, "Video Politics: Early Feminist Projects," *Afterimage* (Summer 1983): 25–27.

4. Quoted in ibid., 10.

5. For more on American feminist artists see Donna Bachman, *Women Artists: An Historical, Contemporary, and Feminist Bibliography* (Metuchen, N.J.: Scarecrow Press, 1994).

6. For more on video art, and Martha Rosler, see Michael Renov and Erica Suderburg, eds., *Resolutions: Contemporary Video Practices* (Minneapolis: University of Minnesota Press, 1996); and Hall and Fifer's *Illuminating Video*.

7. The formats of ½" reel-to-reel and ¾" videotape are outdated, affordable, and professional.

8. For more on these and other early video collectives, see Boyle, *Subject to Change*.

5. Margaret Caples

1. St. Clair Bourne, "Bright Moments: The Black Journal Series," *The Independent* (May 1988): 10.

2. bell hooks, *Ain't I a Woman: Black Women and Feminism* (Boston: South End Press, 1981), 147.

3. Audre Lorde, "Age, Race, Class, and Sex: Women Redefining Difference," in *Out There: Marginalization and Contemporary Cultures*, ed. Russell Ferguson, Martha Gever, Trinh T. Minh-ha, and Cornel West (New York: New Museum of Contemporary Art, 1990), 283.

4. For more on women in early cinema, see Cari Beauchamp, *Without Lying Down: Frances Marion and the Powerful Women of Early Hollywood* (New York: Scribner, 1997); Acker, *Reel Women*; Karyn Kay and Gerald Peary, eds., *Women and the Cinema: A Critical Anthology* (New York: Dutton, 1977); Martin Norden, "Women in the Early Film Industry," *Wide Angle* 6:3 (1984): 58-67; Anthony Slide, *Early Women Directors* (New York: A. S. Barnes, 1977).

5. For more on women in the studio system see Acker, *Reel Women*; Claire Johnston, ed., *The Work of Dorothy Arzner: Toward a Feminist Cinema* (London: BFI, 1975); Judith Mayne, *Directed by Dorothy Arzner* (Bloomington: University of Indiana Press, 1994); Lizzie Francke, *Script Girls: Women Screenwriters in Hollywood* (London: BFI, 1994).

6. Foster, *Women Filmmakers of the African and Asian Diaspora*, 1.

7. Quoted in Boyle, *Subject to Change*, 68.

8. Don Adams and Arlene Goldbard, "Social Studies: Public Policy and Media Literacy," *The Independent* (August/September 1989): 36–37.

9. Ibid., 36.

6. Julia Reichert

1. The film makes use of a significant percentage of the footage shot.

7. Michelle Citron

1. See discussion of these and other feminist filmmakers in 1970s editions of the journals *Screen*, *m/f*, and *Camera Obscura*.

2. See, for example, "The Realist Debates in Feminist Film," in E. Ann Kaplan, *Women and Film: Both Sides of the Camera* (New York: Methuen, 1983), a chapter in which she gives an overview of debates about the theories and strategies of realism in both feminist documentary practice and "avant-garde theory films."

3. Eileen McGarry, "Documentary, Realism, and Women's Cinema," *Women and Film* (summer 1975): 53.

4. Kaplan, *Women and Film*, 131.

5. Claire Johnston, "Women's Cinema as Counter Cinema," in Johnston, *Notes on Women's Cinema*, 214.

6. Martineau, "'Talking About Our Lives and Experiences,'" 260.

7. Michelle Citron, "Fleeing from Documentary," in Walker and Waldman, *Feminism and Documentary*, 280.

8. Citron, "Women's Film Production: Going Mainstream," in E. Deirdre Pribaum, *Female Spectators*.

9. Rich, *Chick Flicks*, 376.

10. Citron, *Home Movies*, 50.

11. For more on these filmmakers and avant-garde filmmaking, see David James, *Allegories of Cinema*; Stan Brakhage, *Film at Wit's End: Eight Avant-Garde Filmmakers* (Kingston, N.Y.: Documentext, 1989); P. Adams Sitney, ed. *The Avant-Garde Film: A Reader of Theory and Criticism* (New York: Anthology Film Archives, 1987); Sitney, *Visionary Film* (New York: Oxford University Press, 1979).

12. Gene Youngblood, *Expanded Cinema* (New York: E. P. Dutton, 1970).
13. Adrienne Rich, *Of Woman Born* (New York: Norton, 1976).
14. Roland Barthes and Christian Metz are influential French poststructuralist/psychoanalytic semi-oticians who wrote about film and other textual systems in the '70s. See, for example, Roland Barthes, *Image/Music/Text* (New York: Hill and Wang, 1977) and *Critical Essays* (Evanston, Ill.: Northwestern University Press, 1972); Christian Metz, *The Imaginary Signifier*.
15. For further discussion of Dorothy Arzner, see Johnston, *The Work of Dorothy Arzner*; Mayne, *Directed by Dorothy Arzner*. And for more on women in Hollywood, see Acker, *Reel Women*.
16. For more on Agnes Varda, see Agnes Varda, *Varda par Varda* (Paris: Cahiers du Cinema, 1994); for more on European women filmmakers, see Annette Kuhn and Susannah Redstone, eds., *The Women's Companion to International Film* (Berkeley and Los Angeles: University of California Press, 1994); Acker, *Reel Women*.

8. Vanalyne Green

1. Cecilia Dougherty, "Stories from a Generation: Early Video at the LA Woman's Building," *Afterimage* (July/August 1998): 9.
2. For more on the Feminist Art Program and feminist art in general, see Norma Broudet and Mary Garrard, *The Power of Feminist Art: The American Movement of the 1970s* (New York: H. N. Abrams, 1994).
3. Kelley, "The Body Politics of Suzanne Lacy," 222.
4. For more on American feminist artists, see Bachman, *Women Artists*.
5. JoAnn Hanley, *The First Generation*, 10.
6. See Cary Nelson and Stephen Watt, *Academic Keywords: A Devil's Dictionary for Higher Education* (New York: Routledge, 1999); Cary Nelson, ed., *Will Teach for Food: Academic Labor in Crisis* (Minneapolis: University of Minnesota Press, 1997).
7. For more on Su Friedrich and other feminist experimental filmmakers, see Redding and Brownworth, *Film Fatales*.
8. Dorothy Dinnerstein, *The Mermaid and the Minotaur* (New York: Harper and Row, 1976); Jessica Benjamin, *The Bonds of Love* (New York: Pantheon, 1988); Shulamith Firestone, *The Dialectic of Sex* (New York: Morrow, 1970).
9. The Scholar and the Feminist IX Conference (1982) at Barnard College was a visible public forum where feminists debated pornography and other manifestations of nonmutual sexuality. Papers from the conference and discussion of its place in the feminist sex wars are collected in Carole Vance, ed., *Pleasure and Danger: Exploring Female Sexuality* (London: Pandora, 1989).

9. Constance Penley

1. Hogeland, *Feminism and Its Fictions*, 10.
2. For more on Chantal Akerman, see Ivone Margulies, *Nothing Happens: Chantal Akerman's Hyperrealist Everyday* (Durham, N.C.: Duke University Press, 1996).

10. Susan Mogul

1. Ann-Sargent Wooster, "The Way We Were," in Hanley, *The First Generation*, 21.
2. Since the interview, Mogul produced *Sing, O Barren Woman* (2000), a documusical about women who are childless by choice.
3. Elayne Zalis worked as an archivist at the Long Beach Museum of Art Video Annex, where this interview with Mogul was shot.
4. *On-lining* refers to broadcast-quality editing that allows for special effects, transitions, and titles. Betacam SP is a professional format video stock.

11. Carol Leigh

1. Patricia Aufderheide, "Underground Cable: A Survey of Public Access Programming," *Afterimage* (Summer 1994): 5, quoting the Cable Communications Policy Act of 1984, U.S. House of Representatives.
2. Boyle, *Subject to Change*, 139.
3. Aufderheide, "Underground Cable," 5.
4. See my "Our AutoBodies/Ourselves: Representing Real Women in Feminist Video," *Afterimage* (February 1994), for more discussion of explicit feminist sexuality in video art.
5. Jennie Klein, "Transgressive Tapes," *Afterimage* (January 1995): 12.
6. Ti-Grace Atkinson, *Amazon Odyssey* (New York: Links Books, 1974).

12. Juanita Mohammed

1. Frances Negrón-Muntaner, "The Ethics of Community Media," *The Independent* (May 1991): 20.
2. Ellen Spiro, "What to Wear on Your Video Activist Outing (Because the Whole World Is Watching)," *The Independent* (May 1991): 22.
3. See Barbash and Taylor, *Cross-Cultural Filmmaking*, for contact information for these and other media arts centers.
4. For a history of Challenge for Change, see Barnouw, *Documentary*. For a history of Newsreel, see Downing, *Radical Media*.
5. My book *AIDS TV* centers on my work with the Women's AIDS Video Enterprise within a broader history and theory of AIDS activist video.

13. Wendy Quinn

1. Women Make Movies celebrated its twenty-fifth anniversary in 1997 with a retrospective and a special edition of the journal *Wide Angle* dedicated to exploring the impact of the organization's tenure. See *Wide Angle* 20:4 (Spring 1999).

14. Victoria Vesna

1. Bill Viola is one of the only video artists consistently recognized and supported by the art world.

15. Valerie Soe

1. Michelle Sidler, "Living in McJobdom," in Heywood and Drake, eds.: 38.
2. Proposition 187 was California's 1994 successful anti-immigration voter's initiative that sought, among other things, to deny state services like education and healthcare to illegal aliens and their children. Most of its mandates have since been found unconstitutional.

16. Yvonne Welbon

1. See Welbon, "Black Lesbian Film and Video Art," *P-Form* 35 (Spring 1995); "Left in the Dust: Lesbians Become More Visible on Screen . . . Sort Of," *Windy City Times*, December 1992; "Black Lesbian Film and Video Artists," *P-Form* (Spring 1995).
2. Redding and Brownworth, *Film Fatales*, 13.
3. Welbon, "Black Lesbian Film and Video Art."

17. Frances Negrón-Muntaner

1. *Anatomy of a Smile* (Berkeley, Calif.: Third Woman Press, 1998); *Puerto Rican Jam: Rethinking Nationalism and Colonialism* with Ramón Grosfoguel (Minneapolis: University of Minnesota Press, 1994); *Shouting in a Whisper/The Limits of Silence: Latino Poets in Philadelphia* (Chile: Asterion Press and Pennsylvania Council on the Arts, 1994).
2. Laura Mulvey, "Visual Pleasure and the Narrative Cinema," *Screen* 16:3 (1975): 6–18.
3. For more on Latino media history, see Noriega and López, *The Ethnic Eye*.

18. Cheryl Dunye

1. For more on video art and Martha Rosler, see Michael Renov and Erica Suderburg, eds., *Resolutions*; and Hall and Fifer, *Illuminating Video*. For more on Michelle Parkerson, see Gloria Gibson, "Identities Unmasked/Empowerment Unleashed: The Documentary Style of Michelle Parkerson," in Waldman and Walker, *Feminism and Documentary*. Michelle Parkerson, Ada Gay Griffin, and many other women filmmakers are featured in Redding and Brownworth, *Film Fatales*.
2. Miller, *Getting Personal*, 21.
3. Zoe Leonard and Cheryl Dunye, *The Fae Richards Photo Archive* (San Francisco: Artspace Books, 1996).
4. Camille Billops is a experimental documentary filmmaker of such films as *Suzanne, Suzanne* (1977) and *Finding Christa* (1981). For more on her, see Valerie Smith, "Telling Family Secrets," in Carson, Dittmar, and Welsch, *Multiple Voices*.
5. For discussion of these and other black lesbian mediamakers, see Yvonne Welbon, "Black Lesbian Film," "Left in the Dust," and "Determined to Create a Presence."
6. Leni Riefenstahl, considered one of the greatest and also most controversial documentarians,

made several of her most important films as propaganda for the Third Reich. See Heck-Rabi, *Women Filmmakers: A Critical Reception.*

19. Eve Oishi

1. For more on this movie, see Julie Dash's book *Daughters of the Dust.*

Afterword

1. AnnJanette Rosga and Meg Satterthwaite, "Notes from the Aftermath," in DuPlessis and Snitow, *Feminist Memoir Project,* 476.

Contributors

PEARL BOWSER is the founder of African Diaspora Images, which specializes in African and African American film. She is codirector of the award-winning documentary *Midnight Ramble: Oscar Micheaux and the Story of Race Movies.*

MARGARET CAPLES is the executive director of the Community Film Workshop, Chicago.

MICHELLE CITRON is an award-winning independent filmmaker and the author of *Home Movies and Other Necessary Fictions* (Minnesota, 1999). She is currently creating a series of narrative CD-ROMs. She is a professor in the Department of Radio/Television/Film at Northwestern University.

MEGAN CUNNINGHAM is the owner of Magnet Media, LLC, a documentary production and sales company. She is the director and producer of *Starting Out,* and coproducer of *Women of Vision* and *Girls of Gold.*

CHERYL DUNYE is a filmmaker and videographer. She made the award-winning feature film *The Watermelon Woman,* as well as several short, experimental videos. She recently shot her second feature, *Stranger Inside.*

VANALYNE GREEN is a videomaker and the chair of the video department at the School of the Art Institute of Chicago. Her videos include *Trick or Drink, A Spy in the House That Ruth Built, What Happens to You?,* and *Saddle Sores.*

BARBARA HAMMER is an internationally recognized film/videomaker of eighty films and videos. *Nitrate Kisses, Tender Fiction*, and *History Lessons* complete her trilogy on lesbian history.

KATE HORSFIELD is cofounder and executive director of the Video Data Bank and served on the board of the Independent Television Service for six years. She served as the president of the Lyn Blumenthal Fund for ten years.

ALEXANDRA JUHASZ is associate professor of media studies at Pitzer College. She is the author of *AIDS TV: Identity, Community, and Alternative Video* and the producer of educational videotapes on feminist issues from AIDS to teen pregnancy. She produced Cheryl Dunye's feature film *The Watermelon Woman*. She completed the feature documentary *Women of Vision* (a companion project to this book) in 1998.

CAROL LEIGH is a videomaker and sex worker who was one of the founding members of ACT UP/San Francisco. Her works include *Blind Eye to Justice: HIV Positive Women in California Prisons*; *Yes Means Yes, No Means No*; *Pope Don't Preach (I'm Terminating My Pregnancy)*; and *Die Yuppie Scum*. She curates the San Francisco Sex Worker Film and Video Festival.

SUSAN MOGUL is an artist and filmmaker. Her films have been broadcast nationally on public television and have received prizes at film festivals nationally and internationally. She just completed *Sing, O Barren Womon* (2000), a short documusical that satirizes and celebrates voluntary childlessness.

JUANITA MOHAMMED is a videomaker whose works include *Homosexuality: One Child's Point of View* and *Two Men and a Baby*. She worked with the Gay Men's Health Crisis in New York City on the *Living with AIDS Show* for most of the 1990s.

FRANCES NEGRÓN-MUNTANER is a filmmaker, writer, and the founder of Polymorphous Pictures. Her films include *AIDS in the Barrio: Eso no me pasa a mí* and *Brincando el charco*. She is the coeditor (with Ramón Grosfoguel) of *Puerto Rican Jam: Rethinking Nationalism and Colonialism* (Minnesota, 1997). She received her Ph.D. in comparative literature from Rutgers University.

EVE OISHI is assistant professor of women's studies at California State University, Long Beach, and curator of experimental film and video by queers of color.

CONSTANCE PENLEY is chair and professor of the film studies department at the University of California, Santa Barbara. She is a founding coeditor of *Camera Obscura* and the author of *The Future of an Illusion: Film, Feminism, and Psychoanalysis* (Minnesota, 1989) and *NASA/TREK: Popular Science and Sex in America.* Her edited books include *Feminism and Film Theory* and *The Analysis of Film* by Raymond Bellour. Her coedited books include *Technoculture* (with Andrew Ross; Minnesota, 1991), *Male Trouble* (with Sharon Willis; Minnesota, 1993), and *The Visible Woman: Imaging Technologies, Gender, and Science* (with Paula Treichler and Lisa Cartwright). Her latest project, Primetime Art by the GALA Committee, can be seen at www.arts.ucsb.edu/mpart.

WENDY QUINN was the director of Women in the Director's Chair Film Festival from 1995 to 1997.

JULIA REICHERT is a filmmaker and professor. Her films with James Klein include *Growing Up Female, Methadone: An American Way of Dealing, Union Maids, Men's Lives,* and *Seeing Red.* Her first feature film is *Emma and Elvis,* and her most recent work is as producer of *The Dream Catcher.*

CAROLEE SCHNEEMANN is an installation artist, merging film and video, photography, and sculpture. Her films include *Fuses, Plumb Line, Kitch's Last Meal,* and *Viet Flakes*; her videos include *Known/Unknown-Plague Column, Vespers Pool, Imaging Her Erotics,* and *Interior Scroll The Cave* (1993–95), the last two of which were made with Maria Beatty. Her book *Imaging Her Erotics: Projects, Essays, Interviews* is forthcoming.

VALERIE SOE is a videomaker and a lecturer in Asian American studies at San Francisco State University. Her videos include *"ALL ORIENTALS LOOK THE SAME," Picturing Oriental Girls: A (re) Educational Videotape, Mixed Blood,* and *Beyond Asiaphilia.*

VICTORIA VESNA is a computer artist and the chair of the Department of Design at the University of California, Los Angeles. Her work includes the WWW interactive installations *Bodies© INCorporated, Datamining Bodies,* and *Life in the Universe with Stephen Hawking* (CD-ROM).

YVONNE WELBON is a Chicago-based filmmaker. She received her M.F.A. from the School of the Art Institute of Chicago. Her films include *Remembering Wei Yi-fang, Remembering Myself . . .; Missing Relations;* and *Living with Pride: Ruth C. Ellis @ 100.*